D0897869

From
Jesus
to
the
Gospels

To Gisela

From Jesus to the Gospels

Interpreting the New Testament in Its Context

HELMUT KOESTER

Fortress Press
Minneapolis

FROM JESUS TO THE GOSPELS
Interpreting the New Testament in Its Context

Cover image: Rivulet flowing into the Lake of Galilee, Israel. Photo © Erich Lessing/Art Resource, NY
Cover design: Brad Norr Design
Book design and typesetting: H. K. Scriptorium

Library of Congress Cataloging-in-Publication Data

Koester, Helmut, 1926–
    From Jesus to the gospels : interpreting the New Testament in its context / Helmut Koester.
      p. cm.
    Includes bibliographical references and index.
    ISBN-13: 978-0-8006-2093-6 (alk. paper)
    1. Bible. N.T. Gospels—Criticism, interpretation, etc. 2. Jesus Christ—Person and offices.
I. Title.
    BS2555.52.K64 2007
    226'.06—dc22

                                    2007010691

The paper used in this publication meets the minimum requirements of American National Standard for Information Sciences—Permanence of Paper for Printed Library Materials, ANSI Z329.48-1984.

Printed in Canada

10 09 08 07 06 1 2 3 4 5 6 7 8 9 10

CONTENTS

PREFACE

Gospels and Gospel traditions have been in the center of my scholarly endeavors from the very beginning, from my doctoral dissertation on the *Synoptic Traditions in the Apostolic Fathers,* which was supervised by Rudolf Bultmann at the University of Marburg and submitted in 1953, and my second thesis on *Septuagint and Synoptic Traditions in Justin Martyr,* submitted 1956 to the University of Heidelberg in order to qualify as a university teacher in my own right (*venia legendi*).The next work, a more general book on *Gospels in the Second Century* that I planned after that time did not reach its final stages until much later. The discovery and first publication of the *Gospel of Thomas* in 1958 forced me to reconsider many major issues in our understanding of the development of the extant Gospel literature. That completion of my efforts finally appeared 1990 as *Ancient Christian Gospels: Their History and Development.*

This volume of collected essays reflects my sojourn in this research from the very beginnings, but it also includes several essays that demonstrate my thinking after the publication of that book. In the selection of articles I have tried to avoid duplications with the work published in 1990 and also excluded some essays that had been republished previously in other venues, especially those that were included in the volume *Trajectories through Early Christianity,* published in 1972 together with James M. Robinson. But in order to preserve the integrity of the articles presented here, it was necessary to allow for some overlap with my book of 1990 as well as for the consideration of the same Gospel materials in more than one essay. In some instances, parallel sections were removed from some articles.

The title "From Jesus to the Gospels" may be misleading. I do not start with the historical Jesus and then show, how the Gospels traditions developed from there. On the contrary, the essays of this volume want to demonstrate that the complexity of the traditions about Jesus does not allow any easy or direct access to the historical Jesus. Isolating particular types of traditions as belonging to Jesus of Nazareth—no matter how critical or how conservative this approach is—has proven to be a dead-end road.

This is clearly shown in the more recent literature about Jesus.Whether Jesus is presented as a magician, or as a Cynic philosopher, or as the follower of the female Wisdom goddess, or as revolutionary prophet—it is always a Jesus according to the hermeneutical presuppositions of the modern author. The historian can be liberated from such presuppositions and prejudices only by the establishment of a historical trajectory. In such a trajectory it is necessary to consider the totality of the historical, religious, theological political, and social components of the entire history that reaches from the prophetic tradition of Israel (rarely considered in modern studies of the historical Jesus!) and the Roman imperial eschatology to the reception of the tradition about Jesus in the surviving Gospel materials. It especially important that the latter is not brushed aside in favor of a more genuine Jesus of Nazareth, whether it is the admittedly later understanding of Jesus as the suffering servant or the equally important understanding of Jesus as the teacher of Wisdom. Palestinian, or especially Galilean social milieu, tends to establish a much too narrow context for Jesus' ministry and proclamation. Jesus of Nazareth must be understood as a historical moment that must be situated within the story of Israel and the renewal of its prophecy as well as in the story of the Roman empire and the Augustan eschatological ideology. His ministry was a political event of extraordinary significance, in which also the tradition about Jesus has its share and rightful place. Much work is to be done in order to define this moment more clearly. Only the historian's patience can illuminate this moment more clearly. I trust that the essays of this volume will help to clarify the challenge. The question of the historical Jesus of Nazareth, however, should be laid to rest for the time being.

Also for this second volume of my collected articles I thank Jörg Frey, Professor at the University of Munich, who originally suggested a publication of my collected articles. I am grateful to the editors at Fortress Press, Michael West and especially Dr. Neil Elliott, for encouraging this publication, proposing a division into two volumes (the first of these volumes was published earlier this year under the title *Paul and His World*), and assisting in the selection and editing of articles. Joshua Messner of Fortress Press patiently and faithfully saw the volume through the process of proofreading. I am indebted to my assistants, Stephen Hebert and above all David Jorgensen, both graduate students at Harvard Divinity School, for their help in transferring the older articles into the format required for this publication and for help in the meticulous work of bringing bibliographical references into a unified format. I also thank Margot Stevenson for the English translation of one essay that was originally published in French ("The Farewell Discourses of the Gospel of John"). Translations from German are my own unless noted otherwise.

I am dedicating this volume to Gisela, my beloved wife for more than half a century. Her contribution to my scholarly work has been critical support and joyful encouragement throughout these years. This dedication is but a token of my gratefulness for all that she has been for me and for her steadfast love.

HELMUT KOESTER

ABBREVIATIONS

AB	Anchor Bible
ANRW	*Aufstieg und Niedergang der römischen Welt*
ANTF	Arbeiten zur neutestamentlichen Textforschung
BA	*Biblical Archaeolgist*
BAR	*Biblical Archaeology Review*
BETL	Bibliotheca ephemeridum theologicarum Lovanensium
BFChTh	Beiträge zur Förderung der christlichen Theologie
BhTh	Beiträge zur historischen Theologie
BZNW	Beihefte zur Zeitschrift für neutestamentliche Wissenschaft
CChr	Corpus Christianorum
chap(s).	chapter(s)
ChrW	*Die christliche Welt*
Comm. Eph.	*Commentariorum in Epistulam ad Ephesios libri III*
DGL	de Gruyter Lehrbuch
ET	English Translation
EtB	Études Bibliques
ETL	Ephemerides theologicae lovanienses
EvTh	*Evangelische Theologie*
FRLANT	Forschungen zur Religion und Literatur des Alten und Neuen Testaments
GCS	Griechische christliche Schriftsteller
HNT	Handbuch zum Neuen Testament
HTR	*Harvard Theological Review*
HTS	Harvard Theological Studies
IG	*Inscriptiones graecae*
JBL	*Journal of Biblical Literature*
JECS	*Journal of Early Christian Studies*
JfAC	*Jahrbuch für Antike und Christentum*
JR	*Journal of Religion*
JTS	*Journal of Theological Studies*
KlT	Kleine Texte für Vorlesungen und Übungen
LXX	Septuagint
MS(S)	Manuscript(s)
n(n).	note(s)
NF	Neue Folge
NHC	Nag Hammadi Codex
NHS	*Nag Hammadi Studies*
NovT	*Novum Testamentum*

NovTSup	Supplements to *Novum Testamentum*
NTA	Neutestamentliche Abhandlungen
NTApo	Hennecke-Schneemelcher, *New Testament Apocrypha*
NTS	*New Testament Studies*
NTTS	New Testament Tools and Studies
NumenSup	Numen Supplements
ÖTKNT	Ökumenischer Taschenbuchkommentar zum Neuen Testament
OTP	Old Testament Pseudepigrapha
Pap.	Papyrus
par(s).	parallel(s)
PW	A. F. Pauly and Georg Wissowa, eds., *Real-Encyclopädie der classischen Altetrumswissenschaft*
RE	*Realencyklopädie für protestantische Theologie und Kirche*
RGG	*Die Religion in Geschichte und Gegenwart*
SAC	Studies in Antiquity and Christianity
SBAW	Sitzungsberichte der bayerischen Akademie der Wissenschaften
SBLMS	SBL Monograph Series
SBT	Studies in Biblical Theology
SHAW.PH	Sitzungsberichte der Heidelberger Akademie der Wissenschaften. Philosophisch-historische Klasse
SNTSMS	Society of New Testament Studies Monograph Series
Str-B	[H. Strack and] P. Billerbeck, Kommentar zum Neuen Testament
StTh	*Studia Theologica*
s.v.	sub voce/verbo
TAPA	*Transactions of the American Philosophical Association*
TDNT	*Theological Dictionary of the New Testamenant*
ThBl	*Theologische Blätter*
ThLZ	*Theologische Literaturzeitung*
ThR	*Theologische Rundschau*
ThZ	*Theologische Zeitschrift*
TRE	*Theologische Realenzyklopädie*
TU	Texte und Untersuchungen
VC	*Vigiliae christianae*
v(v).	verse(s)
VuF	*Verkündigung und Forschung*
WMANT	Wissenschaftliche Monographien zum Alten und Neuen Testament
WUNT	Wissenschaftliche Untersuchungen zum Neuen Testament
ZAW	*Zeitschrift für die alttestamentliche Wissenschaft*
ZNW	*Zeitschrift für die neutestamentliche Wissenschaft*
ZRGG	*Zeitschrift für Religions- und Geistesgeschichte*
ZThK	*Zeitschrit für Theologie und Kirche*

ACKNOWLEDGMENTS

1. Apocryphal and Canonical Gospels
   Published in *HTR* 73 (1980) 105–30.

2. Gospels and Gospel Traditions in the Second Century
   Delivered as a keynote address April 2004 in Oxford on the occasion of the anniversary of the publication of *The New Testament in the Apostolic Fathers*; published in Andrew Gregory and Christopher Tuckett, eds., *Trajectories through the New Testament and the Apostolic Fathers* (Oxford: Oxford University Press, 2005) 27–44.

3. The Text of the Synoptic Gospels in the Second Century
   Published in William L. Petersen, ed., *Gospel Traditions in the Second Century: Origins, Recensions, Text, and Transmission* (Christianity and Judaism in Antiquity 3; Notre Dame: University of Notre Dame Press, 1989) 19–37.

4. From the Kerygma-Gospel to Written Gospels
   Main paper presented on August 11, 1988, at the 43rd General Meeting of the Societas Novi Testamenti Studiorum in Cambridge; published in *NTS* 35 (1989) 361–81.

5. The Synoptic Sayings Gospel Q in the Early Communities of Jesus' Followers
   Published in David H. Warren, Ann Graham Brock, and David Pao, eds., *Early Christian Voices in Texts, Traditions, and Symbols: Essays in Honor of François Bovon* (Biblical Interpretation Series 66; Leiden: Brill, 2003) 45–58.

6. The Extracanonical Sayings of the Lord as Products of the Christian Community
   The basis of this essay is a lecture that I delivered in November 1954 before the Faculty of Theology of the University of Marburg in partial fulfillment of the requirements for the degree of Doctor of Theology. It appears here in slightly revised form but unchanged in its basic features. The essay was published in *ZNW* 48 (1957) 220–37, of which Professor Joachim Jeremias was then the editor. An English translation was published in *Semeia* 44 (1988) 57–77. A French translation is published in François Bovon and Helmut Koester, *Genèse de l'écriture chrétienne* (Mémoires premières; Brepols, 1991).

7. Mark 9:43–47 and Quintilian 8.3.75
   Published in *HTR* 71 (1978) 151–53; republished in *BAR* 6:3 (1980) 44-45.

8. The History-of-Religions School, Gnosis, and the Gospel of John
   Published in *Studia Theologica* 40 (1986) 115–36, as the slightly expanded and annotated version of the first Sigmund Mowinckel lecture, delivered at the theological faculty of the University of Oslo on April 18, 1986.

9. History and Cult in the Gospel of John and in Ignatius of Antioch
   Published in *Journal for Theology and the Church* 1 (1965) 111–23. Translated into
   English by Arthur Bellinzoni. Originally published as "Geschichte und Kultus im
   Johannesevangelium und bei Ignatius von Antiochien," *ZThK* 54 (1957) 56–69.
   Inaugural lecture delivered on July 3, 1956 before the theological faculty of the
   University of Heidelberg.

10. The Story of the Johannine Tradition
    Published in *Sewanee Theological Review* 36:1 (1992) 17–32.

11. Dialogue and the Tradition of Sayings in the Gnostic Texts of Nag Hammadi
    Published as "Dialog und Spruchüberlieferung in den gnostischen Texten von Nag
    Hammadi," *EvTh* 39 (1979) 532–56. This essay is the English translation of the only
    slightly expanded version of a lecture that I presented on June 20, 1979, upon the
    invitation of the Philosophical Seminary of the University of Tübingen on the
    occasion of the celebration of the 80th birthday of professor Hildebrecht Hommel
    and on June 28, 1979, at the Theological Forum of the University of Munich. I am
    grateful to the colleagues of both universities as well as to the New Testament col-
    leagues at the University of Marburg for a number of suggestions.

12. The Farewell Discourses of the Gospel of John: Their Trajectory in the First and
    Second Centuries
    Revised English translation of "Les discours d'adieu de l'évangile de Jean: leur tra-
    jectoire au premier et deuxième siècle," in Jean-Daniel Kaestli et al., eds, *La com-
    munauté johannique et son histoire* (Genève: Labor et Fides, 1990) 269–280.

13. Gnostic Sayings and Controversy Traditions in John 8:12–59
    Published in Charles W. Hedrick and Robert Hodgson, Jr., eds., *Nag Hammadi,
    Gnosticism, and Early Christianity* (Peabody, Mass.: Hendrickson, 1986) 97–110.

14. Jesus the Victim
    The presidential address delivered November 23, 1991 at the annual meeting of the
    Society of Biblical Literature held at the Allis Plaza Hotel, Kansas City, Missouri.
    Published in *JBL* 111 (1992) 3–15.

15. The Memory of Jesus' Death and the Worship of the Risen Lord
    Published in *Harvard Theological Review* 91 (1998) 335–50. An earlier version of this
    essay was presented as the first of three Haskell Lectures at Oberlin College in
    March 1997.

16. The Historical Jesus and the Cult of the Kyrios
    "The Annual Faculty Research Lecture at Harvard Divinity School," *Harvard Divin-
    ity School Bulletin* 24,3 (1995) 13–18.

17. The Story of Jesus and the Gospels
    The third of three Haskell Lectures, delivered at Oberlin College in March 1997
    (unpublished).

18. The Sayings of Q and Their Image of Jesus
    Published in William L. Petersen, Johan S. Vos, and Henk J. de Jonge, eds., *Sayings
    of Jesus: Canonical and Non-Canonical; Essays in Honor of Tjitze Baarda* (NovTSup 89;
    Leiden: Brill, 1997) 137–54.

19. The Historical Jesus and His Sayings
    Second Haskell Lecture delivered at Oberlin College in March 1997; unpublished.

20. Eschatological Thanksgiving Meals: From the *Didache* to Q and Jesus
    Published in Ἁγία Γραφὴ καὶ σύνχρονος ἄνθρωπος: Τιμητικὸς Τόμος στὸν Καθηγητὴ Ἰωάννη Δ. Καραβιδόπουλος [Festschrift for Professor Ioannes D. Karabidopoulos] (Thessaloniki: Pournara, 2006) 539–46.

I

GOSPELS APOCRYPHAL
AND CANONICAL

1

APOCRYPHAL AND CANONICAL GOSPELS

The problem addressed in this chapter is implied in the title. The terms "apocryphal" and "canonical" reflect a traditional usage that implies deep-seated prejudices and have had far-reaching consequences. Any standard dictionary, such as Merriam-Webster, will explain the term "apocryphal" as "not canonical; unauthentic; spurious." The synonyms are listed under "fictitious," that is, "invented or imagined rather than true and genuine," and the term "apocryphal" is explained here as follows: "implies a mysterious or extremely dubious source of origin." More than half a century ago, Montague Rhodes James wrote in the introduction to his edition of the apocryphal writings of the NT:

> The old word apocrypha is good enough for my purpose, and I employ it here in the sense of false and spurious, even when I am dealing with writings, which may contain ancient and truthful elements.[1]

The new standard edition of the New Testament Apocrypha in English translation is somewhat more cautious. Wilhelm Schneemelcher grants that some of the apocryphal writings "appear in part . . . to be almost contemporary with the canonical writings and to have been written on the basis of the same traditions."[2] But a distinction in principle between canonical and apocryphal is still maintained:

> Apocrypha are writings . . . which from the point of view of Form Criticism further develop and mold the kinds of style created and received in the NT, whilst foreign elements certainly intrude.[3]

Cautious restraint in formulation is obviously not sufficient to overcome prejudices of long standing, and Schneemelcher's evaluation of the apocryphal literature by no means signals a new era in the appreciation of these writings. This is confirmed by a distinguished scholar whom the Society of Biblical Literature elected as its president in its ninety-ninth year. He described some newly discovered apocryphal writings as "the schlock that is supposed to pass for literature," and he adds: "It has been mystifying,

---

1. *The Apocryphal New Testament* (Oxford: Clarendon, 1924) xiv.
2. Edgar Hennecke and Wilhelm Schneemelcher, *New Testament Apocrypha* (trans. R. McL. Wilson; 2 vols.; Philadelphia: Westminster, 1963–64) 1. 61.
3. Ibid., 1. 27.

indeed, why serious scholars continue to talk about the pertinence of this material to the study of the New Testament."[4]

If apocryphal gospels can be categorized in this way, it is no wonder that the investigation of the canonical gospels and of their sources is still performed without consideration of gospel literature that was not admitted to the canon of the New Testament.[5] A popular and widely used textbook that introduces students of early Christianity to the New Testament in more than 500 pages devotes only one paragraph, comprising fifteen printed lines, to the non-canonical gospels. They are divided into two groups—Jewish-Christian and Gnostic gospels—and are congenially described in the following way:

> The Jewish-Christian gospels are characterized by a grotesque appeal to vulgar taste and are obviously fictitious. The Gnostic gospels are marked by an esoteric wisdom which renders Jesus' message and mission unintelligible save to the initiated few.[6]

Of course, anyone has the right to abstain from dealing seriously with apocryphal literature, though good taste seems to demand that, in this case, one abstain from derogatory remarks about literature that one does not choose to treat. In a book that is devoted to the treatment of the entire early Christian literature, however, like Philipp Vielhauer's work,[7] it is difficult to understand why the apocryphal gospels and acts are separated from their canonical counterparts.[8] Neither the external attestation nor the internal evidence permits such a separation. To be sure, much of the non-canonical material is lost, whereas the later church preserved the canonical gospels in several thousand ancient and medieval manuscripts. But if one considers the earliest period of the tradition, several apocryphal gospels are as well attested as those that achieved canonical status later.

I. The External Evidence

The external attestations consist of datable manuscripts and of quotations and references in other writers. All early manuscripts were discovered in Egypt. Therefore, they give us information about only one limited area and neither prove nor disprove the

---

4. Joseph A. Fitzmyer, "The Gnostic Gospels according to Pagels," *America* (16 February 1980) 123.

5. The learned *Introduction to the New Testament,* by Werner George Kümmel (Nashville: Abingdon, 1973), in its detailed discussion of the source theories of the Synoptic gospels, mentions only one apocryphal gospel, namely, the *Gospel of Thomas,* and only to refute its relevance (pp. 35–38).

6. Robert A. Spivey and D. Moody Smith, *Anatomy of the New Testament* (New York: Macmillan, 1969) 173.

7. *Geschichte der urchristlichen Literatur: Einleitung in das Neue Testament, die Apokryphen und die Apostolischen Väter* (Berlin: de Gruyter, 1975).

8. Vielhauer (*Geschichte,* 252–459) treats the Synoptic gospels and their sources, Luke-Acts and the Gospel of John; pp. 613–92 deal with the apocryphal gospels, pp. 693–718, with the apocryphal acts of the apostles. This is quite peculiar, because Vielhauer believes that the *Gospel of Thomas* is not dependent upon the canonical gospels but represents an independent tradition (cf. pp. 627–29).

existence of such writings elsewhere. Quotations and references sometimes may reflect the preference of an ancient author, although there are several instances of references to writings, which a particular author rejects. But together both types of external attestation provide a fairly reliable *terminus ante quem* for the composition of the writing in question. The attestation of early Christian gospels through manuscript discoveries is as follows:[9]

First half of the second century CE:

𝔭 52	Gospel of John
Pap. Egerton 2	*Unknown Gospel*

End of second century and beginning of third century CE:

𝔭 64 + 67	Gospel of Matthew
𝔭 66	Gospel of John
Pap. Oxy. 1	*Gospel of Thomas*

Third century:

𝔭 1, 53, 70, 77	Gospel of Matthew
𝔭 4, 69	Gospel of Luke
𝔭 5, 9, 22, 28, 39, 80	Gospel of John
𝔭 75	Gospels of Luke and John
𝔭 45	Four canonical gospels
Pap. Oxy. 654, 655	*Gospel of Thomas*
Pap. Bodmer V	*Protevangelium Jacobi*
Pap. Rainer (Fayyum)	*Unknown Gospel*

Quotations of gospels in Christian writers from the first and second centuries involve numerous problems of dating and of identification of sources. The following survey is deliberatively conservative, that is, use of a particular gospel is only listed when it is clearly evident (usage of one gospel by another author of a gospel is not included):

The Apostle Paul	Free sayings of Jesus
Deutero-Pauline Letters	Free sayings of Jesus
1 Clement (96 CE)[10]	Free sayings of Jesus

---

9. For the dates of the NT papyri see Bruce M. Metzger, *The Text of the New Testament* (New York: Oxford University Press, 1964) 247–55; Kurt Aland, *Kurzgefasste Liste der griechischen Handschriften des Neuen Testaments I. Gesamtübersicht* (ANTF 1; Berlin: de Gruyter, 1963); Aland, "Neue neutestamentliche Papyri," *NTS* 3 (1956–57): 261–86; *NTS* 9 (1962–63): 303–16; *NTS* 10 (1963–64): 62–79; *NTS* 11 (1964–65): 1–21; *NTS* 12 (1965–66): 193–210; *NTS* 20 (1973–74): 357–81; see also Nestle-Aland, *Novum Testamentum Graece* (Stuttgart: Deutsche Bibelstiftung, 1979) Appendix 1, pp. 684–89. For the evidence for non-canonical gospels, see the pertinent sections in Wilhelm Schneemelcher, *New Testament Apocrypha* (2 vols.; rev. ed.; Westminster/John Knox, 1991–1992), vol. 1; hereafter referred to as *NTApoc*.

10. *1 Clement* does not seem to have known any written gospels. The sayings quoted in *1 Clem.* 13.2 and 46.8 derive from the free tradition, which is closely related to the *Synoptic Sayings Source*; cf. Helmut Köster, *Synoptische Überlieferung bei den apostolischen Vätern* (TU 65; Berlin: Akademie-Verlag, 1957) 4–23.

Ignatius (110 CE)[11]	Free sayings and other materials
Papias (130 CE)	Free sayings of Jesus
	Gospel of Mark
	Sayings of Matthew (= Q?)[12]
Polycarp (140 CE)[13]	Gospels of Matthew and Luke
Marcion (140 CE)	Gospels of Luke (and Matthew?)
2 *Clement* (150 CE)	Free sayings of Jesus
	Non-canonical materials[14]
Justin Martyr (150 CE)	Free sayings of Jesus
	Non-canonical materials
	Gospels of Matthew and Luke
	Protevangelium Jacobi (?)
	Acts of Pilate (?)[15]
Epistula Apostolorum	Gospel of Matthew
(160 CE)	Free tradition of sayings
	Non-canonical materials
	Infancy Gospel of Thomas (?)

The following witnesses all belong to the last decades of the second century:

Gospel of Truth	Gospel of Matthew
	Non-canonical traditions

---

11. Ibid., 24–61.

12. Papias says that "Matthew composed the sayings in the Hebrew language and that each translated them as best he could" (Eusebius *Hist. eccl.* 3.39.16). This is usually taken as a reference to the canonical Gospel of Matthew. Friedrich Schleiermacher was the first to suggest that Papias did not speak about the canonical Matthew but about a source of sayings that the author of that canonical gospel used and that was originally composed in Hebrew (or rather Aramaic). This hypothesis was addressed by James M. Robinson in Robinson and Helmut Koester, *Trajectories through Early Christianity* (Philadelphia: Fortress Press, 1971) 74–76. The merits of this hypothesis cannot be discussed here in detail. In any case, neither the suggestion of a translation from Hebrew nor the characterization as *logia* fits the canonical gospel of Matthew (even if *logia* also can designate narratives, why does Papias call the Gospel of Mark a book of the things "said *and done* by the Lord"?). This embarrassment is clearly visible in Vielhauer, *Geschichte*, 261–62.

13. The quotations from Matthew and Luke appear in the first chapters of the preserved letter, i.e., in that part which was composed much later than the cover letter to the Ignatian epistles; cf. P. N. Harrison, *Polycarp's Two Epistles to the Philippians* (Cambridge: Cambridge University Press, 1936).

14. The sayings quoted in *2 Clement* derive from a collection of sayings, not from a gospel. However, this collection shows influence from the canonical gospels of Matthew and Luke; it also includes apocryphal material. Cf. Köster, *Synoptische Überlieferung*, 62–111.

15. The *Acts of Pilate* is preserved in a number of medieval MSS and translations as part of the *Gospel of Nicodemus*. The date of the composition of this book is not certain, but the earliest references to *Acts of Pilate* appear in Justin Martyr (*1 Apol.* 35.8–9; 48.2–3). Some scholars believe that Justin did not know this document but simply assumed that a report about Jesus' crucifixion was kept in the Imperial archives (for the discussion of this question see Felix Scheidweiler, "The Gospel of Nicodemus, Acts of Pilate and Christ's Descent into Hell," in Schneemelcher, *NTApoc,* 1. 501–5). However, Justin's references to the *Acts of Pilate* closely parallel his method of referring to the "Memoirs of the Apostles," i.e., the Gospels of Matthew and Luke, which he certainly knew. Furthermore, a passage in Justin *1 Apol.* 48.2 closely resembles a sentence in a *Letter of Pilate,* a second-century writing that Tertullian knew and that is probably preserved in the *Acta Petri et Pauli*.

Valentinians	Gospels of Matthew and John
Carpocratians	*Secret Gospel of Mark*[16]
Clement of Alexandria	Four canonical gospels
	Gospel of the Egyptians
	Gospel of the Hebrews
	Secret Gospel of Mark
Theophilus of Antioch	Gospel of Matthew
Serapion of Antioch	*Gospel of Peter*
Tatian	Four canonical gospels
	Gospel of Thomas (?)[17]
Athenagoras	Gospel of Matthew
Hegesippus	*Gospel of the Hebrews*
	Gospel of the Nazoreans[18]
Irenaeus	Four canonical gospels
	Gospel of the Ebionites[19]

This survey shows clearly that about a dozen gospels were known in the second century and that the evidence for the apocryphal writings compares quite well with the evidence for the canonical gospels. The attestations do not support a distinction between canonical and apocryphal gospels. Writings of both categories were used and are referred to quite early and often by the same writers. Some observations can be made about geographical distribution. The Gospels of Matthew and Luke were known early in Asia Minor (Polycarp; Papias, who also knew about the Gospel of Mark; both Justin and Marcion came to Rome from Asia Minor). But there is no evidence that John's gospel also was known there until the end of the second century (Montanists, Melito of Sardis); Irenaeus, who came from Asia Minor, can be taken as a witness that all four canonical gospels were in use in that area before the end of the second century. But apocryphal gospels are not unknown (Justin). Egypt, on the other hand, demonstrates an early knowledge of the Gospel of John together with a large number of non-canonical gospels: Two "Unknown Gospels," the *Gospel of Thomas*, the *Gospel of the Egyptians*, *Gospel of the Hebrews*, a *Secret Mark*, *Protevangelium Jacobi*, and *Infancy Gospel of Thomas*. The

---

16. On the use of the *Secret Gospel of Mark* by the Carpocratians and Clement of Alexandria's knowledge of this gospel, see Morton Smith, *Clement of Alexandria and a Secret Gospel of Mark* (Cambridge, Mass.: Harvard University Press, 1973).

17. That Tatian used the *Gospel of Thomas* is possible but not certain; cf. Gilles Quispel, "L'Evangile selon Thomas et le Diatessaron," *VC* 13 (1959) 87–117.

18. According to Eusebius (*Hist. eccl.* 4.22.8), Hegesippus quoted from a gospel according to the Hebrews and from the Syriac gospel. The first must have been written in Greek and was probably identical with the *Gospel of the Hebrews* referred to by Clement of Alexandria; the latter, written in Aramaic (or Syriac), was most likely the *Gospel of the Nazoreans*; cf. Philipp Vielhauer and Georg Strecker, "Jewish-Christian Gospels," in Schneemelcher, *NTApoc*, 1. 134 and passim.

19. Irenaeus says that the Ebionites used the Gospel of Matthew but also reports that they had deleted the story of the virgin birth from it. Thus this "Matthew" was probably the heretical revision of Matthew, which is otherwise known as the *Gospel of the Ebionites*; cf. Vielhauer and Strecker, "Jewish-Christian Gospels," 119.

other canonical gospels are less prominent, and manuscript finds witness the remaining popularity of the Gospel of John also for the third century. Syria, perhaps the home-land of three canonical gospels (Matthew, Mark, John), gives little early evidence for their use, but it provides several testimonies to non-canonical gospels: *Gospel of the Nazoreans*, *Gospel of the Hebrews*, and *Gospel of Peter*.

This survey, of course, by no means accounts for all gospels that were in circulation during the first two Christian centuries. Discoveries of manuscripts written in later centuries have added several gospels to the list of the earliest Christian gospel literature and have also provided fuller texts of such writings as were otherwise known only through quotes or fragments. A large portion of the text of the *Gospel of Peter* was dis-covered in a manuscript from the eighth or ninth century.[20] Most significant is the dis-covery of the Nag Hammadi Library, a collection of over fifty ancient Christian writings in Coptic translation, in codices dating from the middle of the fourth century.[21] It gave us not only the complete text of the *Gospel of Thomas,* which until then was known only through three Greek papyrus fragments from Oxyrhynchos, but also at least two other writings that are doubtlessly early Christian gospels: the *Dialogue of the Savior* and the *Apocryphon of James.*[22] Later sources of information about early Christian gospel litera-ture are the canonical gospels themselves, because they used several written sources that must be classified as "gospels."Three of these can be clearly identified, although it is not possible to reconstruct them with absolute certainty: the *Synoptic Sayings Source*, a col-lection of sayings of Jesus with a strong eschatological orientation that was used by both Matthew and Luke; the Johannine *Semeia Source*, a compilation of miracle stories that presented Jesus as a miracle worker of superhuman powers; and a passion narrative uti-lized by both Mark and John for the composition of their accounts of Jesus' suffering and death. In addition to these three early gospels, other written materials were utilized by the authors of the canonical gospels as well as by the writers of so-called apocryphal gospels. But their identification and reconstruction is burdened with greater uncer-tainties, and in some instances they may have been more casual collections in writing of materials that otherwise circulated orally.

In the following discussion I want to demonstrate, through several selected exam-ples, that at least four apocryphal gospels belong to a very early stage in the develop-ment of gospel literature—a stage that is comparable to the sources that were used by the gospels of the NT.[23]

---

20. Further references to the *Gospel of Peter* follow.

21. For a brief account of the Nag Hammadi discovery, see James M. Robinson, *The Nag Hammadi Library in English* (New York: Harper & Row, 1977) 1–25. For text, translations, etc., of the *Gospel of Thomas,* the *Dialogue of the Savior,* and the *Apocryphon of James,* see the following.

22. It must be noted that some writings from this "library" that bear the title "Gospel," such as the *Gospel of Truth* and the *Gospel of Philip,* do not belong to the genre of gospel literature. Nor is the *Sophia Jesu Christi* a gospel, but a secondary version of a philosophical treatise that is without any relation to the transmission of gospel material.

23. The *Secret Gospel of Mark* is not included in this chapter, although it should be discussed here. This gospel, mentioned and quoted in a letter of Clement of Alexandria published by Morton Smith (see n. 17), contains a miracle narrative of the raising of a young man by Jesus that seems to reflect a tradition that is older than the form of the same story in the Gospel of John (John 11). But the discussion of the *Secret Gospel of*

II. The Synoptic Sayings Source
and the Gospel of Thomas

In addition to their use of the Gospel of Mark, Matthew and Luke employed a second common source that is generally known as the *Synoptic Sayings Source*. Apparently, it was not just a random collection of sayings, but a carefully redacted composition produced some time after the middle of the first century CE.[24] It may have circulated anonymously. However, the report of Papias of Hierapolis[25] seems to indicate that this collection of sayings was known under the name of Matthew. The content of this common source of Matthew and Luke can be reconstructed fairly well, though uncertainties remain. The primary problem in the assessment of the *Synoptic Sayings Source* is the difficulty that arises when one tries to determine its literary genre.[26] On the one hand, wisdom materials are obvious. In addition to proverbs and rules for right conduct, there are I-sayings in which Jesus speaks in the first person with the voice of Wisdom[27] and even a quotation from wisdom material.[28] On the basis of such materials, the *Synoptic Sayings Source* would have to be identified as a wisdom book, comparable to such works as the Wisdom of Solomon. On the other hand, a number of sayings reveal a very different theological orientation that is more clearly evident in the sayings about the coming Son of Man.[29] This eschatological expectation has its ultimate origin in the Book of Daniel. It appropriately dominates the Synoptic Apocalypse (Mark 13). Among the wisdom sayings of the *Synoptic Sayings Source*, it is a foreign element. If the genre of the wisdom book was the catalyst for the composition of sayings of Jesus into a "gospel," and if the christological concept of Jesus as the teacher of wisdom and as the presence of heavenly Wisdom dominated its creation, the apocalyptic orientation of the *Synoptic Sayings Source* with its christology of the coming Son of Man is due to a secondary redaction of an older wisdom book.

While it is evident from 1 Corinthians 1–4 that the understanding of Jesus as the teacher of wisdom developed in the earliest decades of Christian history[30]—wisdom sayings were apparently known in Corinth[31]—no direct witnesses for the existence of

---

Mark involves complex issues of the relationship of this gospel to the version of the Gospel of Mark used by Matthew and Luke and the Markan gospel that was ultimately canonized for which I do not know a persuasive solution. This deserves detailed treatment that is not possible in the space of this chapter.

24. For research on the *Synoptic Sayings Source*, see Dieter Lührmann, *Die Redaktion der Logienquelle* (WMANT 33; Neukirchen-Vluyn: Neukirchener, 1969).

25. See n. 12.

26. Cf. James M. Robinson, "*LOGOI SOPHON*: On the Gattung of Q," in Robinson and Koester, *Trajectories*, 71–113.

27. Matt 11:25–30.

28. Luke 11:29–51. On the question of wisdom theology in the *Synoptic Sayings Source*, cf. M. Jack Suggs, *Wisdom, Christology, and Law in Matthew's Gospel* (Cambridge, Mass.: Harvard University Press, 1970) esp. 63–97.

29. See particularly Luke 17:22–32.

30. On the wisdom party in Corinth, cf. Hans Conzelmann, *1 Corinthians* (Hermeneia; Philadelphia: Fortress Press, 1975) esp. 56–69.

31. On the relationship of wisdom material in 1 Corinthians 1–4 to wisdom sayings in the Synoptic

early Christian wisdom gospels have been preserved. But through the discovery of the Nag Hammadi Library, such a wisdom book has come to light: the *Gospel of Thomas*.[32] The relationship of this gospel to the canonical gospels became a controversial question as soon as the writing became known.[33] The Gnostic character of some of its sayings and the fact that the writing is introduced as a book of secret sayings prompted many scholars to assume that the author of this gospel had plundered the canonical gospels in order to fabricate an archaizing Gnostic book.[34] However, redactional changes, which the authors of the gospels of the NT have introduced in the reproduction of their sayings, do not occur in the *Gospel of Thomas*.[35] Sayings of Jesus, usually in very simple form, are placed side by side without any connecting narrative framework. Sometimes sayings are introduced by questions of the disciples; there are also a few short dialogues. But more elaborate polemical, doctrinal, and biographical scenes are missing.

The understanding of Jesus' sayings as "secret" teaching is not necessarily a sign of a later time. The collection of parables used in Mark 4 was already characterized as secret in its pre-Markan stage. The interpretation of the parables to the disciples is private, whereas the parables are told in public in order to conceal the mysteries of the kingdom. There is also good reason to assume that the Corinthians considered the special wisdom of Jesus as secret.[36] It is this old tradition that is made the central theme of the *Gospel of Thomas*. Many of the familiar parables from the Synoptic Gospels are told, often with few secondary alterations. But the section that contains most of the parables is introduced in *Gos. Thom.* 62:

It is to those who are worthy of my mysteries that I tell my mysteries.

The disciples are indeed the recipients of hidden wisdom that gives salvation.[37] In *Gos. Thom.* 17 Jesus says:

I shall give you what no eye has seen and what no ear has heard and what no hand has touched and what has never occurred to the human mind.

---

gospels, cf. my article "Gnostic Writings as Witnesses for the Development of the Sayings Tradition," in Bentley Layton, ed., *The Rediscovery of Gnosticism,* vol. 1: *The School of Valentinus* (Numen Supp 41; Leiden: Brill, 1980) 238–61.

32. Coptic text and English translation were first published by A. Guillaumont et al., *The Gospel According to Thomas* (New York: Harper, 1959). New translations have been published several times, cf. Schneemelcher, *NTApoc*, 1. 117–29; Kurt Aland, *Synopsis Quattuor Evangeliorum* (Stuttgart: Württembergische Bibelanstalt, 1964) 517–30. The quotations here follow the translation of Thomas O. Lambdin, "The Gospel of Thomas," in Robinson, *Nag Hammadi Library*, 118–30.

33. For literature on the relation of the *Gospel of Thomas* to the canonical gospels cf. Robinson and Koester, *Trajectories*, 129–32, 166–86.

34. E.g., Robert M. Grant, *The Secret Sayings of Jesus* (Garden City, N.Y.: Doubleday, 1960) 102–8; Ernst Haenchen, *Die Botschaft des Thomas-Evangeliums* (Berlin: Töpelmann, 1961) 9–12.

35. For such a comparison, see my essay "One Jesus and Four Primitive Gospels," in Robinson and Koester, *Trajectories*, 167–86.

36. 1 Cor 2:6–16.

37. See also the phrase, "Whoever has ears to hear, let him hear," which is often added to a parable: *Gos. Thom.* ## 7, 21, 63, 65, 96; cf. Mark 4:9.

The same saying is quoted in 1 Cor 2:9 but without the first line and as "scripture." It possibly is a quotation from a Jewish apocryphal book (the *Testament of Jacob*?).[38] In the tradition upon which the *Gospel of Thomas* draws, it was transformed into a saying in which Jesus speaks in the first person singular about his own mission. It is indeed the voice of heavenly Wisdom that speaks here. That this is the central christological concept in this gospel is evident from several I-sayings,[39] notably *Gos. Thom.* 28:

> I took my place in the midst of the world,
> and I appeared to them in the flesh.
> And I found all of them intoxicated;
> and found none of them thirsty.
> And my soul became afflicted for the sons of men,
> because they are blind in their hearts
> and do not see that empty they came into the world,
> and that empty too they seek to leave the world.
> But for the moment they are intoxicated.
> When they shake off their wine, then they will repent.

Such I-sayings are familiar from the Gospel of John[40] but also from the Synoptic gospels. A most striking parallel appears in Matthew (11:28–30) to *Gos. Thom.* 90:

> Come unto me,
> for my yoke is easy,
> and my lordship is mild,
> and you will find rest for yourselves.

The wisdom orientation of the *Gospel of Thomas* and some of the same materials appears in very early stages of the early Christian wisdom traditions, that is, in parts of the *Synoptic Sayings Source*, and in the Corinthian wisdom movement.

The apocalyptic expectation of the coming Son of Man, on the other hand, is completely missing from the *Gospel of Thomas*, although there are a number of eschatological and prophetic sayings.[41] Rather than to expect the coming of the kingdom in the future, the disciples are asked to recognize the presence of the kingdom in themselves; cf. *Gos. Thom.* 3:

---

38. Attention was drawn to this parallel by Eckhard von Nordheim, "Das Zitat des Paulus in 1 Kor 2,9 und seine Beziehung zum koptischen Testament Jakobs," *ZNW* 65 (1974) 112–20. He argues that the *Testament of Jacob* could have been the source of Paul's quote in 1 Cor 2:9. The Coptic text of the *Testament of Jacob* was published by J. Guidi, "Il testamento di Isacco e il testamento di Giacobbo," *Rendiconti della Reale Accademia dei Lincei*, ser. 1, vol. 9 (Rome: L'Academia, 1900) 223–64; an English translation by S. Gaselee was published in G. H. Brox, *The Testament of Abraham* (London: SPCK, 1927) Appendix.

39. The I-sayings are discussed in Robinson and Koester, *Trajectories*, 177–79.

40. For the question of the Johannine parallels, cf. Raymond E. Brown, "The Gospel of Thomas and St. John's Gospel," *NTS* 9 (1962–63) 155–77.

41. The prophetic sayings are discussed in Robinson and Koester. *Trajectories*, 168–75.

If those who lead you say to you,
"See, the kingdom is in the sky,"
the birds will precede you.
If they say to you,
"It is in the sea,"
then the fish will precede you.
Rather the kingdom is inside and it is outside you.
When you come to know yourselves, then you will become known,
and you will realize that it is you who are the sons of the Living Father.

It is quite likely that the Coptic text of the *Gospel of Thomas* does not directly reflect the original text of this gospel, and differences between the Coptic version and the Greek fragments from Oxyrhynchos show that the text was not stable. Similar observations can be made for the transmission of other gospels during the second century. The question remains whether it is possible to determine more accurately the date of the composition of the *Gospel of Thomas* in its earliest form, that is, of a document under this title that was on the whole not much different from the Coptic *Gospel of Thomas*. Since dependence upon other gospels is not in evidence, the time span for the date of this composition is from the middle of the first century to the end of the second century (the date of the earliest papyrus with a fragment of this gospel). Sayings 12 and 13 seem to give a clue to the date of its composition. Saying 12 recognizes the ecclesiastical authority of James the brother of Jesus:

> The disciples said to Jesus: "We know that you will depart from us. Who is to be our leader?" Jesus said to them: "Wherever you are, you are to go to James the Righteous, for whose sake heaven and earth came into being."

It is well known from several passages of the New Testament, as well as other traditions,[42] that James the Righteous occupied a position of authority as the leader of the Christian community in Jerusalem until his martyrdom in 62 CE. Saying 13, however, indicates that the authority of James was superseded by that of Thomas:

> Jesus said to his disciples:
> "Compare me to someone and tell me whom I am like."
> Simon Peter said to him: "You are like a righteous angel."
> Matthew said to him: "You are like a wise philosopher."
> Thomas said to him: "Master my mouth is wholly incapable of saying whom you are like."

The saying continues to report that Jesus withdrew with Thomas to tell him three things that he could not communicate to others. This saying is obviously a variant of the so-

---

42. Galatians 2; Acts 15:13; 21:18. Hegesippus's report about James the Just is quoted by Eusebius *Hist. eccl.* 2.23.4–18. A good collection of all early materials about James can be found in Martin Dibelius, *James* (rev. Heinrich Greeven; Hermeneia; Philadelphia: Fortress Press, 1976) 11–21.

called confession of Peter (Mark 8:27–30). In the Matthean form of this passage, Peter's authority is seen in cosmic dimensions that are analogous to *Gos. Thom.* 12: "On this rock I will build my church, and the gates of Hades shall not overpower it. I will give you the keys of the kingdom of heaven ..." (Matt 16:18–19).

Appeals to particular apostolic authorities are well known in the second and third generation of Christianity. They occur in areas where such apostles had formerly been active as missionaries and founders of churches. Pseudepigraphical authorship (which is so clearly evident in Christian literary productions of the last third of the first century) was certainly an important part of this pattern. 2 Thess 2:1–2 gives a telling example:

> We beg you, brothers, not to be quickly shaken in mind or excited, either by spirit, or by word, or by letter purporting to be from us.

A new letter was written, closely imitating the first letter of Paul to his congregation, in order to affirm a particular interpretation of Paul's teaching in a situation in which Paul's authority was quoted on both sides of a controversial issue. In the same way, the Johannine epistles were written to affirm and to interpret the authority of John that is transmitted in the gospel under his name. But a most direct parallel to the juxtaposition of *Gos. Thom.* 12 (ecclesiastical authority of James) and *Gos. Thom.* 13 (secret authority of Thomas) is provided by the last chapter of the Gospel of John. In John 21, a later addition to the original gospel, Peter is established as the leader of the church through Jesus' command: "Tend my sheep!" (John 21:15–17). The Johannine churches thus recognize the ecclesiastical authority of Peter, just as the Thomas community acknowledges the authority of James. At the same time, comparable to the secret authority of Thomas in *Gos. Thom.* 13, John 21:21–23 gives a distinct rank to the "disciple whom Jesus loved" by the mysterious words of Jesus: "If it is my will that he remain until I come, what is that to you?" (John 21:22). It is, furthermore, exactly this disciple who is claimed as the author of the Gospel of John, in John 21:24:

> This is the disciple who is bearing witness to these things, and who has written these things, and we know that his testimony is true.

Thus Thomas is claimed as the author of *Gospel of Thomas* in Saying 1:

> These are the secret sayings which the living Jesus spoke and which Didymus Judas Thomas wrote down. And whoever finds the interpretation of these sayings shall not taste death.[43]

It is most likely that the authorities of James, Peter, and Thomas represent ecclesiastical developments in the last decades of the first century in Syria. The Gospel of John

---

43. It is also intriguing to compare John 21:23 with this saying of the *Gospel of Thomas*: "The word now went out to the brothers that that disciple would not die." Raymond E. Brown (*The Gospel according to John* [AB; Garden City, N.Y.: Doubleday, 1970] 1117–22) demonstrates the embarrassment of scholars of interpreting this sentence.

and the *Gospel of Thomas* also demonstrate that the question of such apostolic authority was connected with the claims of particular gospel writings under the names of
such apostles. Perhaps also a gospel under the name of Peter was known in Syria at that
time.[44] That would explain the reference to Peter in *Gos. Thom.* 13. Why is Matthew also
mentioned in that passage? Papias's reference to the "sayings composed by Matthew"
already has been mentioned. The canonical Gospel of Matthew, of course, is also a writing that must have been composed in the area of Syria/Palestine. Or is *Gos. Thom.* 13,
with its statement of Matthew about Jesus as the "wise philosopher," an allusion to
Matthew as author of the *Synoptic Sayings Source*? If that is too speculative, it will seem
even more hypothetical to see in Peter's designation of Jesus as a "righteous angel" a witness for the appearance of the risen Lord as an angel in the *Gospel of Peter*. In any case,
the *Gospel of Thomas* must be dated to the same time in which the tradition of Matthew's
sayings and of the Gospel of John were defined with respect to Peter's authority, that is,
at the end of the first century CE.

III. Apocryphal Gospels and the Gospel of John

In the year 1935, three papyrus fragments with portions of an *Unknown Gospel* were
published as Papyrus Egerton 2.[45] The editors judged it to be written in a hand that
showed similarities with datable papyri written before 120 CE. After some initial discussion by several scholars,[46] the Japanese scholar Goro Mayeda published his Marburg
dissertation in the year 1946,[47] which came to the conclusion that the text of this gospel
was written independently of the canonical gospels. Although no major attempt has
been made to refute Mayeda's arguments,[48] Joachim Jeremias, in his introduction to the
translation of these fragments in the new edition of the New Testament Apocrypha,[49]
presents the following opinion:

> The juxtaposition of Johannine and Synoptic material and the fact that the Johan-
> nine material is shot through with Synoptic phrases and the Synoptic with Johan-
> nine usage, permits the conjecture that the author knew all and every of the
> canonical gospels.

---

44. On the *Gospel of Peter*, see below pp. 20–23.

45. H. Idris Bell and T. C. Skeat, *Fragments of an Unknown Gospel and Other Early Christian Papyri* (London: British Museum, 1935), and by the same authors (with corrections): *The New Gospel Fragments* (London:
British Museum, 1935).

46. The relationship of the *Unknown Gospel* to the canonical gospels was discussed in numerous publications of the years 1935–1937, but no consensus emerged. The publications are listed in Goro Mayeda, *Das
Leben-Jesu-Fragment Papyrus Egerton 2 und seine Stellung in der urchristlichen Literaturgeschichte* (Bern: Haupt,
1946) 94–95.

47. See n. 47.

48. Papyrus Egerton 2 is rarely discussed in detail. Exceptions are F.-M. Braun, *Jean le Theologien* (3 vols.;
Paris: Gabalda, 1959–1966) 1. 87–94, and Joachim Jeremias, *Unknown Sayings of Jesus* (2nd ed.; London: SPCK,
1964) 18–20.

49. *NTApoc*, 1. 95; the same judgment is repeated by Vielhauer, *Geschichte*, 638; cf. Brown, *The Gospel
According to John*, 229–30.

Jeremias does not question the dating of the papyrus in the early decades of the second century, and if this date is upheld and Jeremias's evaluation accepted, Papyrus Egerton 2 should be treated as a spectacularly early witness for the four-gospel canon of the NT. However, the "History of the New Testament Canon" by Wilhelm Schneemelcher in the very same volume[50] does not so much as mention Papyrus Egerton 2. But regardless of the question of its date, it can be shown that Mayeda's evaluation of the *Unknown Gospel* is correct; that is, this gospel indeed preserves features that derive from a stage of the tradition that is older than the canonical gospels. The first section of the *Unknown Gospel* closely resembles John 5:39; 5:45; 9:29:[51]

> To the rulers of the people he spoke the following saying:
> Search the scriptures, in which you think you have life; these are they which bear witness of me.
> Do not think that I have come to accuse you before my father; there is one who accuses you: Moses in whom you have set your hope.
> And when they said:
> We know that God has spoken to Moses, but as for you, we do not know whence you are.
> Jesus answered to them:
> Now your unbelief accuses you.

This is a carefully constructed unit: a challenge of Jesus in two parallel sentences; a response of the opponents; and a final accusation of Jesus. The statement of Jesus to the rulers consists of two imperative clauses, each followed by an affirmation. The two parallel statements juxtapose the Scriptures as witness and Moses as the accuser. The final statement of Jesus is closely connected to the second statement through the term "accuse." In the Gospel of John, the two parts of the initial statement of Jesus have been separated (John 5:39 and 5:45), and an additional discourse about "taking honor from each other" (John 5:40–44) has been interposed—a theme which is not directly related to the topic "Scripture/Moses." The response of the opponents has been used by the author of the Fourth Gospel in his discourse of the Pharisees with the man born blind (John 9:29), where it supplements a statement that is most certainly a composition of the author (9:28). But not only does the *Unknown Gospel* seem to present a more original composition, in addition, vocabulary and style are less typically Johannine and show several parallels to what is usually considered typical "Synoptic" usage.[52]

After several missing lines, the *Unknown Gospel* reports an incident of hostility against Jesus that could have been the conclusion of the preceding controversy:

---

50. *NTApoc*, 1. 15–34.

51. *Pap. Egerton 2*, frg. 1 *verso*, lines 7–16. The English translations given here follow Jeremias (with minor changes) in *NTApoc*, 1. 96–99.

52. Terms used here and also in the Synoptic gospels are "lawyer" ($\nu o\mu\iota\kappa\acute{o}\varsigma$), "unbelief" ($\dot{\alpha}\pi\iota\sigma\tau\acute{\iota}\alpha$), and "life" (instead of the Johannine "eternal life"). The phrase $\dot{\alpha}\pi o\kappa\rho\iota\theta\epsilon\grave{\iota}\varsigma$ $\kappa\alpha\grave{\iota}$ $\epsilon\grave{\iota}\pi\epsilon\nu$ never occurs in John but appears frequently in the Synoptic gospels. For further documentation, see Mayeda, *Leben-Jesu-Fragment*, 15–27.

... to gather stones together to stone him. And the rulers laid their hands on him that they might arrest him and deliver him to the crowd. But they were not able to arrest him since the hour of his betrayal had not yet come. But the Lord escaped from their hands and turned away from them.[53]

In the Gospel of John, one sentence of this passage has been used in John 7:30 and the remainder in John 10:31 and 39 with a longer, typically Johannine discourse interposed (10:32–38). Again, the passage in the *Unknown Gospel* is less "Johannine" in its vocabulary and shows several phrases paralleled in the Synoptic gospels.[54] Without any connecting remarks, the story of the healing of a leper follows in the *Unknown Gospel*:[55]

And behold, a leper came to him and said: "Master Jesus, wandering with lepers and eating with them in the inn, I myself became a leper. If you will, I shall be clean." Immediately the Lord said to him: "I will, be clean!" And immediately the leprosy departed from him. And the Lord said to him: "Go and show yourself to the priests."

Variants of this story appear in Mark 1:40–45 (= Matt 8:1–4; Luke 5:12–16) and Luke 17:11–19. The version of this story in the *Unknown Gospel* has affinities with several of these Synoptic parallels, but does not reproduce any one of them. It does not show any traces of the redactions or secondary expansions found in the Synoptic versions of the story. The simple act of healing through the word of Jesus alone is usually considered a sign of early traditions, whereas the Synoptic variants report more elaborate healing procedures (especially Luke 17:11–19).[56] Frg. 2 *verso* of *Pap. Egerton 2* apparently reports a miracle of Jesus at the Jordan to which no parallels in other gospels are known (the text is fragmentary). Frg. 2 *recto* poses most puzzling problems. It is an apophthegma, constructed in a style that is well known from the Synoptic gospels. Puzzling is the fact that parallels to the individual parts are found in different sections of all four canonical gospels:

Introduction: ... and they came to him, testing him with questions saying: "Teacher Jesus, we know that you have come from God (= John 3:2); for what you do bears witness beyond the prophets." (cf. *Gos. Thom.* 52).[57]

Question of opponents: "Is it permitted to give to the kings what pertains to their rule?" (cf. Mark 12:14 par.)

---

53. *Pap. Egerton 2*, frg. 1 *recto*, lines 22–31.

54. See Mayeda, *Leben-Jesu-Fragment*, 27–31.

55. *Pap. Egerton 2*, frg. 1 *recto*, lines 32–41.

56. The elaborate report of the reason for the illness is certainly a later feature and reveals that the author had no knowledge of the Palestinian milieu. That, however, only proves that such stories were further developed in the oral and written transmission. It does not say anything about dependence upon the canonical gospels.

57. *Gos. Thom.* 52: His disciples said to him, "Twenty-four prophets spoke in Israel and all of them spoke in you." He said to them, "You have omitted the one living in your presence and have spoken (only) of the dead."

Jesus' reaction: But Jesus, knowing their intention, became angry and said:

Jesus' answer: "Why do you call me teacher with your mouth and do not do what I say?" (= Luke 6:46)

Expansion with OT quotation: "Well did Isaiah prophesy concerning you, when he said: this people honors me with their lips," and so forth. (= Isa 29:13 = Mark 7:6; Matt 15:7)[58]

There are instances of apophthegmata in which Jesus rejects a question and refuses to give an appropriate answer; cf. Luke 12:13–14:

One of the multitude said to him, "Teacher, bid my brother to divide the inheritance with me." But he said to him: "Man, who made me judge or divider over you?"

Also the apophthegma of the *Unknown Gospel* presents Jesus as rejecting a secular affair. The Synoptic passage on the question of tax to Caesar (Mark 12:13–17 par.), on the other hand, expresses more clearly the interest of the Christian community in finding an accommodation to the Roman laws of revenue. That appears to be secondary as compared to the concern with an understanding of Jesus' mission. However, there can be no question that the apophthegma of the *Unknown Gospel* is also—as most other controversy apophthegmata—a secondary composition. The saying which constitutes Jesus' answer was originally transmitted as a free saying; Luke 6:46 quotes it within a series of other sayings. Thus, the whole framework of the saying is a secondary scene for which other materials may have been used which were already parts of the sayings tradition, such as the quote from Isa 29:13 and the reference to the payment of taxes. But there is no reason to assume that those materials were drawn from the canonical gospels. On the contrary, the Johannine parallel would argue for a dependence of John upon the *Unknown Gospel*: here, as in the instances discussed previously, the author of the Fourth Gospel seems to have utilized pieces from the much more tightly composed *Unknown Gospel* in order to construct his elaborate discourses.

These observations suggest that the author of the Gospel of John used source materials for the composition of his discourses and dialogues. The *Unknown Gospel* of Papyrus Egerton 2 further proves that such sources of the Fourth Gospel were directly related to the traditions upon which the Synoptic gospels rest, but also contained "Johannine" elements. These elements are visible in the terminology of the *Unknown Gospel* and in the initial stages of an expansion of sayings into "dialogues" of Jesus.

A development of the sayings tradition related to the Gospel of John is visible also in the *Dialogue of the Savior* from Codex III of the Nag Hammadi Library.[59] The author

---

58. A full accounting of all parallels to this part of the *Unknown Gospel* is given by Mayeda, *Leben-Jesu-Fragment*, 37–51.

59. At the time of the first publication of this material, the *Dialogue of the Savior* (NHC III,5) had not yet been published in its Coptic text except for *The Facsimile Edition of the Nag Hammadi Codices*, published under the Department of Antiquities of the Arab Republic of Egypt (Leiden: Brill, 1976), vol. 3. A full edition of

of this writing apparently used an older dialogue of Jesus with Judas, Matthew, and Mary that is still clearly recognizable in several sections of the present document.[60] The first section of this dialogue can serve as an example for the use of sayings in such a composition, *Dial. Sav.* 125, 18–127, 3:

> The Savior said: "The lamp of the body is the mind; as long as you are upright of heart . . . then your bodies are lights. As long as your mind is darkness, your lights will not be . . ."
>
> His disciples said: "Lord, who is the one who seeks and who is the one who reveals?"
>
> The Lord said: "The one who seeks is also the one who reveals."
>
> Matthew said: "Lord, . . . who is the one who speaks and who is the one who hears?"
>
> The Lord said: "The one who speaks is also the one who hears, and the one who sees is also the one who reveals."
>
> Mariam said: "O Lord, behold, when I am bearing the body, for what reason do I weep, and for what reason do I laugh?"
>
> The Lord said: "If you weep because of its deeds you will abide, and the mind laughs. . . . If one does not stand in the darkness, he will not be able to see the light."

Some sayings are easily recognized, such as the saying of the eye as the lamp of the body (Matt 6:22) and a saying about seeking and finding (Matt 7:7–8 par.; *Gos. Thom.* 92, 94). Other sayings used here are peculiar to the Gospel of John; cf. John 16:13:

> (The Spirit of Truth) will not speak on his own authority, but whatever he hears he will speak.

John 12:35:

> The light is with you for a little longer. Walk while you have the light, lest the darkness overtake you; he who walks in the darkness does not know where he goes.

John 16:20:

> You will weep and lament, but the world will rejoice; you will be sorrowful, but your sorrow will turn into joy.

---

the text with introduction meanwhile has appeared: Stephen Emmels, Helmut Koester, and Elaine Pagels, *Nag Hammadi Codex III, 5: The Dialogue of the Savior* (NHS 26; Leiden: Brill, 1984).

60. NHC 3, 5: 124, 22–127, 19; 131, 19–133,15; 137, 3 to the end (where the text is very poorly preserved). For a detailed analysis, see the final critical edition (n. 59).

There can be little doubt that in all these instances the Gospel of John is quoting traditional sayings which are utilized for the composition of more elaborate dialogues. In several cases the *Dialogue of the Savior* seems to have preserved such sayings in more original forms than the Gospel of John, for example, *Dial. Sav.* 129,14:

> And he knows, let him seek and find and rejoice.

Cf. John 16:23–24:

> If you ask anything of the Father, he will give it to you in my name. Hitherto you have asked nothing in my name; ask and you will receive, that your joy may be full.

There are several other instances in which the dialogue in the *Dialogue of the Savior* contains analogies to the Johannine composition of dialogues and discourses on the basis of traditional sayings.[61] Yet one other writing from the Nag Hammadi Library seems to be based upon the older and independent tradition of sayings of Jesus: the *Apocryphon of James*.[62] In addition to sayings that have parallels in the *Gospel of Thomas* and in the Synoptic gospels,[63] sayings utilized in the Gospel of John occur. A most striking example is *Ap. Jas.* 12,38–13,1:

> Blessed will they be who have known me; woe to those who have heard and have not believed. Blessed will they be who have not seen yet have believed.

The last of these blessings is used by the author of the Fourth Gospel at the end of the story of Jesus' appearance before Thomas—a story that originally was designed to demonstrate the physical reality of the resurrection through the touching of Jesus' body.[64] The Gospel of John, however, does not report the act of touching and adds instead a saying that rejects the materialistic realism of the traditional story, John 20:29:

> Jesus said (to Thomas): "Have you believed because you have seen me? Blessed are those who have not seen and yet believed."

The secondary usage of the saying in John's gospel is obvious, whereas the *Apocryphon of James* has preserved the saying in its more original setting of a sayings collection that was expanded into a discourse of Jesus.

---

61. See Helmut Koester, "Dialogue and the Tradition of Sayings in the Gnostic texts of Nag Hammadi," pp. 148–73 in this volume; and Koester, "Gnostic Writings" (see n. 31).

62. NHC 1,2; ed. M. Malinine et al., *Epistula Jacobi Apocrypha* (Zürich: Rascher, 1968); Francis Williams, "The 'Apocryphon of James,'" in Harold W. Attridge, ed., *Nag Hammadi Codex I (The Jung Codex)* (NHS 22; Leiden: Brill, 1985) 13–53; translation in: Robinson, *The Nag Hammadi Library*, 29–36.

63. Examples for parallels in the *Gospels of Thomas* and in the Synoptic gospels are cited in my article "Dialog and the Tradition of Sayings" (n. 61).

64. Cf. Luke 24:36–42; *Ign. Smyrn.* 2.2–3.

To be sure, the form-critical investigation of the writings from the Nag Hammadi Library has barely begun. Only preliminary suggestions can be made here. But it seems quite possible to me that the sayings in the *Dialogue of the Savior* and in the *Apocryphon of James* do not depend upon the canonical gospels but derive from an independent tradition. Their development of sayings into dialogue and discourses represents a stage in this tradition that must be presupposed for the more elaborate discourses of the Gospel of John.

IV. The Gospel of Peter and the Passion Narrative

Although known by name through the mention by the Syrian bishop Serapion,[65] only the discovery in the year 1886 of a fragment written in the eighth or ninth century made a portion of the *Gospel of Peter* accessible.[66] It preserves most of the passion narrative, the story of the rising of Jesus from the tomb, and the beginning of the story of Jesus' appearance to the disciples at the Sea of Galilee. Formerly, the almost universal judgment of scholars saw secondary compilation on the basis of the canonical gospels in this gospel.[67] The narrative is cast in the style of a report by Peter; Jesus is killed by Herod, while Pilate is completely exonerated; the miracle of the opening of the tomb and Jesus' resurrection is told elaborately; and the cross also rises and speaks. All this contributed to the impression that this gospel is nothing but a secondary, late, and possibly heretical composition.

No doubt, several of these features are the result of secondary development. But there are indications that the basis of the *Gospel of Peter* was a very early form of the passion and resurrection narratives. In an investigation, Jürgen Denker has demonstrated that almost every sentence of the passion narrative of this gospel is composed on the basis of scriptural references. In those instances where a parallel in the canonical gospels exists, the *Gospel of Peter* either agrees with the oldest form of such scripture-based narrative or shows an even more original relationship to the scriptural basis.[68] Two features are particularly striking: (1) The *Gospel of Peter* follows scriptural references more frequently than the canonical gospels, but unlike the later apologetic interest visible in the Gospel of Matthew and in Justin Martyr, it does not try to demonstrate the exact correspondence between prophecy and fulfillment; (2) Features in the narrative that derive from one single scriptural passage occur only in one scene in the *Gospel of Peter*, whereas the canonical gospels have sometimes distributed them over several scenes. For example, descriptions of the mocking of Jesus derived from Isa 50:6 appear in the

---

65. Eusebius *Hist. eccl.* 4.12.

66. For the first publication of the text and translation, see Christian Maurer and Wilhelm Schneemelcher in Schneemelcher, *NTApoc*, 1. 216.

67. All important arguments are reported by Maurer in Schneemelcher, *NTApo*, 1. 218–19.

68. Jürgen Denker, *Die theologiegeschichtliche Stellung des Petrusevangeliums* (Europäische Hochschulschriften 23/36; Bern: Lang, 1975) 58–77; see also Benjamin A. Johnson, "Empty Tomb Tradition in the Gospel of Peter" (Th.D. dissertation, Harvard Divinity School, 1966).

canonical gospels partly in the scene of the mocking before the synedrion (Mark 14:65 par.), partly in the mocking by the soldiers (Mark 15:16–20), but only once in *Gos. Pet.* 3.7–9. Mark and Matthew report two occasions on which Jesus is given something to drink during the crucifixion (Mark 15:23 = Matt 27:34; Mark 15:36 = Matt 27:48), *Gos. Pet.* 5.16 reports the drinking of vinegar *and* gall according to Ps 68:21 only once.[69]

The judgment about the passion narrative of the *Gospel of Peter* and its relationship to the canonical gospels depends upon one's general view of the development of the passion narrative. If one assumes that once there was an older historical report that was later supplemented with materials drawn from scriptural prophecy,[70] the *Gospel of Peter* with its rich references and allusions to such scriptural passages will appear as secondary and derivative. There are, however, serious objections to this hypothesis. Form, structure, and life situation of such a historical passion report and its transmission have never been clarified. The alternative is more convincing: in the beginning there was only the belief that Jesus' suffering, death, and burial, as well as his resurrection, happened "according to the Scriptures" (1 Cor 15:3-4). The very first narratives about Jesus' suffering and death would not have made the attempt to remember what actually happened. Rather, they would have found both the rationale and the content of Jesus' suffering and death in the memory of those passages in the Psalms and the Prophets that spoke about the suffering of the righteous. The passion narrative of the *Gospel of Peter* indeed is written, sentence for sentence, in the spirit of this "scriptural memory." It is closely related to the teaching and preaching of the earliest Christian communities, where the passion of Jesus from the very beginning was probably never told without the framework of such scriptural reference. The canonical gospels, on the other hand, show an increasing historicizing interest, add martyrological features and want more precisely to demonstrate, in apologetic fashion, the correspondence between prophecy and fulfillment. None of these tendencies are present in the passion narrative of the *Gospel of Peter*, where all redactional features of the authors of the canonical gospels also have left no trace. Though in many other respects it is further developed, for example, in the attempt to exonerate Pilate, the *Gospel of Peter* is an independent witness of the formation of the passion narrative.

It is tempting to ask whether the resurrection account of the *Gospel of Peter* also has preserved older traditions of resurrection stories. In the passion narrative, which was used by both the Gospel of Mark and the Gospel of John, the story of the discovery of the empty tomb by the women must have followed immediately upon the account of the burial of Jesus. The actual resurrection was not told in that common source. However, the *Gospel of Peter* reproduces, after the account of the burial (*Gos. Pet.* 6.21–24) and before the discovery of the empty tomb (*Gos. Pet.* 12.50–13.57), a resurrection narrative that has all the proper features of a miraculous epiphany story (*Gos. Pet.* 8.28–11.49):

Introduction: Preparation of the scene through request for soldiers to guard the tomb, securing and sealing of the tomb, seen by witnesses. (8.28–9.34)

---

69. The close connection of this feature to the interpretation of Scripture is demonstrated in *Barn.* 7.5.

70. Rudolf Bultmann, *The History of the Synoptic Tradition* (New York: Harper, 1963) 275–84.

The epiphany: "Now in the night in which the Lord's day dawned, when the soldiers, two by two in every watch, were keeping guard, there rang a loud voice in
heaven, and they saw the heavens opened and two men come down from there
in great brightness and draw nigh to the sepulcher." (9.35–36).

The miracle: "That stone which had been laid against the entrance to the sepulcher started of itself to roll and gave way to the side, and the sepulcher was
opened, and both the young men entered in." (9.37).

The appearance:[71] "They saw again three men coming out from the sepulcher, and
two of them sustaining the other, and a cross following them, and the heads of
the two reaching to heaven, but that of him who was lead of them by the hand
over-passing the heavens." (10.39–40)[72]

The reaction of the witnesses: "When those who were of the centurion's company
saw this, . . .[73] they said: 'In truth he was the Son of God.'" (11:45)

That such a miraculous epiphany story is a sign of later tradition is a rationalistic prejudice. What is secondary here is the attempt to relate the story to the rest of the gospel
and to connect it with the exoneration of Pilate.[74] The story as reconstructed here is
well preserved in its form and could be very old.

What is the relationship of this epiphany story to the canonical gospels? It seems that
various parts of this story are in fact preserved in the canonical gospels; however, they
have been inserted into different contexts and are fragments of an older story that only
the *Gospel of Peter* has preserved intact. The reaction of the witnesses and their confession "In truth he was the Son of God" appears in Mark 15:39; but it is poorly placed
here after the death of Jesus and clumsily motivated by the remark, "when he saw that
Jesus died in this way." Matthew has recognized the inappropriateness of this fragment
and inserted an account of several miraculous occurrences in order to create a better
reason for the centurion's confession (Matt 27:51b–53). Another displaced fragment
seems to be preserved in Matt 27:2–4:

And behold, there was a great earthquake; for an angel of the Lord descended
from heaven and came and rolled back the stone and sat upon it. His appearance
was like lightning, and his raiment white as snow. And for fear of him the guards
trembled and became like dead men.

---

71. *Gos. Pet.* 10.38–39 says that the soldiers reported what they saw. This is a secondary expansion that
tries to involve the centurion and other witnesses.

72. The following reference to the preaching to the dead, the appearance of another person entering the
tomb—he is needed in the tomb for the next story—and the counsel to report to Pilate (10.41–11.43) do
not belong to the original epiphany story.

73. Here follows a description of the report to Pilate that interrupts the context and is only designed to
exonerate Pilate—clearly a secondary motif. This apologetic motif is continued in 11:46–49.

74. See the redactional material mentioned in nn. 71–73.

Indeed, in this context the appearance of the angel, with all appropriate features of an epiphany, only serves as a courtesy to the women: Jesus had already left the tomb—and why was the tomb closed again after Jesus' resurrection? Matthew wanted to use material from the epiphany story, which the *Gospel of Peter* reported in full. That Matthew knew this story is clear from Matt 27:62–66, the report of the setting of the guard at the tomb. This Matthean section usually is labeled an apologetic legend.[75] As it appears in Matthew, it is not a legend at all but only a fragment, the introduction of an epiphany story that Matthew has used for apologetic purposes. Finally, what about the epiphany account itself? Mark 9:2–8 and par. has been designated as a displaced resurrection account.[76] Jesus appears "in garments glistening, intensely white," together with two angelic figures, identified as Moses and Elijah. This epiphany may indeed be nothing more than a very faint echo of the old account of a resurrection-epiphany that the *Gospel of Peter* has preserved in full.[77]

In the vast treasure of non-canonical gospel literature, there are at least some writings that have not found their rightful place in the history of this literary genre. Since all these writings are stepchildren of the scholarly endeavors of students of the New Testament, all I wanted to do here is to draw attention to five of these apocryphal gospels and to suggest that they are perhaps at least as old and as valuable as the canonical gospels as sources for the earliest developments of the traditions about Jesus. They are significant witnesses for the formation of the gospel literature in its formative stages. The term apocryphal with all its negative connotations should not prejudice us any longer.

---

75. Bultmann, *History*, 287.

76. Ibid., 259.

77. Cf. Denker, *Theologiegeschichtliche Stellung*, 99–101.

2

GOSPELS AND GOSPEL
TRADITIONS IN THE
SECOND CENTURY

The Situation One Hundred Years Ago and Thereafter

At the time of the publication of the *New Testament in the Apostolic Fathers* by the Oxford Committee,[1] the four canonical gospels ruled supreme as the almost exclusive source for the knowledge of Jesus' words and deeds. In some respect, interest in the study of the gospel quotations in the Apostolic Fathers was dictated by the quest for the dating of these gospels: if the dates of the writing of the Apostolic Fathers could be ascertained, their gospel quotations could be used as *terminus ante quem* for the writing of the New Testament gospels.

There was, to be sure, a good deal of knowledge about other, so called apocryphal gospels. But full texts of such gospels that could possibly be dated before the end of the second century were rare. One could mention here the *Protevangelium Jacobi* and the *Childhood Gospel of Thomas*. The knowledge of other early apocryphal gospels, such as the Jewish-Christian gospels, the *Gospel of Thomas,* the *Gospel of the Egyptians,* and some other Gnostic gospels, was derived mostly from occasional quotations of the Church Fathers (especially Clement of Alexandria, Origen, Hippolytus, Eusebius, Jerome, and Epiphanius). And there was, of course, the illusive search for the *Gospel of the Hebrews,* believed to have been the Hebrew original of the Gospel of Matthew. Only on rare occasions did these yield information that could help answer the question of the use of gospels in the Apostolic Fathers. The period of the discovery of new gospel materials had just begun in the last two decades of the nineteenth century. The first fragments with sayings of Jesus from Oxyrhynchus (1, 654, 655) had been published in 1897 and 1904 and had generated considerable interest, although there was no knowledge at the time that these were in fact fragments of the Greek original of the *Gospel of Thomas.* Rather, the category under which these fragments were classified was "Extra-canonical Sayings of Jesus," of which Alfred Resch had published a very extensive collection.[2]

---

1. *The New Testament in the Apostolic Fathers* by a committee of the Oxford Society of Historical Theology (Oxford: Clarendon Press, 1905).

2. *Agrapha: Außerkanonische Schriftfragmente gesammelt und untersucht* (2nd ed.; TU NF 15,3–4; Leipzig: Hinrichs, 1906; reprint, Darmstadt: Wissenschaftliche Buchgesellschaft, 1967; 1st ed. published in 1898 as *Agrapha: Außerkanonische Evangelienfragmente* [TU 5,4]). See also James Hardy Ropes, *Die Sprüche Jesu, die in den kanonischen Evangelien nicht überliefert sind: Eine kritische Bearbeitung des von D. Alfred Resch gesammelten Materials* (TU 14,1; Leipzig: Hinrichs, 1896).

Manuscripts of larger portions of the extra-canonical gospels were scarcely available with the exception of a fragment presenting the passion narrative of the *Gospel of Peter* that had been published in 1892.[3]

Although most of the more important discoveries of the twentieth century were yet to come, the careful and balanced assessment of the evidence by the Oxford Committee was at that time a signal for a fresh understanding in the midst of the battle for an early or a late date for the canonical gospels on the basis of the evidence to be derived from the Apostolic Fathers.[4] Its findings often permit the inclusion of traditions that are independent of the canonical gospels. At that time, however, a free oral tradition of Jesus' sayings had not been widely acknowledged, and form criticism was still in its infancy and had not yet been systematically applied to the study of the New Testament. Major non-canonical gospels or fragments of such gospels were still waiting to be discovered—not to talk of the possibility of dating some of such gospels to the time of the Apostolic Fathers.

When I worked on my dissertation in the early fifties of the last century under the guidance of Rudolf Bultmann,[5] a few additional early gospel materials had come to light, most significantly the "Unknown Gospel" of Papyrus Egerton 2,[6] but the Nag Hammadi Library had not yet seen the light of publication. I also profited, of course, from the pioneering works of gospel form criticism by Rudolf Bultmann and Martin Dibelius and others. This enabled me to argue for the presence of a continuing oral tradition as the source of most of the gospel materials referred to in the Apostolic Fathers. After the publication of my dissertation, I intended to work on a book dealing with the gospels of the second century; but the dream of an early completion of such work was shattered providentially by the publication of the gospel materials from the Nag Hammadi Library, in which I took an active part.

The publication of the gospels from the corpus of the Nag Hammadi Library, as well as a few other discoveries during the past half-century, opened up the possibility of a fresh understanding of the development of gospel literature in the second century. Four different insights seem to me to be most valuable.

1. The *Gospel of Thomas* demonstrated the existence at an early time, possibly as early as the second half of the first century, of written collections of the sayings of Jesus.

---

3. Urbain Bouriant, ed., "Fragments du texte grec du livre d'Énoch et de quelques écrits attribués a saint Pierre," in *Mémoirs publiés par le membres de la Mission archéologique française au Caire*, vol. 9 (Paris, 1892); H. B. Swete, *The Apocryphal Gospel of St. Peter: The Greek Text of the Newly Discovered Fragment* (2nd ed.; London: Macmillan, 1893). The so-called Fayyum Fragment had been published in 1887 and the *Strasbourg Coptic Papyrus* in 1900. Although both texts may be fragments of apocryphal gospels, these gospels do not seem to have been written before the year 200.

4. For some literature see Helmut Köster, *Synoptische Überlieferung bei den Apostolischen Vätern* (TU 65; Berlin: Akademie-Verlag, 1957) 1–2.

5. Later published as *Synoptische Überlieferung bei den Apostolischen Vätern*; see n. 4.

6. H. I. Bell and T. C. Skeat, *Fragments of an Unknown Gospel* (London: British Museum, 1935); idem, *The New Gospel Fragments* (London: British Museum, 1935). Preceding this important discovery, the fragments of gospel manuscripts Oxyrhynchus Papyrus 804 and Oxyrhynchus Papyrus 1224 had been published in 1908 and 1914, respectively.

2. Numerous fragments of gospels, as well as quotations and references of the Church Fathers, attest to a proliferation of gospel literature in the second century, whether or not such literature is dependent upon the canonical gospels. Most important here is, among other discoveries, the Papyrus Egerton 2.

3. Several documents attest the development of dialogues of Jesus with his disciples, which are interpretations of traditional sayings of Jesus, also beginning in the second half of the first century. Direct or indirect evidence comes from the *Dialogue of the Savior,* the *Apocryphon of James (Epistula Jacobi),* and the *Gospel of Mary.*[7]

4. The discovery and publication by Morton Smith of the *Secret Gospel of Mark*[8] provides a fresh insight into the question of the stability of the texts of the canonical gospels during the second century before their eventual canonization.

Written Collections of the Sayings of Jesus and the Oral Tradition

The earliest major collection of sayings of Jesus is, of course, the Synoptic Sayings Gospel Q,[9] which was incorporated into the Gospels of Matthew and Luke. It is not possible to know anything about the continued existence of this common source of these two Synoptic Gospels. Most likely, it was no longer copied because it was superseded by the Gospels of Matthew and Luke,[10] just as the Gospel of Mark, which after its incorporation into Matthew and Luke, has left very few traces in the second century.[11]

Another early written collection of sayings of Jesus underlies the *Gospel of Thomas;* however, it cannot be assumed that this collection was identical with the Greek text that was translated into the preserved Coptic text of this gospel. The *Gospel of Thomas,* as it appears in the fourth century in its Coptic translation, is the result of the instability of such sayings collections. It probably would be very difficult to reconstruct the history

---

7. These dialogues and discourses seem to provide the basis for the more extensive "discussions of Jesus with his disciples," such as the *Pistis Sophia* that are characteristic of later Gnostic literature; they will not be included in the discussion in this chapter.

8. Morton Smith, *Clement of Alexandria and a Secret Gospel of Mark* (Cambridge, Mass.: Harvard University Press, 1973); Smith, *The Secret Gospel: The Discovery and Interpretation of the Secret Gospel of Mark* (New York: Harper & Row, 1973).

9. James M. Robinson, Paul Hoffmann, and James S. Kloppenborg, eds., *The Critical Edition of Q* (Hermeneia Supplements; Minneapolis: Fortress Press, 2000). See also Robinson, Hoffmann, and Kloppenborg, *The Sayings Gospel Q in Greek and English with Parallels from Mark and Thomas* (Minneapolis: Fortress Press, 2002).

10. Wilhelm Bousset (*Die Evangelienzitate Justins des Märtyrers* [Göttingen: Vandenhoeck & Ruprecht, 1891]) endeavored to demonstrate that Justin Martyr drew his quotations of sayings of Jesus from Q. This thesis, however, proved to be unconvincing. On Justin Martyr and his use of gospels, see below.

11. The only trace of the Gospel of Mark before Irenaeus and Clement of Alexandria appears in Justin, *Dial.* 106.3, where Justin refers to the sons of Zebedee as βοανεργές. See Mark 3:17 (this special name for the sons of Zebedee is missing in Matthew and Luke). The oldest manuscript of the Gospel of Mark appears about half a century later than the first fragments and manuscripts of Matthew, Luke, and John. On Mark and *Secret Mark,* see below.

of the text of this gospel from its earliest composition to its latest form. But it would give valuable insight into the factors that influenced the ongoing revisions in the transmissions of such collections of sayings.

Evidence for the continued existence of sayings collections is not easy to obtain. Preserved fragments of "apocryphal gospels"[12] often do not yield much evidence, and numerous later quotations of non-canonical sayings may derive from the free oral tradition of sayings, from gospels that have perished, or from additions to the canonical gospel manuscripts.[13] In any case, the free oral tradition continued well into later centuries and influenced both apocryphal and canonical gospel manuscripts. Sometimes the setting for the free transmission of sayings of Jesus is evident. The quotation of the Lord's Prayer in *Didache* 8 derives from the liturgical tradition of the early church.[14] A baptismal setting is evident for the saying about rebirth quoted by Justin Martyr *1 Apol.* 61.3.[15] Other free sayings derive from the catechetical instructions, as the group of sayings quoted in *1 Clem.* 13.3.

The primary source for the existence of sayings collections in the second century is also Justin Martyr. To be sure, Justin uses the first three canonical gospels, and he utilizes both narrative and sayings materials from these gospels. Both the narrative materials and the sayings that appear in Justin's writings are harmonizations of the parallel texts of the Gospels of Matthew and Luke. However, it could be argued that in his quotations of groups of sayings, Justin is not quoting from a gospel harmony that also included the narrative sections of the gospels, but from compositions of sayings derived from this harmony. Some of these clusters of sayings reveal the signs of composition for instructions of the community, especially the sayings composed in *1 Apol.* 15–16. In another instance, *Dial.* 35.3, a collection of prophetic sayings drawn from Matthew and Luke, includes the apocryphal saying ἔσονται σχίσματα καὶ αἱρέσεις. Also, the non-canonical saying Ἐν οἷς ὑμᾶς καταλάβω, ἐν τούτοις καὶ κρινῶ (*Dial.* 47. 5) may come from such a collection of prophetic sayings.[16]

The existence of written sayings collections that are based on the canonical gospels but also include non-canonical materials is confirmed by *2 Clement*. The sayings quoted in this mid-second century writing show mixtures of readings from Matthew and Luke, just like those that appear in Justin Martyr. *Second Clement's* quotations of sayings twice show the same harmonizations of sayings from Matthew and Luke as the quotations

---

12. Oxyrhynchus Papyrus 840 and Papyrus Egerton 2 seem to be portions of gospels that also contained narrative sections.

13. This is the case with respect to the famous apophthegma of the worker on the Sabbath that appears in Luke 6:5 in Codex D. The saying "And only then shall you be glad, when you look on your brother in love" is derived, according to Jerome, from the *Gospel of the Hebrews*.

14. In spite of some criticism, I am not inclined to abandon my earlier arguments (*Synoptische Überlieferung*, 203–7) for an independence of this quotation from the Gospel of Matthew.

15. The form of this saying, as quoted by Justin, is more original than the form that appears in John 3:3, 5. John changes the original ἀναγεννηθῆτε to γεννηθῇ ἄνωθεν and εἰσέλθητε εἰς τὴν βασιλείαν to ἰδεῖν τὴν βασιλείαν (John 3:3; John 3:5 still preserves the original εἰσελθεῖν εἰς τὴν βασιλείαν).

16. Arthur J. Bellinzoni, *The Sayings of Jesus in the Writings of Justin Martyr* (NovTSup 17; Leiden: Brill, 1967).

appearing in Justin Martyr. *2 Clem.* 5.2–4 harmonizes Matt. 10:28 and Luke 12:4–5 in a way that is similar to the quote in Justin *1 Apol.* 19.7.[17] An almost identical harmonization of this saying appears in *Ps.-Clem.Hom.* 17.5.2.[18] In the other instance, *2 Clem.* 4.2, 5, the quotation reflects not only the same harmonizations but also the same combination of sayings from different contexts from Matthew and Luke[19] that appear in the quotations of the same saying in Justin Martyr.[20] At the same time, this harmonized quotation is combined in *2 Clement* with a non-canonical variant that appears as a marginal notation to Matt. 7:5 in the so-called *Gospel Edition Zion* (MS 1424).[21] The sayings collection used by *2 Clement* also reveals the inclusion of non-canonical sayings in its quote, "When the two become one, and the outside like the inside" (*2 Clem.* 12.2, 6), that is paralleled in the *Gospel of Thomas* (22)[22] and the *Gospel according to the Egyptians*.[23] The latter, written before the middle of the second century, also may have been a collection of sayings, although direct relationships to materials of the synoptic tradition are not apparent. There is, however, too little material left in order to make a judgment about its character. Though it was written in Greek, it does not seem to have enjoyed a wider distribution.[24]

It is possible to conclude that although the earlier sayings collection Q soon disappeared in the second century, one or several new sayings collections appeared. These were based on harmonizations of Matthew's and Luke's texts but also included additional free sayings that also found their way into other non-canonical gospels that circulated or were written at that time. It is remarkable that this development does not assign any special dignity to the canonical gospels but could freely combine materials drawn from these gospels with non-canonical materials.

The Proliferation of Gospels during the Second Century

Of the written gospels composed before the end of the second century, the gospels of Matthew and Luke, the latter separated from its original companion, the Acts of the Apostles, began to emerge from their original local context and circulated more widely in Asia Minor and Greece. While Ignatius of Antioch seemed to be dependent mostly upon oral traditions, his younger colleague Polycarp of Smyrna certainly knew Matthew

---

17. On the parallel in Papyrus Oxyrhynchus 4009, most likely a fragment of the *Gospel of Peter*, see below.

18. See my analysis of this quotation in *Synoptische Überlieferung,* 94–102.

19. Matt. 7:21–23; 13:42–43; and Luke 6:46; 13:26–28.

20. *1 Apol.* 16.9–12 and *Dial.* 76.5.

21. Koester, *Synoptische Überlieferung,* 83–94.

22. Ibid., 102–5. Of course, I did not yet know the latter parallel at the time of the publication of my earlier book.

23. Clement of Alexandria, *Strom.* 3.4.63–64.

24. On the *Gospel according to the Egyptians,* see Wilhelm Schneemelcher, "The Gospel of the Egyptians," in Schneemelcher, *NTApo.*

and Luke. These two gospels also were well-known in Rome before the middle of the century, as Justin Martyr and Marcion attest.

On the other hand, the Gospels of Mark, John, and Thomas—all written in their original form before the end of the first century—did not enjoy a more general circulation. That the Gospel of Mark was known in Rome in the middle of the second century is evident in Justin's reference to this gospel, but it remains otherwise hidden until the time of Clement and Irenaeus. However, the *Secret Gospel of Mark* could indicate that Mark's gospel was popular in Egypt early in the second century.[25] The *Gospel of Thomas* was at first used in eastern Syria as the special gospel of a sectarian group. But it was brought to Egypt sometime during the second century, as fragmentary papyri[26] demonstrate.[27] Also the Gospel of John must have remained the property of a small group of churches somewhere in Syria or Palestine for some time. Polycarp of Smyrna, writing before the middle of the second century, did not know this gospel,[28] but a generation later Irenaeus, originally from Smyrna, knew and defended it. But these gospels appear in Egypt at an early time. John appears in Egypt early in the second century, as 𝔭 52[29] attests as well as its use by Valentinus.

The first decades of the second century thus show that there were a number of older gospels in existence that were originally used in limited geographical locations by special groups but had found their way into Egypt at an early date. A note of caution must be inserted here. The available evidence is biased towards Egypt. Not only do all the papyri with gospel fragments come exclusively from Egypt, but the two Church Fathers, Clement and Origen, who give the most valuable evidence for the existence and use of gospels in the second century, also were located in Alexandria. Were it not for the single reference to a passage from Mark in Justin Martyr's *Dialogue*, we would not have any evidence for the presence of that gospel in Rome in the middle of the second century.[30] Nevertheless, it cannot be doubted that in the beginning, written gospels were the property of limited circles of churches or special groups and achieved a more general circulation only during the second and third centuries.

The gospel writings produced in the first century were soon joined by an increasing number of additional writings that claimed to be legitimate presentations of the

---

25. For further discussion of the *Secret Gospel of Mark*, see below.

26. Papyrus Oxyrhynchus 1, 654, 655.

27. Harold W. Attridge, "Appendix: The Greek Fragments," in *Nag Hammadi Codex II, 2–7* (ed. Bentley Layton; NHS 20; Leiden: Brill, 1989) 1. 95–128.

28. Whether Ignatius of Antioch knew the Gospel of John is still debated; see the literature in William R. Schoedel, *Ignatius of Antioch: A Commentary on the Letters of Ignatius of Antioch* (Hermeneia; Philadelphia: Fortress Press, 1985) 9, n. 52.

29. A date in the early second century for this papyrus, however, is not as certain as generally believed; see Dieter Lührmann, *Die apokryph gewordenen Evangelien: Studien zu neuen Texten und zu neuen Fragen* (Leiden: Brill, 2004) 134 (ca. 170 CE).

30. I am, of course, aware of the widespread assumption of scholars that the Gospel of Mark was written in Rome. There is, however, no single piece of evidence. Mark was used by Matthew in Syria and by Luke in Antioch or in Ephesus in the last third of the first century. That a gospel written in Rome should have been brought to the East at such an early time seems most unlikely.

teachings and works of Jesus. It is doubtful, however, whether they appeared under the title "gospel" (εὐαγγέλιον), because this term was not yet used for written documents in the first half of the second century.[31] The title "Gospel according to . . ."[32] was in most instances added later only by scribes in the colophons—and often for writings that had no real relationship to gospel literature, that is, writings that recorded the words and deeds of Jesus of Nazareth. The often-discussed question whether or not any of these gospels were dependent on one or several of the canonical gospels is immaterial for the following survey. What we shall find is a blend of older traditions and sources, free materials, and influence from those gospels that later became canonical.

The *Gospel of Peter*, originating in Syria,[33] was also brought to Egypt before the end of the second century; this is attested by two papyrus fragments (Papyrus Oxyrhynchus 2940 and 4009), which confirm a date before 200 CE.[34] Although the first of these fragments belongs to the passion narrative of this gospel that had become known through the 6th-century Akhmim Codex Papyrus Cairo 10759, the Papyrus Oxyrhynchus 4009[35] presents a combination of Matt 10:16//Luke 10:3 and Matt 10:28//Luke 12:4–5. It resembles the harmonized quotation of these synoptic passages in *2 Clem.* 5.2–4, although the similarities are not close enough to justify the hypothesis that *2 Clement* is dependent upon the *Gospel of Peter.* If it is correct that this fragment indeed belongs to the *Gospel of Peter,* it is evident that this gospel also contained sayings of Jesus, not just a passion narrative. Should one also consider the story of the transfiguration reported by the "eye-witness" Peter in 2 Pet 1:16–18 as possibly derived from this gospel? In that case, the *Gospel of Peter* would have been a gospel writing with narratives and sayings, resembling the Synoptic Gospels of the New Testament canon.[36]

According to the *Stichometry of Nicephorus,* the *Gospel according to the Hebrews* was almost as long as the Gospel of Matthew. It is now generally accepted that this gospel was a Greek writing that must be distinguished from two other Jewish-Christian gospels, the *Gospel of the Ebionites* and the *Gospel of the Nazoreans.*[37] But in spite of numerous references to the *Gospel according to the Hebrews* in antiquity, only seven quotations have been assigned to it by scholars, among these also a saying about finding rest, which is

---

31. See Helmut Koester, "From the Kerygma-Gospel to Written Gospels," *NTS* 35 (1989) 361–81, also included in this volume.

32. With Schneemelcher ("Gospels: non-biblical materials about Jesus: Introduction," in Schneemelcher, *NTApo,* 1. 77–85) I disagree with the assumption of Martin Hengel (*Die Evangelienüberschriften* [SHAW.PH 1984.3; 1984]) that these titles of the canonical gospels were already used at the beginning of the second century.

33. This is suggested by the claim of Peter as the author and by the report of Serapion of Antioch quoted by Eusebius *Hist. eccl.* 6.12.2–6.

34. Papyrus Oxyrhynchus 4009 may be dated as early as the middle of the second century; Lührmann, *Die apokryph gewordenen Evangelien,* 60–67.

35. As it was reconstructed with the help of *2 Clem.* 5. 2–4 by Lührmann, *Die apokryph gewordenen Evangelien,* 74–82.

36. It must remain doubtful whether the Fayyum Fragment PapVindob. G 2325, also presenting a parallel to Mark 14:27–30, can be shown to have been a part of the *Gospel of Peter* (Lührmann, *Die apokryph gewordenen Evangelien,* 87–90).

37. Philipp Vielhauer and Georg Strecker, "Jewish-Christian Gospels," in Schneemelcher, *NTApo,* 1. 134–78.

paralleled in the *Gospel of Thomas*.[38] Considering the information from the *Stichometry of Nicephorus*, this seems precious little. Dieter Lührmann[39] has argued persuasively that the story of the Woman Taken in Adultery, quoted by Didymus the Blind in his *Commentary on Ecclesiastes*,[40] also may have belonged to the *Gospel according to the Hebrews*, although it is introduced by Didymus as coming from "certain gospels" (ἔν τισιν εὐαγγελίοις). Lührmann demonstrates that this story as reported by Didymus cannot have been derived from John 8:3–11[41] but is an independent variant of the same story, which was also known to Papias of Hierapolis as a story that was included in the *Gospel according to the Hebrews* (ἡ τὸ καθ᾽ Ἑβραίους εὐαγγέλιον περιέχει).[42] Whatever is quoted elsewhere from this gospel reveals elements of a gnostic wisdom theology. This has resulted in the conclusion that this gospel essentially was characterized by a mystic piety and shared very little material with the Synoptic Gospels. One other reference in Didymus the Blind, however, may direct further inquiry in a different direction. In his *Commentary on the Psalms*[43] he says that in the *Gospel according to the Hebrews* (ἐν τῷ καθ᾽ Ἑβραίους εὐαγγελίῳ τοῦτο φαίνεται) the Levi of Luke 5:27, 29 is not identical to the tax collector Matthew of Matt 9:9 but to the newly appointed twelfth apostle Matthias (Acts 1:23, 26).[44] This would indicate that the author of this gospel was familiar with materials from the canonical writings and probably included a good deal of material parallel with or even drawn from the Synoptic Gospels. The reference in Papias also gives a firm date of composition before the middle of the second century.

The only other Jewish-Christian gospel that can be dated to the second century is the *Gospel of the Ebionites,* so designated because it was used by a special group calling itself "Ebionites" (its actual title possibly was *Gospel of the Twelve*). It was a harmonizing Greek composition on the basis of the three Synoptic Gospels that shows some similarities with the gospel harmony of Justin Martyr. Non-canonical materials do not seem to have been included.[45] The third of the Jewish-Christian gospels, the *Gospel of the Nazoreans,*[46] an Aramaic translation of the Greek Gospel of Matthew that was expanded with extra-canonical materials, is not attested until the late fourth century; it is not likely to have existed much earlier.[47]

---

38. Ibid., 172–78.

39. *Die apokryph gewordenen Evangelien,* 191–215.

40. Tura Papyrus IV 7, 7–18.

41. The story appears in Greek manuscripts of the New Testament only in the Middle Ages, although it was a part of the text of John in Latin manuscripts much earlier (the Greek version of Codex D may be a translation from Latin; see Lührmann, *Die apokryph gewordenen Evangelien,* 221–28).

42. Quoted in Eusebius, *Hist. eccl.* 3.39.16.

43. *Tura Fragment III,* 184, 9–10.

44. Dieter Lührmann, "Das Bruchstück aus dem Hebräerevangelium bei Didymus von Alexandrien," *NovT* 29 (1987) 265–79; Lührmann, *Die apokryph gewordenen Evangelien,* 182–91.

45. Vielhauer and Strecker, "Jewish-Christian Gospels," in Schneemelcher, *NTApo,* 1. 166–71; Helmut Koester, *History and Literature of Early Christianity* (2nd ed.; New York: de Gruyter, 2000) 208–9; Lührmann, *Die apokryph gewordenen Evangelien,* 231–33.

46. Vielhauer and Strecker, "Jewish-Christian Gospels," in Schneemelcher, *NTApo,* 1. 154–65.

47. On the complex history of the search for the original Hebrew Matthew, based largely on Jerome's claims that he had found this original Hebrew in the *Gospel of the Nazoreans,* see Lührmann, *Die apokryph gewordenen Evangelien,* 233–58.

The only other important evidence for the gospels in the second century is the "Unknown Gospel" of Papyrus Egerton 2. The fragments were first published by Bell and Skeat in the year 1935.[48] A new fragment of this gospel has been identified in Papyrus Köln 255.[49] These gospel fragments preserve the story of the healing of the leper (Mark 1:40–44 par., including a parallel to John 5:14), the discussion about paying taxes to Caesar (Mark 12:13–15 par., with materials also found in Luke 6:46, Mark 7:6–7//Matt. 15:6–9), and the debate about searching the Scriptures and the authority of Moses (cf. John 5:39–47) followed by a reference to an attempt to arrest Jesus (cf. John 10:31; 7:30; 10:39). In addition, the fragments of this gospel present some damaged sentences that seem to introduce materials that have no parallels in other known gospels (apparently a miracle story). The question of whether and to what degree the texts of this gospel are dependent upon the four canonical gospels is a much debated issue. With respect to the three Synoptic Gospels, one could argue that their text has indirectly influenced the composition of materials in the "Unknown Gospel."[50] With respect to the passage paralleling John 5:39–47; 10:31; 7:30; 10:39, however, there can be little doubt that the "Unknown Gospel" preserves a text that is more original than the respective passages in the Gospel of John; all characteristic Johannine elements are missing here.[51] Moreover, the Papyrus Egerton 2 must be dated well before the year 200.[52] That makes it unlikely that the author could have chosen sundry passages from the four canonical gospels and composed them at random to create new units. Rather, we must assume that the composition of this gospel—by all means a full gospel text with narrative materials and sayings—is dependent upon some independent written source (the portion paralleling John 5:39–47), orally transmitted stories and sayings of Jesus (albeit in their wording influenced by the Synoptic Gospel texts), and apocryphal materials.[53] Therefore, the "Unknown Gospel" may stand as a key example for the development of gospel literature in the second century. We find a mixture of written materials, some predating the canonical gospels, memories of sentences from written gospels composed into new units, and oral materials not otherwise attested and paralleled in hitherto known witnesses.

New discoveries during the past one hundred years have unveiled other fragments of gospel materials existing in the second century that cannot be assigned to any known

---

48. Bell and Skeat, *Fragments from an Unknown Gospel*; Bell and Skeat, *The New Gospel Fragments*.

49. Michael Gronewald, "Papyri Colon 7," *Kölner Papyri* 7 (Opladen: Westdeutscher Verlag, 1987) 136–45.

50. I am not certain whether my arguments (presented in *Ancient Christian Gospels: Their History and Development* [Harrisburg: Trinity Press International, 1990] 211–15) that Papyrus Egerton 2 is not dependent upon the Synoptic Gospels can be upheld. Lührmann (*Die apokryph gewordenen Evangelien,* 125–33) expresses some serious doubts; see also Joachim Jeremias and Wilhelm Schneemelcher, "Papyrus Egerton 2," in Schneemelcher, *NTApo,* 1. 96–99. I remain certain, however, that the "Unknown Gospel" is not dependent upon the Gospel of John.

51. Koester, *Ancient Christian Gospels,* 208–11; see also "Apocryphal and Canonical Gospels," pp. 14–16 of this volume.

52. The dates have been debated since its first publication, which dated it early in the second century; the present scholarly consensus prefers a later date, cf. Lührmann, *Die apokryph gewordenen Evangelien,* 127; Jeremias and Schneemelcher, "Papyrus Egerton 2," in Schneemelcher, *NTApo,* 1. 96–98.

53. See the assessment of Philipp Vielhauer, *Geschichte der urchristlichen Literatur* (DGL; Berlin: de Gruyter, 1975) 638.

gospel writing. Here belong the story of the discussion of Jesus with a "Pharisaic Chief Priest" (Papyrus Oxyrhynchus 840),[54] Pharisees and priests challenging Jesus' participation in a meal with sinners (Papyrus Oxyrhynchus 1224),[55] a fragment discussing Mary's and Joseph's flight to Egypt and Mary's encounter with Elizabeth (Papyrus Cairensis 10.735),[56] and a scene at the last meal of Jesus (the so-called Fayyum Fragment).[57] Some of these may belong to the second century. All of these, except Papyrus Oxyrhynchus 840, have parallels in the Synoptic Gospels and may demonstrate some knowledge of these gospels, in whatever way. They attest the fact that memories of gospel texts could be freely expanded, amplified, and joined with "apocryphal" traditions.

Dialogues of Jesus with his Disciples

Dialogues of Jesus with his disciples, often including longer monologue-type discourses of Jesus, became an increasingly popular form of gospel literature beginning at the end of the first century. Such dialogues must be presupposed for the Gospel of John, whose author revised such dialogues in both parts of his gospel. They are not necessarily dialogues of Jesus with his disciples *after* the resurrection. During the second and third centuries, dialogue gospel literature was further developed into what is commonly known as Gnostic gospel literature, where the relationship to older and independent gospel traditions is often no longer visible, and the setting of a discussion of Jesus with his disciples is not more than an artificial framework.[58] I shall present here three such dialogues, which are still related to materials of the gospel tradition and deserve to be dated fairly early.

The *Dialogue of the Savior*[59] is based on an older dialogue of Jesus with his disciples that is composed as a discussion of traditional sayings, possibly closely related to the sayings of the *Gospel of Thomas*. Although external evidence for the dating of this document is lacking, its character and some similarities to the farewell speeches of the Gospel of John argue for a date of the older dialogues of no later than the beginning of the second century. The sayings that are interpreted here, as Jesus talks with Mary, Judas (Thomas!), and Matthew, deal with the topics of the light, seeking and finding, marveling, and finding rest. Sometimes a traditional saying is used to formulate a question of a disciple; at other times a saying is the basis for the answer of Jesus. While in these older dialogue sections no dependence upon extant written gospels can be

---

54. Joachim Jeremias and Wilhelm Schneemelcher, "Oxyrhynchus Papyrus 840," in Schneemelcher, *NTApo,* 1. 94–95.

55. Wilhelm Schneemelcher, "Oxyrhynchus Papyrus 1224," in Schneemelcher, *NTApo,* 1. 100.

56. Schneemelcher, "Papyrus Cairensis 10 735," in Schneemelcher, *NTApo,* 1. 101.

57. Schneemelcher, "The so-called Fayyum Fragment," in Schneemelcher, *NTApo,* 1. 102.

58. This is clearly the case in the *Sophia Jesu Christi* (Nag Hammadi Codex III and V) and in the *Book of Thomas* (Nag Hammadi Codex II; see Hans-Martin Schenke, "The Book of Thomas," in Schneemelcher, *NTApo,* 1. 232–40).

59. Stephen Emmel, ed., *Nag Hammadi Codex III, 5: The Dialogue of the Savior* (NHS 26; Leiden: Brill, 1984); see also Koester, *Ancient Christian Gospels,* 173–87.

established, the later editor, who added several longer speeches of Jesus, is clearly dependent upon several letters of Paul. [60]

The *Apocryphon of James*[61] claims to be a letter of James regarding the transmission of the "secret book" that was revealed to James and Peter by the Lord. But this is only an external framework for what is essentially a discussion of the meaning of Jesus' sayings and parables.[62] The document was originally written in Greek early in the second century, probably in Syria/Palestine. There are close parallels to the sayings and discourses of the Gospel of John[63] as well as to some sayings[64] and parables[65] of the synoptic tradition, but dependence upon that canonical gospel is unlikely. Remarkably, there is also a list of parables (*Apocr. Jas.* 8,1–4): The Shepherds, the Seed, the Building, the Lamps of the Virgins, the Wage of the Workmen, the Didrachma, and the Woman. The author must have had access to a special collection of parables that also included the parable of the Palm Shoot (*Apocr. Jas.* 7, 22–28), which has no synoptic parallel. The dialogues of the *Apocryphon of James,* like those of the *Dialogue of the Savior,* are in any case less developed than those of the Gospel of John and can be characterized as precursors of the dialogues of the Fourth Gospel.

The *Gospel of Mary* also must be mentioned among the early dialogue gospels. It was discovered in 1896 as one of four writings of the fifth century Coptic Papyrus Berolinensis 8502 but was published for the first time in 1955.[66] Meanwhile two Greek fragments[67] have come to light that prove that the Greek original of the *Gospel of Mary* must have been written in the second century. These fragments also prove that the Coptic translator made some significant changes.[68] Unfortunately, the Coptic translation as well as the two Greek papyri are very fragmentary. The first six pages are missing completely in the Coptic text, and there is a major lacuna from page 11 to page 14. Thus much of the initial dialogue is lost. Only the end with a question of Peter, Jesus' answer,

60. The preserved writing that incorporated these dialogue materials may have been written at the end of the second century or later; it reveals some knowledge of the Pauline corpus.

61. Harold W. Attridge, ed., *Nag Hammadi Codex I (The Jung Codex)* (2 vols.; NHS 22–23; Leiden: Brill, 1985) 1. 13–35, 2. 7–37. This writing is also known as the *Epistula Iacobi.*

62. Ron Cameron, *Sayings Traditions in the Apocryphon of James* (HTS 34; Philadelphia: Trinity Press International, 1984); Dankwart Kirchner, "The Apocryphon of James," in Schneemelcher, *NTApo,* 1. 285–291; Koester, *Ancient Christian Gospels,* 187–200.

63. Cf. John 12:35–36; 14:9; 16:23, 26, 29; 20:29.

64. Matt 5:11 (Q).

65. The parable of the sower (Mark 4:26–29) is quoted in *Apocr. Jas.* 8, 16–23 and introduced with an allegorical interpretation (8, 10–15) that is completely different from the allegorical interpretation in the Synoptic Gospels.

66. Walter C. Till, *Die gnostischen Schriften des koptischen Papyrus Berolinensis 8502* (TU 60; Berlin: Akademie-Verlag, 1955; 2nd ed. by Hans-Martin Schenke, 1972).

67. Papyrus Oxyrhynchus 3525 and Papyrus Ryland 463, published in 1983 and 1938, respectively; only the latter papyrus was available for Till's edition. For a reconstruction of the Greek texts with the help of the Coptic version, see Lührmann, *Die apokryph gewordenen Evangelien,* 107–20. A very helpful English translation with the Coptic and Greek parallels side by side can be found in Karen L. King, *The Gospel of Mary of Magdala: Jesus and the First Woman Apostle* (Santa Rosa, Calif.: Polebridge, 2003) 13–18. I am indebted to King's book for my comments.

68. Lührmann, *Die apokryph gewordenen Evangelien,* 107–20.

and the farewell of Jesus is left from the first part of this writing. Although the question of Peter and Jesus' answer are probably based on Romans 7,[69] Jesus' farewell speech includes several allusions to sayings of the gospel tradition. The preserved text consists mostly of a dialogue between Mary and the disciples. Mary consoles the disciples, who are distressed because of Jesus' departure, and tells them what Jesus had revealed to her in a vision. While Andrew and Peter object saying that Jesus could not have revealed all this to a woman, Levi (=Matthew!) sides with Mary and according to the older Greek version of Papyrus Ryland 463, goes alone to fulfill the command of Jesus to go out and to preach the good news. The later Coptic translator tells that all the disciples went out to teach and to preach. Whatever appears as gospel tradition are free sayings of Jesus that can hardly be traced back to an origin in the canonical gospels.[70]

The Gospels That Later Became Canonical in the Second Century

The fluid state of gospels and gospel traditions in the second century that is evident in a number of so-called apocryphal gospels raises the question of whether the gospels that later became canonical were not also subject to changes, additions, and new editions. Except for the small fragment of the Gospel of John in 𝔓 52, no gospel manuscript written in the second century or fragments of such a gospel manuscript have survived. The earliest manuscripts of the canonical gospels date from around the year 200, mostly John and Luke. Matthew appears less often and Mark only 50 years later. What happened to these gospels in the time from their autograph to their earliest manuscript evidence? This does not concern the changes in the texts of the canonical gospels that are evident in the later manuscript tradition, such as the addition of the secondary ending of the Gospel of Mark and the addition of the story of the woman taken in adultery in John 7:59–8:11.

The question is made even more urgent because of what we know about the use in the second century of the four gospels that later became canonical. Marcion radically edited the Gospel of Luke for his new authoritative scriptures. Justin Martyr composed a harmony of the Synoptic Gospels, for the most part neglecting the Gospel of Mark. A bit later, his student Tatian composed a harmony of all four canonical gospels, including also the Gospel of John. Gospels that were later called apocryphal liberally used materials from the gospels that later became canonical and often combined freely their borrowings with surviving older sources and free "apocryphal" materials. Other gospels expanded sayings of Jesus to form dialogues of Jesus with his disciples—a process that already apparently had begun in the last decades of the first century, as is evident in the dialogues and discourses of the Gospel of John. Moreover, the memory of Jesus, especially in his sayings, was alive as the voice of the Savior that spoke again in new pronunciations through prophets and speakers of wisdom.

---

69. King, *The Gospel of Mary of Magdala*, 119–27.
70. See King's careful analysis, ibid., 93–118.

There are a number of indications that the earliest manuscripts of the canonical gospels do not represent the text of the original that circulated right after they were first published. The Gospel of John was originally published without chapter 21—which contains the narrative of Jesus' appearance at the lake[71]—and without the several corrections of John's radically realized eschatology[72] and the eucharistic interpolation in chapter 6.[73] Moreover, the question of the original order of some chapters in the Gospel of John has been discussed repeatedly. Did John 15–17 originally stand after John 13:34–35, and did chapter 6 originally follow directly upon chapter 4?[74] Even if such suggestions for the reordering of the sequence of some chapters are not generally accepted, it must be conceded that the extant manuscripts do not present the Gospel of John in its original form.

While the text of the Gospel of Matthew, as far as can be known, seemed to have been quite stable throughout the second century,[75] the work of Luke has survived in two different versions, the Alexandrian text and the so-called Western text. As the differences of these two text forms persist throughout the Gospel of Luke and the Book of Acts, both versions must have been published before the separation of Luke's work into two different books. Although the Alexandrian text is preferred by most scholars as the original version, the Western text also is known to have been used in the middle of the second century.[76] That the text of Luke's gospel (as also that of the Gospel of Matthew!) was by no means sacrosanct is evident in Justin Martyr's free expansions of Lukan materials in his harmonizations of the texts of the Synoptic Gospels;[77] and also in Marcion's radical new edition of that gospel.

With respect to the Gospel of Mark, it has long been suspected that the text of Mark preserved in the manuscript tradition may not be identical with the text of the gospel that was used by Matthew and Luke. This suggestion is based on the observation of many "common agreements" of the texts of Matthew and Luke, whenever both are dependent upon the text of Mark. Many of these common agreements perhaps could be explained without assuming a different Markan text as Matthew's and Luke's common source.[78] There is also the possibility that the extant text of Luke may have been

---

71. The beginning of a variant of this story stands at the end of the Akhmim fragment of the *Gospel of Peter.*

72. John 5:27b–29 and the phrase "and I shall raise him on the last day" (6:39b, 40b, 44b).

73. John 6:51b–59; see Günther Bornkamm, "Die eucharistische Rede im Johannesevangelium," *ZNW* 47 (1956) 161–69; Raymond E. Brown, *The Gospel according to John* (2 vols.; AB 29–30; Garden City, N.J.: Prentice Hall, 1966–1970) 1. 289–94, 303–4.

74. Rudolf Bultmann, *The Gospel of John: A Commentary* (Philadelphia: Westminster, 1971) 459–60, 209–10.

75. Matthew appears later in a revised version, supplemented with apocryphal sayings, in Aramaic translation known as the *Gospel of the Nazoreans.*

76. See my essay "The Text of the Synoptic Gospels in the Second Century," in William L. Petersen, ed., *Gospel Traditions in the Second Century: Origins, Recensions, Text, and Transmission* (Christianity and Judaism in Antiquity 3; Notre Dame: University of Notre Dame Press, 1989) 19–37, as well as other contributions in that volume. My essay is included in this volume, pp. 39–53.

77. See Koester, *Ancient Christian Gospels,* 360–402.

78. F. Neirynck, *The Minor Agreements of Matthew and Luke against Mark* (BETL 37; Leuven: Leuven University Press, 1979).

influenced by the better-known text of Matthew.[79] However, these possible explanations— even if seemingly persuasive—call for a reevaluation in the light of the publication of a fragment of a letter of Clement of Alexandria, which quotes and discusses two passages from a *Secret Gospel of Mark*.[80] In spite of some doubts regarding the authenticity of the letter,[81] what these references to the *Secret Gospel of Mark* might suggest for the history of the text of Mark's gospel should be given some serious consideration.[82] I have observed that in a number of instances of the canonical text of Mark, there are special Markan features that are absent in the Gospels of Matthew and Luke but fit in very well with the tendency and wording of the story of the raising of a young man that is told in the *Secret Gospel*.[83] The story of the raising of the young man, though no longer present in the canonical text of Mark, is itself remarkable as form-critically much older than the version of this story in John 11. The version of the story of the epileptic boy in Mark 9:14–29 seems to be the product of a later editor, who changed the much simpler account of an exorcism, still well preserved in both Matt. 17:14–21 and Luke 9:37–43a, into a story of the raising of the boy from the dead. This rewriting creates a parallel to the raising of the young man that was inserted in the *Secret Gospel* after Mark 10:34. Closely related is the note in Mark 14:51–52 about a young man letting his linen cloth go and fleeing naked at the arrest of Jesus, which is missing in both Matthew and Luke. It recalls the appendix to the story of the young man who was raised from the dead, of whom the *Secret Gospel* tells that he went to Jesus to be initiated into the mystery (μυστήριον) of the kingdom of God "dressed with a linen cloth over his naked body." Finally, there is the use of the term "mystery" in the singular in Mark 4:11, where both Matthew (1:11) and Luke (8:10) use the much more appropriate plural. Therefore, there are several passages in the extant text of the canonical Gospel of Mark that reveal the changes and additions introduced by the author of *Secret Mark*.[84] The story of Mark's gospel may thus be a paradigm for the instability of the text during the second century of a gospel that later became canonical.

---

79. This possibility is repeatedly discussed in François Bovon, *Luke 1: A Commentary on the Gospel of Luke 1:1–9:50* (Hermeneia; Minneapolis: Fortress Press, 2002) passim.

80. Smith, *Clement of Alexandria and a Secret Gospel of Mark*; English translations of the two quotations from Clement's letter and a listing of relevant literature can be found in Helmut Merkel, "Appendix: The 'Secret Gospel' of Mark," in Schneemelcher, *NTApo*, 1. 106–9.

81. See the previously mentioned contribution of Merkel to Schneemelcher, *NTApo*, where the relegation of this text to an "Appendix" already indicates the gratuitous negative judgment. See also Charles H. Hedrick, Guy G. Stroumsa, and Bart D. Ehrman, "The Secret Gospel of Mark: A Discussion," *JECS* 11 (2003) 133–63.

82. Helmut Koester, "History and Development of Mark's Gospel (From Mark to *Secret Mark* and 'Canonical' Mark)," in Bruce Corley, ed., *Colloquy on the New Testament* (Macon, Ga.: Mercer University Press, 1983) 35–57.

83. See also Koester, *Ancient Christian Gospels*, 275–84, 293–303.

84. There are other instances, not related to the text of the *Secret Gospel*, where the question can be raised of whether the extant text of Mark is identical with the text of Mark used by Matthew and Luke. The most striking example is the expansion of the question of the Great Commandment in Mark 12:28–31 with the quotation of Deut 6:4 ("Hear, O Israel . . .") and Jesus' debate with the scribe, who is not far from the kingdom of God. See Günther Bornkamm, "Das Doppelgebot der Liebe," in Walter Eltester, ed., *Neutestamentliche Studien für Rudolf Bultmann* (BZNW 21; Berlin: Töpelmann, 1954) 85–93.

A Concluding Remark

The time-honored division of canonical gospels and apocryphal gospels falsifies the actual story of gospel literature in the second century. Rather, the extant witnesses attest that there were multiple gospels in circulation that were not distinguished at the time with respect to their authority and authenticity. Nor were their texts considered to be inviolable. On the contrary, their texts could be freely reused in new forms of writing, be expanded by new materials, and be shaped otherwise according to the demands of the community. All these gospels were not primarily produced as "literature" but as writings destined for oral performance; memory of texts heard and interpreted could also find its way into the copying of texts. Some of these gospels seem to have been restricted in their usage geographically or as the special property of one or another group of a very diversified Christianity, while others circulated freely.

The process that eventually resulted in the production of the four-gospel canon at the end of one hundred years of a very rich proliferation of gospel literature cannot be pursued here. It is most likely related to the fact that the gospels that became canonical were the property of Christian groups committed to building socially viable communities and whose central ritual was the Eucharist, interpreted by the memory and reading of the story of Jesus' suffering and death. Only gospels with a passion narrative were authorized for use in the emerging early catholic church.

3

THE TEXT OF THE
SYNOPTIC GOSPELS IN THE
SECOND CENTURY

Since there is no second-century manuscript evidence,[1] the quest for the text of the Synoptic Gospels in the second century is identical with the question of the earliest usage of their text in other writings. The evidence consists not only of such writers as the Apostolic Fathers and early Apologists but also of later gospel writers, such as Matthew and Luke, as external attestations for the text of an older gospel.

There are fundamental differences between a second-century user of a gospel and a fourth- or fifth-century quotation in a Church Father: (1) For a later user, the gospels of the New Testament were available as part of the four-gospel canon; in the period before the year 200 CE, the gospels were usually transmitted separately. (2) In the later period, the gospels were considered holy scripture; no such respect was accorded them in the earliest period. (3) Beginning only with the third century can we assign quotations to certain text types, attested in extant manuscripts, and often confirmed by translations into Syriac, Coptic, and Latin. For the earlier period, we have no manuscript evidence at all, and text types can be identified only by the evidence that comes from those who used gospels.

The problems for the reconstruction of the textual history of the canonical gospels in the first century of transmission are immense. The assumption that the reconstruction of the best archetype for the manuscript tradition is more or less identical with the assumed autograph is precarious. The oldest known manuscript archetypes are separated from the autographs by more than a century. Textual critics of classical texts know that the first century of transmission is the period in which the most serious corruption occurs. Textual critics of the New Testament writings have been surprisingly naïve in this respect.

Moreover, there can be no question that the gospels, from the very beginning, were not archive materials but used texts. This is the worst thing that could happen to any textual tradition. A text not protected by canonical status but used in liturgy, apologetics, polemics, homiletics, and instruction of catechumens is most likely to be copied frequently and is thus subject to frequent modifications and alterations. What then can be learned from these users of gospels about the alterations they introduced and about the texts that they used?[2]

---

1. The fragment of John in 𝔓52 is so small that it is immaterial as a textual witness.

2. François Bovon ("The Synoptic Gospels and the Noncanonical Acts of the Apostles," *HTR* 81 [1988] 19–36) gives examples from the transmission of the apocryphal acts as possible analogies for the way in which the gospels might have been transmitted and copied before their canonization.

Evidence for Matthew's and Luke's Use of Mark

The Synoptic two-source hypothesis asserts that Matthew and Luke used the Gospel of Mark as their primary source. The alterations that they made in their employment of this source have often been discussed and need not be repeated here. They include not only numerous instances of improving Mark's style and language, but also the rearrangement of larger blocks of materials and the addition of similar materials from other sources. Notable is the assembling of the most Markan miracle stories into a single collection by Matthew (chaps. 8–9). Matthew also expanded existing Markan collections. In reproducing Mark's parable collection (chap. 4), Matthew (chap. 13) added a number of parables from his special source. Luke, on the other hand, left the order of Markan pericopes mostly intact. However, he constantly interwove materials from the Synoptic Sayings Source and from his special source with Markan materials. Among the few departures from the Markan order, the most striking is the placement of Mark 6:1–6 (Jesus' Rejection at Nazareth) at the beginning of Jesus' ministry (Luke 4:16–24; following upon Luke 4:14–15 = Mark 1:14–15).[3]

Matthew and Luke not only provide examples for changes in the text of an older gospel, they are also important witnesses for the oldest text of their source. It is possible, to be sure, that there are instances in which Matthew and Luke, independently of each other, made the same stylistic improvements of Mark's text. But there should be no question that the oldest accessible text of the Gospel of Mark is preserved in most instances in which Matthew and Luke agree in their reproduction of their source—even if the extant Markan manuscript tradition presents a different text.

These instances of agreement are numerous. They include cases in which Matthew and Luke agree in the wording of a phrase or sentence that is different from Mark's text and cases in which Markan words, sentences, or entire pericopes are absent from both Matthew and Luke. I cannot repeat the entire material here. It has been presented and discussed in detail by Frans Neirynck in defense of the two-source hypothesis[4] and by Hans-Herbert Stoldt in his criticism of this hypothesis.[5] In the following I shall discuss only some striking examples.

According to the overwhelming majority of textual witnesses, the text of Mark 4:11 reads: "To you is given the mystery of the rule of God" (Ὑμῖν τὸ μυστήριον δέδοται τῆς βασιλείας τοῦ θεοῦ). However, the parallel passages in Matthew (13:11) and Luke (8:10) agree in reading "to know" (γνῶναι) after "is given" (δέδοται) and the plural "mysteries" (μυστήρια) instead of the singular "mystery" (μυστήριον) of Mark 4:11.[6]

---

3. Furthermore, two Markan pericopes have been placed into the Lukan "Travel Narrative" (Luke 9:51–18:14); Luke 10:25–28 = Mark 12:28–31 (The Great Commandment); Luke 11:15–22 = Mark 3:22–27 (Beelzebul Controversy).

4. Frans Neirynck, *The Minor Agreements of Matthew and Luke against Mark* (BETL 37; Leuven: Leuven University Press, 1974); see also C. M. Tuckett, *The Revival of the Griesbach Hypothesis* (SNTSMS 44; Cambridge: Cambridge University Press, 1983).

5. Hans-Herbert Stoldt, *History and Criticism of the Marcan Hypothesis* (Macon, Ga.: Mercer University Press, 1980).

6. There is considerable variation in the manuscript tradition. Both singular and plural occur in manuscripts of all three gospels. However, the occurrence of the singular in manuscripts of Matthew and Luke and

Thus Matthew and Luke agree in their formulations: "To you is given to know the mysteries of the rule of God (Matthew: of the heavens)" = Ὑμῖν δέδοται γνῶναι τὰ μυστήρια τῆς βασιλείας τοῦ θεοῦ (τῶν οὐρανῶν).

As far as the context is concerned, both Matthew and Luke drew everything surrounding this discourse of Jesus with the disciples (the Parable of the Sower and its allegorical interpretation) from the Gospel of Mark, not from a different common source. Thus, they must have preserved the original Markan text also in the statement of Jesus to the disciples in Mark 4:11. Moreover, the plural "mysteries" is appropriate here: each parable is "a mystery," that is, a mysterious saying or a riddle that must be explained.[7] This use is more original,[8] while the singular "mystery" as a designation of the entire preaching of Jesus or of the entire gospel occurs only in later Christian literature.[9]

In numerous instances, Matthew and Luke agree against Mark in the choice of a particular term. One of the most striking cases is the use of ἐγερθῆναι in Matthew and Luke instead of Mark's ἀναστῆναι in two of the Predictions of the Passion. In the first Prediction of the Passion, Matt 16:21 and Luke 9:22 are in agreement in their reading, "and on the third day he will be raised" (καὶ τῇ τρίτῃ ἡμέρᾳ ἐγερθῆναι), while the extant text of their common source, Mark 8:31, says: "and after three days he will rise" (καὶ μετὰ τρεῖς ἡμέρας ἀναστῆναι).[10] In the reproduction of the second and third Predictions of the Passion (Mark 9:31; 10:34), Matthew (17:23; 20:19) also uses the term "he will be raised" (ἐγερθήσεται) instead of Mark's "he will rise" (ἀναστήσεται). In these last two instances, the evidence is less conclusive with respect to the original reading of Mark, because a Lukan parallel to Mark 9:31 is missing and in the parallel to Mark 10:34, Luke (18:33) agrees with Mark's extant text "he will rise" (ἀναστήσεται). But "to be raised" (ἐγερθῆναι) is more common in the oldest Christian

---

the occurrence of the plural in manuscripts of Mark is due to later corruption and is not the survival of a more original reading. The archetype for all Markan manuscripts reads the singular.

7. Joachim Jeremias (*The Parables of Jesus* [2nd ed.; New York: Scribner's, 1972] 13–18) has shown that Mark 4:11–12 is an older and originally independent saying. He points to the antithetical parallelism of the phrases, "to you the mystery is given" and "to those outside it comes in parables." However, Jeremias fails to explain why Mark 4:11 reads the singular "mystery" as antithesis to the plural "parables" (cf. also the plural in Mark 4:34: "to his disciples he explained all these things"). The problem is resolved if the plural form in the first half of the antithesis in Matt 13:11 and Luke 8:10 ("to you it is given to know the mysteries") was also the original reading of Mark 4:11.

8. The *Gospel of Thomas* uses the plural in a saying that introduces several parables: "It is to those who are worthy of my mysteries that I give my mysteries" (62). Paul confirms the analogous usage. When referring to an individual saying, he uses the singular (Rom 11:25; 1 Cor 15:51); otherwise he uses the plural; cf. 1 Cor 13:2: "and if I knew all the mysteries" (see also 1 Cor 4:1; 13:2). See Günther Bornkamm, "μυστήριον," *TDNT* 4 (1967) 802–28.

9. Typical for later usage is the identification of "mystery" and "gospel" or the close association of the two terms; cf. Eph 6:19: "to make known the mystery of the gospel" (see also Eph 3:1–7).

10. Mark's phrase "after three days" instead of "on the third day" is peculiar. It contradicts Mark's own dating of the resurrection: the empty tomb is found on the morning of the third day. Morton Smith (*Clement of Alexandria and a Secret Gospel of Mark* [Cambridge, Mass.: Harvard University Press, 1973] 163–64) points out that "after three days" actually means "on the fourth day" and that there is an interesting parallel in John 11:17 and 39, the Johannine parallel to the story of the raising of the young man reported in the *Secret Gospel of Mark*: Lazarus was raised on the fourth day after his death.

usage (see also 1 Cor 15:4) and is, therefore, most likely the term that appeared in Mark's original text.[11]

The two words "to teach" (διδάσκειν) and "teaching" (διδαχή) were certainly used in the oldest text of the Gospel of Mark. Matthew or Luke or both reproduce them in their usage of the following Markan passages: 1:21, 22; 6:2, 6; (7:7); 11:18; 12:14; 14:49. However, there are a number of Markan passages in which the term occurs without equivalent terms occurring in the corresponding parallels in Matthew and Luke. In Mark 1:27, the witnesses to Jesus' exorcism (1:23–26) respond by saying "a new teaching with authority" (διδαχὴ καινὴ κατ᾽ ἐξουσίαν). The phrase "new teaching" appears only in one other New Testament passage, Acts 17:19: "What is this new teaching that is proclaimed by you?" (τίς ἡ καινὴ αὕτη ἡ ὑπὸ σοῦ λαλουμένη διδαχή). As Acts 17:32 reveals, this new teaching is "the resurrection from the dead." Another important parallel occurs in the gospel fragment from P. Oxy. 1224, 2 v. col. I: "Which new teaching do they say you teach, and which new baptism do you proclaim?" (π[ο]ίαν σέ [φασιν διδα]χὴν καιν[ὴν διδάσκειν ἢ τί β]ά[πτισμ]α καινὸν [κηρύσσειν]. . .).[12]

In Mark 6:7 the Twelve are sent out "with power over the unclean spirits." When they return (Mark 6:30), they announce to him "all they had done and what they had taught" (πάντα ὅσα ἐποίησαν καὶ ὅσα ἐδίδαξαν). The parallel passages (Matt 14:12 and Luke 9:10) do not present the latter phrase καὶ ὅσα ἐδίδαξαν. In the subsequent introduction to the story of the Feeding of the Five Thousand, Mark 6:34 says, "and Jesus began to teach (διδάσκειν) them many things." Matt 14:14 only reports that Jesus healed the sick; Luke 9:11 contains a similar remark and notes that Jesus was "speaking" (ἐλάλει) about the rule of God. Mark 8:31 and 9:31 introduce the first and second Predictions of the Passion with the words "he began to teach" and "he taught"; no such statement appears in the parallels in Matthew and Luke. In addition to these passages, Mark 2:13; 4:1–2; 10:1; 11:17; 12:35, 37, 38 also use the word "to teach" for the activity of Jesus, while Matthew and Luke use different verbs in their parallel passages.

The story of the Healing of the Epileptic Child, Mark 9:14–29, is the most complex miracle narrative in Mark and presents the most difficult problems for the explanation of its origin and its relationship to the parallels in Matthew (17:14–21) and Luke (9:38–43a).[13] Mark's version of the story is more than twice as long as the parallel versions in Matthew and Luke. In addition, Mark 9:14b–16, 21, 22b–24, parts of 25–27, and 28 have no parallels in either Matthew or Luke. It seems that both read a version of this story in their copy of Mark that did not contain these verses. Especially the phrases and sentences of Mark 9:25–27, which are missing in the other two Synoptic Gospels, have the appearance of secondary alterations or additions. Matt 17:18 and Luke 9:42b must have read a common source which reported briefly that Jesus exorcised the unclean spirit

---

11. See the use of ἐγείρειν in other formulaic passages such as Rom 4:24; 1 Thess 1:10.

12. Erich Klostermann, *Apocrypha II: Evangelien*, KlT, no. 8 (3rd ed.; Berlin: de Gruyter, 1929) 26.

13. Commentaries try to explain the complexity of the Markan story as the result of an inept redaction by the author of the Gospel who may have tried to conflate two older stories. However, they do not use the much simpler forms of the story in Matthew and Luke as a guide for the reconstruction of the original story in Mark. For discussion and literature, see Walter Schmithals, *Das Evangelium nach Markus* (ÖTKNT 2/1; Gütersloh: Gütersloher Verlagshaus, 1979) 407–424.

(ἐπετίμησεν κτλ.), that the child was healed (Matt: ἐθεραπεύθη, Luke: ἰάσατο), and perhaps a reaction of the crowd (preserved only in Luke 9:43). The extant text of Mark, however, quotes in full the wording of an exorcistic formula, indeed the longest such formula in the Synoptic Gospels.[14] "You mute and deaf spirit, I command you, go out of him and never enter into him again" (Τὸ ἄλαλον καὶ κωφὸν πνεῦμα, ἐγὼ ἐπιτάσσω σοι, ἔξελθε ἐξ αὐτοῦ καὶ μηκέτι εἰσέλθης εἰς αὐτόν). Surprisingly, this is an exorcism for a deaf-mute person, not for an epileptic child.[15] Apparently, the redactor shows little interest in the healing of the disease. Rather, he wants to describe the effect of a powerful exorcism and thus introduces the following action of Jesus that has no parallel whatever in Matthew and Luke: the demon departs with appropriate demonstration, the boy is left "as if dead" (ὡσεὶ νεκρός), and the bystanders say "he died" (ἀπέθανεν). This prepares for an action of Jesus which is described as the raising of a dead person: Jesus takes him by the hand (κρατήσας τῆς χειρὸς αὐτοῦ), raises him, and he rises (ἤγειρεν αὐτόν, καὶ ἀνέστη).

There are several "major omissions" of Markan pericopes or parts of pericopes that Matthew and Luke share. At least in two instances, they apparently did not appear in the original Markan text that was used by Matthew and Luke.

The Parable of the Seed Growing Secretly (Mark 4:26–29) is not reproduced by either Matthew or Luke. If Matthew found the parable in his copy of Mark, one must resort to the explanation that he replaced it with the Parable of the Tares (Matt 13:24–30). However, the additions to the Markan parable chapter in Matt 13 show that he was eager to expand this chapter.[16] As Luke also does not reproduce this parable in his version of the parable chapter (Luke 8:4–18) nor anywhere else in his gospel, it is more likely that the original text of Mark did not include it.[17] In Mark 12:28–31 (= Matt 22:34–40 and Luke 10:25–28), the pericope about the Great Commandment is provided with an appendix about "the scribe who is not far from the rule of God" (Mark 12:32–34). Günther Bornkamm has demonstrated that this appendix is a later addition to the text of Mark, written from the perspective of Hellenistic propaganda.[18] The scribe acknowledges that Jesus "in truth" (ἐπ᾽ ἀληθείας) puts forward first of all the confession of Hellenistic Jewish and Christian propaganda that "God is one" (εἷς ἐστιν, Mark 12:32)—thus the quote of Deut 6:3, which appears only in Mark (12:29), is also an expansion. He then adds the phrase, "out of your whole understanding" (ἐξ ὅλης τῆς συνέσεως, Mark 12:33), in the repetition of the commandment to love God (Deut 6:5). Finally, he contrasts love of one's neighbor with "burnt offerings and sacrifices,"

---

14. The other exorcistic formulae cited in the Synoptic Gospels are very brief; cf. Mark 1:41; 2:11; 3:5; 10:52; Luke 8:54; 13:12; 17:14.

15. Mark, or a later redactor, has changed 9:17 accordingly (ἔχοντα πνεῦμα ἄλαλον), although the original description of the disease is still visible in Mark 9:18, 20, 22.

16. Cf. Matt 13:33, 44–46, 47–50, 51–52.

17. Philipp Vielhauer (*Geschichte der frühchristlichen Literatur* [Berlin: de Gruyter, 1975] 273–75) considers this the only certain evidence for the thesis that the original text of Mark differed from the canonical text.

18. Günther Bornkamm, "Das Doppelgebot der Liebe," in Walther Eltester, ed., *Neutestamentliche Studien für Rudolf Bultmann* (BZNW 21; Berlin: Töpelmann, 1954) 85–93.

another typical commonplace of Jewish and Christian propaganda. Jesus finally answers that the scribe has spoken "with understanding" (νουνεχῶς, Mark 12:34).[19]

The Evidence from the Apostolic Fathers

At an earlier time in New Testament scholarship, the Apostolic Fathers played a major role in attempts to establish an early *terminus ante quem* for the composition of the canonical gospels.[20] Though one may still find occasional claims that Matthew and Luke were used in the *First Epistle of Clement*, in the *Epistle of Barnabas*, and in the *Didache* or that the Gospel of John was used by Ignatius of Antioch, it is now more generally acknowledged that there is no basis for such assumptions. The careful investigation by a British committee of scholars at the beginning of this century[21] has made scholars more cautious in this respect.[22]

The earliest use of the Gospel of Matthew appears in the letter of Polycarp of Smyrna. In *Phil.* 2.3, he quotes sayings of Jesus from *1 Clem.* 13.2.[23] However, Polycarp does not reproduce these sayings as they appear in *1 Clement*. Rather he revises the text in order to achieve a more exact agreement with the Matthean parallels.[24] It is not certain that this use of Matthew can be dated early in the second century CE. More likely, the part of the letter of Polycarp in which these quotations appear was not written until the middle of the second century, as Harrison has argued quite convincingly.[25]

---

19. I leave aside here the problem of Mark 6:45–8:26, the "Bethsaida section," which is completely missing in Luke. It at least is possible that Luke had a text of Mark in which this section was missing, whether or not this was a defective or a more original copy of Mark. As is well known, this Markan section contains a number of doublets to the preceding chapters. This would support the view that this section is a secondary addition.

20. The classical work was written by Constantin Tischendorf, *Wann wurden unsere Evangelien verfaßt?* (4th ed.; Leipzig: J. C. Hinrichs, 1866); the most comprehensive material was brought together by Theodor Zahn, *Geschichte des neutestamentlichen Kanons* (2 vols.; Erlangen and Leipzig: A. Deichert, 1888–1892). These works were primarily directed against the arguments for second-century dates of the gospels of the New Testament that were based on the lack of certain quotations from these gospels in the Apostolic Fathers; cf. I. H. Scholten, *Die ältesten Zeugnisse betreffs der Schriften des Neuen Testaments* (Bremen, 1867).

21. *The New Testament in the Apostolic Fathers*, by a committee of the Oxford Society of Historical Theology (Oxford: Clarendon, 1905). For a more comprehensive study, see Helmut Koester, *Synoptische Überlieferung bei den Apostolischen Vätern* (TU 65; Berlin: Akademie-Verlag, 1957).

22. The work of Édouard Massaux, *Influence de l'Évangile de saint Matthieu sur la littérature chrétienne avant saint Irénée* (Louvain: Universitaires de Louvain, 1950), now also available in English translation (*The Influence of the Gospel of Saint Matthew on Christian Literature before Saint Irenaeus* [Macon, Ga.: Mercer University Press, 1990–1993), is too uncritical in this respect and assumes the use of Matthew in numerous instances in which reliance on oral or an apocryphal tradition is the more appropriate explanation.

23. That Polycarp is dependent upon *1 Clement* is evident in the quotation formula: μνημονεύοντες δὲ ὧν εἶπεν ὁ κύριος, διδάσκων; cf. *1 Clem.* 13.1: μεμνημένοι τῶν λόγων τοῦ κυρίου Ἰησοῦ, οὓς ἐλάλησεν διδάσκων, οὕτως γὰρ εἶπεν. See Koester, *Synoptische Überlieferung*, 115–18.

24. Knowledge of the text of Matthew is also evident in Polycarp, *Phil.* 7.2, where he combines an allusion to the Lord's Prayer ("Lead us not into temptation") with a sentence spoken by Jesus in the Gethsemane narrative: "As the Lord said, 'the flesh is willing, but the spirit is weak'" (Mark 14:38 = Matt 26:41).

25. P. N. Harrison, *Polycarp's Two Epistles to the Philippians* (Cambridge: Cambridge University Press, 1936).

The information of Papias about Mark and Matthew[26] may indeed refer to the two canonical gospels transmitted under these names.[27] But Eusebius has not preserved anything that Papias may have quoted from these gospels. Thus, nothing can be learned from Papias about the text of these gospels.

The *Second Epistle of Clement*, written around the middle of the second century, is the only writing from the corpus of the Apostolic Fathers in which a number of quotations of sayings of Jesus appear which could be claimed as evidence for the use of canonical gospels. These quotations are very instructive.[28] (1) Nowhere does one find allusions to narrative materials from any written gospel known to us. (2) The sayings quoted here are certainly not taken directly from any canonical gospel by the author of this writing; rather, they derive from a collection of sayings into which apocryphal sayings also have been incorporated.[29] (3) Almost all the sayings are harmonizations of parallel texts of Matthew and Luke, reflecting redactional changes introduced by these two gospel writers.

The third point is evident in *2 Clem.* 4.2, 5, quoting parts of Matt 7:21–23 = Luke 6:46 and 13:22–28. A more fully harmonized text of these sayings occurs in two quotations in Justin Martyr, *1 Apol.* 16.9–12 and *Dial.* 76.5.

2 Clem. [Justin]	Matthew	Luke
οὐ πᾶς ὁ λέγων	οὐ πᾶς ὁ λέγων μοι	τί δέ με καλεῖτε
[εἰσελεύσεται . . .]	εἰσελεύσεται . . .	
ἀλλ᾽ ὁ ποιῶν . . .	ἀλλ᾽ ὁ ποιῶν	
[πολλοὶ ἐροῦσίν μοι	πολλοὶ ἐροῦσίν μοι	τότε ἄρξεσθε λέγειν
ἐφάγομεν		ἐφάγομεν ἐνώπιόν
καὶ ἐπίομεν		σου καὶ ἐπίομεν
καὶ προεφητεύσαμεν	καὶ ἐπροφητεύσαμεν	
καὶ	καὶ τῷ σῷ ὀνόματι	
δαιμόνια ἐξεβάλομεν]	δαιμόνια ἐξεβάλομεν	
καὶ	καὶ τότε	καὶ
ἐρῶ ὑμῖν [αὐτοῖς]	ὁμολογήσω αὐτοῖς	ἐρεῖ λέγων ὑμῖν
[ἀποχωρεῖτε ἀπ᾽ ἐμοῦ]	ἀποχωρεῖτε ἀπ᾽ ἐμοῦ	ἀπόστητε ἀπ᾽ ἐμοῦ
ἐργάται	οἱ ἐργαζόμενοι	πάντες ἐργάται
ἀνομίας	τὴν ἀνομίαν	ἀδικίας

---

26. Cf. Eusebius *Hist. eccl.* 3.39.15, 16.

27. The reference to Matthew has been taken by some scholars as a witness to the Synoptic Sayings Source, although more recent arguments have been presented which reaffirm the traditional view that the canonical Gospel of Matthew was known to Papias. For a more complete discussion, cf. Ron Cameron, *Apocryphon of James* (HTS 34; Philadelphia: Fortress Press, 1984) 93–116.

28. For these sayings, see Koester, *Synoptische Überlieferung*, 70–105.

29. *2 Clem.* 4.5 contains a sentence ("If you were assembled on my breast . . .") that is commonly assigned to the *Gospel of the Nazoreans. 2 Clem.* 12.2, 6 quotes a saying ("When two are one . . .") that Clement of Alexandria (*Strom.* 3.13, 92.2) found in the *Gospel of the Egyptians* and that is now also attested in the *Gospel of Thomas* (22).

The last phrase of this saying is drawn by Matthew and Luke from the Synoptic Sayings Source which in turn uses Ps 6:9: ἀπόστητε ἀπ᾿ ἐμοῦ, πάντες οἱ ἐργαζόμενοι τὴν ἀνομίαν.[30] It is likely that this wording appeared in the Synoptic Sayings Source. Matt 7:23 changed the beginning of the sentence to ἀποχωρεῖτε ἀπ᾿ ἐμοῦ . . . , whereas Luke 13:27 changed only the second half of the sentence to πάντες ἐργάται ἀδικίας. That *2 Clement* and Justin present a mixture of these redactional changes is evident. It is unlikely that this is just an accidental mixture of the parallel versions. Other parallels in Justin's quotations confirm that these harmonized sayings derive from a systematic harmonization of Matthew and Luke; special features of Mark's text never occur.

Justin Martyr as a Witness to the Text of the Gospels

The mixture of synoptic parallels in the quotations of sayings of Jesus in Justin Martyr has, of course, been observed for a long time. Many solutions have been proposed, ranging from use of a pre-synoptic source,[31] exclusive use of the canonical gospels,[32] use of an apocryphal gospel,[33] and careless quotation from memory[34] to the employment of a systematic harmony of the canonical gospels.[35] In an investigation of all sayings quoted in Justin's writings, Arthur Bellinzoni has demonstrated that Justin's quotations rest on a systematic harmonization of written gospels and that only the gospels of Matthew and Luke have been used to produce these harmonized texts.[36] However, Bellinzoni does not believe that Justin possessed a full harmony of these two gospels. Rather, for the sayings, he presupposes a written catechism for which harmonized forms of the sayings were produced. The occasional appearance of non-canonical sayings in Justin's writings is explained as deriving from the use of "traditional" sources, such as liturgical texts or early Christian handbooks known in similar form to other fathers in the early church.[37] The reference to one or several catechisms with a harmonized text may seem a satisfactory explanation of the sayings in Justin. The question, however, remains whether the "catechisms" from which Justin quotes are composed as harmonies on the basis of the two separate gospels of Matthew and Luke, or whether they are excerpts from a previously composed harmony of Matthew and Luke. It seems to me that the

---

30. For a presentation of all parallels, see Koester, *Synoptische Überlieferung*, 88.

31. Wilhelm Bousset, *Die Evangeliencitate Justins des Märtyrers in ihrem Wert für die Evangelienkritik* (Göttingen: Vandenhoeck & Ruprecht, 1891).

32. Édouard Massaux, "Le texte du Sermon sur la Montagne de Matthieu utilisé par Saint Justin," *ETL* 28 (1952) 411–48; Massaux, *Influence de l'Évangile de St. Matthieu,* passim.

33. Adolf Hilgenfeld, *Kritische Untersuchungen über die Evangelien Justins, der Clementinischen Homilien und Marcions* (Halle: C. A. Schwetschke, 1850).

34. Theodor Zahn, *Geschichte des neutestamentlichen Kanons* (Erlangen: A. Deichert, 1888) 1. 2, passim.

35. Ernest Lippelt, *Quae fuerint Justini Martyris APOMNEMONEUMATA* (Halle: E. Karras, 1901).

36. Arthur J. Bellinzoni, *The Sayings of Jesus in the Writings of Justin Martyr* (NovTSup 17; Leiden: Brill, 1967). See ibid. for a full bibliography on the various hypotheses summarized above.

37. Bellinzoni, *The Sayings of Jesus,* 138; cf. Bellinzoni, "The Source of the Agraphon in Justin Martyr's Dialogue with Trypho 47:5," *VC* 17 (1963) 65–70.

way in which Justin's catechisms move from one saying to another suggests that he is not composing a catechism and at the same time harmonizing the readings of the two gospels for that particular purpose. Rather, the sayings he included in his catechism were already harmonized in his *Vorlage*. Whoever produced this *Vorlage*—and I am inclined to think that it was Justin himself or his "school"—did not intend to construct a catechism but was composing the *one* inclusive new gospel that would make its predecessors, Matthew and Luke (and possibly Mark), obsolete.

To illustrate the method used by the composer of this harmony, I shall consider one example that also includes the passage already cited above in the discussion of *2 Clement*: Justin *1 Apol*. 16.9–13.[38]

1 Apol. 16.9	=	Matt 7:21 = Luke 6:46.
1 Apol. 16.10	=	Luke 10:16, which is a variant of Luke 6:47 with a phrase from Luke 6:46 not quoted in *1 Apol*. 16:9.
1 Apol. 16.11	=	harmonization of Matt 7:22–23 and Luke 13:26–27.
1 Apol. 16.12	=	harmonization of Matt 13:42–43 and Luke 13:28.
1 Apol. 16.13	=	combination of Matt 24:5 with Matt 7:15–16, 19.

The writer of this new gospel used Matthew 7 as the basis, moved from Matthew 7 to the proper Lukan parallel (6:46), replaced the following verse in Luke (6:47) with a variant found in Luke 10:21, returned to the Matthean context (7:22–23), harmonized it with the Lukan parallel (13:26–27), quoted the following Lukan verse (13:28) and harmonized it with the appropriate Matthean parallel (13:42–43), then returned to another saying from Matthew 7 (vv. 15–16), and combined it with a variant from Matthew 24 (verse 5).[39] This is a complex procedure that the composition of catechetical materials would hardly require, but could well be the result of a systematic composition of a new gospel on the basis of several older sources. The procedure resembles that of Matthew, who frequently combines and amalgamates parallels from his two sources Mark and Q, whereas Luke more often reproduces such variants twice in separate sections of his Gospel.

The harmonized quotations of gospel narrative materials in Justin also call for an explanation. More detailed analysis would demonstrate that, also in this respect, Justin follows the "School of St. Matthew." Justin (or his source) wants to bring the narrative texts into closer agreement with scriptural prophecy. In almost all instances, Justin quotes such narrative materials from the gospels in order to demonstrate the fulfillment of biblical prophecies, and his choice of sentences and phrases from either Matthew or Luke is dictated by the requirements of such scriptural proof. One example must suffice here, a section from the passion narrative quoted as a proof for the fulfillment of Psalm 21:8–9.

---

38. This passage is also discussed in Bellinzoni, *The Sayings of Jesus*, 98–100.
39. It is, of course, possible that the quote stood before Matt 7:21 in Justin's *Vorlage*.

Psalm 21:8-9	Justin, *Dial.* 101.3[40]	Synoptic Gospels
		Luke 23:35:
πάντες οἱ	οἱ	εἰστήκει ὁ λαὸς
θεωροῦντές με	θεωροῦντες αὐτὸν	θεωρῶν
		Matt 27:29:
ἐκίνουν κεφαλὴν	τὰς κεφαλὰς ἕκαστος	κινοῦντες τὰς
	ἐκίνουν	κεφαλὰς
ἐλάλησαν ἐν	καὶ τὰ χείλη	
χείλησιν	διέστρεφον	
		Luke 23:35:
ἐξεμυκτήρισάν με	καὶ τὰς μυξωτῆρσιν	ἐξεμυκτήριζον
	ἐν ἀλλήλοις	καὶ οἱ ἄρχοντες
	διαρρινοῦντες ἔλεγον	λέγοντες
	εἰρωνευόμενοι	
		Matt 27:40:
ἤλπισεν ἐπὶ κύριον	υἱὸν θεοῦ αὐτὸν	εἰ υἱὸς εἶ τοῦ θεοῦ
	ἔλεγε	
ῥυσάσθω αὐτόν	καταβὰς περιπατεῖτο	καὶ κατάβαθι ἀπὸ
		τοῦ σταυροῦ
σωσάτω αὐτόν.	σωσάτω αὐτὸν ὁ θεός.	σῶσον σεαυτόν.

It is well known that Matthew's changes of Mark's text in the passion narrative are often based on the desire to establish a closer agreement with the text of the prophetic biblical passages.[41] Justin's further improvement of the gospel texts—in his case, the texts of Matthew and Luke—continues this process. But while Matthew does not always quote the biblical reference for his development of the text of Mark, Justin lays his cards on the table, quoting his biblical texts in full. The process, however, is exactly the same as the procedure that must be assumed for Matthew. Like Matthew, Justin is creating a new text of the "Gospel," harmonizing what he has inherited, adding phrases which are missing in the texts of Matthew and Luke. That Justin is not doing this ad hoc, but is relying on a previously composed new gospel text, is evident in the passage quoted above: in his quotation of Ps 21:9 in *Dial.* 101.3, the phrase σωσάτω αὐτόν is actually missing in his quote from the Psalm, while the corresponding phrase appears in his quotation of the gospel text. On the other hand, Justin does not list only those phrases that prove the fulfillment of Scripture; he also includes such phrases from the text of the gospels that do not have a scriptural base.

The hypothesis I am proposing here is that Justin (or someone in his "school") continues the literary activity that is most clearly evident in Matthew. Justin wants to cre-

---

40. A similar, but less complete, harmonization of parallel passages from Matthew and Luke appears in *1 Apol.* 38.8. This parallel demonstrates that Justin did not compose such harmonizations ad hoc but relied on previously redacted written materials.

41. The most striking example is Matt 27:34, where Matthew substitutes μεμιγμένον for Mark's ἐσμυρνισμένον οἶνον (Mark 15:23) in order to establish closer agreement with Ps 68:22.

ate again the *one* Gospel, now combining Matthew and Luke, strengthening at the same time the close bond between prophecy and fulfillment, and thus expanding the text of this Gospel to achieve an even closer agreement than is evident in Matthew.

Another instance of bringing the text of the gospels into closer conformity to the Scripture is a "Western Text" reading in Justin's quotation of the account of Jesus' baptism in *Dial.* 88.8 and 103.6: instead of "You are (Matt: this is) my beloved son in whom I am well pleased" (Matt 3:17; Mark 1:11; most manuscripts of Luke 3:22) which mirrors Isa 42:1, Justin reports the heavenly voice in an exact quote from Ps 2:7: "You are my son, today I have begotten you." This latter reading appears in Luke 3:22 in Codex D, in manuscripts of the Vetus Latina, and in several fathers.[42] Justin's reading is usually quoted as evidence for the original text of Luke. There is indeed one Lukan feature in *Dial.* 88.8: ἐν εἴδει περιστεράς (Matt: ὡς περιστεράν). But ἅμα τῷ ἀναβῆναι in Dial. 103.6 (cf. Matt: ἀνέβη) reveals that Justin was using a harmonized text also in this instance. This makes it difficult to consider Justin as a witness for an early Lukan text. The quotation from Ps 2:7 was probably contributed by the author of Justin's harmony in an attempt to bring its text closer to a scriptural prophecy. The possibility that Ps 2:7 was inserted ad hoc by Justin himself is unlikely; he never refers to Ps 2 in the context of his quotations from the story of Jesus' baptism.[43]

There are more "Western Text" readings in Justin's quotations which cannot be discussed in detail here. Is Justin a witness for the early existence of the Western Text, especially for the Gospel of Luke? Or is the Western Text a testimony for the influence of Justin's gospel harmony? And is Justin's new gospel also responsible for the large number of harmonized readings found in subsequent gospel quotations from Clement of Alexandria and Irenaeus to the *Apostolic Constitutions* and other Church Fathers?

What was the motivation and purpose of the composition of a new gospel on the basis of Matthew and Luke? And why was the composer of this gospel interested in strengthening the ties to the prophecy of the Scriptures? Justin knew Marcion, opposed him, and even composed a *Syntagma* against Marcion, which is, unfortunately, lost.[44] Marcion was the first Christian theologian who called a writing that contains the words and deeds of Jesus a "Gospel,"[45] and Justin must have learned this designation from Marcion. There is no evidence for the use of this designation before Marcion and Justin.[46] It is not unlikely, then, that the harmony of Matthew and Luke, which Justin

---

42. Numerous editions adopt this reading as the original text of Luke: Huck, Huck-Greeven, Boismard. Yet, Aland and Nestle-Aland have the reading of the majority of manuscripts (= Mark 1:11).

43. Psalm 2:7-8 is quoted in full in Justin, *Dial.* 122:6; but there is no reference to the story of Jesus' baptism.

44. For Justin against Marcion, see *1 Apol.* 26.8 (*Syntagma* against all heresies); Irenaeus, *Haer.* 4.6.9; Eusebius, *Hist. eccl.* 4.11.8 (*Syntagma* against Marcion).

45. Hans von Campenhausen, *The Formation of the Christian Bible* (Philadelphia: Fortress Press, 1972) 147–65. For a fuller account of this argument, see the chapter "From the Kerygma-Gospel to Written Gospels" in this volume.

46. In a few instances, Justin explicitly states that what he otherwise calls "Memoirs of the Apostles" are called "Gospels." In *1 Apol.* 66.3 he relates: "In the memoirs that the apostles have composed which are called Gospels (ἃ εὐαγγέλια καλεῖται) they transmitted that they had received the following instructions. . . ." In *Dial.* 10.2, Justin introduces Trypho the Jew, his partner in the dialogue, as saying: "I know that your

composed and/or used, was also produced in the context of the reaction to Marcion's work. While Marcion severed the ties between gospel and scripture, Justin's harmony wants to reestablish the close relationship between prophecy and fulfillment and thus continued the work that is already evident in Matthew's harmony of Mark and Q.

Canonical and Secret Mark

The quote of a portion of a *Secret Gospel of Mark* in a letter of Clement of Alexandria[47] has been the subject of controversy ever since its publication.[48] I shall base the following discussion on the assumption that the quotations from the *Secret Gospel* are genuine.[49] There are several peculiar features in the extant canonical text of the Gospel of Mark that seem to be related to the quote from the *Secret Gospel* in the letter of Clement of Alexandria. I have discussed these in an article.[50] Let me point to the four most striking peculiarities.

(1) In the *Secret Gospel*, the young man (νεανίσκος) who has been raised by Jesus "looks at Jesus and loves him" (ἐμβλέψας αὐτῷ ἠγάπησεν αὐτόν). In Mark's version of the story of the "Rich Man" (Mark 10:17–22) Jesus "looks (at the rich man) and loves him" (ἐμβλέψας αὐτῷ ἠγάπησεν αὐτόν, 10:21). There is no parallel to this sentence in either Matthew or Luke. However, in the Johannine version of the story of the raising of Lazarus, Jesus weeps as he comes to the tomb and the Jews say: "Behold, how he loved him" (ἴδε πῶς ἐφίλει αὐτόν, John 11:36). This feature does not belong in the story of the Rich Man but may have been a genuine part of the story of the raising of the youth/Lazarus. The latter story has been introduced into the text of Mark by the *Secret Gospel* after Mark 10:32. It could be argued that the same redactor inserted Mark 10:21 in order to establish the identity of the rich man who had encountered Jesus with the youth who was raised by Jesus. This is confirmed by the remark included in the *Secret Gospel* that the youth was rich (ἦν γὰρ πλούσιος)—a feature that is missing in the Johannine version, that is, it is due to the redactor who inserted the story into the Gospel of Mark.[51]

---

commandments which are written in the so-called gospel (ἃ γέγραπται ἐν τῷ λεγομένῳ εὐαγγελίῳ) are so wonderful and great that no human being can possibly fulfill them."

47. Morton Smith, *Clement of Alexandria and a Secret Gospel of Mark*. The text, plates, and translation are found on pp. 445–54. The Greek text has been republished in Otto Stählin and Ursula Treu, eds., *Clemens Alexandrinus*, vol. 4.1: *Register* (GCS; 2nd ed.; Berlin: Akademie-Verlag, 1980) xvii–xviii.

48. For discussion on this controversy, see Morton Smith, "Clement of Alexandria and Secret Mark: The Score at the End of the First Decade," *HTR* 75 (1982) 449–61.

49. Even if the letter of Clement of Alexandria should not be genuine, it must be an ancient forgery written in order to defend the *Secret Gospel of Mark* as apostolic. The gospel text quoted here is certainly genuine and possibly written early in the second century. The story of the raising of the youth told in the quote from the *Secret Gospel* is a version of a story that is form-critically earlier than the story of the raising of Lazarus of John 11.

50. "History and Development of Mark's Gospel: From Mark to Secret Mark and 'Canonical' Mark," in Bruce C. Corley, ed., *Colloquy on New Testament Studies: A Time for Reappraisal and Fresh Approaches* (Macon, Ga.: Mercer University Press, 1983) 35–58.

51. It can be argued that Mark 10:24 also is due to this same redactor. After Jesus' saying about the diffi-

(2) The *Secret Gospel* reports that the young man (νεανίσκος) comes to Jesus to be initiated into the mystery of the kingdom of God "dressed in a linen cloth over his naked body" (περιβεβλημένος σινδόνα ἐπὶ γυμνοῦ). Mark 14:51–52 reports that, when Jesus was arrested in the Garden of Gethsemane, a young man "dressed in a linen cloth over his naked body" (νεανίσκος περιβεβλημένος σινδόνα ἐπὶ γυμνοῦ) lets go of his linen cloth and flees naked. There are no parallels to this brief Markan pericope in either Matthew or Luke. No satisfactory explanation for this episode in Mark's gospel has ever been proposed,[52] nor has anyone been able to explain why both Matthew and Luke should have deleted it completely without any trace. If this account was missing in the copy of Mark that Matthew and Luke used, it is reasonable to suggest that it was added by the redactor of the *Secret Gospel*.

(3) The original edition of the text of the *Secret Gospel* had already proposed that the six-day instruction by Jesus that the youth receives after he is raised must be understood as the preparation for baptism, which here is understood as a secret initiation rite.[53] In Mark 10:38b/39b Jesus refers to the disciples receiving "the same baptism with which I am baptized." This statement, which is usually taken as a reference to martyrdom, is problematic. It is not included in the Matthean parallel (Matt 20:23-24 = Mark 10:38a/39a), which only refers to "drinking the same cup which I am drinking."[54] This latter expression is attested early as a metaphor for martyrdom; but "baptism" is never used as a martyrological metaphor in the early period of the Christian church.[55] In the earliest text of Mark, there was probably no reference to "baptism," but only to the "cup" as symbol of martyrdom.[56] After the parallel sentence referring to "baptism" had been added, Mark 10:38–39 no longer referred to martyrdom, but to the Christian "sacraments" of baptism and Eucharist (= the cup). Was the redactor of the *Secret Gospel* responsible for this addition?

(4) According to the letter of Clement of Alexandria, the *Secret Gospel* not only reported the story of the raising of the youth after Mark 10:34, but also told of an encounter after Mark 10:46a ("And they came into Jericho"): "And the sister of the youth whom Jesus loved and his mother and Salome were there and Jesus did not receive them." In the extant text of Mark 10:46, the two clauses, "And they came into Jericho," and "when he came out of Jericho," seem to be remnants of this episode, thus creating the strange statement that Jesus and his disciples went into Jericho for no reason

---

culty of the rich people to enter the kingdom of God (Mark 10:23 = Matt 19:23 and Luke 18:24), Mark mentions the amazement of the disciples (ἐθαμβοῦντο) and repeats Jesus' saying, but without reference to wealth: "Children, how difficult it is to enter the kingdom of God." There are no parallels in either Matthew or Luke.

52. Rudolf Bultmann (*A History of the Synoptic Tradition* [New York: Harper, 1963] 1–17) suggested that this was a remnant of an ancient historical report. Few exegetes after him have seriously entertained this explanation.

53. Morton Smith, *Clement of Alexandria and a Secret Gospel of Mark*, 174–88.

54. A Lukan parallel is missing, because Luke skips the entire pericope.

55. Hans von Campenhausen, *Die Idee des Martyriums in der alten Kirche* (2nd ed.; Göttingen: Vandenhoeck & Ruprecht, 1953) 60–61.

56. Cf. also the use of "cup" in the Gethsemane pericope (Mark 14:26 and parallels).

whatsoever. Matthew only speaks of Jesus coming out of Jericho, introducing the situation of the healing of the (two) blind men (Matt 20:29).[57] This may be exactly what stood originally in the Markan text.

If the *Secret Gospel* redaction of the original text of the Gospel of Mark has left traces in the extant manuscript text of Mark, the conclusion is unavoidable that the canonical text is the result of a further redaction of the *Secret Gospel of Mark*, an edition in which some of the questionable passages were omitted. One may debate whether any of the other peculiarities in the canonical text of Mark, discussed in the first part of this chapter, also are the product of the redaction of the *Secret Gospel*. This is most likely the case with respect to the singular μυστήριον (Mark 4:11), the only instance of the singular in the canonical gospels. There is a parallel in the statement of the *Secret Gospel*: ἐδίδασκε αὐτὸν . . . τὸ μυστήριον τῆς βασιλείας τοῦ θεοῦ. Also the present form of the healing narrative of Mark 9:14–29 was probably created by the same redactor who thus presented a story of the raising of a child that shared many features with the story of the raising of the youth inserted into the following chapter of Mark. As a result, the *Secret Gospel of Mark* presents a story reporting the raising of a person by Jesus between the first and second prediction of the passion and resurrection, as well as between the second and third of these predictions.

Conclusion

This chapter has not surveyed all of the available evidence for the second-century text of the Synoptic Gospels. Further corroboration would have to come from the investigation of those apocryphal gospels that are dependent upon the canonical gospels.[58] An investigation of the apocryphal acts of the apostles, the Pseudo-Clementines, and a number of writings from the Nag Hammadi corpus would also be required. Finally, the further history of gospel harmonies and harmonized readings in the Church Fathers would probably confirm that Justin Martyr's harmony of Matthew and Luke was an influential document.

All of the evidence presented here points to the fact that the text of the Synoptic Gospels was very unstable during the first and second centuries. With respect to Mark, one can be fairly certain that only its revised text has achieved canonical status, while the original text (attested only by Matthew and Luke) has not survived. With respect to Matthew and Luke, there is no guarantee that the archetypes of the manuscript tradition are identical with the original text of each gospel. The harmonizations of these two gospels demonstrate that their text was not sacrosanct and that alterations could be expected, even if they were not always as radical as in the case of Marcion's revision of Luke, the *Secret Gospel's* revision of Mark, and Justin's construction of a harmony.

---

57. Luke locates the encounter with Zacchaeus at Jericho (Luke 18:35–19:9).

58. Especially the *Gospel of the Ebionites* that presents some harmonized readings similar to those found in *2 Clement* and Justin Martyr. *The Gospel of Thomas, The Dialogue of the Savior, The Apocryphon of James, The Gospel of the Egyptians,* and *The Gospel of the Hebrews* are most likely independent of the gospels of the NT canon.

New Testament textual critics have been deluded by the hypothesis that the arche-types of the textual tradition which were fixed ca. 200 CE—and how many archetypes for each gospel?—are (almost) identical with the autographs. This cannot be confirmed by any external evidence. On the contrary, whatever evidence there is indicates that not only minor, but also substantial revisions of the original texts have occurred during the first hundred years of the transmission. The story of the text of the Gospel of Mark and the revisions of its text—documented by Matthew, Luke, and the *Secret Gospel of Mark*—illustrates this, as well as the harmonizations of Matthew and Luke in Justin and in other witnesses.

4

FROM THE KERYGMA-GOSPEL
TO WRITTEN GOSPELS

This chapter addresses the question why and how the term εὐαγγέλιον, originally a term for the early Christian proclamation, became the designation of a certain type of literature. The following closely related problems have been discussed repeatedly in New Testament scholarship for several generations:[1] (1) the origin of the term εὐαγγέλιον; (2) the consistency and uniformity of its meaning in its Christian usage; (3) the question of the literary genre of the writings that later became known as gospels. I shall comment on the second and third of these problems insofar as they concern the question addressed in this chapter, but I shall leave aside the question of the background and origin of the term.[2]

I. The Pauline Usage

The earliest and at the same time overwhelming evidence for the use of the terms εὐαγγέλιον and εὐαγγελίζεσθαι comes from the genuine Pauline letters. Both words designate the Christian message and its proclamation.[3] Whether Paul says "the gospel of God" (τὸ εὐαγγελιον τοῦ θεοῦ, 1 Thess 2:2, 8–9; 2 Cor 11:7) of which he is the apostle (Rom 1:1; 15:16), or "the gospel of Christ" (τὸ εὐαγγέλιον τοῦ Χριστοῦ, Rom

---

1. A comprehensive treatment was presented by Detlev Dormeyer and Hubert Frankemölle, "Evangelium als literarischer und als theologischer Begriff: Tendenzen und Aufgaben der Evangelienforschung im 20. Jahrhundert, mit einer Untersuchung des Markusevangeliums in seinem Verhältnis zur griechischen Biographie," *ANRW* 2.25/2 (1984) 1541–1704. Dormeyer and Frankemölle also treat the history of scholarship and give extensive bibliographies.

2. On this question, cf. Gerhard. Friedrich, "εὐαγγέλιον," *TDNT* 2 (1964) 721–736. For the use of the noun in the Roman imperial period, see especially Julius Schniewind, *Euangelion: Ursprung und erste Gestalt des Begriffs Evangelium* (BFChTh 13; Gütersloh: Bertelsmann, 1927; reprint, Darmstadt: Wissenschaftliche Buchgesellschaft, 1970) 113–258.

3. The noun εὐαγγέλιον occurs 48 times in the genuine Pauline letters. In 26 of these occurrences it is used absolutely, without a following genitive; 14 times the genitive "of God" (τοῦ θεοῦ) or "of Christ" (τοῦ Χριστοῦ) follows. Τὸ εὐαγγέλιον ἡμῶν (2 Cor 11:4; 1 Thess 1:5) means "the gospel that we preach." ἕτερον εὐαγγέλιον (2 Cor 11:4; Gal 1:6) is used in such a way that the implication is unmistakable: there is no such thing as "another gospel." The term has a somewhat different meaning in the phrase τὸ εὐαγγέλιον τῆς ἀκροβυστίας (Gal 2:7): it is the office of preaching to the uncircumcised but not a different gospel that is preached to them. "My gospel" (τὸ εὐαγγέλιόν μου) in Rom 16:25 is certainly not Pauline; Rom 3:16, where the same phrase appears, may also be a later interpolation; cf. 2 Tim 2:8.

15:19; 1 Cor 9:12; 2 Cor 12:12; etc.), he always refers to the same and only gospel. Most frequently he uses the term without a genitive as a *terminus technicus* for both the action of the proclamation and for the content of the message (Rom 1:16; 1 Cor 4:15; 9:14; etc.). He presupposes that the content is understood and requires no further definition.

The verb εὐαγγελίζεσθαι does not have the same technical meaning. In 1 Thess 3:6, Paul speaks of the arrival of Timothy "who brought the (good) message" (εὐαγγελισαμένου) of the Thessalonians' faith and love. But in 1 Cor 1:17 ("Christ did not send me to baptize, but to preach [the gospel]") the verb designates the Christian missionary's activity.[4] However, other verbs are used with the same meaning; cf. Phil 1:14–17, where "to say the word" (λόγον λαλεῖν), "to announce" (κηρύσσειν), and "to proclaim" (καταγγέλλειν) are used side by side.[5]

There is no fixed formulation describing the content of the "gospel," although some passages use words derived from kerygmatic formulae. The earliest of these appears in 1 Thess 1:9–10. In the most famous of these passages, 1 Cor 15:1–5, the content is the proclamation of the death, burial, and resurrection of Christ. What is called "gospel" seems to be a formula that was handed down like a piece of tradition. Paul wants to emphasize that the gospel preached by him is the common gospel of the entire enterprise of the Christian mission. But the emphasis upon "receiving" and "transmitting" of the gospel does not imply that the formulation of its content was stable. Neither the formula quoted in 1 Cor 15 nor any other formulaic statement of the gospel in Paul is ever repeated.

II. The Kerygma-Gospel Hypothesis

In a famous essay of 1923, Karl Ludwig Schmidt[6] presented a criticism of attempts to understand the genre of the gospels in analogy to Greek biography. Schmidt referred to Franz Overbeck's distinction between Christian "primitive literature" (*Urliteratur*) and patristic literature.[7] According to Overbeck, the letters and gospels of the New Testament belong to the former category, because they owe their existence to the special

---

4. The verb appears 19 times in the genuine Pauline letters. It can be used in a technical sense insofar as it means not only "to announce," "to proclaim" (1 Cor 9:16, 18; Gal 1:16, 23; 4:13; 1 Thess 3:6), but also in the full sense "to preach the gospel" (Rom 1:15; 15:20; 1 Cor 1:17; 2 Cor 10:16; Gal 1:8–9). For emphasis, Paul can also say εὐαγγελίζεσθαι τὸ εὐαγγέλιον (2 Cor 11:7; cf. Gal 2:11; 1 Cor 15:1).

5. Full equivalents of εὐαγγελίζεσθαι are κηρύσσειν ("to proclaim," Rom 10:8, 14, 15; 1 Cor 1:23; 9:27; 15:11; Gal 2:2), καταγγέλλειν ("to announce," 1 Cor 2:1; 9:14; 11:26; Phil 1:17–18), λάλειν ("to speak," Phil 1:14; 1 Thess 2:2, 4, 16). In the Acts of the Apostles, διαμαρτύρεσθαι appears frequently as the equivalent of εὐαγγελίζεσθαι (Acts 2:40; 8:25; 10:42; 18:5; 20:21, 24; 28:23).

6. Karl Ludwig Schmidt, "Die Stellung der Evangelien in der allgemeinen Literaturgeschichte," *ΕΥΧΑΡΙΣΤΗΡΙΟΝ für Hermann Gunkel* (2 vols.; FRLANT 36; Göttingen: Vandenhoeck & Ruprecht, 1923) 2. 50–135.

7. Franz Overbeck, "Über die Anfänge der patristischen Literatur," *Historische Zeitschrift* 14 (1882) 417–72; reprinted in book form: Darmstadt: Wissenschaftliche Buchgesellschaft, 1954 and 1966.

circumstances of Christian beginnings. Writings of this genre could not be reproduced in the later period, because these special circumstances no longer obtained.[8] Patristic literature, on the other hand, belongs to the "high literature" (*Hochliteratur*) of antiquity, because it is influenced by established literary genres of the ancient world. In addition to utilizing Overbeck's questionable distinction, Schmidt employed the insights of the form-critical works of Rudolf Bultmann[9] and Martin Dibelius,[10] as well as his own work,[11] that the gospels of the New Testament were collections of materials that had been formed in the oral stages of their transmission. Schmidt concludes that the genre of the gospels cannot be determined on the basis of a comparison with the products of literary culture. They are casual literature *sui generis*.

A few years after the appearance of Schmidt's essay, Julius Schniewind published a noted review article of works on the Synoptic Gospels[12] in which he proposed a further elaboration of Schmidt's arguments with respect to the term "gospel" as a designation of a literary genre. Noting the close relationship in form and content between the Synoptic Gospels and the early kerygma, Schniewind concluded that gospels constituted a special literary genre which reflected the structure of the kerygma:

> There can be no doubt: only because there was a kerygma proclaiming a human being who lived "in the flesh" as "the Lord," is it possible to understand the origin of our gospels, including any forms of Christian literature that preceded them.[13]

This explanation of the origins of this literature and of its designation as "gospel" had been widely accepted.[14] More recent discussion of the genre of the gospel has reopened the question of the gospels as biography, however cautiously.[15] With respect to Hellenistic models for the genre of biography, Albrecht Dihle has warned that the search for adequate models in Greco-Roman literature may be futile. But at the same time, he encouraged the understanding of the gospels as biographies.[16] Detlev Dormeyer, "Evan-

---

8. In the discussion of the synoptic problem in his *Christentum und Kultur* (ed., Carl Albrecht Bernoulli [Basel: Schwabe, 1919; reprint, Darmstadt: Wissenschaftliche Buchgesellschaft, 1963] 78–79) Overbeck characterizes the Gospel of Luke as a tasteless and disastrous attempt to transform the *Urliteratur* into a piece of literary historiography.

9. Rudolf Bultmann, *The History of the Synoptic Tradition* (2nd ed.; New York: Harper, 1968). The first German edition had been published two years before the appearance of Schmidt's essay: *Die Geschichte der synoptischen Tradition* (FRLANT 29; Göttingen: Vandenhoeck & Ruprecht, 1921).

10. Martin Dibelius, *From Tradition to Gospel* (New York: Scribner's, 1934). First German edition: *Die Formgeschichte des Evangeliums* (Tübingen: Mohr/Siebeck, 1919).

11. Karl Ludwig Schmidt, *Der Rahmen der Geschichte Jesu* (Berlin: no publisher, 1919; reprints, Darmstadt: Wissenschaftliche Buchgesellschaft, 1964, 1969).

12. Julius Schniewind, "Zur Synoptiker-Exegese," *ThR* NF 2 (1930) 129–89.

13. Ibid., 183.

14. Cf. Günther Bornkamm, "Evangelien, formgeschichtlich," *RGG* 2 (3rd ed.) 750.

15. Most of this literature is treated in Dormeyer and Frankemölle, "Evangelium: Gattung und Begriff," cited above in note 1.

16. Albrecht Dihle, "Die Evangelien und die griechische Biographie," in Peter Stuhlmacher, ed., *Das Evangelium und die Evangelien* (WUNT 28; Tübingen: Mohr/Siebeck, 1983) 383–411.

gelium als literarische Gattung,"[17] has pursued this question more vigorously. The primary strength of his thesis lies in the use of Klaus Baltzer's work on the biography of the prophets.[18] Especially the Gospel of Mark, on the basis of this hypothesis, becomes understandable as an office biography.[19] The further elaboration of this hypothesis would have to take into account the genre of the *commentarius*, the autobiography of the Roman official, to which Dihle has pointed as an important analogy.[20] Less convincing is the attempt of Dormeyer and Frankemölle to relate the development of this biographical genre to the kerygma as it appears under the term εὐαγγέλιον combined with the assumption that this term is a linguistic metaphor with a presupposed implicit meaning. In particular, Dormeyer's arguments with respect to the key passage Mark 1:1[21] puts too much burden of proof on this Markan text. Is it possible to draw a direct line from the Pauline meaning of the term εὐαγγέλιον to the use of this word as a designation of gospel literature? How was the term εὐαγγέλιον understood in other Christian writings?

III. The Deutero-Pauline Use of the Term Εὐαγγέλιον

1. The Letters of Ignatius of Antioch.[22] As in Paul's letters, the gospel is in general the preaching of Jesus Christ. In *Phld.* 8.1, Ignatius juxtaposes the "gospel" to the "archives," that is, the Scriptures in which his opponents claim to possess the basis for Christian faith. In this context (*Phld.* 9.2), he states as the specific content of the gospel: the coming (παρουσία) of our Lord Jesus Christ, his suffering (πάθος), and his resurrection (ἀνάστασις).[23] In such formulaic expressions, Ignatius occasionally includes additional topics, like Christ's birth through the virgin and his baptism (*Eph.* 18.2) and, especially in anti-docetic contexts, phrases that emphasize the full humanity of the

---

17. In Dormeyer und Frankemölle, "Evangelium: Gattung und Begriff," 1545–1634.

18. Klaus Baltzer, *Die Biographie der Propheten* (Neukirchen: Neukirchener Verlag, 1975). However, it is difficult to understand Dormeyer's hesitation with respect to the acceptance of this model, which he justifies with the reference that this genre of the biography of the prophets had come to an end with the time of the exile. The biography of Nehemiah as well as the biographical substratum of Deutero-Isaiah is postexilic. Moreover, George Nickelsburg ("The Genre and Function of the Markan Passion Narrative," *HTR* 73 [1980] 153–84) has shown that this biographical genre finds its postexilic continuation in the narrative of the suffering righteous and his vindication.

19. On this question, see also Dieter Lührmann, *Das Markusevangelium* (HNT 3; Tübingen: Mohr/Siebeck, 1987) 42–44.

20. Dihle, "Die Evangelien und die griechische Biographie," 407-11.

21. Detlev Dormeyer, "Die Kompositionsmetapher 'Evangelium Jesu Christi, des Sohnes Gottes' Mk 1.1: Ihre theologische und literarische Aufgabe in der Jesus-Biographie des Markus," *NTS* 33 (1987) 452–68. See also Dormeyer and Frankemölle, "Evangelium als Begriff," 1639–94.

22. On the use of the term gospel in Ignatius's letters, see Helmut Koester, *Synoptische Überlieferung bei den apostolischen Vätern* (TU 65; Berlin: Akademie-Verlag, 1957) 6–10; William R. Schoedel, *Ignatius of Antioch: A Commentary on the Letters of Ignatius of Antioch* (Hermeneia; Philadelphia: Fortress Press, 1985) on *Phld.* 8.2; 9.2. There is no evidence that Ignatius used any of the written gospels known to us.

23. Other passages in which suffering or death and cross and resurrection appear together in formulaic language are Ign. *Eph.* 7.2; *Magn.* 11; *Trall.* 9.1; *Smyrn.* 5.3; 7.2; 12.2.

coming of Jesus Christ (cf. *Trall.* 9.1–2). However, quotations of such kerygmatic materials are not designated as εὐαγγέλιον. The term is also missing in the context of the extensive combination of traditional sentences and formulations into a kind of a credal statement in *Smyrn.* 1.1–2.[24]

There is no basis for the assumption that the εὐαγγέλιον in Ignatius designates any fixed formula describing the coming, birth, life, ministry, suffering, death, and resurrection of Christ, and it certainly does not refer to any written text enumerating the basic topics of Jesus' appearance.[25] Rather, the εὐαγγέλιον is the message of salvation in general, of which Christ's death and resurrection are constitutive parts.[26] Ignatius, writing half a century after Paul, simply continues the Pauline usage of the term.

2. The Deutero-Pauline Epistles and the Book of Acts. Eph 3:6 speaks of the fulfillment of the plan of salvation that the Gentiles should also inherit the promise διὰ τοῦ εὐαγγελίου, cf. Eph 3:8: "(Paul) has been appointed to preach (εὐαγγελίζεσθαι) to the Gentiles the inexhaustible richness of Christ." But neither here nor in Colossians nor in 2 Thessalonians is there any attempt to define the content of the εὐαγγέλιον as a sequence of events or a "story." Nowhere are fixed credal formulations called gospel. Its content is presupposed: the Pauline message of salvation, especially his preaching to the Gentiles.[27] Also in the Acts of the Apostles, the term εὐαγγέλιον designates in general Paul's message of salvation that is preached to the Gentiles (Acts 15:1; 20:24).

In the Pastoral Epistles, probably written in the first half of the second century CE, the εὐαγγέλιον becomes the guarantee for the correct Christian proclamation, which is closely associated with the person of Paul and his work as founder of the church.[28] This is evident in the peculiar phrase "my gospel"; cf. 2 Tim 2:8: "Remember Jesus Christ, risen from the dead, from the seed of David, according to my gospel (κατὰ τὸ εὐαγγέλιόν μου)."[29] This formulation as well as the references to suffering in the context of the use of the term in 2 Tim 1:8, 10 demonstrates that cross and resurrection of Christ are the traditional content of the gospel. Εὐαγγέλιον, by no means a key term of the theology of the Pastoral Epistles, is used only whenever the author connects the right doctrine to Paul and to the message that he preached.

---

24. See on this passage and on its traditional elements Schoedel, *Ignatius of Antioch,* on *Smyrn.* 1.1–2. Schoedel argues convincingly that Ignatius does not quote a long traditional formula here; rather he combines individual traditional phrases with sentences from Paul's letters.

25. Gilles Wetter (*Altchristliche Liturgien: Das christliche Mysterium* [FRLANT 30; Göttingen:Vandenhoeck & Ruprecht, 1921] 1. 121–22) understands εὐαγγέλιον in the letters of Ignatius as a central feature of the enactment of Christian cult, a text that represents the Christian myth of salvation so that its reading "creates life." Heinrich Schlier (*Religionsgeschichtliche Untersuchungen zu den Ignatiusbriefen* [BZNW 8; Gießen:Töpelmann, 1929] 165–66) has further elaborated this suggestion.

26. See especially *Smyrn.* 7.2: ". . . to pay attention to the prophets and in particular to the gospel, in which the passion is shown us and the resurrection accomplished."

27. See further on these letters Georg Strecker, "Das Evangelium Jesu Christi," in Strecker, ed., *Jesus Christus in Historie und Theologie: Festschrift Hans Conzelmann* (Tübingen: Mohr/Siebeck, 1975) 531–33.

28. Ibid., 533–55.

29. The phrase τὸ εὐαγγέλιόν μου in Rom 2:16 and 16:25 reflects this same later usage.

IV. The Term Εὐαγγέλιον in the Gospels of the New Testament

1. The Gospel of Luke, the latest of the gospel writings of the New Testament, was written by an author who is familiar with both the noun εὐαγγέλιον and the verb εὐαγγελίζεσθαι. But he uses the former only in the Book of Acts,[30] the latter in both parts of his work. The verb either refers to the action of preaching or to the content of the Christian message, which, however, is never clearly defined.[31] The formulaic enumeration of the events of Jesus' coming, ministry, suffering, death, and resurrection in several of the speeches of Acts have been singled out as reproductions of older traditions giving the basic outline of gospel literature.[32] However, these outlines must be understood as Lukan compositions[33]—dependent upon the framework of the gospel story as it is presented by Mark—and they are never called gospel by the author of Acts. Nor does Luke understand the first part of his own work as the Gospel. On the contrary, Luke 1:1 designates the work, that is, both the Gospel and the Acts of the Apostles, as a "narrative" (διήγησις) of the events that took place.

2. The Gospel of Matthew. The absence of the noun in the Gospel of Luke is surprising, because the preserved text of Mark employs the noun repeatedly. However, Matthew also reproduces only a few of the Markan occurrences of the term. On the other hand, he uses the term also in non-Markan contexts and in two instances adds the phrase "and he preached the gospel of the kingdom" (καὶ κηρύσσων τὸ εὐαγγέλιον τῆς βασιλείας) to a Markan summary statement about Jesus' activity (Matt 4:23; 9:35; cf. Mark 1:39; 6:6). The following table shows the use of the term in the respective Markan and Matthean passages.

	Mark[34]		*Matthew*
1:1	Ἀρχὴ τοῦ εὐαγγελίου		— —
	Ἰησοῦ Χριστοῦ		— —
1:15a	κηρύσσων	4:17a	ἤρξατο . . . κηρύσσειν
	τὸ εὐαγγέλιον τοῦ θεοῦ		— —

---

30. It occurs only twice here: 15:7 and 20:24; see above.

31. In both the Gospel of Luke and in the Acts of the Apostles the verb εὐαγγελίζεσθαι can simply mean "to announce" (Luke 1:19; 2:10; Acts 14:15). But in most instances, it designates the missionary proclamation. In Luke 3:18; 4:18 (= Isa 61:1); 7:22; 9:6; 20:1; Acts 8:25, 40; 14:7, 21; 16:10, the verb has no direct object. Thus it means either simply "to preach," or the direct object is implied: "to preach the gospel." Sometimes the object of the verb is made explicit: "the rule of God" (Luke 4:3; 8:1; cf. 16:16; Acts 8:12), "Christ Jesus" (Acts 5:42; 8:35; 11:20), "the word (of the Lord)" (Acts 8:4; 15:35), "peace" (Acts 10:36), "the promises to the fathers fulfilled" (Acts 13:32), "Jesus and the resurrection" (Acts 17:18).

32. Especially Charles Harold Dodd, *The Apostolic Preaching and its Development* (New York: Harper & Brothers, 1936; 2nd ed. 1944).

33. Ulrich Wilckens, *Die Missionsreden der Apostelgeschichte: Form und traditionsgeschichtliche Untersuchungen* (WMANT 5; 3rd ed.; Neukirchen: Neukirchener Verlag, 1974).

34. There is a further occurrence of the term in the secondary, longer ending of Mark: "Go into all the world and proclaim the gospel to every creature" (Mark 16:15).

Mark (cont.)		Matthew (cont.)	
1:15b	μετανοιεῖτε καὶ πιστεύετε ἐν τῷ εὐαγγελίῳ	4:17b	μετανοεῖτε — —
8:35	ἕνεκεν ἐμοῦ καὶ τοῦ εὐαγγελίου	16:25	ἕνεκεν ἐμοῦ — —
10:29	ἕνεκεν ἐμοῦ καὶ ἕνεκεν τοῦ εὐαγγελίου	19:29	ἕνεκεν τοῦ ἐμοῦ ὀνόματος — —
13:10	πρῶτον δεῖ κηρυχθῆναι τὸ εὐαγγέλιον	24:14	καὶ κηρυχθήσεται τοῦτο τὸ εὐαγγέλιον τῆς βασιλείας
14:9	ὅπου ἐὰν κηρυχθῇ τὸ εὐαγγέλιον	26:13	ὅπου ἐὰν κηρυχθῇ τὸ εὐαγγέλιον τοῦτο

The term εὐαγγέλιον appears in Mark 13:10 and 14:9 (also in 16:15) without a qualifier.[35] But in the two instances in which Matthew reproduces gospel passages from Mark, he adds the demonstrative "this" (τοῦτο) to the word gospel and in the second instance also the qualifying genitive "of the kingdom" (τῆς βασιλείας). What message is meant, is not immediately clear.[36] The phrase εὐαγγέλιον τῆς βασιλείας appears independently of Mark, also in Matt 4:23 and 9:25. In these two passages (as well as in Matt 24:14) the meaning of the phrase is evident: it is Jesus' proclamation of the coming of the kingdom of the heavens. It is Jesus' message as already it was the message of John the Baptist (compare Matt 4:17 with 3:2), but not the gospel about Jesus' death and resurrection. Matthew never uses the term gospel in this latter meaning. Characteristically, the term εὐαγγέλιον is missing in the commissioning of the disciples in Matt 28:18–20. The difference between Matt 28:18–20 and Mark 16:15 is striking. While in the (albeit secondary) ending of Mark Jesus commands the disciples to go into all the world to proclaim the gospel (κηρύξατε τὸ εὐαγγέλιον), Matthew reports Jesus' mission command as a charge to the "Eleven" to make all the nations disciples, to baptize them, and to teach them to observe everything that he had taught.

3. The Gospel of Mark. Two problems exist with respect to the understanding of the term εὐαγγέλιον in Mark: (1) Does the term belong to the original text of Mark in the passages where it occurs in the extant manuscripts? (2) What is the content of the gospel in Mark?

In Mark 8:35 and 10:29, the phrase καὶ (ἕνεκεν) τοῦ εὐαγγελίου is redundant after ἕνεκεν ἐμοῦ, and it is indeed missing in the Matthean parallels (16:25; 19:29). There is also no Matthean correspondence to the use of the term in Mark 1:14 and 15b (= Matt 4:17).[37] In three of these passages (Mark 1:15b; 8:35; 10:29), the term

---

35. For the meaning of the term in these Markan passages, see below.

36. All modern commentaries agree that "this gospel" in Matt 26:13 cannot refer to Matthew's gospel. The phrase is variously understood as the gospel of Christ, the proclamation of the passion of Jesus, or the announcement of the coming of the kingdom of heaven.

37. Willi Marxsen (*Der Evangelist Markus* [FRLANT 67; Göttingen: Vandenhoeck & Ruprecht, 1956] 81) argues persuasively that Matthew used Mark 1:15, not only in 4:17, but also in Matt 4:23 and 9:35. See

εὐαγγέλιον appears without a genitive designating its content. This corresponds to the Pauline use of εὐαγγέλιον as a technical term.[38] In the juxtaposition "on behalf of me and on behalf of the gospel," gospel even assumes the same dignity that is accorded to Christ himself. But do the other occurrences of gospel in Mark confirm this meaning of the term?

The occurrences of the term in Mark 13:10[39] and 14:9 are confirmed as part of the original text of Mark by Matt 24:14 and 26:13. While the worldwide proclamation of this gospel is emphasized, nothing indicates that it is the gospel that has as its content the proclamation of Christ's suffering, death, and resurrection.

Only the beginning of the Gospel of Mark gives a clue to the author's understanding of the term. "The gospel of God" in Mark 1:15a is, as 1:15b shows, the proclamation of the nearness of the kingdom of God through Jesus and the call for repentance.[40] Mark 1:14–15 must be understood together with Mark 1:1; the term εὐαγγέλιον in Mark 1:1 and 1:14 forms an *inclusio*. It is not impossible that a scribe added the phrase "Beginning of the gospel of Jesus Christ" in order to indicate the point in his manuscript at which the text of another writing began.[41] If it is an original part of Mark's work, it is a reference to a message that is introduced by the Baptist's preaching of repentance and is begun by Jesus' announcement of the nearness of the kingdom, which resumes the call for repentance.[42] Nothing in the text indicates that this phrase should be understood as a designation of Mark's entire work.[43] Ancient writings either begin

---

further on this question Helmut Koester, "History and Development of Mark's Gospel: From Mark to Secret Mark and 'Canonical' Mark," in Bruce C. Corley, ed., *Colloquy on New Testament Studies: A Time for Reappraisal and Fresh Approaches* (Macon, Ga.: Mercer University Press, 1983) 43–44.

38. Peter Stuhlmacher (*Das paulinische Evangelium I* [FRLANT 95; Göttingen:Vandenhoeck & Ruprecht, 1968]) argues for a close relationship between Mark's use of the term and the Pauline understanding of the content of the gospel.

39. Mark 13:10 interrupts the close connection between 13:9 and 13:11. Can 13:10 be considered a secondary intrusion into the text of Mark from the parallel in Matthew? Commentaries usually ask whether v. 10 was inserted into an older tradition, either by Mark or in a pre-Markan stage of the text; cf. Rudolf Pesch, *Das Markusevangelium* (2 vols.; Herders Kommentar; Freiburg: Herder, 1977) 2. 285; see also Pesch, *Naherwartungen* (Düsseldorf: Patmos, 1968) 129–31. On the term in Markan usage in general, see Willi Marxsen, *Markus*, 77–92; Lührmann, *Markusevangelium*, 40–41 and *passim*. Both Marxsen and Lührmann argue that all passages in which the term εὐαγγέλιον appears in Mark are redactional.

40. The expression πιστεύειν ἐν is peculiar and without parallel in the NT. However, it is hard to interpret this phrase in any other way than as an equivalent of the common πιστεύειν εἰς = "to believe in"; see Marxsen, *Markus*, 90. Marxsen also argues that the term εὐαγγέλιον always occurs in redactional materials and never in any traditions or sources used by Mark. The peculiar phrase of Mark 1:15 cannot be explained by recourse to an older Aramaic tradition used by Mark (against Pesch, *Markusevangelium*, 105). Dormeyer ("Die Kompositionsmetapher," *NTS* 33 [1987] 454-55) explains the choice of the preposition ἐν as a deliberate Markan finesse by which Mark wants to indicate that the "gospel" preached by Jesus in 1:14–15 is not the entire gospel but only one of its ingredients (*Teilmenge*).

41. Cf. Walter Schmithals, *Das Evangelium nach Markus* (ÖTKNT 2/1; Gütersloh: Gütersloher Verlagshaus, 1979) 73–74.

42. Cf. Lührmann, *Markusevangelium,* 33–34, 41.

43. Marxsen, *Markus*, 87–88. Dormeyer ("Die Kompositionsmetapher," 452–68) has recently tried to demonstrate that the "genitive-syntagma" ἀρχὴ τοῦ εὐαγγελίου can be reversed to "gospel of the beginnings" and thus become the title of a writing.

with a formal dedication describing the purpose (such as in Luke/Acts) or with a sentence marking the first subject treated, but never with cryptic phrases that mysteriously suggest their true genre to the modern interpreter. Neither Matthew nor Mark suggests that the term εὐαγγέλιον is restricted to a technical designation of the preaching of Christ's suffering, death, and resurrection. There is no indication whatsoever by any of the authors of the New Testament gospels that εὐαγγέλιον would be an appropriate title for the literature they produced.

V. Εὐαγγέλιον in the First Half of the Second Century

1. The Apostolic Fathers.[44] Traditionally the writings of the Apostolic Fathers had been viewed as witnesses for the use of written gospels,[45] and their references to the gospel were understood as designations for gospel writings. Later research has recognized that this is untenable.[46]

In the *First Epistle of Clement*, the term gospel means preaching in general: "as Paul wrote to you in the beginning of his preaching (εὐαγγέλιον)" (*1 Clem.* 47.2). The author did not know any written gospel. The sayings of Jesus in *1 Clem.* 13.2 and 46.8 are drawn from the oral tradition.[47]

In the *Epistle of Barnabas*, written at the same time or a few decades later, εὐαγγέλιον refers to the oral proclamation: Jesus chose the apostles in order that they should preach his "message" (*Barn.* 5.9). More difficult to determine is the use of the word gospel in the *Didache*. In its present form, the *Didache* is a compilation of several sources; some of the older components have preserved the terminology of an earlier period.[48] On the other hand, redactional passages reveal the vocabulary of the later editor. One part of older liturgical instructions in *Did.* 8.2, the Lord's prayer, is introduced with the words: pray "as the Lord has commanded in his gospel" (ὡς ἐκέλευσεν ὁ κύριος ἐν τῷ εὐαγγελίῳ αὐτοῦ). The form and wording of the Lord's prayer are almost identical with Matt 6:7–15. However, a few details in the *Didache* version are more original than the parallel expressions in Matthew.[49] Moreover, the verb in the quotation formula

---

44. For the occurrences of the term in the letters of Ignatius of Antioch, see above.

45. Most characteristic for this position is the very influential work of Theodor Zahn, *Geschichte des neutestamentlichen Kanons* (2 vols.; Erlangen: Deichert, 1888–1889) 1. 840, 916–41. Zahn even believed that Papias of Hierapolis, the second century bishop who argued strongly for the trustworthiness of the oral tradition, drew his "Sayings of the Lord" from a written gospel.

46. The first challenge to the traditional view came from *The New Testament in the Apostolic Fathers* by a committee of the Oxford Society of Historical Theology (Oxford: Clarendon Press, 1905). I see no reason to alter the results of my *Synoptische Überlieferung* (1957) with respect to Ignatius's, *1 Clement's*, and *Barnabas's* independence of any written gospel. For a more detailed discussion of the *Didache* and *2 Clement*, see below.

47. This is borne out by their form and wording, which does not reveal any redactional features of a known gospel author, and by the quotation formula that appears in the past tense: "he said" (εἶπεν), i.e., the Lord said when he was preaching and teaching. Cf. Koester, *Synoptische Überlieferung*, 6.

48. J. M. Creed, "The Didache," *JTS* 39 (1937) 370–378; Jean-Pierre Audet, *La Didache: Instructions des Apôtres* (EtB; Paris: Gabalda, 1958) 104–20; more recently, with full discussion of literature, Klaus Wengst, *Didache (Apostellehre), Barnabasbrief, Zweiter Klemensbrief, Schrift an Diognet* (Schriften des Urchristentums 2; Darmstadt: Wissenschaftliche Buchgesellschaft, 1984) 18–32.

49. Koester, *Synoptische Überlieferung*, 103–9.

appears in the past tense: "his (i.e., the Lord's) gospel" is best understood as a reference to the preaching of Jesus. In the next part of the *Didache*, dealing with instructions for church officers, the following formula occurs twice: "(do this) as you have it in the gospel" (ὡς ἔχετε ἐν τῷ εὐαγγελίῳ, *Did.* 15.3 and 15.4); cf. 11.3: κατὰ τὸ δόγμα τοῦ εὐαγγελίου οὕτως ποιήσατε. This suggests a document in which the respective instructions were written down. But these phrases stem from the hand of the later editor of the *Didache*, while the materials quoted in this context are derived from older traditions.[50] Nothing in the context of these references indicates that Matthew or any other gospel writing was the source of these materials. In the one instance in which the final redactor actually quotes gospel materials, *Did.* 1.3–5, the sentences are not drawn from Matthew but from a gospel harmony.[51]

The so-called *Second Epistle of Clement*, written about 150 CE or later,[52] repeatedly quotes sayings of Jesus. The verbs in the quotation formulae vary. In two instances, a saying is introduced by "the Lord said" (εἶπεν ὁ κύριος, *2 Clem.* 4.5; 9.11), but in other instances, the present tense of the verb (λέγει) is used in the quotation formula (*2 Clem.* 3.2; 5.2). The present tense, customarily employed for the introduction of quotations from Scripture, would suggest that *2 Clement* quotes from a written document. *2 Clem.* 8.5, introducing a saying of Jesus with the words "because the Lord says in the gospel" (λέγει γὰρ ὁ κύριος ἐν τῷ εὐαγγελίῳ), could be a reference to a book, called "gospel," in which the Lord presently speaks to the church. Several of the sayings quoted in *2 Clement* indeed reveal redactional features of Matthew and Luke.[53] On the other hand, only sayings are quoted. There is no indication that the author knew narrative materials. If he drew his sayings from a written document, it was most likely a sayings collection based on a harmony of Matthew and Luke.

2. Gnostic writings. The *Gospel of Thomas* does not use the term εὐαγγέλιον. It only occurs in the colophon of the scribe. On the other hand, the *Gospel of Thomas* comes with a title and the name of its author. Both are most likely very old: "The Secret Sayings which Jesus Spoke and which Didymus Judas Thomas wrote Down." A similar title appears at the beginning of the *Apocryphon of James*: "The Secret Book which was revealed to me (i.e., James) and Peter by the Lord" (NHC 1/2, 1.10–12).[54] Titles like

---

50. It must be maintained (against Wengst, *Didache*, 61–63) that there is no external evidence that would force us to date the final composition of this book before the end of the second century. Materials and sources used in the final composition are certainly much older; but at least three of the four references to the gospel come from the hand of the final redactor.

51. To maintain his hypothesis of the dependence of the *Didache* upon Matthew, Wengst (*Didache*, 18–20) calls these verses a later interpolation.

52. For the date of *2 Clement,* see Wengst (*Didache*, 222–27): 130–150 CE. The use of sayings based on Matthew and Luke and of apocryphal materials would allow any date before the end of the second century. Martin Hengel (*Die Evangelienüberschriften* [SHW. Philosoph-historische Klasse 1984.3; Heidelberg: Winter, 1984] 34: "einige Jahrzehnte vor Justin") and especially Karl Paul Donfried (*The Setting of Second Clement in Early Christianity* [NovTSup 38; Leiden: Brill, 1974] 55–56) give no convincing arguments for an earlier date.

53. Koester, *Synoptische Überlieferung,* 70–99.

54. The incipit of the work in its present form, "[James] writes to [. . .] those: Peace . . ." (1,13), is secondary and was added by a later hand.

these must have appeared originally also in the incipits of the canonical gospels, and it is unlikely that the term εὐαγγέλιον was ever used in them.[55] In fact, the term does not occur in any title of a gospel writing from the Nag Hammadi Library which reproduces gospel materials; e.g., *The Dialogue of the Savior, The Book of Thomas*.

On the other hand, the *Gospel of Truth*, a writing probably composed by Valentinus around the middle of the second century, uses εὐαγγέλιον in its opening sentence (16,31) and in the text (17,2; 18,11). Although the author certainly knew and used written gospels, in each instance εὐαγγέλιον designates the message of salvation. Gospel as the designation of a writing appears for the first time in the *Treatise on the Resurrection*,[56] which must be dated into the second half of the second century.

VI. From the Oral Tradition to the Written Gospel

In the first decades of the second century, gospel writings were variously known and used. But they did not have the authority of Holy Scripture, nor was their dignity enhanced by the title εὐαγγέλιον. Authoritative scripture was exclusively what was later called the Old Testament. Any additional authority was present in a great variety of traditions that were still undefined. Sometimes they were transmitted orally, sometimes in written form. These authorities could be called "the sayings of the Lord,"[57] "the pronouncements of the apostles,"[58] "the traditions of the elders,"[59] or they could appear as the proclamations or the writings of Christian prophets.[60]

----

55. Hengel (*Evangelienüberschriften*) has tried to renew the thesis that the titles of the canonical gospels, as they appear in the earliest manuscripts ca. 200 CE, already existed in the same form at the beginning of the second century. Hengel is correct in his claim that these gospels must have circulated under the name of a specific author from the very beginning. But there is no evidence that their original book titles were identical with the later "Gospel according to . . ." (εὐαγγέλιον κατὰ . . .). On the contrary, the incipits of some apocryphal gospels, as well as the evidence from Papias (see below), prove that there was no uniformity in the original book titles and that the term εὐαγγέλιον was not used as a designation for such books. See also François Bovon, "The Synoptic Gospels and the Canonical Acts of the Apostles," *HTR* 81 (1988) 19–36.

56. "For if you remember reading in the Gospel that Elijah appeared and Moses with him . . ." (48,8).

57. Acts 20:35; *1 Clem.* 2.8; 13.1; 46.8; *Did.* 8.2. Even the quotations of Jesus' sayings in *2 Clement*, although they are drawn from a written source, are usually introduced as words of the Lord (3.2; 4.5; 5.2–4; 6.1; 8.5; 9.11; 12.2); cf. also Polycarp *Phil.* 2.3.

58. However, there is no particular tradition that is connected with the authority of the apostles. *1 Clement* 44 relates the offices of the church to the apostles but in very general terms. 2 Pet 3:2, where the apostles appear as guaranteeing the commandment of the Lord (μνησθῆναι . . . τῆς τῶν ἀποστόλων ὑμῶν ἐντολῆς τοῦ κυρίου καὶ σωτῆρος), reflects the situation of a later time (probably after Marcion and Justin Martyr). *Didache inscr.* (διδαχὴ κυρίου διὰ τῶν δώδεκα ἀποστόλων) is difficult to date, but is most likely a title that was added later. On the entire question, see Hans von Campenhausen, *Ecclesiastical Authority and Spiritual Power* (Stanford, Calif.: Stanford University Press, 1969); Helmut Koester, "The Apostolic Tradition and the Origins of Gnosticism"; included in volume 1 of my collected articles: *Paul and His World: Interpreting the New Testament in Its Context* (Minneapolis: Fortress Press, 2007).

59. The oldest witness for the teaching authority of the "elders" (πρεσβύτεροι) is Papias of Hierapolis (in Eusebius *Hist. eccl.* 3.39.3–4). More abundant evidence comes from Irenaeus and Clement of Alexandria; see Günther Bornkamm, "Πρεσβὺς κτλ.," *TDNT* 6 (1968) 651–83; von Campenhausen, *Ecclesiastical Authority*, 162–77.

60. In the early church, prophets were not only concerned with predicting the future (e.g., Acts 11:28;

1. Papias of Hierapolis illustrates this well.[61] He says about Mark that he wrote "what was said and done by the Lord" (τὰ ὑπὸ κυρίου ἢ λεχθέντα ἢ πραχθέντα), and about Matthew that he composed "the oracles" (τὰ λόγια).[62] It is evident that Papias did not think of Matthew and Mark as "gospels." Authority came from those who guaranteed the tradition, that is, the disciples of the Lord and those who had followed them. In their written form, these traditions about Jesus and of Jesus' words did not carry any greater authority than that which was transmitted orally. Written accounts of Jesus' words and deeds, of course, were not transmitted without titles and/or names of authors. But εὐαγγέλιον was not used as the title for such books, although Papias's references to Matthew and Mark/Peter show that apostolic names guaranteed the faithfulness of what was written. Titles of these books were probably something such as "The Sayings of the Lord written by Matthew (in Hebrew[63])." What Papias says about both Matthew and Mark reveals that these "gospels" originally had incipits that were similar to those still preserved in the gospels from the Nag Hammadi Library.

Decisive for the trustworthiness of a written or oral gospel tradition was that it was "remembered." The word "remember" (μνημονεύειν) plays an important role in the earliest quotation formulae for sayings of Jesus.[64] Papias says that he wants to write down "what he has learned and remembered well" (ὅσα καλῶς ἔμαθον καὶ καλῶς ἐμνημόνευσα), and that Mark composed in his writing "what he remembered" (ὅσα ἐμνημόνευσεν) from Peter's teachings, and that Mark did not sin when he wrote things down just as he "remembered" (ἀπομνημόνευσεν) them.

A close parallel to Papias's report appears in the *Apocryphon of James*, a writing that must be dated in the early second century.[65] It reports the following in its opening scene (2, 7–15):

> . . . the twelve disciples [were] all sitting together at the same time and remembering what the Savior had said to each one of them, whether in secret or openly, and [putting it] in books.

The terminology of "remembering" is deliberate, and as Vielhauer already had remarked about Papias,[66] it is part of the controversy with the Gnostics. Gnostic writers were

---

21:10–11; Rev 22:6–7); they also occur often as instructors and church leaders, together with "teachers" (διδάσκαλοι); cf. Acts 13:1; *Did.* 10.7; 11.7–13.7. Prophetic writings also claim authority for the regulation and the renewal of the life of the church; see the Revelation of John and the *Shepherd of Hermas*.

61. The date for his writings is usually given as some time between 100 and 150 CE.

62. Quoted in Eusebius *Hist. eccl.* 3.39.14–16.

63. It is worth noting that the incipit of the *Apocryphon of James* says that the book was written in "the Hebrew alphabet." Papias's reference to Matthew writing in Hebrew may rest upon such a statement in the original incipit of the book.

64. Acts 20:35; *1 Clem.* 13.1–2; 46.7–8.

65. This date was originally proposed by Willem van Unnik, *Evangelien aus dem Nilsand* (Frankfurt am Main: Heinrich Scheffler, 1960) 93–101. Van Unnik's argument was that this writing contains gospel materials that are still dependent upon oral tradition. In spite of some criticisms of this early date (see F. E. Williams, "The Apocryphon of James," in Harold W. Attridge, ed., *Nag Hammadi Codex I* [NHS 22; Leiden: Brill, 1985] 26–27), van Unnik's arguments have been confirmed by Ron Cameron, *Sayings Traditions in the Apocryphon of James* (HTS 34; Philadelphia: Fortress Press, 1984) 91–124.

66. Philipp Vielhauer, *Geschichte der urchristlichen Literatur* (Berlin: de Gruyter, 1975) 762.

composing their written documents on the basis of the claim that they remembered well from the apostles and from those who had followed them.[67] For written documents containing the words and deeds of Jesus, it was important (1) that they could claim to rest on legitimate memory, and (2) that they carried apostolic authority.[68] There was no concern with respect to the title that was given to a particular book.[69]

2. Marcion. Hans von Campenhausen[70] suggested that the impulse for a radical change came from the Christian reformer Marcion. The impact of Marcion's reforms, especially his rejection of the "Law and the Prophets," that is, of the Holy Scripture of the Christians, forced a reevaluation of the status and authority of the Christian tradition and thus also of the standing of the gospel literature as a part of this tradition. Marcion was convinced that the traditions and writings transmitted under the authority of the apostles and the elders, upon which the church based its teachings, including the oral and written "Remembrances of the Apostles," had been contaminated by Judaizing interpretations. He thus attacked a universally recognized authority, that is, traditions guaranteed by names of various apostles and accepted both by the orthodox church and their Gnostic opponents.

For this apostolic authority, Marcion substituted his revised edition of the letters of Paul, written documents under the authority of the only apostle who had fought against the Judaizers. In these letters, he found references of Paul to "my gospel" and "our gospel."[71] Because of his fundamental doubts regarding the oral tradition, Marcion understood these phrases as references to a written document called "gospel." He may have known more than one writing with reports of Jesus' words and deeds. But it is no longer possible to determine with certainty whether he was acquainted with Matthew and John as well as with Luke. It is obvious that Matthew's pervasive references to the prophecies of Israel would have made his book an unlikely choice. In any case, Marcion believed that it must have been the Gospel of Luke to which Paul had been referring as "my/our gospel."

There is no evidence that anyone before Marcion called a gospel writing εὐαγγέλιον.[72] But all reports about Marcion agree that he called his revised edition of

---

67. On this entire question, see the chapter "Remembering the Words of Jesus" in Cameron, *Sayings Traditions in the Apocryphon of James*, 91–124.

68. On this latter point, see Koester, "The Apostolic Tradition and the Origins of Gnosticism."

69. Hengel (*Evangelienüberschriften*, 8–18) argues that Papias already presupposes the title Εὐαγγέλιον κατὰ . . . with the implied meaning that this is the one gospel according to Matthew, Mark, etc. This is anachronistic. That the one gospel was extant in different written gospels under apostolic names became a problem only after Marcion (see below). For Papias's time, all emphasis lies upon the apostolic names, no matter what title appeared in the incipit of a particular book.

70. *The Formation of the Christian Bible* (Philadelphia: Fortress Press, 1972) 147–63.

71. The phrase τὸ εὐαγγέλιόν μου appears in Rom 2:16 (Rom 16:25 is part of a secondary addition to Paul's letter); τὸ εὐαγγέλιον ἡμῶν is found in 2 Cor 4:3; 1 Thess 1:5; 2 Thess 1:8; 2:14, but see also Gal 1:1. Since Marcion did not know the Pastoral Epistles, 2 Tim 2:8 is not relevant.

72. The evidence assembled by Hengel (*Evangelienüberschriften*) to demonstrate the early use of this title for the canonical gospels consists exclusively of materials from the second half, or even the very last decades, of the second century. Hengel simply projects these data back into the beginning of the second century and assumes that no changes took place in the course of the century. For a critique of Hengel's thesis, see Bovon, "The Synoptic Gospels," especially p. 23.

Luke "εὐαγγέλιον."[73] This is the first instance in which a Christian used the term as a title of a written document. Marcion introduced this novel usage in conscious protest against the still undefined and mostly oral traditions to which the churches of his day referred as their dominical and apostolic authority. Thus, Marcion's new ecclesiastical organization was not only the first Christian church with its own "scripture," it also possessed for the first time a written document called "the gospel." According to the witness of Justin Martyr,[74] this church quickly, that is, within a decade after Marcion's excommunication, established itself throughout the whole world. It soon constituted a veritable threat to all those Christian churches that continued to insist that theology and ecclesiastical organization must be based upon the Law and the Prophets, the "Holy Scripture" of Christendom, and upon the traditions of the apostles.

VII. Justin Martyr

Justin's writings, composed in the later years of Antoninus Pius (150 to 160 CE), make extensive use of written gospels and quote both sayings of Jesus and narrative materials in numerous instances. In most cases, Justin refers to these written gospels as the "Remembrances of the Apostles" (ἀπομνημονεύματα τῶν ἀποστόλων). In three instances he identifies these same writings also as εὐαγγέλια.

1. Justin's ἀπομνημονεύματα τῶν ἀποστόλων. Justin saw written documents as records that were more reliable than the oral traditions about Jesus. This is evident in their designation as the "Remembrances of the Apostles" (ἀπομνημονεύματα τῶν ἀποστόλων).[75] This term has been explained as a title designed to raise these documents to the status of Greek memoirs of a philosopher.[76] However, the term used by

---

73. Adolf von Harnack, *Marcion: Das Evangelium vom fremden Gott* (reprint, Darmstadt: Wissenschaftliche Buchgesellschaft, 1960) 184.

74. On Justin about Marcion, see *1 Apol.* 26.5–8; 58.1–2. Cf. Eusebius *Hist. Eccl.* 4.11.10.

75. The designation occurs rarely in *1 Apol.* (only 66.3 and 67.3); but cf. also *1 Apol.* 33.5: "As those who remembered (οἱ ἀπομνημονεύσαντες) everything about the savior Jesus Christ have taught" (a quote of Luke 1:31 follows). All other occurrences of the term are found in *Dial.* 100–107 where Justin systematically uses gospel materials for his interpretation of Psalm 21 (*Dial.* 100.4; 101.3; 102.5; 103.6, 8; 104.1; 105.1, 5, 6; 106.1, 3, 4; 107.1).

76. This suggestion was first made by E. Köpke, *Über die Gattung ἀπομνημονεύματα in der griechischen Literatur* (Programm der Ritterakademie zu Brandenburg, 1857). It has been repeated by most authors, because the name seemed to be "well-chosen and very appropriate in order to give to the educated Greeks the right ideas about the character of the gospels" (Zahn, *Kanon*, 1. 471). However, the term was not used for philosophers' memoirs before the Second Sophistic in the second century CE. The primary older example commonly cited is Xenophon's *Memorabilia of Socrates* (this Latin title was used for the first time by Johann Lenklau in the year 1569 for the Latin version of his edition of Xenophon). The term ἀπομνημονεύματα—Latin *Commentarii* (the latter first in Aulus Gellius [2nd century CE] *Noct. Att.* 14.3.5: *quod Xenophon, in libris quos dictorum atque factorum Socrates commentarios composuit*)—does not appear in Xenophon's writings, but only as a title of his work in later manuscripts, Ξενοφῶντος Σωκράτους ἀπομνημονευμάτων βιβλίον πρῶτον, and in the pseudepigraphical letter 18 of Xenophon from the time of the Second Sophistic (πεποίημαι δέ τινα ἀπομνημονεύματα Σωκράτους, [11] ed. Hercher, *Epist. Graec.*, 623); cf. also Diog. L. 4.2; 7.4, 36, 163. Xenophon uses the term διαμνημονεύω once in his *Memorabilia* (τουτὸν δὲ γράψω ὁπόσα ἂν

Justin, composed with the prefix ἀπο-, does not occur among the designations of philosophical memoirs.[77] On the other hand, the simple form of the verb "to remember" (μνημονεύειν), as we have observed, occurs frequently in the quotation formulae for orally transmitted sayings of Jesus.[78] The composite form of the verb "to remember" (ἀπομνημονεύειν) had been used by Papias as technical term for the transmission of oral materials about Jesus. Richard Heard therefore had proposed to understand Justin's term ἀπομνημονεύματα τῶν ἀποστόλων as a continuation of this traditional Christian usage.[79] Luise Abramowski has discussed the frequent occurrence of the term ἀπομνημονεύματα τῶν ἀποστόλων in *Dial.* 100–107, Justin's interpretation of Psalm 21—most likely an earlier composition by the same author that was later incorporated into the Dialogue.[80] She suggests that this earlier treatise on Psalm 21 was written with an anti-gnostic intention and that Justin coined the phrase ἀπομνημονεύματα τῶν ἀποστόλων in the context of this controversy.[81] Justin thus continues the tradition which is evident in Papias and in the *Apocryphon of James*, but now emphasizes that "it is written that these things really happened" (γέγραπται γενόμενον, *Dial.* 104.1).[82]

2. **Justin's use of εὐαγγέλιον.** In each of the three passages in which the term occurs it designates written gospels. It is also clear that these gospels are identical with the "Remembrances of the Apostles." In *1 Apol.* 66.3 he relates:

> In the memoirs which the apostles have composed which are called gospels (ἃ γέγραπται ἐν τῷ καλεῖται εὐαγγελίῳ) they transmitted that they had received the following instructions . . .

In *Dial.* 10.2 Justin introduces his fictitious partner, the Jew Trypho, as saying:

διαμνημονεύω, 1.3.1). That Justin should have known this term from its very occasional use in the Second Sophistic is possible. But it is highly unlikely that his choice of the term as a designation for the gospels was dependent upon this usage.

77. Such writings did not enjoy a special technical designation; they could be called by several terms, such as ὑπομνήματα (= *commentarii*), συγγράμματα; see LSJ, svv.

78. Acts 20:35; *1 Clem.* 13.1; cf. 46.7; Polycarp *Phil.* 2.3; cf. *2 Clem.* 17.3; cf. Koester, *Synoptische Überlieferung*, 4–6; see above.

79. Cf. Richard Heard, "The ἀπομνημονεύματα in Papias, Justin, and Irenaeus," *NTS* 1 (1954–55) 122–29. This hypothesis has been criticized by Nils Hyldahl, "Hegesippus Hypomnemata," *StTh* 14 (1960) 70–113. Hyldahl, however, does not appreciate the differences between ὑπομνήματα, συγγράματα, and ἀπομνημονεύματα, or the fact that the latter term occurs relatively late in Greek literature; see above.

80. Luise Abramowski, "Die 'Erinnerungen der Apostel' bei Justin," in Peter Stuhlmacher, ed., *Das Evangelium und die Evangelien* (WUNT 28; Tübingen: Mohr/Siebeck, 1983) 341–53.

81. Ibid., 352.

82. See ibid., 350. Abramowski (p. 353) agrees that Justin must have known Papias or analogous traditions, because his reference to the "Remembrances of Peter" in *Dial.* 106.3 in the context of a citation from Mark (3:16–17) shows that he was familiar with the tradition that connected the Gospel of Mark with Peter like the Elder of Papias (Eusebius *Hist. eccl.* 3.39.15). However, the general observation that second-century authors prefer the oral tradition and do not value the written documents very highly is no longer valid for Justin (*pace* Eric Francis Osborn, *Justin Martyr* [BhTh 47; Tübingen: Mohr/Siebeck, 1973] 125–26).

I know that your commandments which are written in the so-called gospel (ἃ γέγραπται ἐν τῷ λεγομένῳ εὐαγγελίῳ) are so wonderful and so great that no human being can possibly fulfill them.

For Justin, therefore, a gospel is a book and since Justin uses the plural gospels, he must have known more than one writing with this designation.

For Justin, these gospel writings possess the authority of written records. But they are not "Holy Scripture" (γραφή) like the Law and the Prophets. The authority of the latter is enhanced by the inspiration of the prophecies that they record,[83] but Justin never considers the gospels or the memoirs of the apostles as inspired. While he regularly quotes the Law and the Prophets with the formula "it is written" (γέγραπται), he uses this term only rarely for a quotation from the gospels. In the few instances where he does so, he combines it with other verbs. Introducing gospel quotations, the term does not mean "it is written in Holy Scripture," but "it is recorded in a written document that Jesus said" (ἐν τῷ εὐαγγελίῳ δὲ γέραπται εἰπών, *Dial.* 100.1).[84]

3. Justin Martyr and Marcion. Justin was involved in the earliest phase of the Marcionite controversy; he reports that he had published a book against Marcion.[85] But we do not know the details of his arguments because this writing as well as his *Syntagma* against all heresies are lost. However, Justin's extant writings show the impact of Marcion's challenge. Most noticeable is the suppression of Paul and his letters. Although earlier writers, even in Rome, never hesitated to refer to Paul as their authority,[86] there is not a single quote from the Pauline corpus in Justin's writings, nor is the apostle ever mentioned. On the other hand, Justin's writings abound with quotations from the gospels of Matthew and Luke.

Justin adopts Marcion's concept of a written gospel and distances himself from the oral tradition. He agrees with Marcion: the gospel of the church must be a written document. However, while Marcion emphasized the irreconcilable contradiction between the written gospel and Israel's scripture, Justin tied the "Remembrances of the Apostles" or "Gospels" as tightly as possible to the Law and the Prophets. While Marcion revised the Gospel of Luke in order to eliminate all references to the Law and the Prophets, Justin did not hesitate to revise the texts of Matthew and Luke in order to

---

83. *1 Apol.* 32. However, Justin does not ascribe the inspiration to the text of the Septuagint translation or to the Hebrew text, but rather to the prophets themselves, whose words were recorded in Hebrew and translated into Greek.

84. Justin uses the quotation formula "it is written" also in connection with the "Memoirs of the Apostles" (*Dial.* 103.6, 8; 104.1; 105.6; 106.3, 4; 107.1).

85. On Justin against Marcion, see *1 Apol.* 26.8 (*Syntagma* against all heresies); Irenaeus *Haer.* 4.6.9; Eusebius *Hist. eccl.* 4.11.8 (*Syntagma* against Marcion).

86. In addition to numerous allusions to Paul's letters, there are several explicit references in *1 Clement*: 32.5–6 = Rom 1:29–32; *1 Clem.* 37.5 = 1 Cor 12:21–22; *1 Clem.* 47.1–3 = Phil 4:15; cf. *1 Clem.* 49.5 = 1 Cor 13:5. With respect to the debated question of the dependence of 1 Peter (also written in Rome) upon Paul, see Francis Wright Beare, *The First Epistle of Peter* (3rd ed.; Oxford: Blackwell, 1970) 28–29, 212–16.

establish an even closer verbal agreement between the prophecies of the Greek Bible and the record of their fulfillment.

As records of this nature the gospels are, indeed, the foundations of the truth of the Christian beliefs and they substantiate the validity of the Christian kerygma. That this is the case is not related to their "kerygmatic" character or structure. Rather, Justin sees the gospels as reliable historical records. As the testimony of true divinity is the fulfillment of prophecy,[87] the gospels as reliable records of history provide the evidence for the fulfillment of prophecy in the story of Jesus. The Christian kerygma that proclaims this Jesus is trustworthy divine revelation because it is confirmed by the historical record provided by the gospel.

VIII. Conclusion

The evidence of all extant sources from the first and early second centuries reveals that εὐαγγέλιον is always and everywhere understood as the proclamation of the saving message about Christ or the coming of the kingdom. There are no indications that such understanding of the term gradually developed into the designation of written documents as gospels. Not one of the authors of a gospel writing understands his work as a written gospel, nor do the authors of the gospels of Mark, Matthew, Thomas, and John even reveal any consciousness that they are producing works of the same type of literary genre that is representative of the εὐαγγέλιον, that is, the proclamation of and about Jesus Christ.

Luke is the first author of a written gospel who is aware of the literary genre of his work and of the relationship of his work to previous similar writings. He calls it a "narrative" (διήγησις, Luke 1:1–4)—a term that characterizes both parts of his work (including the Acts of the Apostles). Even a later writer like the author of the *Gospel of Truth*, who knows and uses such literary products as the Gospel of Luke, reserves the term εὐαγγέλιον as a designation for the oral proclamation.

The employment of the term εὐαγγέλιον as a technical designation for a written document by Marcion, therefore, appears as a revolutionary novelty.[88] It is prompted by Marcion's conviction that the Christian tradition had been contaminated by a Judaizing interpretation and that the original gospel of Paul could be recovered only by a critical edition of extant written works. He had learned from Paul (Gal 1:6–9) that there could only be *one* gospel, which he restored in his purified edition of Luke's work.

---

87. Justin *1 Apol.* 12.10: "It is the work of God to announce something before it happens and then to demonstrate that it happened as it was predicted." In a brilliant formulation, this principle occurs in Tertullian *Apologeticum* 20.3: *testimonium divinitatis veritas divinationis* ("The testimony of divinity is the truth of divination").

88. I wish to acknowledge gratefully a suggestion that was made by Professor Henry Chadwick at the annual meeting of the Societas Novi Testamenti Studiorum in Cambridge in August 1988. He pointed to the likelihood that the liturgical reading of written gospels had been established by that time. Such readings could have been introduced as "the gospel." This might have given rise to a more common understanding of the εὐαγγέλιον as a written document. In this case, Marcion would have elevated such popular understanding to a theologically conscious literary usage.

The effects of Marcion's innovative use of the term εὐαγγέλιον are clearly visible in Justin's treatment of the gospels of Matthew and Luke (and probably Mark): though he knows of a plurality of such writings, he harmonizes these gospels and connects them more intimately with the prophecy of the Scriptures. Indeed, Marcion's emphasis upon the uniqueness of the one gospel is continuing to be effective in the subsequent production of Tatian's *Diatessaron*, in Irenaeus' defense of the fourfold written form of the one gospel of Christ, and finally in the designation of the canonical gospels as "the Gospel according to (τὸ εὐαγγέλιον κατά) Matthew, Mark, Luke, and John."

5

THE SYNOPTIC SAYINGS GOSPEL Q
IN THE EARLY COMMUNITIES
OF JESUS' FOLLOWERS

Among the numerous questions that are discussed regarding the Synoptic Sayings Gospel Q, I shall consider three issues in this chapter:[1] (1) The geographical location of the community that preserved the sayings tradition that resulted in the composition of Q, (2) the stratification of the document Q, and (3) the problem of the life situation (*Sitz im Leben*) of the materials in Q and related traditions. Arguments against the assumption of a relatively isolated community in Galilee that produced the Synoptic Sayings Gospel are formidable.[2] I myself have been critical of the "Galilee only" hypothesis for the origin of Q. But there are substantial problems not only with locating Q in Jerusalem but also with the attempt to understand Q within the context of mainline early-Christian developments. Arguments against a literary stratification of Q, which was proposed in an eminently persuasive way by John Kloppenborg[3] have been brought forth a number of times,[4] including by Paul Hoffmann,[5] who is also one of the editors of the recently published critical edition of Q.[6]

---

1. This chapter has been developed on the basis of a response that I was asked to give to Birger Pearson's critique of recent hypotheses about the Synoptic Sayings Gospel Q (unpublished). His paper and my response were presented at the annual meeting of the Society of Biblical Literature in Denver in November 2001. Birger Pearson affirms the validity of the Q hypothesis, but he wants to assign the document to Jerusalem as a kind of supplemental handbook. I do not pretend to be able to address all related issues of the debate—indeed I am not well enough acquainted with all the relevant literature. However, I will elaborate my position as it reflects my more recent thinking on some of the issues.

2. This was one of the arguments in the paper presented by Birger Pearson. He argued instead for Jerusalem as the place of origin; see also Marco Frenschkowski, "Galiläa oder Jerusalem: Die topographischen und politischen Hintergründe der Logienquelle," in Andreas Lindemann, ed., *The Sayings Source Q and the Historical Jesus* (BETL 158; Leuven: Leuven University Press, 2001) 535–59.

3. John S. Kloppenborg, *The Formation of Q: Trajectories in Ancient Wisdom Collections* (SAC; Philadelphia: Fortress Press, 1987).

4. See the review by John S. Kloppenborg, "The Sayings Gospel Q: Literary and Stratigraphic Problems," in Risto Uro, ed., *Symbols and Strata: Essays on the Sayings Gospel Q* (Göttingen: Vandenhoeck & Ruprecht, 1996) 1–66.

5. "Mutmaßungen über Q: Zum Problem der literarischen Genese von Q," in Lindemann, *The Sayings Source Q*, 255–88.

6. James M. Robinson, Paul Hoffmann, and John S. Kloppenborg, eds., *The Critical Edition of Q: Synopsis Including the Gospels of Matthew and Luke, Mark, and Thomas* (Hermeneia Supplements; Minneapolis: Fortress Press, 2000).

Finally, if more weight is shifted to the oral tradition, the life situation must be more rigorously defined as situation in the life of the community, for which the materials preserved in the *Didache* might serve as a helpful guide.

I. The Question of Geographical Isolation

More than thirty years ago, James Robinson and I proposed that the development of diverse early responses to the ministry, preaching, suffering, and death of Jesus presupposes formations of different traditions from and about Jesus in groups that existed in relative geographical isolation from each other.[7] Eventually, such groups committed their traditions, in the beginning preserved orally, to writing. Moreover, these older traditions and sources represent in each instance different answers to the question of Jesus' significance as a lasting source for salvation. Literature from the last third of the first century, that is, from the third generation after Jesus, demonstrates an effort to bring those different writings together, as is especially evident in the Gospels of Matthew and Luke, but also must be presupposed for the composition of the Gospel of John—efforts that still bear witness to the conflicting christological agendas of the older literatures and traditions. The most fundamental differences can be observed in the comparison of two major early developments: There is, on the one hand, the proclamation of Jesus' death and resurrection as the turning point of the ages and the subsequent development of the passion narrative and on the other hand, the cultivation of the memory of Jesus' sayings together with their further enrichment and interpretation. These two traditions cannot have been wrought and cultivated in one and the same circle of the communities of the first and second generation. Each of them is self-sufficient. They were, to be sure, combined at a later stage; but these later combinations show that it was problematic to reconcile the different inherent theological biases of these two different answers to the significance of Jesus.

It is comparatively simple to delineate the development of the proclamation of the suffering, death, and resurrection of Jesus and of the passion narrative. This is because the letters of Paul, and the traditions upon which Paul relies, are accessible as direct sources that give evidence even for the very beginnings of this proclamation. An investigation of these traditions demonstrates that a formulation of "the gospel" of Jesus' death, burial, resurrection, and epiphanies existed before Paul's call, that is, in the very first years after the death of Jesus. Similarly, together with this gospel, a tradition that interpreted the Eucharist in view of the death was simultaneously established in these very first years. Moreover, the two traditional formulae in 1 Cor 11:23–25 and 15:1–7 reveal that this interpretation of Jesus' suffering and death used the story of the suffering servant as the key to an understanding of the significance of Jesus for the understanding of salvation. Both the introduction to the words of institution, "in the night in which he was handed over," and the gospel formula, "he died for our sins according to

---

7. James M. Robinson and Helmut Koester, *Trajectories through Early Christianity* (Philadelphia: Fortress Press, 1971).

the Scriptures," point to Isaiah 53.[8] Sayings of Jesus and stories about his miracles, although they were known in the context of these developments, did not play any role whatsoever in the interpretation of Jesus' significance for salvation.

The location of the development of the gospel/Eucharist tradition is evident. Most likely, this appeared in the Greek-speaking church, probably in Antioch; the allusions to Isaiah 53 presuppose the Greek rather than the Hebrew text. The missionary efforts of Paul and his associates carried this gospel to the major cities of the Aegean—Thessalonike, Corinth, and Ephesus. Also the deutero-Pauline letters were written in this geographical area, and the collection of the Pauline corpus was most likely brought together in Ephesus. How this tradition is related to Jerusalem is not clear. But the Jerusalem agreement between Paul, Barnabas, and Titus on the one hand, and James, Peter, and John, on the other hand (Gal 2:1–10), would suggest that the authorities in Jerusalem at least did not object to this understanding of the saving significance of Jesus' death and resurrection. Indeed, the list of people to whom Jesus appeared after his death includes the names of the Jerusalem authorities, Peter, and James (1 Cor 15:5–8).

It is much more difficult to reconstruct the process in which the tradition of Jesus' sayings was developed as a continuing instrument for the understanding of salvation. Although the genuine Pauline letters were written in the fifties of the first century, there is no direct written documentation for the sayings tradition that can be dated to before 70 CE. The Synoptic Sayings Gospel, in the form in which Matthew and Luke knew it, was not composed before the end of the Jewish War.[9] This late date is further confirmed by Egon Brandenburger's investigation of Mark 13. He establishes a close connection between the Son of Man sayings and the Jewish War or at least the unrest immediately before the war.[10] The *Gospel of Thomas* is certainly based upon earlier collections of sayings. In its extant versions (the Greek fragments and the Coptic translation), however, it must be assigned to some time in the second century. The Gospel of John and the *Dialogue of the Savior* presuppose an interpretation of the sayings of Jesus in which the meaning of these sayings was further explored in the form of dialogue between Jesus and his disciples. But the extant written documents cannot be dated any earlier than to the very end of the first century.

On the other hand, the understanding of the sayings of Jesus as instruments of salvation must have begun very early after the death of Jesus. But to understand this process, it is necessary to investigate the possibility of written sources and oral traditions that were used by the authors of the extant documents. With respect to the second common source for the Gospels of Matthew and Luke, this task has been successfully completed in the publication of the reconstructed document Q. Did this document as it is now reconstructed depend on an earlier written version? In an earlier essay that was

---

8. Helmut Koester, "The Memory of Jesus' Death and the Worship of the Risen Lord," *HTR* 91 (1998) 335–50; included in this volume (chap. 15).

9. On the dating of Q, see Robinson, Hoffmann, and Kloppenborg, *Critical Edition of Q*, xlvii–lvii. The close relationship of some of the Q material to the events of the Jewish War makes it impossible to uphold a dating around or before 50 CE.

10. Egon Brandenburger, *Markus 13 und die Apokalyptik* (FRLANT 134; Göttingen: Vandenhoeck & Ruprecht, 1984).

published in 1965[11] and then republished in *Trajectories through Early Christianity*,[12] I indicated that there must have been an earlier layer of the sayings tradition. I then followed Kloppenborg's thesis in my later work.[13] But like Kloppenborg, I am fully aware of the hypothetical character of reconstructing an earlier version of a document that is itself the result of a reconstruction, however carefully that reconstruction was done. As far as the *Gospel of Thomas* is concerned, a good many of its sayings can be dated to the first century, perhaps even to a time corresponding to an earlier stage of Q. The judgment here, however, to a large degree depends upon finding parallel sayings in the canonical gospels. Furthermore, it is not certain whether they already expressed a gnosticizing interpretation at the time of their incorporation into the earliest version of the *Gospel of Thomas*. We may be on safer ground with respect to the sayings traditions used in the Gospel of John. These sayings traditions presuppose developments that must have occurred before the writing of the Fourth Gospel: their meaning was explored in the form of dialogues and discourses, and these dialogues interpreted the sayings in a gnosticizing manner.[14]

What geographical locale can be assigned to the development of the sayings tradition as the saving words of Jesus? The Gospel of John contains a number of place names that reveal familiarity with Palestine, especially Samaria, Galilee, and the area of the Jordan Valley. The Samaritans appear as the first converts of Jesus' ministry (John 4). The use of the Son of Man title also points to the area of Palestine and Syria outside of Antioch. Even after the acceptance of the passion narrative in the Johannine communities and the composition of the gospel, the writing must have remained in a fairly isolated location. It was brought to Egypt early in the second century, as the find of 𝔓52 demonstrates but did not reach Asia Minor until the middle of the second century; Polycarp of Smyrna does not yet show any knowledge of the Gospel of John, although he was familiar with the Gospels of Matthew and Luke. Can we therefore locate the tradition of John in a specific area? It would be foolhardy to suggest a specific place (e.g., Samaria or one of the cities of the Decapolis). On the other hand, some place or places in Greek-speaking Syria and Palestine are likely, while Jerusalem and Antioch and certainly Ephesus can be convincingly excluded.

The *Gospel of Thomas* should be located in some close proximity to the Gospel of John. The latter is the only gospel in which the apostle Thomas occurs several times. Moreover, Thomas appears to be the one who expects a gnostic answer from Jesus as, for example, in his quest for the way to the heavenly mansions in John 14. Furthermore, the Gospel of John knows and utilizes a number of sayings that have parallels only in the *Gospel of Thomas*. Even if the authority of Thomas later is used primarily in eastern

11. Helmut Koester, "GNOMAI DIAPHOROI: The Origin and Nature of Diversification in the History of Early Christianity," *HTR* 58 (1965) 279–318.

12. James M. Robinson and Helmut Koester, *Trajectories through Early Christianity* (Philadelphia: Fortress Press, 1971) 114–57.

13. Helmut Koester, *Ancient Christian Gospels: Their History and Development* (Philadelphia: Trinity Press International, 1990) 128–71.

14. Ibid., 173–87.

Syria, these connections to the Fourth Gospel suggest that it originated in the area of southern Syria and Palestine. That is, of course, underlined by the many parallels to the sayings of the *Gospel of Thomas* in the Synoptic tradition (not only in Q, but also in the special materials of Matthew and Luke). Remarkable, however, is the total absence of the Son of Man sayings in spite of its close relationship with other Synoptic materials. Thus the tradition contained in the *Gospel of Thomas* was originally closely associated with that preserved in the Synoptic tradition but went a separate path at a fairly early time.

As far as the Synoptic Sayings Gospel Q is concerned, we unfortunately have no particular name that can be assigned as an authority for the tradition it preserves. Names are helpful because they can demonstrate the continuity of a tradition in spite of theological discontinuity. Consider the case of the Pastoral Epistles as part of the Pauline corpus. They certainly belong to the area of the Pauline mission in Western Asia Minor. It would be helpful if we were certain that Papias's remark about "Matthew who composed the sayings" indeed referred to some version of Q.[15] It would establish a link between Q and the Gospel of Matthew and the area of western Syria. This, however, is debated. But there are some telltale signs that point to one specific area rather than to another. It is well known that names of places in Galilee appear frequently in the sayings of Q, especially in the second stage of Q. It still may be questioned whether this points to Galilee as the location of those sayings in the oral tradition or to the place of Q's final composition.

There is, however, one other indication for the location of the final composition, or at least for the final development, of the sayings tradition preserved in Q—the designation of Jesus as the coming Son of Man, which is limited to Q, Mark, and the Gospel of John. Matthew and Luke do not count as independent witnesses because they draw that title, together with the respective materials, from Mark and Q. Even Mark is not necessarily a direct witness for the location in which this title originated, because the title may have come to him via the tradition of sayings that are collected in the Synoptic Apocalypse of Mark 13. This chapter is not an original Markan composition, and although Mark was written somewhere in Phoenicia or Syria (not in Rome!), chapter 13 must belong to a different locale, namely Palestine. The title Son of Man cannot be assigned to the earliest traditions of sayings of Jesus. It is absent in the *Gospel of Thomas* and never appears in Paul's writings, although Paul was certainly familiar with some sayings of Jesus. Where and when did the Son of Man sayings arise? I have been impressed by Egon Brandenburger's study of Mark 13.[16] He argues persuasively that the announcements of the sudden coming of the Son of Man were prophetic utterances that called Jesus' followers away from the growing messianic fervor that permeated the Jewish society in Galilee and Judea during the years immediately before the Jewish War. With the

---

15. On the discussion of the possible relationship of Papias's statement about "Matthew who composed the sayings (τὰ λόγια = "oracles") in the Hebrew Language," see Dieter Lührmann, "Q; Sayings of Jesus or Logia?" in Ronald A. Piper, ed., *The Gospel Behind the Gospels: Current Studies on Q* (NovTSup 75; Leiden: Brill, 1995) 97–116. See also Robinson, Hoffmann, and Kloppenborg, *Critical Edition of Q*, xx–xxxiii.

16. Brandenburger, *Markus 13 und die Apokalyptic*, passim.

prophetic announcement of the expected sudden return of Jesus as the Son of Man, Jesus' followers distanced themselves from those people in Palestine who believed that an uprising against Rome would bring about the messianic age for Israel. These sayings pronounce that Jesus' followers should not be engaged in messianic-inspired war and violence. If Brandenburger's hypothesis is right, we would have to look for the community of Q as well as for the author of the Markan apocalypse somewhere in Palestine.

There are several reasons, however, which argue against too narrow a localization of Q in Lower Galilee. The Son of Man sayings that are at the basis of the Markan apocalypse point to a wider area. Mark 13:14 says that those in Judea must flee to the mountains. The final form of Q, on the other hand, contained an oracle against Jerusalem (Q 13:34–35). The Gospel of John is also dependent upon the identification of Jesus with the Son of Man, and its tradition may not have originated in Lower Galilee. It is therefore necessary to establish a wider geographical area in southern Syria/Palestine as the place for the development of this sayings tradition and its eventual written form as it is present in Q.

The essential weakness of the hypothesis that the community of Q with its traditions of Jesus' sayings was located and remained in Galilee for many years disregards an important fact about the early expansion of the movement deriving from Jesus, namely, that the expansion was explosive. Twenty years after Jesus' death, Paul was already in Macedonia, and a few years later he wrote to the Romans that from Jerusalem to Illyricum there was no longer any area in which the gospel had not yet been proclaimed (Rom 15:19). To be sure, this early expansion also implied a considerable diversity of traditions. But it is unlikely that any part of this rapidly expanding movement should have remained stuck in the small towns and villages of Lower Galilee for many decades.

The development of the oral tradition in these circles of followers of Jesus did not take place in a community settled in the same place over more than one generation, but in a quickly moving missionary enterprise. Moreover, as Paul went to the major city centers of the Greek world, it is likely that those who preached salvation through Jesus of Nazareth's saving words were also on the move. This is reinforced by the fact that the sayings tradition of Q from its very beginning reveals a clear eschatological urgency, driven by the expectation of the coming of the kingdom of God. I am not at all impressed by the thesis that the Q people were some kind of wandering Cynic philosophers,[17] although they were certainly a community that was on the move away from the rural milieu of Jesus' preaching to the cities of Syria and Palestine. It is interesting that even the *Gospel of Thomas* indicates a change from the rural milieu to the city.[18] It is necessary to draw a circle for the Q community and its traditions much wider than the small town milieu of Lower Galilee.

---

17. For literature and a critical discussion of the Cynic hypothesis, see John S. Kloppenborg Verbin, "A Dog Among the Pigeons: The 'Cynic Hypothesis' as a Theological Problem," in John A. Asgeirsson, Kristin de Troyer, and Marvin W. Meyer, eds., *From Quest to Q; Festschrift for James M. Robinson* (Leuven: Leuven University Press, 2000) 73–117. For a defense, see Leif E. Vaage, "Jewish Scripture, Q and the Historical Jesus: A Cynic Way with the Word?" in Lindemann, *The Sayings Source Q*, 479–95.

18. Cf. the Parable of the Banquet, saying 64.

Two features stand out: (1) this community was either bilingual or Greek-speaking, but the preaching of Jesus seems to have stayed within the rural and small-town Aramaic-speaking world of Galilee; (2) it must have preserved some ties to Jewish people in Palestine (be that Judea and/or Galilee). Evidence for an Aramaic substratum may exist, but it is not very strong. If the *Didache* preserves an Aramaic phrase like *Maranatha*, so does Paul.[19] Certainly there was never a written predecessor of Q in Aramaic, no matter how early one wants to date the earliest version of Q. There were a large number of Greek-speaking cities in Syria (e.g., Damascus), in Phoenecia, and even in Palestine itself, such as Caesarea Maritima and the cities of the Decapolis that would have allowed for an expansion of the community without direct conflict with the missionary activity of Antioch. On the other hand, even though Gentile mission cannot be excluded,[20] there is an obvious Jewish constituency. There is no polemic against the observance of the Sabbath, although the Pharisees are criticized. (Note that one does not have to go to Jerusalem to find Pharisees. Paul, one of the best-known Pharisees of the time, came from a Greek city outside of Palestine, perhaps from Damascus rather than Tarsus.)

Finally, the Son of Man sayings point to a connection with Jewish communities of followers of Jesus in Palestine. The Synoptic Apocalypse Mark 13 became known outside of Palestine very soon after the Jewish War. Similarly, the written gospel of the community of Q became known in the areas of the Antioch mission at the latest during the seventies of the first century and was used by Matthew in the eighties. A decade later, the same document had been brought to Ephesus, if that was the place where Luke wrote his gospel. But did Q originate in Jerusalem? Quite unlikely—and certainly not with the Hellenists of the time right after the death of Jesus! Barnabas, and most likely also Peter, were associated with the gospel of Paul, not with the preaching of either the coming kingdom of God or with the expectation of the Son of Man. On the other hand, if the final composition of Q took place only after the Jewish War, Jerusalem is the most unlikely place in the world.

The major writing that emerged from the tradition of Jesus' sayings, namely Q, arrived in the areas of the Pauline mission only after the Jewish War. But smaller collections of sayings that belong to this tradition were known in these areas much earlier. A clean geographical separation of the diverse traditions even in the earlier period of oral transmission is not possible in any case. Paul himself is familiar with smaller collections of the sayings of Jesus. In Romans 12 he alludes to two sayings that are paralleled in the inaugural sermon of Q.[21] First Corinthians 1–4 reveals that sayings related to the tradition of the *Gospel of Thomas* and to Q had made their way to the wisdom-hungry Corinthians.[22] The author of the Gospel of Mark, who was not familiar with Q, used a number of collections of sayings, apophthegmata, and parables as well as an

---

19. *Did.* 9.6; 1 Cor 16:22.

20. See again Q 13:28–29.

21. For Rom 12:14 and 17, cf. Q/Luke 6:27 and 29; see Koester, *Ancient Christian Gospels*, 53; Charles H. Talbert, "Tradition and Redaction in Romans XII," *NTS* 16 (1969/70) 87.

22. Helmut Koester, "Gnostic Writings as Witnesses for the Development of the Sayings Tradition," in Bentley Layton, ed., *The School of Valentinus* (vol. 1 of *The Rediscovery of Gnosticism*; NumenSup 41; Leiden: Brill, 1980) 23–61; Koester, *Ancient Christian Gospels*, 55–62.

apocalypse composed of sayings of Jesus. Matthew and Luke, in addition to their use of Q, had access to major collections of sayings and parables of Jesus. A small catechism of Jesus' sayings strayed as far as Rome, where it was used in *1 Clement* 13.[23] On the other hand, Q contained a miracle story of Jesus, and it is indeed the case that some of the Q sayings presuppose a knowledge of Jesus' death and allude to it. The question is not whether such materials were known, but whether they functioned in defining the central religious concern of the community, that is, whether they functioned christologically.[24]

Birger Pearson, in his address at the 2001 meeting of the Society of Biblical Literature,[25] questioned the possibility of reconstructing an earlier stage of the composition of Q, as did Paul Hoffmann in a major article.[26] I am, of course, partially responsible for the hypothesis of the existence of an earlier stage of the sayings tradition or even its composition in a written document.[27] I did this following the lead of Dieter Lührmann[28] and combined it with my own observation that the Son of Man sayings and Q's judgment sayings left no trace in the sayings tradition that is preserved in the *Gospel of Thomas*. I therefore proposed that there must have been a stage of the development of the sayings tradition that did not contain the Son of Man sayings. Furthermore, if arguments for the literary and thematic consistency of Q are problematic,[29] why does the hypothesis of an older written version of Q remain so controversial? The most obvious problem with the reconstruction of Q1 is its bias towards rediscovering the historical Jesus, be he now a prophetic revolutionary or a mild-mannered Cynic philosopher. Moreover, if it is difficult to move from a hypothetical document written shortly after the year 70 (= Q2) to an earlier version of this document written perhaps ten or twenty years earlier, it is perilous to jump from that earlier version of the document over a distance of more than two decades to the historical Jesus![30] That is especially the case if the reconstruction of that earlier version is dictated by a particular image of the historical Jesus—although John Kloppenborg cannot be accused of such a motivation. His reconstruction of Q1 is not dictated by an interest in the historical Jesus or by the isolation of theological motifs that distinguish the different layers of Q. Rather, his arguments are based on literary observations.[31]

---

23. Helmut Koester, *Synoptische Überlieferung bei den apostolischen Vätern* (TU 65; Berlin: Akademie-Verlag, 1957) 12–19; Koester, *Ancient Christian Gospels*, 66–68.

24. On the implicit christology of the Q tradition, see Jacques Schlosser, "Q et la christologie implicite," in Lindemann, *The Sayings Source Q*, 289–316.

25. See above, n. 1.

26. Paul Hoffmann, "Mutmassungen über Q: Zum Problem der literarischen Genese von Q," in Lindemann, *The Sayings Source Q*, 255–88.

27. Koester, "GNOMAI DIAPHOROI," 114–57.

28. Dieter Lührmann, *Die Redaktion der Logienquelle* (WMANT 33; Neukrichen-Vluyn: Neukirchener Verlag, 1969).

29. In spite of the efforts of Paul Hoffmann ("Mutmassungen über Q," 255–88), I am not convinced.

30. See the recent criticism of such attempts by Dieter Lührmann, "Die Logienquelle und die Leben-Jesu-Forschung," in Lindemann, *The Sayings Source Q*, 191–206.

31. John S. Kloppenborg, "The Sayings Gospel Q and the Quest for the Historical Jesus," *HTR* 89 (1996) 307–44.

It is essential that the question of the historical Jesus be excluded from the search for an earlier stage of Q. Just as the passion narrative, even in its earliest stages, cannot tell us anything about the way in which Jesus actually suffered and died, the earliest stage of the sayings tradition or the first written version of Q cannot be considered as a direct witness to the preaching of Jesus. On the other hand, those who deny the existence of an earlier written version of Q still face serious problems—*pace* all the difficulties of reconstructing an earlier version of a hypothetical document. The hypothesis of an earlier version of Q has one great advantage: it can explain the transition from a tradition in which the announcement of the coming kingdom of God was the guiding theological principle to a later version that emphasizes instead the sudden coming of Jesus as the Son of Man on the clouds of heaven for the final judgment. I am aware of the fact that this is a history-of-religions rather than a literary argument. That is to say, the reconstruction of Q1 must proceed on the grounds of literary criteria. But the result can be instructive regarding a problem of the religious development within the history of the community of Q.

Philipp Vielhauer's elucidation of the fundamental difference between the proclamation of the kingdom of God and the expectation of the Son of Man, proposed about half a century ago, should not be forgotten.[32] These two different eschatological concepts are not easily reconciled with each other. As the final version of Q as well as the Synoptic Gospels demonstrate, these two different eschatological expectations could well be combined later into one and the same literary document. The latest version of Q presents an uneasy and conflicting harmonization of the two—clearly a secondary development. It is a development that is not visible in the *Gospel of Thomas* or the letters of Paul. If one wants to throw out the hypothesis of an earlier version of Q, theologically dominated by the proclamation of the impending kingdom of God, it is necessary to explain why this expectation appears in combination with the secondary eschatological concept of the sudden appearance of the Son of Man in the final version of Q. In other words, denying the earlier version of Q does not get rid of the problem; it is simply passing the solution of the problem to the oral tradition.

II. The Situation of Q and Its Traditions in the Life of the Community

Perhaps the challenge should be accepted and the functions of materials in the oral tradition should be explored further, rather than reconstructing an earlier written version of Q. But in recent research this is burdened with a difficulty, because what form criticism had defined as the *Sitz im Leben* of the oral tradition has now been miraculously metamorphosed into the search for ideas held by individuals vis-à-vis social situations and, moreover, to the search for a social situation in a very small geographical area, such as Lower Galilee. It seems to have become a sacrilege even to speak of the political life

---

32. Philipp Vielhauer, "Reich Gottes und Menschensohn in der Verkündigung Jesu," in *Festschrift für Günther Dehn* (Neukirchen-Vluyn: Neukirchener Verlag, 1957) 57–79.

situation of a community, not to mention communal religious identity and practices such as preaching, instruction for baptism, ritual, inter-community relationships, and moral motivation. Unless future research is liberated from this stranglehold of only social definitions as the *Sitz im Leben* and is willing to consider questions of theology, christology, and religious experience, no progress can be made. Some recent scholarship does not always abide by the definitions of the *Sitz im Leben* as they were proposed in the beginnings of form criticism by Martin Dibelius,[33] Rudolf Bultmann,[34] and others.[35] It is necessary to relate oral traditions as well as any written versions of the sayings tradition to political and religious life situations of a community and to liberate them from their present captivity, as if these traditions were bearers of individuals' ideas regarding narrowly defined social circumstances. It is the great merit of Egon Brandenburger's[36] explanation of the origin of the Son of Man sayings that he tried to demonstrate how political events could leave deep impressions in the understanding of the existence of a community and prompt a fundamental revaluation of previously held convictions. To disregard the momentous impact that the Jewish War must have had for those living in Palestine would be tantamount to saying that the September 11 attack upon the World Trade Center did not have any effects upon the American self-definition as a nation.

If the question of the *Sitz im Leben* is short-circuited to the situation of religious or philosophically concerned individuals in a secular social situation, it is easy to move back from the life situation of such individuals to an analogous situation in the life of another individual, such as Jesus. This, however, is not how *Sitz im Leben* should ever be understood, else we fall once more into the trap of Joachim Jeremias, who tried to find for the Synoptic traditions the *Sitz im Leben Jesu*.[37] Rather, *Sitz im Leben* refers to the situation and function of a tradition in the life of a community. What was the situation and function of the traditions incorporated in Q in the life of the religious community that formed and transmitted these traditions? It goes without saying that such an understanding of the situation of traditions in the life of a community cannot be used directly for an understanding of the historical Jesus. Whatever Jesus may have said has been transformed—Kloppenborg uses the term "inscribed"[38]—into tradition on the basis of the life situation of a community, just as the memory of Jesus' suffering and death has been transformed by the image and language of the suffering servant.

It has been repeatedly stated that the Synoptic Sayings Gospel Q does not present enough information about the organization and rituals of the community. There may be hints; liturgical materials like the Lord's Prayer are present. Also instructions for the conduct of brothers and sisters in the community can be found. If Q sayings speak about the meal in the coming kingdom of God, does this imply that the community

---

33. Martin Dibelius, *From Tradition to Gospel* (2nd ed.; New York: Scribner's, 1934).

34. Rudolf Bultmann, *The History of the Synoptic Tradition* (2nd ed.; New York: Harper, 1968).

35. For a bibliography, see Helmut Koester, "Formgeschichte/Formenkritik II: Neues Testament," *TRE* 2 (1983) 286–99.

36. See above, n. 10.

37. Joachim Jeremias, "Kennzeichcn der ipsissima vox Jesu," in *Synoptische Studien: Festschrift für A. Wikenhauser* (Munich: Zink, 1953) 86–93.

38. Kloppenborg, "The Sayings Gospel Q," passim.

celebrated eschatological thanksgiving meals in anticipation of the coming meal in God's kingdom? Admittedly, Q itself offers only very limited information. There is, however, very ancient liturgical and instructional material preserved in another document for which a meaningful life situation has not been found, namely the materials in the *Didache*. This book preserves Eucharistic prayers about the cup and the bread that do not make explicit reference to the suffering and death of Jesus; it preserves instructions for wandering apostles and prophets; it knows other Synoptic materials that are not dependent upon the canonical gospels; finally, it presents a form of the Lord's Prayer that is almost identical with, but not dependent upon, the form presented in the Gospel of Matthew.[39]

Most remarkable are the Eucharistic prayers of the *Didache*.[40] These prayers give witness to a community of followers of Jesus who celebrated a meal of the cup and the bread in the expectation of the coming kingdom of God and called for the coming of "the Lord," evident in the final words of the Eucharistic liturgy, *Maranatha*. Cup and bread here have a meaning that is analogous to the Eucharist to which Paul provides evidence in 1 Corinthians 10 and 11. In both cases, the cup is the symbol of the covenant; in both cases, the bread is the symbol of the oneness of the community. But, unlike Paul's words of institution, the prayers of the *Didache* do not reflect on the significance of the death of Jesus. Rather, the prayer for the bread gives thanks "for the life and knowledge that you have revealed through Jesus, your servant."[41] The prayer after the meal gives thanks "for the knowledge, faith, and immortality that you have revealed to us through Jesus, your servant."[42]

Is it possible to relate these Eucharistic prayers to the community of Q? I am not the first to make this suggestion, but I agree that it is most likely that the Q community celebrated a common meal that must have been accompanied by prayers like the ones found in the *Didache*, namely Jewish meal prayers with an eschatological outlook.[43] There is a saying in Q about the coming meal in the kingdom of God (Q 13:28–29). The Lord's Prayer in Q connects the petitions for the coming kingdom and the will of God to be done on earth with the petition for the bread. Someone must have preserved the Eucharistic prayers that belong to a practice of common meals with an eschatological outlook. If this were not the community of Q, we would have to invent a similar community of followers of Jesus. It is another question whether this meal practice and these prayers derive from Jesus himself.[44] But these are typical Jewish meal prayers[45] and if the members of the community of Q ever ate together (which is not

---

39. Koester, *Synoptische Überlieferung*, 203–9; Kurt Niederwimmer, *The Didache: A Commentary* (Hermeneia; Minneapolis: Fortress Press, 1998) 135–38.

40. *Didache* 9–10.

41. *Did.* 9.2.

42. *Did.* 9.3.

43. "The next chapters, [*Didache*] 9 and 10, offer an archaic liturgical formulary without peer in the early period of Christian literature. In *Didache* 9–10 we have the oldest formula for the Christian eucharistic liturgy" (Niederwimmer, *Didache*, 139). For a full discussion of these prayers, see ibid., 139–43.

44. Koester, "The Memory of Jesus' Death," 335–50; included in this volume (chap. 15).

45. Niederwimmer, *Didache*, 110 and special reference to Jewish prayer parallels on the following pages in the commentary.

unlikely), they would have spoken these prayers with an eschatological outlook to the coming kingdom of God. A community that preserved these prayers as part of its central religious ritual had no need to reflect on the death of Jesus, as long as Jesus' words were the saving message, not Jesus' death and resurrection.

As a final note on this question, it is evident that also the following instructions for the reception of apostles and prophets in *Did.* 11.4–12 belong in the context of the milieu of the Q communities.[46] While the instructions for missionaries in Q/Luke 10:2–12 are directed to the apostles regarding their behavior and rights, the instructions of the *Didache* address the communities' behavior with respect to wandering missionaries. The original situation in the life of the community can clearly be seen here. The materials in this section with parallels in Q show that they are analogous to a very early stage of the tradition of sayings of Jesus. This is especially evident in the command not to test any prophet who speaks in the spirit (*Did.* 11.7). In the form in which this command appears here, it predates the more elaborate form preserved in Q/Luke 12:10.[47]

Regarding the understanding of the traditions preserved in the Synoptic Sayings Gospel Q, the life situation of their development is the community. This is underlined by the parallels in the *Didache*. The *Didache* also demonstrates that some of these traditions, such as the exact wording of the Lord's Prayer, the Eucharistic prayers, and the instructions for the reception of missionaries, were committed to writing at an early date; that is, before the production of the Son of Man sayings and the crisis of the Jewish War.[48] It is all the more probable that the final editor of Q also relied on an earlier written compilation of relevant Sayings of Jesus that communities outside of the circle of the mission of Antioch and the Pauline churches had developed, probably in the forties or fifties of the first century, in an area of Syria and Palestine outside of, but not unrelated to, Galilee and Judea. Kloppenborg's reconstruction of Q indeed has a great deal of merit, especially since it is done on the basis of a literary analysis and not in the search for the historical Jesus, although I myself would be inclined to give a greater value to the external witness of the *Gospel of Thomas* in such a reconstruction. The final redaction of Q, however, cannot be dated until the end of the Jewish War. The further redaction of Q, the question of a Q-Matthew and a Q-Luke, and the question of the Sermon on the Mount as an independent document are issues beyond the scope of this chapter.[49]

---

46. With respect to the instructions for the reception of apostles, Niederwimmer (*Didache,* 175) writes: "The subject here is an archaic institution, preceded by the group of Jesus' disciples and spreading thereafter within certain regions of the post-Easter church. . . . It should probably be located in the border region between Palestine and Syria."

47. Niederwimmer, *Didache,* 179: "Our version of the Logion can scarcely be traced to Mark/Matthew or to Q (or Matthew/Luke), but probably presents a separate form of the tradition." See also Koester, *Synoptische Überlieferung,* 215–17; Koester, *Ancient Christian Gospels,* 92–93.

48. Note that a reference to the Son of Man is missing in the saying *Did.* 10.7 (cf. Q/Luke 12:10); see Niederwimmer, *Didache,* 179.

49. If the Sermon on the Mount, as reconstructed by Hans Dieter Betz (*The Sermon on the Mount: A Commentary on the Sermon on the Mount, including the Sermon on the Plain* [Hermeneia; Minneapolis: Fortress Press, 1995]) is dependent upon Q2, it must also be dated to a time after the Jewish War.

6

THE EXTRACANONICAL SAYINGS OF THE LORD AS PRODUCTS OF THE CHRISTIAN COMMUNITY

The extracanonical sayings of Jesus have usually not received the attention they deserve. The primary reason for this neglect is certainly the almost exclusive use of the criterion of "authenticity" in the determination of their value. It is quite true, as a matter of fact, that a demonstration of their authenticity is possible only in a few instances and that these few probably authentic extracanonical sayings of Jesus add little to our understanding of the preaching of Jesus that has come from the investigation of the canonical gospels. It is questionable, however, whether this criterion of authenticity does justice to the extracanonical tradition of sayings.

Around the turn of the last century, Alfred Resch collected all known extracanonical materials in an immensely detailed investigation.[1] He found 194 "Agrapha"—unwritten sayings of Jesus that had been transmitted orally—and in addition ninety-seven "Apocrypha"—sayings transmitted in apocryphal writings. As a result of a careful analysis of this material, Resch stated that of these almost three hundred sayings, only thirty-six could be considered as authentic sayings of Jesus. In a critical review of all the materials collected by Resch, James Hardy Ropes demonstrated that a considerable number of the thirty-six sayings considered genuine by Resch did not really deserve to be called authentic.[2]

Half a century later, a considerable number of additional extracanonical sayings of Jesus had been found, especially through the discovery of several papyrus fragments. The entire corpus has once again been investigated by Joachim Jeremias.[3] His critical sifting of the extracanonical materials leaves a total of twenty-one sayings that he considers to be "historically valuable." However, with respect to ten of these sayings, Jeremias himself has some doubts; only eleven remain as certainly authentic. In his review of Jeremias' book, Werner Georg Kümmel demonstrated that this small number could be reduced even further.[4]

We should be grateful that Jeremias once again has drawn attention to the problem of the extracanonical sayings of Jesus.[5] Yet the result is quite sobering. Does this imply

---

1. Alfred Resch, *Agrapha: Aussercanonische Schriftfragmente* (2nd. ed.; Leipzig: Hinrichs, 1906; reprint: Darmstadt: Wissenschaftliche Buchgesellschaft, 1967).

2. James Hardy Ropes, *Die Sprüche Jesu* (Leipzig: Hinrichs, 1896).

3. Joachim Jeremias, *Unknown Sayings of Jesus* (London: SPCK, 1957). Translation of *Unbekannte Jesusworte* (2nd ed., 1951).

4. Werner-Georg Kümmel, "Review of Jeremias, *Unbekannte Jesusworte*." *ThLZ* 78 (1953) 99–101.

5. I gladly acknowledge that I have learned much from the work of Jeremias and am in his debt for many suggestions. The following critical discussion should be understood in this context.

that our search for valuable materials in the extracanonical sayings of Jesus should be terminated?

Form-critical investigation of the Synoptic Gospels during the twentieth century demonstrated that the tradition of the sayings of Jesus should not be viewed only from the perspective of the criterion of authenticity. The limitation of the verdict "historically valuable" to those sayings that could possibly be considered as authentic sayings of Jesus is not legitimate. This concerns not only the canonical tradition, but also the extracanonical materials. In both cases, it is not the historical Jesus whose voice is heard in a saying—apart from whether or not a saying is authentic—but instead, it is the voice of the exalted Lord through the agency of his church. If one approaches the extracanonical sayings on the basis of this insight, it is evident that in principle, all of them could be termed "historically valuable." All of them provide evidence for the history of the churches, because they testify to the quest of the Christian communities for that which "the Lord" has said.

I would like to illustrate the significance of this insight in yet another respect in this conversation with Jeremias. Jeremias knows quite well that the question of authenticity is a dead end in the investigation of the Agrapha, and he states that explicitly.[6] It is a positive element in Jeremias's approach that he proposes to proceed with a different criterion; he seeks to present all those sayings which, in his opinion, have the same historical value as the sayings of Jesus that are preserved in the canonical gospels.[7]

Unfortunately, this new criterion is confusing. The four canonical gospels contain so great a variety of sayings materials that they cannot provide a uniform criterion. Even the Synoptic Gospels, taken by themselves, present nearly every type of material from the various stages of the development of the traditions of sayings of Jesus, ranging from the Jewish *mashal* that had not yet been transformed by Christian concerns, to possibly authentic sayings of Jesus and on to formulations of the Palestinian community and revelation sayings of Hellenistic character. Even if the criterion were narrowed to the Synoptic Gospels, a useful measurement for the judgment "historically valuable" would not emerge; the matter is even less clear if the Gospel of John is included.

It also seems that Jeremias has not been very successful in the application of his criterion: half of his "historically valuable" sayings still remain suspect with regard to their authenticity, to the extent that he is concerned with the *ipsissima verba* of Jesus. Why Jeremias nevertheless interprets these sayings from the context of the historical Jesus is difficult to understand. Each saying should be interpreted within the context to which it owes its origin, in which it has its *Sitz im Leben*—whether that is the life of Jesus or the life of the Christian community. The same requirement is required for the investigation of the extracanonical sayings of Jesus. Only when they are seen in their proper *Sitz im Leben* do they gain their true historical value and become immune to the verdict "spurious," even if their original *Sitz* is not the life of Jesus but the life of the church.

A further aspect is also important in this context. If the question about *Sitz im Leben* is determinative for both the canonical and the extracanonical tradition, there is a pri-

---

6. Jeremias, *Unknown Sayings of Jesus*, 32.
7. Ibid., 30.

ori no qualitative difference between the canonical and the extracanonical tradition. For the historian, a "spurious" extracanonical saying of Jesus has in principle the same value as a "spurious" canonical saying, just as, vice versa, Jeremias has demonstrated in his book that the "authentic" extracanonical sayings have the same status as "authentic" canonical sayings.

A differentiation between canonical and extracanonical, of course, did not yet exist in the earliest period of Christianity. A conscious elimination of the extracanonical sayings did not begin until the last decade of the second century CE. We find only a marginal attestation of the so-called extracanonical material (compared to the canonical tradition) mostly because of the anti-heretical polemics of the Church Fathers, who attacked and burned everything that was not orthodox.

Nevertheless, quite a few extracanonical sayings have been preserved, apart from the small number that survived under canonical protection in the writings of the New Testament outside of the four gospels (e.g., Acts 20:35; 1 Thess 4:15). The following sources for these sayings outside of the canon are well known:[8]

1. A number of variants in manuscripts of the canonical gospels.

2. Quotations in ancient Christian writers from the Apostolic Fathers to Augustine, especially in *2 Clement*, Justin Martyr, Clement of Alexandria, Origen, Eusebius, Jerome, and Epiphanius (Resch even tried to demonstrate that there were extracanonical sayings in writers from as late as the high Middle Ages).

3. The papyri, especially the discoveries at Oxyrhynchus in Egypt, begun in 1897, and Papyrus Egerton 2, published in 1935.

In what follows I have chosen several especially clear examples in order to demonstrate how extracanonical sayings came into existence and how one can determine their *Sitz im Leben*. However, I shall not restrict my examples to the 21 sayings identified by Jeremias, nor discuss all of them; but on occasion I shall point to Jeremias's interpretations and discuss them critically.

1 Clem. **13.1–2**

One of the earliest references to sayings of Jesus is found in *1 Clem.* 13.1–2:

Remember the words of the Lord Jesus which he said, . . . thus he spoke:
"Be merciful, so that you will find mercy,
forgive, so that you will be forgiven,
as you do, so it will be done to you,
as you give, so it will be given to you,
as you judge, so you will be judged,
as you are gentle, so you will experience gentleness,
with whatever measure you measure, so it will be measured to you."

---

8. See on these sources ibid., 4–21.

Where do these words of Jesus come from? In the form in which they are presented here, they cannot be found in the canonical gospels. The Golden Rule ("as you do, so it will be done to you") was well known in Judaism before the time of Jesus. To be sure, it also appears in the Synoptic Gospels, but in a form different from that found in *1 Clement*: "Everything that you want people to do to you, do also to them" (Matt 7:12 par.). If one looks for parallels to the other sentences of *1 Clem.* 13.2 in the Synoptic Gospels, one finds: "With whatever judgment you judge, you will be judged" (Matt 7:2), and: "Give and it will be given to you" (Luke 6:38). But synoptic parallels to the remaining sentences of this passage are more remote. For "Be merciful so that you will find mercy" the parallel in Matt 5:7 reads: "Blessed are the merciful, because they will receive mercy." And for "Forgive so that you will be forgiven" the parallel in Mark 11:25 reads: "Forgive if you have anything against someone, so that your heavenly Father will also forgive you"; or one could compare the fifth petition of the Lord's Prayer: "Forgive us our debts, as we forgive our debtors" (Matt 6:12 par). For one of the sentences of *1 Clem.* 13.2—"As you are gentle, so you will experience gentleness"—there is no parallel at all in the Synoptic Gospels.

While the Synoptic Gospels provide us with several parallels in different contexts, each of them is formulated differently; *1 Clement* presents a composition of sayings formed according to one uniform pattern. Although different topics appear (forgiveness, mercy, giving, judging, etc.), they are all cast in the same form. It is hardly reasonable to assume that someone selected the various sayings from different passages of two or three gospels and then composed them into this uniform pattern. It is much more likely that one or two sayings formed the nucleus of the composition—whether these were Jewish proverbs or authentic sayings of Jesus—and that subsequently more sayings were added, including finally a completely new saying constructed by analogy to the form and content of the other sayings. The reason for the formation of such collections can be found in a need of the Christian communities for teaching materials, that is, for a catechism. Apparently *1 Clem.* 13.2 is such a catechism of the church, consisting of sayings of Jesus. In the formation of these early Christian catechisms, it made no difference where the materials came from or whether they were authentic or spurious. The early church even took over an entire Jewish catechism as a whole and adapted it to the purposes of Christian instruction, namely, the "Teaching of the Two Ways," which is preserved in *Barnabas* 18–20 and *Didache* 1–6. There the catechism is presented under the authority of the Twelve Apostles; in *1 Clem.* 13.2 a smaller catechism is given under the authority of the Lord. It is possible that "authentic" sayings of Jesus are preserved in both catechisms (cf. *Did.* 1.3–5). Another catechism has in fact been admitted into a canonical gospel: Matthew 18.

No doubt we could select a few authentic words of Jesus from each of these catechisms with various degrees of success. But that is a question that the early church did not ask. For the early church, it was important to possess a canon of virtues authorized by having been spoken by the risen Lord, whether through the agency of a teacher or of an apostle.

The hyperbolic radicalization of the commandment of love in Jesus' preaching is well known: "Love your enemies." It is almost surprising that this saying is still preserved in this form. In the early Christian period there was little interest in this particular wording of the command, which was usually understood in quite a different way.

We see this expressed in quotations of the command in which the wording was changed accordingly: "Pray for your enemies." In this form, this saying is quoted in *Did.* 1.3, and Justin Martyr cites it in the same form no less than five times (*1 Apol.* 13.3; 15.9; *Dial.* 35.8; 96.3; 133.6), but the well-known wording of Matt 5:44 occurs only once in his writings (*Dial.* 85.7). "Pray for your enemies" is also found in one of the Oxyrhynchus papyri with sayings of Jesus (1224) and in the *Syriac Didascalia* (108.4).[9] Polycarp of Smyrna says at the end of his *Letter to the Philippians* (12.3):

> Pray also for the kings . . . and for your persecutors, and for those who hate you, and for the enemies of the cross.

Even if here Polycarp comes close to the wording of the canonical gospels, he does not quote the first sentence of Matt 5:44–45: "Love your enemies." Only those sentences that are useful for his practical advice for prayer are repeated. This clearly shows how Jesus' radicalization of the commandment of love into the commandment of loving one's enemies was rendered innocuous by being transformed into an admonition for prayer.

This also explains why the exact wording of Matt 5:44 ("Love your enemies") begins to assert itself only later, at a time when the texts of the canonical gospels are gaining in authority (for the first time in *2 Clem.* 13.4). In the earlier period, the practical and legalistic orientation of early Christian piety was strong enough to shape the wording of Jesus' sayings according to its needs. It is quite in accord with this orientation that *Did.* 1.3 continues its quotation with the words ". . . and fast for your persecutors." No parallel exists to this command in the texts of the canonical gospels. The need to enforce the rules of fasting in addition to those for prayer produced a new formulation by analogy to a traditional saying of Jesus. Also belonging in this context is the saying of Jesus that is transmitted by Clement of Alexandria in *Strom.* 1.24, 158:

> Pray for the great things,
> then the small things will be added for you.

In Origen (*Or.* 2.2; 14.1) the same saying can be found, also under the authority of Jesus, but it has received a characteristic continuation:

> Pray for the heavenly things (τὰ ἐπουράνια)
> and the earthly things (τὰ ἐπίγεια) will be added for you.

Compare with these sayings the composition of sayings "On Earthly Cares" in Matthew 6, where the final sentence (6:33) reads:

> Seek first the rule of God . . . ,
> and all the other things (food, clothing, etc.) will be added for you.

---

9. Hans Achelis and Johannes Flemming, eds., *Die Syrische Didaskalia, übersetzt und erklärt* (Leipzig: Hinrichs, 1904).

There can be no doubt that the saying quoted by Clement of Alexandria and Origen is formulated by analogy to this saying from the Synoptic Gospels. But the difference is also apparent. No longer is the impending arrival of the rule of God a concern for which people should give up all earthly cares; rather, the question is knowledge of the heavenly things: how could someone who strives for higher wisdom even contemplate asking God for such mundane earthly matters? For the formulation of these new sayings, certain traditional patterns were used, determined by such antitheses as "small/great" or "heavenly/earthly," as can also be seen, for example, in John 3:12:

> If I tell you of earthly things (τὰ ἐπίγεια)
> and you do not believe,
> how could you believe,
> if I tell you the heavenly things (τὰ ἐπουράνια)?

Cf. also *Barn.* 19.8:

> If you share together the thing which is imperishable (ἐν τῷ ἀφθάρτῳ) how much more the things which are perishable (ἐν τοῖς φθαρτοῖς)?

In *2 Clem.* 8.5, the synoptic saying, "Whoever is faithful with the smallest thing is also faithful with much" (Luke 16:10), has been expanded with an analogous formulation according to the formal pattern "small/great":

> If you do not preserve the small thing,
> who will give you what is great?

Logia from Extracanonical Gospels

Some examples will show how the tradition adopted rules of the community as sayings of Jesus on a large scale.

Jerome quotes the following rule as a saying from the *Gospel of the Hebrews* (*In Ez.* 18.7):

> Whoever causes grief to the spirit of his brother is guilty of the greatest crime.

This sentence about causing grief to the spirit of one's brother must be understood on the basis of a phrase that is attested in the New Testament (Eph 4:30), a phrase that also plays an important role in Hermas *Mand.* 10: λυπεῖν τὸ πνεῦμα τὸ ἅγιον (to cause grief to the Holy Spirit; *Herm. Mand.* 10.2.4; 3.4). Hermas also reveals what this means and why causing grief to the spirit is such a serious crime: grief (λύπη) drives out the Holy Spirit dwelling in the human soul (*Herm. Mand.* 10.1.2; 2.1). Thus the term *spiritus* in the saying quoted by Jerome does not mean the mind of the brother, but the share of the Holy Spirit which every Christian possesses.

This concept is not of Christian origin, no more than the understanding of "grief" (λύπη) as a vice.[10] In the citation of Jerome, these concepts have been put secondarily into the mouth of Jesus: a rule of the community has become a commandment of the Lord. It is characteristic for the origin of these concepts that Jerome found this saying in the probably Jewish-Christian *Gospel of the Hebrews*.

Another variant of the commandment of love was found by Jerome (*Comm. Eph.* 5.4) in the *Gospel of the Nazoreans*, also a Jewish-Christian gospel:

The Lord had said to his disciples:
"And never shall you be joyful
unless you look upon your brother with love."

That this saying was originally formulated in Aramaic has been demonstrated by Harnack[11] and Jeremias[12] (*in caritate* corresponds to the Aramaic ב and must be translated as "with"). This Aramaic background fits well with an origin of the saying in the Aramaic *Gospel of the Nazoreans*. However, it does not prove that the saying can be derived directly from the lips of Jesus. The claim that this saying "corresponds exactly to the teaching given in the Gospels about the brotherly love towards their fellow countrymen that Jesus requires"[13] employs a general criterion that does not permit precise historical judgment. It would be more accurate to state that this saying is a rule of the community, which makes brotherly love a prerequisite for joyful celebration. Thus it is a variant of those rules that demand reconciliation as prerequisite for sacrifice (Matt 5:23–24) or for prayer (Mark 11:25) or for participation in the Lord's Supper (*Did.* 14.2).

As it interpreted the central commandment of love, the church tried to regulate specific instances of its community life and fixed and established those regulations in the form of "sayings of the Lord." Such rules of the community derive from a wide variety of backgrounds, including Jewish proverbs as well as Gnostic ascetic laws.

The saying "It is more blessed to give than to receive" (μακάριόν ἐστιν μᾶλλον διδόναι ἢ λαμβάνειν), which Acts 20:35 transmits as a saying of Jesus, was originally a Jewish saying. It is also found in *Did.* 1.5, but we cannot be sure that the *Didache* understood this saying as a word of the Lord. *1 Clem.* 2.1 alludes to the same rule without any indication that it is pointing to a saying of Jesus, though sayings of Jesus are otherwise explicitly termed such in this writing (*1 Clem.* 13.1–2; 46.7–8). No literary relationships exist between the *Didache*, *1 Clement*, and the Book of Acts. The saying was transmitted orally.

In terms of its content, this saying would fit Jewish parenesis very well;[14] nor is its

---

10. It is already found in *T. Dan* 4.6, later in *Corp. Herm.* 13.7. Here and in *Herm. Sim.* 9.15.3, it appears within a catalogue of vices. Cf. Martin Dibelius, *Der Hirte des Hermas* (HNT Ergänzungsband 4; Tübingen: Mohr/Siebeck, 1923) ad loc.

11. Adolf von Harnack, "Über einige Worte Jesu, die nicht in den kanonischen Evangelien stehen," SBAW (1904) 175.

12. Jeremias, *Unknown Sayings of Jesus,* 82.

13. Ibid., 83.

14. That a Semitic basis must be assumed for the different Greek versions has been demonstrated convincingly by Jeremias, *Unknown Sayings of Jesus,* 78–79.

form specifically Christian. To be sure, macarisms are transmitted in our gospels, but these characteristically speak not of the blessedness of a particular moral action. Rather they speak instead of the blessedness of being, seeing, or of an attitude with respect to Jesus or of a specific behavior related to his word, such as, "Blessed are the poor" (Luke 6:20) or "Blessed are those who hear the word of God" (Luke 11:28). The macarisms of Jesus look to the coming judgment; they belong to his prophetic words. Macarisms about moral actions, on the other hand, are typical of Jewish proverbial wisdom and the didactic poems of the Old Testament. This is the context from which the macarism of giving is derived—another example of how the church adopted Jewish rules according to its needs and transformed them into sayings of Jesus.

In the same way, however, the church also borrowed encratite rules from its Hellenistic surroundings and transformed them into sayings of Jesus. Clement of Alexandria has preserved several passages from the *Gospel of the Egyptians* which clearly bear the stamp of Gnostic sexual asceticism, for example, *Strom.* 3.13, 92:

> When Salome [who often appears in the *Gospel of the Egyptians* as a speaker] asked when what she had inquired about would be known, the Lord said: "When you have trampled upon the garment of shame and when the two will become one, and the male with the female is neither male nor female."

It should not be said that this saying reveals nothing but the taste of some extreme heretical circles. The same saying is quoted in *2 Clem.* 12.2–5, that is, in a writing widely accepted in orthodox circles of the church. Only here the question is formulated: "When does the rule of God come?" It is generally assumed that *2 Clement* was not written in Egypt, but either in Rome or in Corinth.[15] Thus such "tendentious" sayings must have found a wider distribution.

The designation "tendentious" does not help us answer the question of the origins of sayings of this kind. A particular tendency must be ascribed to all sayings of Jesus, to extracanonical sayings as well as to those from the canon. The decisive question relates to the historical place of these sayings, that is, how the tendency of a saying as it is expressed in its external form and in its content helps to determine its *Sitz im Leben*, its original situation in the life of the church.

Pseudo-Clementine Homilies 19.20.2 and Parallels

The *Pseudo-Clementine Homilies* (19.20.2) as well as Clement of Alexandria (*Strom.* 5.10, 63) and Theodoret (*In Psalm.* 65, T. 1, p. 1049; Schmidt) preserve a saying which was designed to enforce an arcane discipline on the basis of a commandment of Jesus:

> Preserve my mysteries for me and for the sons of my house.

There is no doubt that this saying arose in a mistranslation of Isa 24:16 in some of the Greek witnesses. The still untranslatable Hebrew רזי in this passage was understood by

---

15. Vernon Bartlet, "The Origin and Date of 2 Clement," *ZNW* 7 (1906) 123–35.

Symmachus, Theodotion, Lucian, and the Hexapla on the basis of the late biblical רֹז = "mystery," רֹזִי = "my mystery." This resulted in the Greek translation to: μυστήριόν μου ἐμοὶ (καὶ τοῖς ἐμοῖς).

The sentence in this form is a variant of the wisdom saying "Do not give holy things to the dogs" (Matt 7:6). Theodoret also cites this apocryphal saying in the context of the synoptic saying. How was it possible that Christians could take this sentence from the Greek Bible and transform it into a saying of the Lord? In the time of early Christianity, no distinction was made between the *Kyrios* who was speaking in the Old Testament and the Christ who spoke in the gospels. Therefore, a sentence from the Old Testament could become a saying of the Lord—spoken by Jesus. The following saying, preserved in Clement of Alexandria (*Exc.* 2.2), came into existence in the same way:

Save yourself and your life!

Its Greek wording

Σῷζου σὺ καὶ τὴν ψυχήν σου

is a simple alteration of Gen 19:17:

σῴζων σῷζε τὴν σεαυτοῦ ψυχήν.

Deriving a special value for this saying of Jesus from the fact that it states explicitly καὶ τὴν ψυχήν = Save yourself *and your soul*[16]—Jesus also cares for the soul of a human being—is impossible. If this saying were spoken in the realm of Palestinian Christianity, the word ψυχή would be understood as נֶפֶשׁ = "throat," that is, naked life. However, it is unlikely that this saying came into existence during the lifetime of Jesus. It is rather the result of later exegetical efforts in the interpretation of the Old Testament. In that context, ψυχή may have had a meaning different from "physical life."

A confirmation that the saying "Save yourself and your life" is derived from the Old Testament comes from the fact that another saying of the three quoted in Clement of Alexandria, *Excerpta ex Theodoto* (9), is also a variation of an Old Testament passage. "Go out of the house of my father" adapts the well-known command of God to Abraham in Gen 12:1: "Go out of your country and from your relatives and from the house of your father."

Of course, the meaning of Gen 12:1 has been completely distorted in the saying of the *Excerpta*, but this new understanding does not transcend the limits of the methods of interpretation that were current at that time, especially in Gnostic circles. No special importance was assigned to historical faithfulness in the reproduction of an Old Testament passage; but it was important that the authority of the Lord could be claimed to regulate the needs of the community.

---

16. Jeremias, *Unknown Sayings of Jesus*, 61–64.

Epistle of Barnabas 7.11 and 7.4–5

A similar and quite simple method of lending to some statement the authority of a saying of the Lord appears in the *Epistle of Barnabas*. In two instances, this writing gives a quotation of a statement of the Lord as the conclusion to an exegetical discussion. In his discussion of the meaning of Jewish sacrificial rites (*Barn.* 7.11), the author asks: "What does it signify that wool is placed between the thorns? This is a type of Jesus, designed for the church; for whoever wants to take the scarlet-red wool must suffer much, because the thorns are terrible, and [one must] with tribulations master them." Then he proceeds in the style of an I-saying of Jesus, quoted with φησίν:

> Therefore those who want to see me and enter my kingdom must lay hold of me with tribulations and suffering.

As Barnabas interprets the entire sacrificial rite typologically, such a saying of Jesus can arise from the Jewish prototype without any special effort.

Barnabas 7.4-5 presents another example of this method: "Only the priests shall eat from the offal of the sacrifice unwashed with vinegar. Why?" Barnabas now introduces the Lord himself to give the answer to this question:

> Because, when I am about to offer my flesh for the sins of my new people, you will give me vinegar and gall to drink; therefore, you shall eat alone, while the people fast and mourn in sackcloth and ashes.

Jesus himself prophesies here that he will receive vinegar and gall to drink, as the gospels report. The identification of the *Kyrios* who prophesies in the Old Testament with the Jesus of the gospels is here carried out with utmost consistency. This opens the way for the formation of a potentially limitless number of sayings of Jesus derived from the Old Testament prophecies—though this opportunity was not used very often.

Another Logion from the *Gospel of the Nazoreans*

With these last examples, our discussion has already left the area of parenesis and has demonstrated how theological motives—in Barnabas the proof from prophecy—have led to the creation of new sayings of Jesus. There are a number of additional theological motives that caused the transformation of older sayings and the formation of new sayings of Jesus. One of these is the question of repeated repentance after conversion to Christianity—a much-debated question in the early church. A solution supported by the quotation of a saying of the Lord would carry much weight in such discussions.

The traditional rule about an obligation to forgive one's brother must have been a welcome argument in such debates. It is transmitted in the Synoptic Gospels in two different versions and appears in a third version in the *Gospel of the Nazoreans* (Jerome *Pelag.* 3.2). The original rule is probably preserved in Luke 17:3 ("If your brother sins, admonish him; and if he repents, forgive him"). A comparison of the three expanded versions is interesting.

Luke 17:4:

If your brother sins against you seven times a day, and yet returns to you seven times a day saying, "I repent," you shall forgive him.

Matt 18:21-22 has expanded this saying to form a dialogue and added an exaggeration:

Then Peter approached him and said: "Lord, how often may my brother sin against me and I am to forgive him? Seven times?" Jesus said to him: "I do not say seven times, but seventy times seven."

The *Gospel of the Nazoreans* has combined the Matthean and Lukan versions and added a further sentence:

"When your brother sins with words and gives you satisfaction, receive him seven times a day." His disciple Simon said to him: "Seven times a day?" The Lord answered and said to him: "I even say to you: up to seventy times. For sinful speech has been found even in the prophets, after they had been anointed with the Holy Spirit."

Some peculiarities, such as the restriction to sinning in words, can be left aside here. What is important for our context is the last sentence from the *Gospel of the Nazoreans*: "For sinful speech has been found even in the prophets, after they had been anointed with the Holy Spirit." The "anointment of the prophets" is a fixed term that is not necessarily related to Christian baptism. Nevertheless, the term *unctio* (in the Latin text of Jerome's quote) or χρισθῆναι (in the Greek version of the Gospel edition Zion, MSS 566 and 899, which preserve the same saying in the marginalia to Matt 18:22) was used very early for Christian baptism (cf. 2 Cor 1:21). If this apocryphal expansion of Matt 18:22 understands the anointing of the prophets by analogy to Christian baptism—and I think that is most likely the case—it is attempting to say this: just as the prophets were not without sinful speech after their anointment but were not rejected, so also the Christians can receive forgiveness for such sins after their χρῖσμα, that is, after their baptism. The sentence that was added to the traditional saying about forgiveness can therefore be understood as a defense of repeated repentance and forgiveness after baptism. But even if this interpretation is not completely certain, there is no doubt that the *Gospel of the Nazoreans* has transformed a theological motivation for repeated forgiveness into a saying of Jesus.

Sayings about forgiveness are repeatedly found as words of Jesus. In the apocryphal *Acts of Peter* (chap. 10), Marcellus comes to Peter to ask his forgiveness. As a justification for his request, he points to Peter's own weakness as the one "who began to doubt on the waters." This is certainly a reference to the legend of Peter's attempt to walk on water. What is significant here is the addition of a further motivation by Marcellus in the form of a saying of Jesus:

For I have heard that he (i.e., Jesus) also said this:
"Those who are with me did not understand me."

Is this a lament of Jesus, his greatest sorrow, that even his own disciples did not understand him?[17] That is very unlikely. This saying is better understood as a secondary creation to serve as a rationale for the forgiveness of sins. It is not difficult to discern the text from which this saying originated: it is the immediate context of the story of walking on the water in the Synoptic Gospels. At the end of the Matthean version, Jesus says to Peter: "Oh you of little faith, why did you doubt?" (Matt 14:31). And at the end of the Markan parallel, pointing back to the story of the feeding of the five thousand, it is stated: "For they did not understand about the bread" (Mark 6:52). It is one of the sayings belonging to the theological complex of the disciples' failure to understand that occurs repeatedly in the Gospel of Mark. The author of the *Acts of Peter* knew these texts; indeed, he reported the entire story about Jesus' walking on the water in the same chapter of his work. Subsequently, he used the remarks about the disciples' lack of understanding in order to formulate this new saying: "Those who are with me have not understood me." As a result, a new saying of Jesus was created which could serve as a support for the forgiveness of sins. In the *Gospel of the Nazoreans* the prophets served as a foil in order to justify forgiveness; in the *Acts of Peter* the foil is provided by the disciples themselves. But in each case, it is the Lord himself who authorizes forgiveness through the appropriate saying.

The pericope of the adulteress inserted by some manuscripts in the text of the Gospel of John after 7:52 may also be classified among these secondary motivations for the forgiveness of sins that were ascribed to Jesus himself. Johannes Waitz once stated that it was "generally accepted" that this pericope relied "on a tradition that is as old as it is authentic."[18] He also assumed that it must have been a part of the oldest text of Matthew. But there is no basis for such conjectures. The pericope has all the characteristics of a secondary composition and cannot be salvaged as a report from the life of the historical Jesus. In fact, this story has no interest in reporting an incident from his life. Its sole purpose is to contribute to the issue of whether deadly sins can be forgiven—in this case the sin of adultery. Such questions had already played a role in the earliest period of the Christian churches, as Paul's recommendation of excommunication for incest demonstrates (1 Corinthians 5). Even if this pericope about the adulteress is very old, it does not belong in Jesus' lifetime. Rather, it arose from the debates of the early church about the question of whether adultery can be forgiven, and it authorizes a positive answer to this question by means of a story of an incident in the life of Jesus.

1 Thess. 4:15–17

The reformulation and creation of sayings of Jesus was by no means restricted to the two topics that have been mentioned so far, namely, the question of scriptural proof and the issue of forgiveness. In these two instances as well as in other theological discussions, extracanonical sayings tended to utilize already existing traditions or older sayings of Jesus.

---

17. Jeremias (*Unknown Sayings of Jesus,* 77) seeks to interpret the saying in this way.

18. Hans Waitz, "Die judenchristlichen Evangelien in der altkirchlichen Literatur," in Edgar Hennecke, ed., *Neutestamentliche Apokryphen* (Tübingen: Mohr/Siebeck, 1924) 11–12.

The best-known example is probably the saying of the Lord on which Paul bases his argument in 1 Thess 4:15–17 to dispel doubts about the parousia that arose due to the Christians who had already died.

What is quoted here by Paul is not a saying of Jesus in terms of its form (Paul uses the first-person plural), nor is it possible to find a place for the content of Paul's statements in Jesus' own proclamation. The delay of the parousia is clearly presupposed, something that had no part in the situation of Jesus, but instead reflects the situation of the church in the transition from the first to the second generation.[19] That is the context from which this "Word of the Lord" originated, even if individual elements may possibly relate to genuine sayings of Jesus (as, e.g., Matt 24:30–31). Concepts like the sounding of the trumpet, the descending of the Lord from heaven, and the gathering of the elect (1 Thess 4:16–17) are certainly traditional and must have been part of the saying to which Paul is alluding in this passage. Therefore, what Paul is using here is either a transformation of an older saying of Jesus or a piece of Jewish apocalyptic tradition that had by then become a saying of Jesus. However, the most important part of the statement in this pointed form, namely, that those who have died will not be at a disadvantage at the time of the parousia as compared to those who are still alive, must have been a product of the Christian community addressing the problem of the delay of the parousia.[20]

As Jesus more and more assumed the features of the Gnostic revealer in many circles of early Christianity, it is understandable that Gnostic discourses of revelation were also ascribed to him, as was done by the author of the Gospel of John. There are also numerous examples outside of the canonical gospels (cf. writings like the *Pistis Sophia*, the various discourses of Jesus with his disciples after the resurrection, and the apocryphal Gnostic literature in general). The Gospel of John demonstrates that quite "orthodox" ecclesiastical circles had no hesitation in presenting Jesus in such a role or at least to accept such a writing as canonical.

That "orthodoxy and heresy" were not neatly separated in this respect is evident in Pap. Oxyrhynchus 1, which also presents, alongside typical "synoptic" sayings of Jesus, the following saying of the Lord:[21]

I stood in the midst of the world
and I appeared to them in the flesh
and I found all of them intoxicated
and no one among them did I find thirsty.
And my soul suffers because of humankind,
because they are blind in their heart and do not see . . .

The first four lines of this saying are certainly Gnostic in character, perhaps also the last line. Blindness and intoxication are typical Gnostic concepts. The sentence ἔστην μέσῳ

---

19. Günther Bornkamm, "Die Verzögerung der Parusie," in Werner Schmauch, ed., *In Memoriam Ernst Lohmeyer* (Stuttgart: Evangelisches Verlagswerk, 1951) 116–26.

20. I hope to demonstrate this in the near future in a special investigation of 1 Thess 4: 13ff. [One of the many rash and still unfulfilled promises of a young scholar—H.K.]

21. It should be noted here that the article upon which this chapter is based was written before the publication of the *Gospel of Thomas,* to which this saying belongs.

τοῦ κόσμου derives from concepts of the Gnostic redeemer myth. One might debate, however, whether the second line, ἐν σαρκὶ ὤφθην αὐτοῖς, was perhaps influenced by John 1:14 (cf. 1 Tim 3:16).

Yet the phrase "blind in their heart" seems to allude at the same time to the well-known passage from Isaiah about hardening of hearts (Isa 6:9f.).[22] But even more clearly formulated in terms of the Old Testament—and this is very interesting in this saying—is the last clause: καὶ πονεῖ ἡ ψυχή μου. Πόνος τῆς ψυχῆς appears in Isa 53:10. These are words that described, for Christianity, the sufferings of the servant of God.

Therefore, the sentence "And my soul suffers because of humankind" is most likely not a testimony to the great personal saving patience of Jesus.[23] Instead this phrase demonstrates that it was possible to combine a Gnostic concept of the redeemer with an interpretation of the figure of the servant of God of Isaiah 53 and to authorize this theological combination by presenting it as a revelatory speech of Jesus.

Anti-Gnostic polemic also created new sayings of Jesus. We can leave the question undecided whether the refutation in Luke 24:36–43 of the thought that Jesus appeared as a "Spirit" was already motivated by anti-Gnostic polemic. But this purpose is clearly present in the parallel to Luke 24:36 that is quoted in Ign. *Smyrn.* 3.2–3 (also transmitted in Jerome, *Vir. ill.* 16), where the Lord appears to his disciples after the resurrection and says:

I am not a bodiless demon.

This saying claims that even the resurrected Lord still exists in the body and is not, as docetic Gnosticism claimed, a spiritual being that only reluctantly assumed a human body during this earthly life in order to leave this body behind in his death. Since Jesus himself speaks the sentence, "I am not a bodiless demon," this polemic receives special emphasis.

P. Oxy. 1.5

As a last example, I shall now present alterations of one and the same saying that are characteristic of the liberty with which the church formed, transformed, and re-created sayings of Jesus.

For the Jewish scholar, God was present wherever the Torah was studied; this is expressed in Aboth 3.2:

Wherever two sit together
and words of the Torah are between them,
the *shekina* dwells among them.

---

22. This sentence ὅτι τυφλοί εἰσιν τῇ καρδίᾳ αὐτῶ[ν] καὶ [οὐ] βλέπ[ουσι has, however, its closest parallel in a sentence of the New Testament that also occurs in the context of Gnostic concepts, 2 Cor 4:4: ὁ θεὸς τοῦ αἰῶνος τούτου ἐτύφλωσεν τὰ νοήματα τῶν ἀπίστων εἰς τὸ μὴ αὐγάσαι . . .

23. This is the understanding of Jeremias (*Unknown Sayings*, 72–73).

In its adaptation of this Jewish saying, the Christian church formulated a saying of Jesus that guarantees the presence of the Lord through the invocation of his name in the assembly of the congregation:

> Wherever two or three are gathered together in my name, I am in their midst (Matt 18:20).

For the Christian pantheist and mystic, however, the presence of Jesus is bound neither to Holy Scripture nor to the Christian assembly and calling upon his name. The Lord is everywhere. Our saying of Jesus has therefore been transformed and has received a mystical continuation:[24]

> Where there are two, they are not without God.
> And where one is alone, I say, I am with him.
> Lift the stone, and you will find me there;
> split the wood, and I am there.[25]

Observations

This small segment from the rich history of the extracanonical sayings was designed to demonstrate the following:

1. Any restriction of the history of the sayings of Jesus to the canonical gospels is historically irresponsible. Form criticism has been correct in not accepting this restriction. But restriction of the criterion for evaluation to "compatible with the canonical gospels" will also necessarily lead to a method which does not do justice to a large portion of the extracanonical materials. The few that are accepted as valuable are then forced into an interpretation that seeks to understand them in the context of the life of the historical Jesus, while all other sayings are tarred with the verdict "tendentious."

It should not be overlooked that the very scanty preservation of our extracanonical materials contrasts sharply with their actual historical significance. This is reason enough to pay much more attention to these traditions in the investigation of the history of the sayings of Jesus. What Walter Bauer demonstrated in his work *Orthodoxy and Heresy in Earliest Christianity*[26] also is valid for the sayings of Jesus: Items separated later as "orthodox" and "heretical" enjoyed equal rights at the beginning of Christian history, where they were still closely intertwined and undifferentiated. It is only due to the process of canonization that a relatively small segment from the rich history of the sayings of Jesus has been well preserved by admission to the canon of the New Testament.

---

24. Neither here can I follow Jeremias (*Unknown Sayings*, 96–98), who understands this saying as a comment of Jesus on the blessings of hard work.

25. P. Oxy. 1.5. At the time of the original writing of this material, the *Gospel of Thomas*, to which this saying belongs, had not yet been published.

26. *Orthodoxy and Heresy in Earliest Christianity*. Translated from the German 2nd ed. with appendices by Georg Strecker, R. A. Kraft, and Gerhard Krodel (Philadelphia: Fortress Press, 1971).

2. Only fragments of the extracanonical sayings have been preserved. Nothing is gained if a very small portion of this fragmentary tradition is occasionally used whenever it seems to fit the already existing picture of the historical Jesus and of the earliest orthodox community. Nothing new can be learned from the extracanonical tradition by such a procedure. How did early Christianity understand itself, and how was the risen Lord present in this self-understanding of the Christian community? How did he speak in this community as their living Lord? If we want to learn from this question as theologians, the extracanonical sayings (whether or not they are "authentic" words of Jesus) must be included as weighty documents for the history of earliest Christianity. From this perspective, the extracanonical sayings may be found to have considerable value. They may provide a more lively testimony to the history of early Christianity than many familiar documents.

Postscript 26 July 1986

I have been asked to prepare an English translation of the material in this essay, which I completed twenty-nine years ago—a year before I came to the United States, and two years before I first read the *Gospel of Thomas*. I have left the original essay as I wrote it then and have made only a few minor corrections that do not alter the substance in any way.

Had I written the essay today, its basic thesis would have remained the same. Of course, with the availability of the entire *Gospel of Thomas* (of which I only knew those sayings that are preserved in the Oxyrhynchus fragments) and of other newly discovered documents such as the *Dialogue of the Savior* and the *Apocryphon of James*, I would have had access to a much richer base of material for the documentation of my thesis, and my argument in favor of the relatively early age of the extracanonical tradition would have been stronger. I also could have strengthened my arguments by referring to several scholarly publications by colleagues and students that have appeared during the last three decades and contributed much to the understanding of the extracanonical traditions about Jesus.

But the battle which I began with Joachim Jeremias 31 years ago is far from over. There are still those who reject the entire *Gospel of Thomas* and other Gnostic gospels as entirely tendentious, and there are still those who want to "collect apologetic figs from critical thistles" (an authentic "extracanonical" saying of Rudolf Bultmann) by claiming some of the materials from these writings for the historical Jesus. Arguments for a relatively early date for some apocryphal gospels and for the tradition of sayings that they represent do not threaten the authority of the canonical gospels as authentic records for the historical Jesus—that is a fiction anyway. Such arguments challenge the authority of the canon as the exclusive record of the earliest history of Christianity. This history was much richer than the canon would suggest, and in theological terms it was more controversial and more interesting, because the "Living Jesus" spoke in many different ways to different people who confessed him as their Lord. The historian must never solve this problem by using the labels "orthodox" and "heretical," nor should responsible Christians and theologians try to do that any longer today.

7

MARK 9:43–47 AND
QUINTILIAN 8.3.75

The following saying in Mark 9:43–47 has always been a puzzle:

If your hand offends you, cut it off. It is better to enter into life crippled than with both hands to depart for hell, to the unquenchable fire.

And if your foot offends you, cut it off. It is better for you to enter into life lame than with both feet to be thrown into hell.

And if your eye offends you, pluck it out. It is better for you to enter into the kingdom of God with one eye than with two eyes to be thrown into hell.

The context in Mark does not give any clue, because the connection with the preceding saying about "not offending the little ones" (Mark 9:42) is secondary, caused by the catchword "offend" (σκανδαλίζειν).

The saying is often understood as hyperbolic demand for radical and uncompromising discipleship. If there is anything that might cause separation from God and his kingdom, one must be prepared for the most painful sacrifice.[1] But other interpretations also have been offered: "The advice which Jesus here gives is that we are not to provoke danger and call it forth. Far better to nip it in the bud, and to pray, 'Lead us not into temptation.'"[2]

Matt 5:29–30 presents a variant of this saying in the context of the antithesis "On Adultery" (Matt 5:27–28). This has suggested interpreting the saying more specifically as a warning against sexual sin: "It is requested that one fight one's own desires which, according to Jewish thinking, are located in the members of the human body."[3] It is indeed possible that Matt 5:29–30 is more original insofar as it speaks only to the offense

---

1. Ernst Haenchen, *Der Weg Jesu* (Berlin: Töpelmann, 1966) 329.

2. C. G. Montefiore, *The Synoptic Gospels* (London: MacMillan, 1927) 1. 223. Francis Wright Beare (*The Earliest Records of Jesus* [New York: Abingdon, 1962] 149), following Adolf Schlatter, interprets the saying on the basis of Mark 9:42: "Christian believers must avoid becoming a cause of offense to their fellows, and must discipline themselves without waiting for the Church to pronounce sentence, out of fear of the inescapable judgment of God."

3. Erich Klostermann, *Das Markusevangelium* (HNT 3; 4th ed.; Tübingen: Mohr/Siebeck, 1950) 96. Rabbinic discussion of Exod 20:14 and Isa 1:15 ("Your hands are full of blood")—in the discussion of the law of purity with respect to menstruation—requests that the hand of a male offender be cut off; cf. Str-B 1. 302–3.

of the eye and hand,[4] but the quotation of the offense of the eye as the first part of the saying and its interpretation as a warning against the "lustful eye"—cf. Matt 5:28, "everyone who looks at a woman lustfully"—are certainly secondary and cannot give a clue for understanding the saying.

To be sure, this interpretation was widespread in the ancient church. Justin Martyr *1 Apol.* 15.2 quotes it together with Matt 5:28 and 19:12 (eunuchs for the kingdom of God). The *Sentences of Sextus* 13 cite the advice "to cut off any member of the body which persuades you not to be chaste" (μὴ σωφρονεῖν, *contra pudicitiam*).[5] But it may be doubted that the saying was originally designed to convey such advice, whether it is taken literally or metaphorically.

Quintilian *Institutio oratoria* 8.3.75 quotes among the parables (*similitudines*) which are generally understood (*volgaria*) and useful (*utilia*) the following:

> As the physicians cut off the members of the body which are estranged (from it) through sickness, thus also evil and corrupting people, even if they are related to us through bonds of blood, must be cut off (ut medici abalienata morbis membra praecidant, ita turpes ac perniciosos, etiam si nobis a sanguine cohaereant, amputandos).[6]

A parable similar to Mark's is used here. But there is no attempt to relate it hyperbolically to the moral behavior of the individual. Rather, it is applied to the concept of the health of the community. This corresponds to the general use of the image of the body and its members in the ancient world, especially in Stoic philosophy.[7] The image of the body as a communal metaphor is so widespread that one must assume that the saying of Mark 9:43–47 was originally designed to serve as a rule for the community: members of the Christian church who give offense should be excluded. Paul, in 1 Cor 5:1–13, gives an example of the application to this rule. He does not, to be sure, use the saying of Mark 9—though he uses the familiar image of the human body in 1 Cor 12:12–27—but he underlines his command by quoting Deut 17:7: "Drive out the wicked person from your midst." But even in 1 Cor 12:26 there is some corroboration of the interpretation suggested by the Quintilian passage: "And when one member suffers, all the members suffer with it."

One difficulty remains. The parable would be simpler if it said: "It is better for you to live as a cripple than with both hands to perish." The expression "to enter into life" or "into the kingdom of God" and "to depart for/to be thrown into hell" are not needed for its communal application. They are a hyperbolic transgression of the parameters of the parable. It is, of course, not impossible that an individualistic interpretation had

---

4. In his reproduction of Mark 9:43–47, Matt 18:8–9 also reduces the three parts of Mark's saying to two: offense of the hand and foot in the first part, offense of the eye in the second.

5. Ed. Henry Chadwick (Texts 5; Cambridge: Cambridge University Press, 1959).

6. Ed. Helmut Rahn (Texte zur Forschung 2; Darmstadt: Wissenschaftliche Buchgesellschaft, 1972 and 1975); the translation is my own.

7. The examples are collected by Hans Conzelmann, *1 Corinthians* (Hermeneia; Philadelphia: Fortress Press, 1975) 211.

already caused the hyperbole in this saying as it occurs in Mark 9:43–47 and Matt 18:8–9. However, this seems unlikely. Mark 9:42, the command not to offend the little ones, is a rule for the community. Matthew makes use of the whole section Mark 9:43–49 in order to introduce his discourse on community regulations (Matt 18:8–9); rules on reproving and excommunication follow (Matt 18:15–18). 2 Corinthians 13 demonstrates that destruction of the whole community can be the alternative to excommunication of an individual.[8] Also, 1 Cor 5:6 warns that "a little leaven ferments the whole lump." For early Christianity the choice between eternal life and destruction was not seen as a choice of the individual, but rather as a demand for the preservation of the Christian community as a whole. This could explain the formulations of the sayings that emphasize eternal life and death or kingdom of God and hell as the choices, not of the individual, but of the community as a whole. As a rule of the community, the similitude of the offending hand justifies excommunication. It is only Matt 5:28–29 which introduced the misleading interpretation of this saying as hyperbolic advice to abstain from sexual desire, and only the particular context of Matthw 5, not the saying itself, suggests such an interpretation. The parallel in Quintilian reminds us that in general usage, the image of the body and its (sick) members was understood as a communal parable.

---

8. That Paul quotes the rule about two or three witnesses in 2 Cor 13:1 = Matt 18:16 may not be accidental.

II

THE GOSPEL OF JOHN

8

THE HISTORY-OF-RELIGIONS SCHOOL, GNOSIS, AND THE GOSPEL OF JOHN

1. The History-of-Religions School

More than a hundred years ago, Albrecht Ritschl, Professor of Theology at the University of Göttingen, was advertising his new theology as the enlightened perfection of the Lutheran Reformation. Next to the Reformation's discovery of the sinner's justification by grace alone, a second focus of the Christian revelation, equally important, was Jesus' proclamation of the Kingdom of God. This Kingdom of God, according to Ritschl, was to be built in this world as the perfection of human culture, to be accomplished through the moral education of humankind.[1]

But during the most successful and effective years of Albrecht Ritschl's career (roughly from 1875 to his death in 1891), there existed a new generation of young scholars at the University of Göttingen. All were deeply influenced by Ritschl but were united in their protest against this great theologian's arbitrary use of biblical texts in the service of his theological system.[2] This group of younger scholars later was called "The History-of-Religions School."[3] Many remarkable people who eventually became famous in the twentieth century were members of this group:

William Wrede, born 1859, Inspector of the Theologische Stift in Göttingen from 1884, then pastor (1887–89), was a bit older than the others and seems to have been a convener of the group. He became Dozent in 1891, then professor in Breslau in 1893. His book, *The Tasks and Methods of the So-called New Testament Theology*,[4] states one of the

---

1. Johann Meyer, "Geschichte der Göttinger theologischen Fakultät," *Zeitschrift der Gesellschaft für niedersächsische Kirchengeschichte* 42 (1937) 7–107; E. Schott, "Ritschl, Albrecht," *RGG* 5 (3rd ed., 1961) 1114–17 (with further literature); O. Ritschl, "Ritschl, Albrecht Benjamin," *RE* 17 (1906) 22–34.

2. "What called forth the protest of the young theologians was the danger of all historicizing dogmatism from which Ritschl also could not escape; i.e., the necessity to construct a system based on the statements of the New Testament, made it impossible to do justice to the variety of the statements preserved in this document and forced a violation of their integrity" (Werner Klatt, *Hermann Gunkel: Zu seiner Theologie der Religionsgeschichte und zur Entstehung der formgeschichtlichen Methode* [FRLANT 100; Göttingen: Vandenhoeck & Ruprecht, 1969] 20). All translations from German are my own.

3. "Die religionsgeschichtliche Schule." According to J. Hempel ("Religionsgeschichtliche Schule," *RGG* 5 [3d ed., 1961] 991), this term was first used by A. Jeremias in the year 1904 in a polemical fashion.

4. William Wrede, *Über Aufgabe und Methode der sogenannten neutestamentlichen Theologie* (Göttingen: Vandenhoeck & Ruprecht, 1897). On Wrede, see especially Georg Strecker, "William Wrede," *ZThK* 57 (1960) 67–91.

important new insights of the "school": New Testament theology should disregard the limitations of the canon and become a history of early Christian religion and theology.

Hermann Gunkel, born 1862, studied in Göttingen, then in Gießen where he heard Adolf Harnack (1882–83). After his return to Göttingen, he became Dozent in 1888. Like most others in this circle of friends, he began as a New Testament scholar but was persuaded to accept a position as a teacher of Old Testament interpretation in Halle a year later. In 1907 he was called to Gießen where Sigmund Mowinckel became his student; in 1920 he returned to Halle for the final years of his career.[5] His dissertation, "The Working of the Holy Spirit,"[6] demonstrates that the early Christians understood the Holy Spirit as a magic and miracle-working power, not as a rational-moral principle.

Wilhelm Bousset, born 1865, began his studies in Erlangen in 1884, where he met Ernst Troeltsch, with whom he established a life-long friendship. After a brief stay in Leipzig, he went to Göttingen in 1886, where he became Dozent in 1891 and where he stayed as "Professor extraordinarius" (Associate Professor) until 1916. His political convictions and activities as a liberal (he was closely associated with Friedrich Nau-mann) as well as his wife's feminist engagement made a call to a chair in a Prussian university impossible. Finally, in 1916, he became "Professor ordinaries" (Full Professor) in Gießen as Gunkel's colleague but died after only a few years (1920). But during his long teaching career in Göttingen, he contributed substantially to the education of several younger scholars who entered "the History-of-Religions School." Hugo Gressmann, Wilhelm Heitmüller, and Gillis P:son Wetter were his students during those years.[7]

Ernst Troeltsch, born 1865, had already met Wilhelm Bousset in Erlangen. He joined the circle of friends when he continued his studies in Göttingen; he became Dozent there in 1891. A year later he moved to Bonn and in 1894 to Heidelberg. The only scholar in this circle of friends whose special field was not biblical interpretation, Troeltsch thought of himself as "the systematic theologian of the History-of-Religions School."[8]

Johannes Weiss, born 1863, was only a casual member of the group. He became Dozent in Göttingen in 1888. His dissertation, "The Preaching of Jesus of the Kingdom of God,"[9] demonstrated the mythical-eschatological dimensions of Jesus' concept of

---

5. On Gunkel, see the comprehensive treatment of Werner Klatt, *Hermann Gunkel*, cited in n. 2; see also H. Schmidt, "In Memoriam Hermann Gunkel," *ThBl* 11 (1932) 97–103; François Bovon, "Hermann Gunkel, historien de la religion et exégète des genres littéraires," in Bovon and Grégoire Roullier, *Exégèsis* (Neuchâtel/Paris: Delachaux & Niestlé, 1975) 86–97; Reinhard Wonneberger, "Gunkel, Hermann," *TRE* 14 (1985) 297–300.

6. Hermann Gunkel, *Die Wirkungen des Heiligen Geistes nach der populären Anschauung der apostolischen Zeit und der Lehre des Apostels Paulus* (Göttingen: Vandenhoeck & Ruprecht) 1888.

7. On Bousset, see Anthonie F. Verheule, *Wilhelm Bousset: Leben und Werk* (Amsterdam: Van Bottenburg, 1973). See also Hermann Gunkel, "Gedächtnisrede auf Wilhelm Bousset," *Evangelische Freiheit* 42 (1920) 142–62; Johann Michael Schmidt, "Bousset, Wilhelm," *TRE* 7 (1981) 97–101.

8. Cf. H. Benckert, "Troeltsch, Ernst," *RGG* 6 (3rd ed., 1962) 1044–47; Heinz-Horst Schrey, "Ernst Troeltsch und sein Werk," *ThR* N. F. 12 (1940) 130–62.

9. Johannes Weiss, *Die Predigt Jesu vom Reiche Gottes* (Göttingen: Vandenhoeck & Ruprecht, 1892; English translation: Richard Hyde Hiers and David Larrimore Holland, trans. & eds., *Jesus' Proclamation of the Kingdom of God* (Philadelphia: Fortress Press, 1971; Chico, Calif.: Scholars Press, 1985).

the Kingdom and thus constituted the most fundamental attack upon the biblical base of Ritschl's theology. Johannes Weiss was professor in Marburg from 1895 to 1908 where Rudolf Bultmann became his student. However, Weiss moved to Heidelberg in 1908 and therefore did not supervise Bultmann's dissertation.[10]

Among somewhat younger scholars who can be counted as members of the "school," two men were most influential in the continuation of the history-of-religions approach to biblical studies: Wilhelm Heitmüller and Hugo Gressmann. Wilhelm Heitmüller, born 1869, became a student of Wilhelm Bousset and in 1902, Dozent in Gottingen. His dissertation, on the use of the name of Jesus in early Christianity,[11] deals with the close association of religious thought and cult (baptism). As professor in Marburg from 1908, where he succeeded Johannes Weiss, he supervised Rudolf Bultmann's dissertation.[12] Hugo Gressmann, born 1877,[13] also had studied with Bousset in Gottingen. He became Gunkel's most intimate and congenial friend, and later he expanded and revised Bousset's monumental work on the religious thought of Judaism in the late Hellenistic period.[14]

It is well known that the name "school" is a misnomer for these young scholars in Göttingen. They did not have a common teacher to whom they owed allegiance. The designation "History-of-Religions School" was a nickname, reluctantly accepted by this circle of friends. Attempts have been made to identify particular teachers or scholars whose thoughts could have inspired this new departure. Hermann Usener, professor of classical philology in Bonn, has been mentioned; his student Albrecht Dieterich, then about the same age as the members of the Göttingen circle, wrote several books that were wholly congenial with the quest of his Göttingen contemporaries.[15] Paul de Lagarde, the father of the scientific study of ancient Near-Eastern languages and advocate of the Romantic concept of a purified national Germanic Christianity, has been explicitly cited as the founder of the history-of-religions school.[16] De Lagarde taught in Göttingen from 1869 to his death in 1891,[17] and Hermann Gunkel took some

---

10. On Johannes Weiss, see Rudolf Bultmann, "Johannes Weiss zum Gedächtnis," *ThBl* 18 (1939) 242–46; Karl Prümm, "Johannes Weiss als Darsteller und religionsgeschichtlicher Erklärer der paulinischen Botschaft," *Biblica* 40 (1959) 815–36.

11. Wilhelm Heitmüller, *Im Namen Jesu: Eine sprach- und religionsgeschichtliche Untersuchung zum Neuen Testament* (FRLANT 1,2; Göttingen: Vandenhoeck & Ruprecht, 1903).

12. A most informative monument is the memorial by Rudolf Bultmann, "Wilhelm Heitmüller," *ChrW* 40 (1926) 209–13.

13. Karl Galling, "Gressmann, Hugo," *RGG* 2 (3rd ed., 1958) 1856; Reinhard Wonneberger, "Gressmann, Hugo," *TRE* 14 (1985) 212–13; Arthur Titius, Theodore H. Robinson, Ernst Sellin, and Johannes Hempel, "Dem Gedächtnis Hugo Gressmanns," *ZAW* 45 (1927) iii–xxiv.

14. Wilhelm Bousset, *Die Religion des Judentums im späthellenistischen Zeitalter* (HNT 21; 3rd ed. by Hugo Gressmann; Tübingen: Mohr/Siebeck, 1926).

15. Albrecht Dieterich, *Abraxas: Studien zur Religionsgeschichte des späteren Altertums: Festschrift Hermann Usener* (Leipzig: B. G. Teubner, 1891; reprints 1905; Aalen: Scientia-Verlag, 1973); Dieterich, *Nekyia: Beiträge zur Erklärung der neuentdeckten Petrusapokalypse* (Leipzig: B. G. Teubner, 1893; 2nd ed. 1913; 3rd ed. Darmstadt: Wissenschaftliche Buchgesellschaft, 1969).

16. Hans-Walter Schütte, "Theologie als Religionsgeschichte: Das Reformprogramm Paul de Lagardes," *Neue Zeitschrift für systematische Theologie und Religionsphilosophie* 8 (1966) 111–20.

17. On Paul de Lagarde's theological ideas, see Lothar Schmidt, *Paul de Lagardes Kritik an Kirche, Theologie*

courses in Semitic languages from him. But Gunkel later stated explicitly that he and his friends were not strongly influenced by either de Lagarde or any other famous scholars except, of course, Ritschl.[18]

Obviously, there was not one particular scholar who inspired these young biblical scholars. But they all were indebted to a common older friend and mentor, the church-historian Albrecht Eichhorn. He was born in 1856, and thus three years older than Wrede and nine years older than Bousset and Troeltsch. He was in Göttingen in 1884–85 in order to prepare his dissertation; became Dozent in Halle in 1886, where he taught until he was called to a professorship in Kiel, which he held from 1901 to 1913 until forced to retire because of poor health, and died in 1927. When he was at Halle, he frequently returned to Göttingen to visit his friend, William Wrede, and on these occasions met others of the circle. A few years later, when Gunkel had gone to Halle, Eichhorn's influence was mostly channelled through him. Gunkel dedicated his book *Schöpfung und Chaos in Urzeit und Endzeit,* which was written during those years, to his friend Eichhorn.[19] Later Hugo Gressmann created a lasting monument to this otherwise not very well-known scholar with his book *Albrecht Eichhorn und die religionsgeschichtliche Schule.*[20]

The peculiar influence that Eichhorn had upon this group of friends was characterized later by Gunkel and Troeltsch in letters to Gressmann. "He was a critic of the first order," Gunkel writes,[21] "a merciless critic of every prejudice, political, scholarly, ecclesiastical, liberal, or conservative. . . . He had a strong sense of reality! Therefore his interest in history. . . ."[22] "The leading concept in all matters was the real understanding, the *historical* understanding of *religion:* thus the designation *Religionsgeschichte* which was chosen with good reason and describes the intention accurately. . . ."[23] Troeltsch's letter underlines the Socratic character of Eichhorn's role: "There were suggestions, flashes of words, casual remarks, paradoxical brain-waves, cleverly formulated questions—that is what we heard from him. And that had its lasting effects, God knows how and when."[24]

Eichhorn, himself a historian, certainly reinforced the emphasis upon a historical understanding of all religious phenomena. Moreover, the indirect and direct influence of the scholarly work of such historians as Adolf Harnack should not be underestimated.[25] In any case, the last decades of the nineteenth century witnessed a general rise in the number of historical works as well as an increasing interest in the study of religions and of the phenomena of religious life. But the basic insights that were developed by this circle of friends in Göttingen, with the particular emphasis upon the understanding of Bible and Christianity as "religion," seem to have their peculiar roots in

---

und Christentum (Tübinger Studien zur systematischen Theologie 4; Stuttgart: W. Kohlhammer, 1935); Wilhelm Rott, "Nationale Religion und Entstaatlichung der Kirche bei Paul de Lagarde," *EvTh* 5 (1938) 58–67.

18. Hermann Gunkel, "Die Richtungen der alttestamentlichen Forschung," *ChrW* 36 (1922) 64–67.

19. 1894; 2nd ed. Göttingen: Vandenhoeck & Ruprecht, 1921.

20. Göttingen: Vandenhoeck & Ruprecht, 1914.

21. Werner Klatt, "Ein Brief von Hermann Gunkel über Albert Eichhorn an Hugo Gressmann," *ZThK* 66 (1969) 5.

22. Ibid., 3.

23. Ibid., 5.

24. Letter of July 4, 1913; quoted in Klatt, *Hermann Gunkel.*

25. Gunkel dedicated his commentary on the book of Genesis to him.

common backgrounds and experiences that all, or most of them, shared. With one exception, they were all from northern Germany.[26] Bousset came from Lübeck; Johannes Weiß from Kiel; all others from the area of the Lutheran church of Hannover. Heitmüller was the son of a farmer; Johannes Weiss of a New Testament professor (Bernard Weiss); all the others were pastors' children. Gunkel later wrote that the basic "insight that all phenomena of the mind, in literature and religion, had to be understood historically," was formed before he entered the university.[27] This insight was formed in the atmosphere of a Lutheran parsonage in a town or a village and during the years in high school and became a theological protest when these young students sat at the feet of the much admired and famous systematician, Albrecht Ritschl, in Göttingen. It became a protest because they felt that their sense of the historical reality of the biblical stories was violated in those lectures. "It was a thoroughly inner-theological movement which had taken its beginnings in this circle of friends of young theologians. . . . It endeavored to become free from the barriers of the scholarly establishment of that time . . . to get away from barriers of the canon and from the ecclesiastical dogma about the Bible, from the one-sidedness of a dogmatizing 'Biblical Theology' and from a hyper-philological literary criticism . . . also from the isolation of the Old and New Testaments from their historically given connections with other religions in order to enter midstream into the flowing river of the real history of the Biblical religion."[28]

Let me summarize some of the insights which have become part of the heritage of this "school" for scholarship until today:[29]

1. Religion is not a subcategory of culture, but an independent fundamental phenomenon of the human striving for life, insofar as this striving endeavors to reach its goal through a relationship with higher powers.

2. Religion is part of the nature of all human beings. Mowinckel wrote: "Religion proves to be a feature among all human beings as a correlative to a common human need, or more accurately: to a general human experience."[30]

3. A distinction between natural and revealed religion is impossible, because revelations of divine powers and divine beings belong to the experience of all human religion.

4. Religion and its verbal expressions are both universal and syncretistic; its basic experiences are comparable, and concepts and metaphors can be transferred from one religion to another.

5. Religion is not primarily present in systems of theology and rational dogma, but in the basic manifestations of its own life: cult, prayer, celebration, mysticism, magic, and myth.

---

26. Only Troeltsch came from southern Germany; he was the son of a physician in Augsburg.
27. Klatt, *Hermann Gunkel*, 17–18.
28. Hermann Gunkel, "Die Richtungen der alttestamentlichen Forschung," *ChrW* 36 (1922) 66.
29. I am formulating these principles on the basis of Wilhelm Bousset, *Das Wesen der Religion dargestllt an ihrer Geschichte* (Tübingen: Mohr/Siebeck, 1903; 4th ed. 1920).
30. Sigmund Mowinckel, *Religion und Kultus* (Göttingen: Vandenhoeck & Ruprecht, 1953) 132.

The consequences of this fresh approach to biblical scholarship and the new insights that have resulted from it are well known to all of us today. The more original expressions of biblical religion were found in the forms and genres of oral traditions that belong to the festivals of Israel's annual calendar and to the cult of the Kyrios Christos in the early Christian communities. Spiritual phenomena, enthusiasm, ecstasy, prophecy, glossolalia, miracles, and magic were seen as the moving forces of religious life. It was demonstrated that the religious language of the Bible is shared, to a very large degree, with other religions of the ancient Near East from Babylon to Egypt and from Persia to Hellenistic Rome. As Israel emerged as just one variant of the development of Near Eastern religions, early Christianity was seen as one of the several mystery religions of the Hellenistic world.

2. Myth and Gnosis

There is one particular part of the primary manifestations of religion which remained difficult and controversial among scholars of the history of religions: the place and function of myth. All other verbal expressions of primary religion—liturgical formulae and priestly instructions, curses and blessings, psalms and hymns, prayers and doxologies, prophetic utterances, and magic incantations—can be related to, or identified with, specific actions and experiences of religious life. But where does myth belong? How is myth related to the life of religion and its manifestations?

In the article "Mythus" in the first edition of *Die Religion in Geschichte und Gegenwart*,[31] Hugo Gressmann wishes to disassociate myth from the verbal expressions of primary religion, because myth, he argues, is too complex a phenomenon, often dominated by the poetic license of the narrator or by the speculative interests of the theologian. On the other hand, in the third edition of the same work, published half a century later, Sigmund Mowinckel states in his article on "Mythus": "Myth in its true sense narrates in epic form the 'salvation' which has been enacted (or re-enacted) and experienced in cult."[32] In his book on religion and cult, Mowinckel says:

> True myth is tied to the cult, has arisen out of the cult and expresses that which is happening there and has once happened in a founding event—the "fact of salvation"—which is brought back to "memory" as it is experienced again. . . . If we have said before that the cult represents the myth of the god, we have formulated this somewhat inaccurately; the relationship should rather be stated the other way around: Myth expresses in epic form what is happening in the cult.[33]

This definition is useful as long as there is a known cultic setting and as long as the further development of the myth is understood as closely associated with the development of a specific cult or reflects changes in the ongoing interpretation of the

---

31. Hugo Gressmann, "Mythus und Mythologie, Religionsgeschichtlich," *RGG* 4 (1st ed.; 1913) 618–21.

32. *RGG* 4 (3rd ed.; 1960) 1274–78.

33. Sigmund Mowinckel, *Religion und Kultus*, 94.

experiences that this cult provides. But if myths seem to be the only extant witnesses of an ancient religion, how can they be used to understand the origins of a religion and of its developments?

History-of-religions scholars in the field of the New Testament were confronted with this question with respect to the most important and most vexing problem of myth in early Christianity, namely the question of Gnostic myth. The answer has been: One must reconstruct the most original form of the myth and understand the meaning of Gnostic religion on that basis, although nothing seems to be known about the cult to which this myth was related. This is exactly the procedure that Wilhelm Bousset and others after him have used in their investigations of the Gnostic religion. In this way, scholars of the history-of-religions school were able to challenge the traditional opinion that held that Gnosticism was nothing but an aberration from orthodox Christianity, a wrong and falsifying interpretation of the apostolic tradition and of its canon.

In his book *Hauptprobleme der Gnosis,* published in 1907, Wilhelm Bousset carefully investigates all mythological elements that appear in Gnostic materials. On that basis, he reconstructs what is, in his opinion, the most original form of the Gnostic religion.[34] The myth tells of a primordial unnamed and unfathomable deity, a god whose essence is pure light. Associated with this god is a female figure, the primordial mother with her eight emanations, the *Ogdoad.* Under this original divine pleroma, at a lower level of the cosmic order, are the semi-demonical Seven with their archon Yaldabaoth (who is later identified with the creator god of the book of Genesis and also called Sabaoth). He is the demiurge who creates the world and who fashions human beings out of the portions of the primordial *Anthropos* who somehow fell under his power.

The myth of creation teaches initiates about that process and gives them the knowledge that they have in themselves as an element from the sphere of the primordial divine light. The Gnostic mysteries, therefore, must have been rituals in which the mystagogue instructed the participants about the instruments and secret passwords that were to be used after death in order to rise through the hostile cosmic spheres into the realm of pure light.[35]

At this point Bousset notes, and this is very important: "It is remarkable that there is, in some of these Gnostic sects, not yet any figure of a redeemer."[36] He then proceeds to summarize the various elements of this Gnostic myth with respect to their origin (the major part of the book contains careful and rich documentation for this summary): the primordial *Anthropos* stems from Iranian concepts of the cosmic "Urmensch"; the concepts of the light pleroma and of the Seven are derived from Babylonian astrology; the primordial female figure is derived from oriental beliefs in a mother-goddess who is also the deity of the heavens. Yaldabaoth with his characteristic lion-head is the Babylonian Kewan whom the Greeks identify with Kronos-Saturn.[37] Any Jewish elements Bousset ascribes to a later stage of Jewish adaptation of this originally pagan myth. Wherever

---

34. See also Wilhelm Bousset, "Gnosis," and "Gnostiker" in Pauly-Wissowa 7,2 (1912) 1503–33 and 1534–47; reprinted in Bousset, *Religionsgeschichtliche Studien* (ed. Anthonie F. Verheule; NovTSup 50; Leiden: Brill, 1979) 44–96.

35. Bousset, *Hauptprobleme,* 319–21.

36. Ibid., 321.

37. Ibid., 321–22.

Jesus appears in these systems, this is also considered to be a secondary addition to the salvation myth of an originally pagan religion.[38]

Bousset's ingenious and learned reconstruction of this original myth of the Gnostic religion has determined scholarship on the phenomenon of Gnosis ever since, in spite of various criticisms that mostly tried to revive the older assumption that Gnosticism was nothing but an aberrant form of Christianity. Richard Reitzenstein gave further strength to Bousset's construct by supplying the missing redeemer myth from a hypothetical Iranian Gnostic mystery of salvation.[39] Thus, Rudolf Bultmann could include among the presuppositions of New Testament theology a description of Gnostic thought, including a redeemer myth and a full picture of the Gnostic system, albeit mythological, of a pre-Christian religion.[40]

The weaknesses and problems of this hypothesis have been pointed out frequently. Criticism was directed in particular against Reitzenstein's construct of a pre-Christian redeemer myth of Iranian origin—well-justified criticism.[41] But the real problem must be defined with more precision: Is it possible to locate the origins and the development of Gnosticism in an actually existing religious group with its cultic performances and social structures? And since the answer to this question has proved to be so immensely difficult, is perhaps this rediscovered original Gnostic myth nothing but a theoretical reconstruction of learned scholars?

What is required is the demonstration of the relationship of myth to a particular group that can be identified with respect to its religious tradition and its cultic practices. If one is confronted with this question with respect to Gnosticism, the specific modifications or reinterpretations of older mythical materials and traditions must be clarified insofar as they relate to a particular group and to specific institutions and cults. In order to establish such criteria, I want to discuss a specific case of the new formation of a cult and a closely related reinterpretation of older mythical materials from the early Roman imperial period. Although this new cult is not at all connected with the problem of Gnosis, I trust that it will provide some helpful criteria.

3. The Cult of Palaimon/Melikertes in Isthmia[42]

In the middle of the second century CE, Pausanias visited Isthmia during his tour of Greece, on his way from Athens to Corinth along the coast of the Saronic Gulf. As he reaches the Isthmus, he tells the following:

---

38. Ibid., 324–26.

39. *Das iranische Erlösungsmysterium* (Bonn: A. Marcus & E. Weber, 1921). On the development of this hypothesis of Reitzenstein, see Carsten Colpe, *Die religionsgeschichtliche Schule: Darstellung und Kritik ihres Bildes vom gnostischen Erlösermythus* (FRLANT 78; Göttingen: Vandenhoeck & Ruprecht, 1961).

40. Rudolf Bultmann, *Theology of the New Testament* (New York: Scribner's, 1951) 164–83.

41. For a critique of the underlying concept of myth, see Colpe, *Religionsgeschichtliche Schule*, 191.

42. For a more detailed discussion of all literary and archaeological evidence, see my essay "The Cult of Palaimon-Melikertes in Isthmia," in David L. Balch, Everett Ferguson, Wayne Meeks, eds., *Greeks, Romans, and Christians: Essays in Honor of Abraham J. Malherbe* (Minneapolis: Fortress Press, 1990) 355–66; reprinted in Helmut Koester, *Paul and His World* (Minneapolis: Fortress Press, 2007) 180–91.

Farther on the pine tree still grew by the shore at the time of my visit, and there was an altar of Melikertes. At this place, they say, the boy was brought ashore by a dolphin; Sisyphus (the legendary first king of Corinth) found him lying and gave him burial on the Isthmus, establishing the Isthmian games in his honor.[43]

Pausanias then proceeds inland to the Temple of Poseidon in Isthmia. At the end of his description of the magnificent temple statues of Poseidon and Amphitrite that had just been given to the temple by Herodes Atticus, the benefactor of so many Greek cities, Pausanias says:

and there is the boy Palaimon upright on a dolphin.[44]

He then continues:

Within the enclosure (τοῦ περιβόλου, i.e., of the Temple of Poseidon), there is on the left a Temple of Palaimon with images in it of Poseidon, Leukothea, and Palaimon himself. There is also what is called Adyton (ἄλλο ἄδυτον καλούμενον), and an underground descent to it, where they say that Palaimon is concealed. Whosoever, whether Corinthian or stranger, swears falsely here can by no means escape from his oath.[45]

The myth or story of Palaimon, also called Melikertes, to which Pausanias refers, can be reconstructed fully from ancient sources. Ino, the sister of Semele, daughter of Kadmus, is the victim of Hera's wrath, because she had nursed the child of her sister, Semele, by Zeus, the young Dionysus. Stricken with madness by Hera, Ino finally jumps into the sea with her own boy Melikertes. However, Poseidon is persuaded by Dionysus (or some other god) to transform both into deities: Ino becomes Leukothea, her son Melikertes becomes Palaimon; the latter is carried to the shores of Isthmia by a dolphin where he is found by Sisyphus, the legendary king of Corinth, who establishes the Isthmian games in his honor.[46]

The story has all the makings of an ancient aetiological myth, related to an actually existing cult that was closely associated with the Isthmian games. The myth does not tell much about the specifics of the cult. But Pausanias knows of an *Adyton* and of sacred oaths, which were sworn there. Philostratus, describing a picture of the discovery of Palaimon by Sisyphus, gives additional information about the rites:

Sisyphus sacrifices a black bull. The meaning of the sacrifice, the garb worn by those who conducted it, the offerings (τὰ ἐναγίσματα), ... and the use of the knife (τὸ σφάττειν) must be reserved for the rights (τὰ ὄργια) of Palaimon, for the doctrine is holy and altogether secret.[47]

---

43. Pausanias 2.1.3; translations here and in some other instances are from LCL (modified).
44. Pausanias 2.1.8.
45. Pausanias 2.2.1.
46. Pausanias 1.44.7–8; Apollodorus *Bibl.* 3.4.3; Hyginus *Fabulae* 2.5; 3.4; 4.1–2, 5. See also n. 55. More materials are quoted in J. G. Frazer, *Pausanias' Description of Greece* (New York: Biblo & Tannen, 1965) 2. 549.
47. *Imagines* 2.16. In this context, Philostratus also tells the story of Ino and Palaimon.

The excavations at Isthmia have brought to light some very interesting facts. First of all, there was indeed a temple and a cult of Palaimon Melikertes. The foundations of a small circular temple with an underground chamber were found "within the enclosure on the left," exactly as Pausanias says.[48] A statue base of white marble with the name Sisyphus inscribed on it was excavated a few meters away from the temple foundations.[49] A long inscription of the priest Iuventianus tells of the renovation and decoration of the precinct of Palaimon.[50] Corinthian coins show the round temple with a dolphin and a figure lying on its back. Furthermore, the excavations have brought to light three burning pits in the immediate vicinity of the temple foundations; all three were still half full of the ashes and bones of bulls and showed evidence of intense heat.[51] Also found in or near these pits were large numbers of peculiar lamps which must have been used in the cult, that is, nocturnal sacrifices in which bulls were burnt.

But all this archaeological evidence for the cult of Palaimon must be dated in the Roman imperial period. There is no trace of the existence of such a cult from an earlier time, although the entire site has been thoroughly searched. There is not a single find relating to Palaimon-Melikertes dating to the period before the destruction of Corinth by the Roman general Mummius in the year 146 BCE. All archaeological finds from that period are related to Poseidon[52] and to some other Greek gods (Demeter, Dionysus) who were worshipped in a nearby sacred grove. According to the archaeological evidence, the cult of Palaimon-Melikertes was introduced only after the refounding of Corinth by Caesar as a Roman colony with foreign settlers in the year 44 BCE. During the intervening 102 years, while Corinth lay waste, the games were transferred to Sikyon; no cultic rites were celebrated and no games were held at Isthmia during that period.

A closer scrutiny of the ancient literary sources confirms the archaeological evidence. In the classical period, it is common knowledge that the Isthmian games were celebrated every two years in honor of Poseidon. No classical author mentions Palaimon or Melikertes in connection with the Isthmian games. On the other hand, Ino-

---

48. Oscar Broneer, "Excavations at Isthmia. Third Campaign 1955–56," *Hesperia* 26 (1957) 15–17; Broneer, "Excavations at Isthmia. Fourth Campaign 1957–58," *Hesperia* 28 (1959) 317–19; Broneer, *Isthmia* (Princeton, N.J.: Princeton University Press, 1971) 2. 106–12.

49. The base carries the inscription Σείσιφος on both sides. It was published by Oscar Broneer, "Excavations at Isthmia. Third Campaign 1955-56," *Hesperia* 26 (1957) 22–23.

50. This second-century CE Isthmian inscription (*IG* 4, No. 203) was found in the nineteenth century and brought to Italy (now in the Museo Lapidario in Verona, Inventory No. 73). The Isthmian excavations have brought to light a statue base with the inscription; cf. Broneer in *Hesperia* 26 (1957) 23. In his *Geschichte der Kunst des Altertums* (= *History of Ancient Art* [New York: F. Ungar Pub. Co., 1968] 2. 280–81), Winckelmann reported that the name of the same priest also appeared on the head of a dolphin at the feet of a large statue of Neptune that was found in Corinth, together with a "statue of Juno, so-called." These statues, however, have since disappeared. The inscription is published in *IG* 4, No. 202.

51. The largest and latest of these three pits measures 4.05 by 3.57 m., is preserved to a height of 1.10 m., and was filled with ashes and animal bones as well as quantities of lamps up to a height of 0.75 m. The first two pits date from the first century CE; the third burning pit was in use during most of the second century CE. Cf. Oscar Broneer, "Excavations at Isthmia. Fourth Campaign 1957–58," *Hesperia* 28 (1959) 312–17; Broneer, *Isthmia*, 2. 100–106.

52. Cf. Broneer, *Isthmia*, vol. 1.

Leukothea and her child Palaimon are well known. Ino-Leukothea is mentioned as early as Homer,[53] and Ino and Palaimon together appear in Euripides.[54] They are deities of the sea, helpers of sailors in distress. The story that Ino, persecuted by Hera, threw herself into the sea together with her son is also known in the earlier period. But her son is never called Melikertes, nor is the place located near Isthmia. The identification of Palaimon with Melikertes as well as the Isthmian localization of the event of their deaths appear for the first time after the refounding of Corinth by Caesar.

One must, therefore, conclude that the myth of Palaimon-Melikertes in the form in which it relates to the Isthmian games and its cult is an interpretation of older mythological materials for the purpose of creating the aetiology for a new cult that was introduced to Isthmia in the Roman imperial period. Ovid, in his *Metamorphoses* as well as in his *Fasti,* clearly reveals the interests which form the background for this novel formation of the myth. As he retells the story of Ino and Palaimon, he also reports the prophecy of a priestess from Tegea to Ino, revealing her future divine status:

You shall be a divinity of the sea; your son, too, shall have his home in the ocean. Take you both different names in your own waters. You shall be called Leukothea by the Greeks and Matuta by our people, your son (Melicerta) will have authority over harbors; he whom we name Portunus will be named Palaimon in his own tongue.[55]

The syncretistic interests of the myth, as it appears in Ovid, are obvious in the identification of the Roman Matuta with the Greek Leukothea, and of the Roman Portunus with the Greek Palaimon.

Why is the latter also called Melicerta? It has been suggested that the Phoenician god Melqart appears in this name.[56] In fact, the identification of Melqart and Palaimon is not as novel as it might seem, because Palaimon was a well-established surname of Herakles, and the identification of Herakles and Melqart is as old as the cult of Herakles-Melqart on the island of Thasos in the classical period.[57] The Melqart of the city of Tyre, originally a dying-and-rising fertility deity, was called Herakles by the Greeks, and after the time of Alexander the Great his iconography became completely identical with that of Herakles. When the Phoenicians brought their god Melqart to the western Mediterranean as one of the great gods of Carthage, he also became a deity of

---

53. Homer *Od.* 5.333–34 calls the sea goddess Leukothea the daughter of Kadmus.

54. Euripides *Iph. taur.* 1282–89: "O child of the ruler Leukothea, guardian of ships, lord Palaimon, be merciful to us!"

55. *Fasti* 6.543–50. In *Fast.* 6.495–96, Ovid also describes the Corinthian Isthmus as the locality of Ino's and Melicerta's deaths. Ovid wrote the *Fasti* just before his exile in 8 CE. Ovid had told the story of Ino and Melicerta a few years earlier in his *Metamorphoses* (4.416–542), but the only location that is indicated there is "in the broad Ionian Sea." Thus Ovid's *Fasti* is the first reference to Isthmia in connection with Ino and her son in extant ancient literature. Virgil had mentioned Melicerta, Ino's son, only in general as a divinity of the sea.

56. The older literature on this question is cited in John G. Hawthorne, "The Myth of Palaimon," *TAPA* 89 (1958) 92–98.

57. Herodot 2.44 (cf. Pausanias 5.25.12); Lycophron *Alexandria* 633; Plautus *Rudens* 160. See also Pauly-Wissowa, RESuppl. 3. 964.

the sea. In addition to the Melqart sanctuary in Carthage, there were sanctuaries in Sicily, Sardinia, and Spain. The Romans who learned about Melqart from the Carthaginians called the city of Tyre on Sicily with its Melqart sanctuary "Heraclea Minora."[58] Since the new name for Palaimon appears for the first time in Latin literature, one must assume that the Greek Μελικέρτης is a transcription of the Latin *Melicerta* (traditionally the Greek transcription for Melqart had been Μέλκαθρος).

It is quite possible that some of the archaeological finds also point to a Phoenician origin of the Isthmian cult of Palaimon-Melikertes. To my knowledge, whole-burnt offerings of bulls in special pits are rare in Greece; and the peculiar lamps which were used in the nocturnal rites are without any analogues in Greece. Phoenician settlers, brought to Corinth by Caesar and Augustus, probably from the western Mediterranean, must have introduced this cult to Isthmia where it replaced the older Greek cult of Poseidon during the Roman period.[59] It is also noteworthy that the Isthmian victor's crown, traditionally made of wild celery, was later often replaced by a crown made of pine—possibly understood as a symbol of Melikertes, whose pine tree grew near the altar of Melikertes on the shores of the Isthmus.

But one should not expect to find too many signs of the old Syrian cult of Melqart in Isthmia. No doubt, the cult had been thoroughly Hellenized, a process which could have begun even before the cult was introduced to Isthmia. Elements of Greek hero cult as well as mystery features are clearly present in the cult of Melikertes. The boy Melikertes, assumed to be dead and alive in his sanctuary, is worshipped like a Greek founding hero. Athletes and musicians coming to the games swear their oaths by Melikertes in a mystery ceremony of initiation and enthusiasm (Aelius Aristides speaks of τελετή and ὀργιασμός).[60]

What is the role of myth as it relates to the cult of Melikertes? The establishment of the cult is clearly the primary event; to this cult belong the ritual, the institution of the games, and the mystery celebration with its initiation. The myth is the vehicle of communication that justifies the existence of the cult. It utilizes fragments from older Greek mythology, that is, from the religious language that will be understood in Greece, of which Isthmia is a part. In its most complete form, the myth is a secondary compilation that has benefited from the religious syncretism of the early Roman imperial period. Although the myth appears to be old, everything in it that matters is new: the arrival of the cult here from the sea on a dolphin, the god who is both dead and alive, and finally, the name Melikertes.

---

58. On Melqart, see Karl Preisendanz, "Melkart," Pauly-Wissowa, RESuppl. 6. 293–97; Hartmut Gese, "Die Religion Altsyriens', in Preisendanz, Maria Höfner, Kurt Rudolph, *Die Religionen Altsyriens, Altarabiens und der Mandäer,* Die Religionen der Menschheit 10,2 (Stuttgart: W. Kohlhammer, 1970) 1–232; cf. p. 194 on the spread of the Melqart cult in the western Mediterranean, p. 196 on the iconography of Melqart.

59. The large classical altar of Poseidon (40 m. in length) was destroyed by Mummius in 146 BCE and never rebuilt (Broneer, *Isthmia*, 1. 98–101). There is a Roman foundation further to the east of the temple and a few meters to the south; i.e., not centered on the axis of the temple. It is assumed that this was the foundation of the Roman altar of Poseidon (Broneer, *Isthmia*, 2. 73–74), though the location is very strange for an altar of the Poseidon temple. In any case, this Roman foundation was situated under the floor of the East Stoa that was built in the second century CE.

60. Aelius Aristides, p. 375 ed. Keil; cf. Plutarch *Theseus* 25: nocturnal celebrations with cultic hymns.

4. The Origin of Gnostic Religion
and the Gospel of John

According to the paradigm of the myth of Melikertes, we cannot expect to discover the origin of Gnosticism by means of a reconstruction of the original Gnostic myth. Rather, one has to find a specific community with its cult and religious institutions in which a Gnostic interpretation of ritual and tradition appears. Only then will it be possible to ask how myth justifies and communicates such Gnostic interpretation of an already existing cult with its traditions. In the following, I discuss the rise of myth on the basis of a gnosticizing interpretation of cult and tradition in the Johannine community, that is, in the historical process that eventually resulted in the composition of the Gospel of John and related documents, such as the Johannine Epistles and the *Acts of John*.

In the analysis of this historical process, it would not be advisable to presuppose the existence of a Gnostic myth. But one can presuppose certain more general factors that have played a role in the development of religions in the early Roman imperial period. These presuppositions are closely related to, if not identical with, those that made the development of the new cult of Palaimon-Melikertes in Isthmia possible: The migration of people to new places of residence that brought them into contact with other religious traditions and their cults and mythical lore; the impetus for a new syncretism that arose in the time of Augustus and is related to his political universalism (clearly present in the works of the Roman poets Virgil and Ovid with their deliberate religious syncretism); the hero cult and the veneration of the divine man; the tendency to understand religious performances as mystery rites; and, finally, the pervasive dualism, whether in its Platonic-philosophical or in its oriental-mythological form.

But while all these factors are general presuppositions that determine the entire cultural milieu, the actual story must begin with a specific group, the disciples and followers of Jesus of Nazareth who soon emerged as a special group within the early Christian movement. More research has made it possible to determine with a certain degree of probability the several stages of the development and history of this "Community of the Beloved Disciple" and of its traditions.[61]

The earliest stage seems to be represented by a number of traditional pieces that show Jesus in controversy with his Jewish opponents, comparable with some of the Synoptic apophthegmata. The question discussed in these oldest units is often that of Jesus' authority, whether it is confirmed by 'scripture' or by Moses and Abraham (e.g., John 5:38–40, 45–47; 8:31–50, also some material used in John 9). These units must have been formulated while the disciples of Jesus were still part of the Jewish synagogue.[62]

At the second stage one finds traditions which reflect that the community has been separated from the Jewish synagogue; there is reference to excommunication from the

---

61. Raymond E. Brown, *The Community of the Beloved Disciple* (New York: Paulist Press, 1979); Oscar Cullmann, *The Johannine Circle: Its Place in Judaism, among the Disciples of Jesus, and in Early Christianity* (London: S.C.M. Press, 1976).

62. For the use of such older traditions in the Gospels of John, see my essays "Apocryphal and Canonical Gospels," and "Gnostic Sayings and Controversy Traditions in John 8:12–59," which are both included in this volume, pp. 3–23 and pp. 184–96.

synagogue (9:22)—and subsequently this community also may have moved to a new geographical location. At this point, the disciples began to form their own cultic structures: baptism and Eucharist. There can be no doubt that these "sacraments" were celebrated, because too much of the discussion preserved in the Fourth Gospel is concerned with their understanding and interpretation (John 3; 6; 15). Two characteristic genres of traditions are developed at this stage: (1) the miracle stories and (2) the sayings of Jesus.

The miracle stories are religious propaganda materials that demonstrate that the community had moved into the Hellenistic world beyond the confines of the Jewish synagogue. They go beyond the miracle stories of the Synoptic Gospels by incorporating, in typical syncretistic fashion, a story that originally belonged to the Greek god Dionysus (the wine miracle at Cana, John 2:1-11). In these stories, Jesus is indeed the divine being walking on the earth, a god who has supernatural insights (cf. the story of Jesus and the Samaritan Woman, John 4) and who even commands the dead (the raising of Lazarus, John 11).

Sayings of Jesus may have served, at least initially, as community regulations. They are concerned with the sacraments: there is a saying on baptism (John 3:3, 5), probably sayings on the bread from heaven, and the true vine (John 6; 15). There are also sayings about conduct (walking in the light, John 11:9–10 and so forth and loving each other) and community authority (John 13:16). But there is also a peculiar group of sayings that is concerned with the question of finding salvation:

If you remain in my word, you will truly be my disciples, and you will know the truth, and the truth will make you free (John 8:31–32).

or:

Those who drink from the water that I give them, will never thirst into eternity (John 4:14).

or:

Whosoever keeps my word, will not see death into eternity (John 8:51).

or:

I am going to the one who sent me; you will seek me and not find me (John 7:33).

All these sayings are wisdom sayings in which Jesus speaks with the voice of heavenly Wisdom. It is remarkable that there are frequent parallels to these Johannine sayings in the *Gospel of Thomas,* where wisdom sayings in which Jesus speaks also predominate.[63]

The next stage of the development in the Johannine community is visible in the

---

63. See n. 62 above; also Raymond E. Brown, "The Gospel of Thomas and St. John's Gospel," *NTS* 9 (1962–63) 155–77.

process of the interpretation of these sayings of Jesus. It can be demonstrated that the typical Johannine discourses and dialogues are the result of an interpretation of traditional sayings. The texts from Nag Hammadi have brought to light three writings in which the process of the development of such discourses and dialogues can be observed: the *Gospel of Thomas,* the *Dialogue of the Savior,* and the *Apocryphon of James.*

In this interpretation of sayings, the question of Gnosis arises for the first time. Initially it appears in simple modifications of the traditional saying. The baptismal saying that is quoted in John 3:3 is preserved in its most original form by Justin Martyr (*1 Apol.* 61): "Unless you are reborn (ἀναγεννηθῆτε) you cannot enter the kingdom of God." In John the saying is subtly changed: "Unless someone is born *from above* (γεννηθῆ ἄνωθεν), one cannot *see* the kingdom of God."[64] The saying about walking in the light (John 11:9–10) has been altered in its last clause: "If someone walks in the night, he stumbles, because the light is not *in him.*"

More obvious and explicit is the tendency toward a gnosticizing interpretation in longer dialogues that were developed on the basis of traditional sayings. The *Dialogue of the Savior* has preserved several units of this type that demonstrate the Gnostic tendency of this interpretation. One passage from this writing from Nag Hammadi is a dialogical interpretation of a traditional saying about entering the place of life (132, 2–19):[65]

Jesus said: "... and enter the place of life in order that he might not be confined in this impoverished world."

Matthew said: "Lord, I wish to see that place of life, that place in which there is no evil, but rather it is pure light."

The Lord said: "Brother Matthew, you cannot see it, as long as you wear the flesh."

Matthew said: "Lord, even if I cannot see it, let me know it."

The Lord said: "Everyone who has known himself, has seen it; everything that is fitting for him to do, he does it, and he has been doing it in his goodness."[66]

The parallels of this passage to John 14:2–12 are evident. Also in John, the dialogue begins with a statement of Jesus about the place of light ("the mansions in the house of the father"); a request "to see" follows: Philip says: "show us the father." And also in John there is a final statement of Jesus about the works: "Whoever believes in me will also do the works that I do." Equally evident are the differences: there is no parallel in

---

64. Note that the repetition of the saying in John 3:5, which explicitly refers to the birth through baptism ("through the water and the spirit"), also preserves the more original wording: "Unless someone is born ..., one cannot *enter* the kingdom of God." With most exegetes, I believe that ὕδατος καί is part of the original text.

65. I have discussed this passage in more detail in my article "Dialogue and the Tradition of Sayings in the Gnostic Texts of Nag Hammadi," included in this volume.

66. The reconstruction of this fragmentary text is problematic.

the *Dialogue of the Savior* to the Ἐγώ εἰμι-saying of Jesus "I am the way and the truth and the life" (John 14:6). Another difference appears at the end of the dialogue. The *Dialogue of the Savior* defines the true "seeing" in a typical Gnostic way as the knowledge of one's true self out of which the works of one's own goodness are flowing. The Gospel of John, however, states that "seeing" is believing in Jesus and that the resulting works repeat the works which Jesus has done.

I would assign the dialogue as it is preserved in the *Dialogue of the Savior* to an earlier stage of the development, John 14 to a later stage. At the earlier stage of the interpretation of the sayings, Jesus is not the redeemer or savior, but the teacher, exemplar, and leader. There is no redeemer myth. Rather, the interpretation speaks about the divine origin of the true human self and the recognition of this true self as it is mediated through Jesus' words. The sacraments are interpreted in the same way: baptism is the true water that Jesus gives (John 4:14; 7:37–38); the Eucharist is the true bread that has come down from heaven which Jesus gives (John 6:27, 32).

Not until the next stage in the development of these dialogue materials is Jesus seen as the redeemer and savior. This stage is present in the conscious christological interpretation of older dialogue traditions by the author of the Gospel of John. It is important to dismiss once and for all the hypothesis that the Ἐγώ εἰμι-sayings of the Gospel of John are traditional Gnostic formulation.[67] On the contrary, throughout the Fourth Gospel they are formulations of the evangelist. Older sayings used in these Johannine Ἐγώ εἰμι-sentences were originally formulated in the second or third person. Some of these are still preserved in the Gospel of John in this more original form, for example, the saying about walking in the light (John 11:9–10; 12:35–36). But the form in which it appears in John 8:12—"I am the light of the world"—has been created by the author of the gospel. It must be noted that sayings in this Ἐγώ εἰμι form are extremely rare in the Gnostic dialogues and sayings of the *Gospel of Thomas*, the *Dialogue of the Savior*, and the *Apocryphon of James*.

The redeemer figure and its myth of the Son who has come down from heaven, who *is* the bread of life, the true light, the way, and the resurrection in a unique sense, and who accomplishes his task of salvation in his glorification on the cross is, therefore, the critical Johannine answer to the Gnostic interpretation of the traditional sayings of Jesus. Only at this stage are the ingredients ready for the development of a Gnostic version of this redeemer myth, a new myth that communicates and justifies the religious experience of alienation and other-worldly salvation.

This process took place within the Johannine community—but not only here—as a consequence of the continuing controversies between the Gnostic interpreters of Jesus' sayings and of the sacraments on the one side, and on the other side, those who believed in Jesus as the savior who died on the cross. The *Acts of John* have developed a

---

67. This is a widespread assumption. Rudolf Bultmann, in his commentary on the Gospel of John (*Das Evangelium des Johannes* [Göttingen: Vandenhoeck & Ruprecht, 1941 (1st of 18 eds.)]; English translation: *The Gospel of John: A Commentary* [Philadelphia: Westminster Press, 1971]) used these sayings as a key element in the reconstruction of the source of Gnostic revelation discourses. Johannes Becker (*Die Reden des Johannesevangeliums und der Stil der Gnostischen Offenbarungsrede* [FRLANT 68; Göttingen: Vandenhoeck & Ruprecht, 1956]) makes them a standard introduction of the "Gnostic kerygma."

myth of the Gnostic Jesus who did not really take on human flesh and never really died, but is *deus praesens,* the lord of the dance of salvation in whose mysterious ritual the Gnostics know themselves as they become who he *is* and always has been. On the other hand, the First Epistle of John protests: "Whoever does not confess that Jesus Christ has come *in the flesh,* is not from God" (1 John 4:1–2).[68]

But analogous processes of the development of Gnostic myth took place also in other religious communities, Christian, Jewish, and pagan—wherever adherents of a specific religious tradition discovered that salvation could be found in the gnosis of their own ultimate divine self. In Jewish Gnosticism, the resulting myth utilizes materials from a syncretistic Genesis interpretation in which the creation story had already been re-mythologized with the help of Babylonian astrology and in which Sabaoth had already been identified with the lion-headed Yaldabaoth-Saturn. This Gnostic Genesis interpretation found the symbolic-mythical prototype of the true Gnostic in such figures as Seth and Norea. A number of only superficially Christianized writings from Nag Hammadi give rich evidence for this myth-creating process of Gnosticism which took place in syncretistic Jewish circles.[69]

Was there an original Gnostic religion with its original pre-Christian myth? The answer to this question must be negative. But there certainly were Gnostic religions and gnosticizing interpretations of religious traditions and mythical materials, pre-Christian and Christian, Jewish, and pagan. They may have been committed to different cults, and they developed different myths because in each instance, as also in the case of Melikertes in Isthmia, the formation of such myth is the result of the interpretation of quite different materials, traditions, writings, and rituals. All share common presuppositions that are characteristic for the late Hellenistic and early Roman imperial period. And all these Gnostic religions, in spite of the vast differences of the materials they interpret, exhibit a high degree of affinity and congeniality. It is therefore quite legitimate to speak of the phenomenon of "Gnosis" in general, as we also speak of the phenomenon of mystery religion or imperial cult, although these terms are generalizations that comprise a large number of religions with their distinct cults, rituals, and traditions.

But the protest of the history-of-religions school against Albrecht Ritschl should be remembered. Just as Christian religion, in the early Christian period as well as today, cannot be grasped in the abstraction of a theological and cultural system, Gnostic religion in its origin and development cannot be understood through the reconstruction of a general system in mythological and philosophical terms, but only in the analysis of Gnostic interpretations of the traditions of myth and cult in specific religious communities.

---

68. Cf. also 2 John 7; Polycarp *Phil.* 7.1.

69. E.g., *The Hypostasis of the Archons* (NHC 2,4), *The Apocryphon of John* (NHC 3,1, etc.), *The Apocalypse of Adam* (NHC 5,5).

9

HISTORY AND CULT IN
THE GOSPEL OF JOHN AND
IN IGNATIUS OF ANTIOCH

I. The Problem

Few men of the first hundred years of Christianity have as much in common as do the author of the Gospel of John and Ignatius of Antioch. They use nearly the same language; they employ closely related terminology; and in their theological thought, both are apparently influenced by Gnosticism. Moreover, both stand in close proximity in time—the Gospel of John was written shortly before the turn of the century; the epistles of Ignatius one or two decades after the turn of the century—and both probably come from the same geographical vicinity, that is, from Syria.[1]

There is less certainty with regard to the question of literary relationship. Did Ignatius know the Gospel of John? Is it possible to prove the presence of quotations? Until the beginning of the twentieth century the answer to this question was almost always affirmative, for example, Dietrich Völter: "The acquaintance of the author (of the epistles of Ignatius) . . . with the Fourth Gospel can be taken as absolutely certain."[2] However, since the investigation of von der Goltz,[3] the opposite opinion has prevailed: "Even though the Fourth Gospel already existed, which cannot be doubted, the bishop of Antioch did not know it, in any case did not know it in such a way that his mode of thinking could be traced back to the fact that he had read it." This is the way von der Goltz formulates his solution, and most scholars have followed suit, while at the same time emphasizing the common history-of-religions background more strongly.[4]

A major investigation of this subject comes from Christian Maurer.[5] Maurer tries to make the hypothesis of a literary dependence again respectable. He argues that Ignatius is combining various passages from the Synoptic Gospels, from John, and from Paul, and it is for this reason that it is so difficult to recognize that real quotations are involved

---

1. For John, see Walter Bauer, *Das Johannesevangelium* (HNT 6; Tübingen: Mohr/Siebeck, 1933) 243–44.

2. Dietrich Völter, *Die Apostolischen Väter neu untersucht* (Leiden: Brill, 1910) 112; similar conclusions were reached by Ferdinand Christian Baur, Adolf Hilgenfeld, G. Volkmar, Heinrich Julius Holtzmann, Bernhard Weiss, Theodor Zahn, and J. B. Lightfoot.

3. Eduard von der Goltz, *Ignatius von Antiochien als Christ und Theologe* (TU 12, 3; Leipzig: Hinrichs, 1894).

4. E.g., Walter Bauer, Gerhard Krüger (in Edgar Hennecke, *Neutestamentliche Apokryphen* [Göttingen: Vandenhoeck & Ruprecht, 1904]); Heinrich Schlier, Hans Werner Bartsch, and Rudolf Bultmann.

5. Christian Maurer, *Ignatius von Antiochien und das Johannesevangelium* (Zürich: Zwingli, 1949).

here. For Maurer, Ignatius's literary dependence upon the Gospel of John is, however, beyond question, once his method of conflating quotations has been clarified. On the other hand, Maurer now puts the emphasis upon the essential difference between the two writers, also with respect to their history-of-religions background. The dividing line between gospel and Gnosticism separates John and Ignatius. Whereas John is still completely filled with the "Old Testament spirit of the Bible," Ignatius is proclaiming a Christian Gnosis and a Christian Mysterion.

Inasmuch as Maurer's hypothesis regarding Ignatius's method of conflating quotations is contestable, the question of the literary relationship of John and Ignatius remains uncertain even after his investigation. This problem will not be pursued here.[6] It appears to me, however, that in principle, Maurer is quite right in his emphasis upon the fundamental and essential difference between John and Ignatius.[7] Yet, Maurer's formula for this difference is much too simple. As much as John does not think simply in "Old Testament" terms, Ignatius is not just a representative of Gnosticism. It is necessary to add, moreover, that such a classification does not automatically imply a theological judgment of the subject matter. One certainly has to recognize the shades of difference in their history-of-religions background. But this does not mean that it is possible to explain the terminological relations as literary dependence and to deny flatly the proximity in terms of history-of-religions background. After all, an essential difference does not have to result exclusively from a difference in history-of-religions motives and thought forms. Such essential differences also might result from a difference in decision with respect to theological questions in each case.

In my opinion, Ernst Fuchs has correctly grasped the basic intention that is consistently carried through in the Gospel of John: "He (the evangelist) has seen that theology is not permitted to put the problem of the historical past of Jesus into parenthesis . . . , but that theology must be developed on the basis of the distance of faith from the historical Jesus."[8]

That is a "theological" question that enables us, as I believe, to lay open an important difference between John and Ignatius, precisely in view of their strong relationship in terminology and history-of-religions background. How did the author of the Gospel of John solve this problem of the distance from the historical Jesus? Did Ignatius see this problem at all? How did he solve it? In the same way in which the author of the Gospel of John solved it? Or do fundamental differences appear here?

Taking this formulation of the question as the starting point, I will examine two topics in John and Ignatius: 1) the work of Jesus and its appropriation; 2) the unity of

---

6. Cf. the critical review of Ernst Käsemann, "Ein neutestamentlicher Überblick," *VuF* (1951–52) 205–7, and the favorable evaluation of Eduard Schweizer, review of Christian Maurer, *Ignatius von Antiochien und das Johannesevangelium, ThZ* 5 (1949) 463–66.

7. One should not overemphasize the fact that literary knowledge and essential misunderstanding always go hand in hand in Ignatius. On the contrary, it is certainly true that with respect to the relationship of Ignatius to Paul, Ignatius knew and made full use of the Pauline Epistles and at the same time, he understood and interpreted Paul very well and much better than many others, as Bultmann has shown in his essay "Ignatius and Paul," in Schubert M. Ogden, ed., *Existence and Faith* (New York: Meridian, 1960) 267–77.

8. Ernst Fuchs, *Hermeneutik* (Bad Cannstatt: Müllerschön, 1954) 242.

the church and Christian existence. The concern here is primarily to contribute to the understanding of the Gospel of John rather than focusing upon Ignatius. The latter will be referred to only as an example of a theological point of view that is quite similar in appearance, but in reality is rather different.[9]

II. The Redeemer in Ignatius and John

Ignatius is capable of describing the work of the Redeemer in the colors and terms of the Gnostic myth, as he does most noticeably in *Ephesians* 19.[10] The virginity and parturition of Mary as well as the death of the Lord are secret facts of which the ruler of this aeon does not receive any knowledge. It is only with the ascension of the Redeemer that the accomplished work of salvation is made known. From then on, all works of the old dominion are in the state of dissolution: "Witchcraft, bond of evil, ignorance, death" (μαγεία, δεσμὸς κακίας, ἄγνοια, and θάνατος).[11]

This Gnostic cosmological aspect of salvation shows similarities throughout with the statements of the Gospel of John, although the latter lacks a coherent myth of descent and ascension. But single features of this myth also are present in John: The Son of Man descended from heaven, and he will ascend into heaven again (John 3:13; 6:33, 50, 62; 20:17). Faith in the Redeemer is characterized as "to know" (γινώσκειν; the corresponding negative ἄγνοια does not appear in John). The believer has gone from death into life (John 5:24; 1 John 3:14)—this corresponds to the dissolution of death in Ignatius *Eph.* 19.3.

In the Gospel of John, however, these concepts do not have a cosmological but an existential meaning. Consequently, there is nothing in John that corresponds to "witchcraft" (μαγεία) and "bond of evil" (δεσμὸς κακίας), and nothing is said about the appearance of the star of the ascending Redeemer. The exaltation (δοξασθῆναι) refers to the cross (John 7:39; 12:16 and passim). Whoever sees him who became flesh sees the "glory" (δόξα, John 1:14). This is plainly the fundamental statement of the Gospel.

But such a comparison between Ignatius and John still falls too short, because also for Ignatius, the emphasis is not on the myth of secret descent and spectacular ascension, but similarly on the coming of the Redeemer into the flesh. To be sure, in *Eph.* 19.3, Ignatius speaks only in colorless terms about the "The God who was revealed in a human form" (θεὸς ἀνθρωπίνως φανερουμένος), yet in other places he says, "the God who has become flesh" (ἐν σαρκὶ γενόμενος θεός, *Eph.* 7.2; cf. *Smyrn.* 3) or "the fleshly Christ" (Χριστὸς σαρκικός, *Eph.* 7.2); in kerygmatic formulations also "Christ who is from the seed of David according to the flesh" (Χριστὸς ὁ κατὰ σάρκα ἐκ γέ-

---

9. I make no claim that the details of the following discussion are new. My intention is solely to re-examine the comparison between John and Ignatius under a fresh formulation of the question, with the result that much already said elsewhere must be repeated.

10. See Heinrich Schlier, *Religionsgeschichtliche Untersuchungen zu den Ignatiusbriefen* (BZNW 8; Giessen: Töpelmann, 1929) 5ff.

11. As in Paul in 1 Cor 15:26, "death" is emphasized here by its position at the end.

νους Δαυίδ, *Eph.* 20.2). Ignatius far exceeds the Gospel of John in the frequency of emphasis upon the fleshly appearance of Jesus, even if the ". . . became flesh" (σάρξ ἐγένετο) of John 1:14 is lacking in Ignatius. Yet this unanimity is only an apparent one. "Flesh" (σάρξ) does not mean the same to John and Ignatius.

For Ignatius "flesh" (σάρξ) is a sphere that corresponds to the other sphere of the "spirit" (πνεῦμα). Therefore, the statement of the fleshly appearance of Jesus is always joined together with the other statement of his pneumatic existence:

Eph. 7.2:
There is one physician,
both fleshly and spiritual
begotten and unbegotten,
come in flesh, God, in death, true life,
both of Mary and of God,
first passible and then impassible,
Jesus Christ, our Lord.
(εἷς ἰατρός ἐστιν,
σαρκικός τε καὶ πνευματικός,
γεννητὸς καὶ ἀγέννητος,
ἐν σαρκὶ γενόμενος θεός, ἐν θανάτῳ ζωὴ ἀληθινή,
καὶ ἐκ Μαρίας καὶ ἐκ θεοῦ,
πρῶτον παθητὸς καὶ τότε ἀπαθής,
Ἰησοῦς Χριστὸς ὁ κύριος ἡμῶν.)

Smyrn. 3.3:
. . . he ate and drank with hem as a being of flesh,
although spiritually united with the Father.[12]
(. . . συνέφαγεν αὐτοῖς καὶ συνέπιεν ὡς σαρκικός,
καίπερ πνευματικῶς ἡνωμένος τῷ πατρί.)

Even if this terminology is dualistic in origin, the examples presented here (they can easily be multiplied) show that Ignatius's thought is not essentially dualistic, but rather a soteriological "monism." Two spheres, flesh and spirit, things procreated and things unbegotten, man and God, are made a unity in Christ. There is no irreconcilable antagonism like the one that is characteristic of genuine dualism, where the battle is to the end, and the battle cry is irreversible separation. In Ignatius the theme is synthesis and unity, which is present in perfection with the person of the Redeemer who is both flesh and spirit at once. The presupposition for this description of the Redeemer and his work is the Hellenistic concept of substances, which makes possible the thought of a unification of two spheres if they are conceived of as substances. According to Ignatius, this unification has been accomplished in Christ, who being spirit, took on flesh also.

---

12. Translation from William R. Schoedel, *Ignatius of Antioch: A Commentary on the Letters of Ignatius of Antioch* (Hermeneia; Philadelphia: Fortress Press, 1985) 59 and 225. All other translations are mine.

In the Gospel of John, especially in the prologue, a truly dualistic concept seems to appear: the light shines in the darkness, and the darkness did not comprehend it (John 1:5). The statement "light *and* darkness" is impossible for the Gospel of John. The opposites are irreconcilable. Yet the statement about the Logos becoming flesh neither belongs in the categories of such an antithetical dualism nor does it intend to describe the accomplishment of a synthesis as it does in Ignatius.

The term "flesh," rare in the Gospel of John, as a rule is neutral and simply designates the world in terms of the things that are in existence, in terms of that which belongs to humans and to history—but never the world as hostile to God (John 1:14; also 8:15; 17:2).[13] "Flesh" is used in contrast to "spirit" only twice: John 3:6 and 6:63. Both times, however, we are not dealing with a dualistic statement, but with a general maxim about the impossibility of taking possession of the divine by means of natural criteria: It is the spirit that gives life, the flesh is useless.

If "flesh," therefore, is the neutral sphere of that which belongs to humanity and history, the fundamental assertion of John 1:14, "The Word became flesh" (ὁ λόγος σὰρξ ἐγένετο), says that the divine Logos comes into the historical realm of human existence, not to bring about a uniting of metaphysical substances, but to work as the historical word of a historical man.

III. The Work of the Redeemer in Ignatius

As far as the work of the Redeemer is in question, the differences between John and Ignatius lie in the same direction. In Ignatius's epistles, the Redeemer appears to be speechless. Not only is the completion of the three secrets of *Ephesians* 19 (virginity and parturition of Mary, the death of the Lord) brought about in the "silence of God," but also "what he (Christ) has done silently, is worthy of the Father" (*Eph.* 15.1). That indicates that according to Ignatius, the work of Christ is not word, is not address, neither as a whole nor in what he happens to have said;[14] it is rather the accomplishment of a unification of substances, a work that is concerned with metaphysical principles and elements. Consequently he says about Christ: "He was born and baptized in order to purify the water through suffering" (*Eph.* 18.2). Thus the meaning of Jesus' baptism is the consecration of the baptismal water for the Christians.

Above all, his coming in the flesh had the purpose of mediating the sacred food to his people. The Eucharist is the flesh of the Redeemer (*Smyrn.* 7.1). His flesh is the medicine of immortality (*Eph.* 20.2), which is effective because in Christ the unity of flesh and spirit is present. Therefore, whoever eats his flesh partakes of this unity and consequently also of the spirit. Stated paradoxically: "You are made alive through the blood of God" (*Eph.* 1.1); "What I desire is the bread of God, which is the flesh of Jesus Christ, who is of the seed of David; and for drink I desire his blood which is an imperishable meal of love" (*Rom.* 7.3).

---

13. Rudolf Bultmann, *The Gospel of John: A Commentary* (Philadelphia: Westminster, 1971) 60–62.

14. The designation of Jesus as the διδάσκαλος, however, is strikingly rare in Ignatius (only *Eph.* 15.1; *Magn.* 9.1–2); what its meaning is must be discussed in another context.

The appropriation of salvation is possible through sacramental means and possible only in this way. At the same time, one understands why it was a must for Ignatius to argue in terms of a strict anti-docetism. The absolute denial of the fleshliness of Jesus would have implied the impossibility of obtaining salvation, because then the sacrament also would be only a semblance. The ultimate purpose of the mysterious coming of the Redeemer into the flesh, therefore, is not understood in terms of Gnosticism as the deception of the rulers (one is tempted to interpret *Ephesians* 19 in this way at the first reading); it is rather to bring about the unification of flesh and spirit in order to give to those who are flesh the possibility of partaking of the spirit through the sacrament.

IV. Historical or Sacramental Redemption in John?

Returning to the Gospel of John, in chapter 6 we find a number of sentences that seem to fit rather well into Ignatius's understanding of the sacrament and of salvation, to wit, the controversial passage John 6:51b–59. In agreement with Ignatius, these verses designate the Eucharistic bread as the flesh of Jesus: "The bread which I shall give for the life of the world is my flesh" (v. 51b); "He who eats my flesh and drinks my blood has eternal life" (v. 54). The Ignatian term "medicine of immortality" lies within close proximity of this passage. Exegetes have observed and noticed this fact again and again. Indeed, the Eucharistic character of these verses is beyond any doubt.

What is to be doubted, however, is whether these words are an original part of the text of the Gospel of John; these doubts must be raised in spite of attempts to retain them as genuine.[15] Günther Bornkamm[16] takes as his starting point the observation that the offence caused by Jesus' words, which is discussed in John 6:60–63, cannot refer to the questionable passage John 6:51b–59, as many exegetes maintain.[17] Actually, v. 63 is only a maxim that does not say anything with respect to "flesh" as a (sacramental) element, nor anything about Jesus as being "in the flesh." As Jesus' words in v. 62 indicate, the subject matter in question is rather Jesus' claim to be the bread from heaven; v. 62: "What if you now see the Son of Man ascend where he was before?" refers back to v. 50: "This is the bread which has descended from heaven." The verses in which the *flesh* of Jesus is spoken of as the food that gives life are not in view at all. Therefore, in addition to other, older arguments against the authenticity of John 6:51b–59,[18] there is further reason for eliminating these verses. This is how far Bornkamm's argumentation brings us.[19]

Rather, it seems to be necessary to admit that this sacramental passage, John 6:51b–59, characterizes the view of Ignatius and should not be employed for the interpreta-

---

15. Eduard Schweizer has spoken for the genuineness: "Das johanneische Zeugnis vom Herrenmahl," *EvTh* 12 (1952–53) 358–61.

16. Günther Bornkamm, "Die eucharistische Rede im Johannesevangelium," *ZNW* 47 (1956) 161–69.

17. So again, Schweizer, "Das johanneische Zeugnis," 358.

18. Cf. Bultmann, *The Gospel of John* and Ergänzungsheft (1953) on John 6:51–59.

19. At the same time Bornkamm's interpretation shows convincingly that one cannot separate John 6:60 from 6:1–51 as Bultmann has done (*The Gospel of John*, on John 6:60–71).

tion of Johannine thought. It should not be overlooked, however, that even after the elimination of this passage, there remain certain elements in the words about the "bread of life" (ἄρτος τῆς ζωῆς) in John 6 that possibly are determined by cultic language. To be sure, the background may be a metaphor originating in Gnosticism; yet a Christian of the second generation could hardly speak about the "bread of life" without thinking of the Eucharist. First, "bread" in early Christianity is the technical term for the Eucharistic food; second, the comparison of the bread that Jesus gives (or is himself) with the manna of the fathers always occurs in the context of the Eucharist (with John 6:31, 49 compare 1 Cor 10:3–4 and Rev 2:14, 17).

The reference to the Eucharist, however, is not the case in point in the argumentation of John 6. Rather, the discourse only starts from the abovementioned term (bread of life) in order to point in another direction, that is, to the words which Jesus speaks. To the sentence 6:51a: "He who eats of this bread (which has come down from heaven, which I am) will live in eternity," corresponds v. 63b: "The words which I have spoken to you are spirit and life." The case in point is the words of the Revealer who has come into history, the words to which Peter confesses: "You have words of eternal life" (ῥήματα ζωῆς αἰωνίου ἔχεις, 6:68).

V. The Transposition of Cultic Categories into Historical Categories in John

In John 6 we have observed the tendency to appropriate cultic terminology and by means of it to refer back to the revelation that has the character of a historical event. This same tendency also can be noticed in other passages of the Gospel of John.

John 3:5: "Whoever is not born again of water and the spirit cannot enter the Kingdom of God." *Water* and spirit can only refer to baptism. Bultmann also recognizes this.[20] In his opinion, however, "of water" (ἐξ ὕδατος) is a later addition that belongs to the redaction of the church, which subsequently wanted to introduce a connection to baptism into this passage.[21] But is this connection to baptism not present even without this controversial word?

I think the connection with baptism is already quite certain through the phrase "to be born anew/from above" (ἄνωθεν γεννηθῆναι, v. 3), because this expression is obviously formulated with reference to the terms "new birth" (ἀναγέννησις, 1 Pet 1:23) and "rebirth" (παλιγγεννησία, Titus 3:6), terms that are always designations of baptism (cf. λοῦτρον, Titus 3:6). Furthermore, the saying quoted in John 3:3 as the theme for the following discourse also occurs in Justin *1 Apol.* 61.3–4 in a reading that cannot be derived from the Gospel of John: "Unless your are born again you will not enter the kingdom of the heavens" (Ἀν μὴ ἀναγεννηθῆτε, οὐ μὴ εἰσέλθητε εἰς τὴν βασιλείαν τῶν οὐρανῶν), but which apparently depends on older oral tradition.[22] Justin uses the saying as a proof for baptism.

---

20. *The Gospel of John*, 98.
21. Ibid.
22. I refer to the proof offered by Wilhelm Bousset *(Die Evangelienzitate Justins* [Göttingen:Vandenhoeck

Wherever there is mention of "rebirth" in early Christianity, the idea of baptism is always present.[23] This connection would have suggested itself quite naturally and is traditional. It would be present in John 3:3–5 even if "from water" (ἐξ ὕδατος) were not to appear in 3:5. The saying quoted in John 3:3 already apparently contains a reference to baptism. Accordingly, there is no reason to assume that the Evangelist could not possibly also have written ἐξ ὕδατος in 3:5. However, the quest of the Gospel of John is not about the meaning and significance of the element of the sacrament, but about the "Mystery of the Son of Man." This title which Bultmann gives to the section 3:9–21 is very much to the point.[24] It is the Son of Man to whom the community bears witness (3:11: "We bear witness to what we have seen"), that is, the one who has come down from heaven (3:13). Here, too, the witnessing community takes its starting point from the sacrament of baptism only in order to point back to the Word that has become flesh—to the Jesus of history!

On the basis of the understanding of baptism and Eucharist given by John 3 and 6, it also is necessary to interpret the equally controversial passage John 19:34b–35.

Bultmann also tries to solve the difficulty in this passage by a deletion.[25] Verse 34b ("and immediately blood and water flowed out" [καὶ ἐξῆλθεν εὐθὺς αἷμα καὶ ὕδωρ]) and v. 35 as a whole ("and he who has seen it gave witness, and his testimony is true") he considers as additions of the church redactor, who at a later time wanted to tie baptism and Eucharist to the cross by means of an eye-witness. Also, vv. 34b-35 interrupt the connection between the piercing of his side (v. 34a) and the quotation of Zech 12:10 (John 19:36–37) that reflects upon it.

The latter observation is certainly correct. This connection, however, is not typically Johannine. It belongs rather to the narrator whose passion narrative John has used.[26] The Gospel also shows that elsewhere the author of the Gospel of John is accustomed to disrupting a traditional connection, and what has been brought into this passage appears to me to be typically Johannine. It is questionable, however, whether it is really the purpose of this insertion to authenticate the sacrament through the suffering of Jesus.

The phrase "blood and water" (αἷμα καὶ ὕδωρ) and the reference to the witness (ὁ ἑωρακὼς μεμαρτύρηκεν) in John 19 must be compared to the following passages in the First Epistle of John:

1 Jn 3:11: "We give witness to what we have seen" (ὃ ἑωράκαμεν μαρτυροῦμεν).

& Ruprecht, 1891] 116–20), a proof that in my opinion is still valid: It is very doubtful whether Justin knew the Gospel of John. Justin's use of this gospel can in no case be established with any certainty.

23. We should also refer to *Ps.-Clem. Hom.* 9.26.2 (cf. Bousset), where the same saying is quoted in connection with baptism. As in the case of Justin, here, too, εἰς τὴν βασιλείαν τῶν οὐρανῶν (John: τοῦ θεοῦ) and ἀναγεννηθῆναι (John: ἄνωθεν γεννᾶσθαι) speak against dependence on John and for dependence on the free tradition.

24. *The Gospel of John*, 102.

25. Ibid., 525ff.

26. Martin Dibelius has demonstrated this point conclusively in "Die alttestamentlichen Motive in der Leidensgeschichte des Petrus- und Johannesevangeliums," in Dibelius, *Botschaft und Geschichte* (2 vols.; Tübingen: Mohr/Siebeck, 1953–1956) 1. 235–36. Zech 12:10 already must have been applied to the passion before John and independently of him; cf. Rev 1:7; *Barn.* 7.9; etc.

1 Jn 1:2: "And we have seen and we give witness" (καὶ ἑωράκαμεν καὶ μαρτυροῦμεν).

1 Jn 5:7–8: "There are three that give witness: water, blood, and spirit" (τρεῖς εἰσιν οἱ μαρτυροῦντες· ὕδωρ, αἷμα καὶ πνεῦμα).

What is being witnessed here is not the sacrament, but the reality of the historical existence of the Revealer. This is shown by the use of the verb "to witness" in the Gospel and the Epistles of John. For John the concern is not with the sacrament that also can be conceived of apart from the historical reality of salvation. Jesus is not merely the one who brings the water of life ("not only in the water," οὐκ ἐν τῷ ὕδατι μόνον, 1 John 5:6), but he who has come through water and blood, that is, he who really was and who really suffered. In this way the Evangelist points from the sacramental term back to the reality of history.

The Evangelist and the author of 1 John are not aiming at sacramental participation, but rather at the recognition that the historical Jesus is the Revealer who brings life. This recognition is given by the "spirit." Therefore "the spirit" in 1 John 5 is the third witness. For this reason, even if John 3:5 first formulates "from water and the spirit" (ἐξ ὕδατος καὶ πνεύματος), John 3:8 can say simply, "The one who is born by the spirit" (ὁ γεγεννημένος ἐκ τοῦ πνεύματος).

Our considerations fully confirm what Günther Bornkamm notes with respect to John 19:34–35, namely, that John remains quite within the framework of sacramental concepts.[27] John indeed uses such sacramental concepts and terms, but he employs them in such a way as to point back to the history of Jesus. What corresponds to the sentence, "the word became flesh" (ὁ λόγος σὰρξ ἐγένετο), in the beginning of the Gospel is the remark "and blood and water flowed out" (καὶ ἐξῆλθεν εὐθὺς αἷμα καὶ ὕδωρ) in the conclusion of the Johannine passion narrative.

VI. The Church as a Historical Actuality in John

The spirit bears witness that the Jesus of history is the Revealer; the same spirit, as the Paraclete, recalls this revelation in the flesh. In keeping with this "remembering" of the Paraclete, the narrative of the foot-washing (John 13:1–17) indicates that the Evangelist wants the church to depart from the understanding that the past presence of Jesus simply can be extended into the present in such a way as it is possible in the cult. He refers the church back to the historical "once for all" of Jesus' coming.

The context of the last supper of Jesus is no doubt presupposed in John 13. A reader of the Gospel in that time had to expect that the institution of the sacramental meal would follow after the entry into Jerusalem. Already in the tradition that Paul uses, the institution of the Eucharist by the Lord is placed in the context of the last supper (1 Cor

---

27. Günther Bornkamm, "Das Anathema in der urchristlichen Abendmahlsliturgie," in Bornkamm, *Das Ende des Gesetzes: Paulusstudien* (Munich: Kaiser, 1952) 128–29.

11:23). Thus, the author of John must have known what it meant that the institution of the sacrament was *not* reported at this point.

Obviously the Evangelist consciously avoids making the last meal of Jesus a legend that institutes a cult. In the Fourth Gospel, the service of the historical Jesus takes the place of the institution of the sacrament. This is emphasized in two respects:

First, through the singularity of the service. He who is washed is pure and needs no further washing (John 13:10). This feature probably was already part of the source that John uses here and that polemicized against repeated washings as were practiced, for example, among the Essenes. According to the intention of the Evangelist, however, the concern is not to justify the unrepeatable act of baptism, but to emphasize the "once and for all" of the historical ministry of Jesus. For what takes place in the foot-washing is, to be sure, not the institution of the sacrament of baptism or any other sacrament, but is the symbolization of the service that Jesus does to those who belong to him.

Second, at the same time this service establishes, in a non-sacramental fashion, the new existence of the church and the unity thereby effected. That is what the second interpretation that the Evangelist adds to the foot-washing (vv. 12-17) says: "I have given you an example in order that you do to each other as I have done to you." Divorced from the symbolization through the foot-washing, the same thing is said in John 13:34: "That you love one another as I have loved you, in order that you also love one another." It is this love in which the unity of the church as the disciples of Jesus is founded: "By this all men will know that you are my disciples, if you have love for one another" (John 13:35).

The scene of the designation of the traitor that follows the foot-washing (John 13:18–30) is also intended to avert a sacramental interpretation. Closely associated with the disavowal of the sacramental communion is the repudiation of misconceived effects of the sacrament. The service of Jesus is valid even for the traitor. The notion that this service might have results that come about by way of magic necessity is thereby explicitly excluded. The remark at the conclusion of the discourse on the bread from heaven must be interpreted accordingly: "My words are life and are spirit; but there are some who do not believe; for Jesus knew from the beginning who would betray him" (John 6:64–65, 70–71).

Thus, according to the Evangelist, there is no guarantee for the unity and for the purity of the church. Even the sacrament cannot give this guarantee. There are only words and commands of Jesus with which the church is confronted time and again; they are to be "remembered" by the church, and they call the church to the service of love.

These statements of John 13 are further developed in John 15.[28] The myth of the tree of life probably provides the background for the discourse of the true vine in John 15.[29] The fact, however, that this tree of life is not conceived of as an olive tree, or as an ash

---

28. I am inclined to agree here with Rudolf Bultmann (*The Gospel of John,* 249–50 and 401–2) who places chapter 15 immediately after 13:31–34.

29. Eduard Schweizer, *Ego Eimi* (FRLANT n.s. 38; Göttingen: Vandenhoeck & Ruprecht, 1939) 39ff.

or pine or any other plant,[30] but precisely as a vine, perhaps points again to a cultic background.

One of the reasons for this assumption is the occurrence of the vine in the Eucharistic prayers in *Did.* 9.2:"We praise you for the holy vine of David which you have made known to us through Jesus, your servant." Second, the image of the vine elucidates the unity of the disciples among themselves and with Jesus. Elsewhere, however, this concept belongs to the Eucharist (1 Corinthians 10, also 11; cf. *Did.* 9.4; furthermore Ignatius, see the following section). Third, the "joy" (χαρά, John 15:11 and passim) also belongs to the context of the concepts associated with the Eucharist.

Through his use of this image, however, the Evangelist does not elucidate the sacramental unity, but rather the unity in the word and in love that has its basis in the love of the human Jesus and in his word. John 15:7:"If you remain in me, my words also will remain among you." John 15:10:"If you keep my commandments, you will remain in my love, because I have kept my Father's commandments and remain in his love." It is on account of this historical work in which the Son is united with the Father that the church lives in love, which is the historical unity of the church's work with Jesus, with his word, and his service. Thus, obedience to the word and acting in this love constitute the unity of the church.

VII. The Cultic Unity of the Church in Ignatius

If in conclusion we look back once more at Ignatius, there emerges a quite different picture.

Here the unity is already arranged beforehand in the one and only Christ, who as the one and only bread, both bodily and spiritually, is always present as the foundation of the church. His existence is focused upon, not in terms of history but in terms of metaphysics. This by no means excludes the fact that the church is addressed in the imperative mode, just as it also includes the aspiration of the martyr to imitate in his own fate the fate of the Redeemer in order to achieve the final perfection of this unity. The road of the martyr, however, remains an "exceptional case." What is true for the martyr is not at the same time a demand directed to all Christians. These, nevertheless, have all reached perfection in the unity of the church, when they gather together with one mind in obedience to the bishop, in one faith, one prayer, one hope, and at one altar, to break one bread that is the medicine of immortality (*Eph.* 20.2; *Magn.* 7.1–2; *Phld.* 4 and passim).

This unity of the church is the presupposition for everything else. It is guaranteed solely through community with the bishop. Those who do anything without the bishop are serving the devil (*Smyrn.* 9.1). Only those who are within the boundaries of the realm of the altar are "pure," that is, in unity with the bishop and the board of presbyters (*Trall.* 7.2). How differently purity is defined in John! According to Ignatius, it is as a

---

30. Bultmann, *The Gospel of John*, 407 n. 6.

consequence of this unity that love comes into existence (*Magn.* 6.2), and not the other way around.

With this sacramental unity, all attacks of Satan are in vain. If gatherings of the congregation are held frequently, all attacks of Satan fail because of this unity of faith (*Eph.* 13.1). Heretics are those who stay away from the Eucharist and from prayer (*Smyrn.* 7.1). For Ignatius this argument is quite consistent and authentic; for it concerns people who do not confess that Christ has come in the flesh, that is to say, who therefore would have no interest in the cultic documentation of the flesh of Christ. Thus, for Ignatius also, what continues to be the criterion for heresy is christology, and by no means a self-appointed concept of unity with the bishop.

This, however, should not be allowed to mislead us. Actually, if Ignatius holds on to the concept that Jesus was in the flesh, he is holding on to something quite different from what the author of the Gospel of John expounds as the content of the statement that the Word became flesh in Jesus. To be sure, the terminology and history-of-religions motifs of John and Ignatius are closely related; anti-docetism is also common to both authors. But in John it is the once-and-for-all historical event that is placed against docetism; in Ignatius, however, it is the supra-historical Henosis of flesh and spirit, understood in terms of metaphysics, extended into the sacrament, as Christ is truly in the flesh even after his resurrection and is not a "bodiless demon" (*Smyrn.* 3).[31] John also maintains, to be sure, that Christ is in the flesh after the resurrection, but he places such an emphasis side by side with the sentence: "Blessed are those who do not see and yet believe!" (John 20:29). He is thus taking seriously the historical distance of the believing church from the Jesus of history, and he solely trusts the word that alone is capable of making past history present. Of this historical distance, Ignatius is quite unaware because to begin with, he understands the event of salvation in terms of metaphysics rather than in terms of history.

If the sacrament is thus understood in metaphysical terms as a *Christus prolongatus*, the cult as such gains ultimate significance and with it also the bishop who demands obedience. As a consequence, the only possibility that remains is the service of the altar and submission. Faith and love are only a subsequent effect. Ignatius has thereby sacrificed everything that constitutes the essence of a historical revelation, that is, the knowledge that there is a claim of Jesus on my history and that there is a ministry of the history of Jesus for my sake that constitutes my own existence in history. Only in the way in which John understands it is Christian existence able to remain an existence of obedience to the word and of the service of love. Only if understood as the appeal to the historical service of the Jesus of history can the cult represent the demand of a historical act of salvation.

---

31. With respect to the difference in terms of history-of-religions perspectives, it is necessary to point out that John's dualistic concept of realms has been replaced in Ignatius by a metaphysical concept that thinks in terms of substances.

10

THE STORY OF
THE JOHANNINE TRADITION

This chapter is an attempt to tell a story.[1] Instead of beginning with the text of the Fourth Gospel and then proceeding analytically to identify sources and older traditions, I shall start where it all began. Thus I shall try to depict the development of traditions in the Johannine community from its beginnings to the writing of the gospel that is ascribed to "John."[2]

Beginnings

We cannot be sure about the name of the apostle who founded the community in which this gospel was formed. The tradition of the later second century knows this writing as the Gospel of John and claims that Jesus' disciple, John the son of Zebedee, produced it in Ephesus.[3] However, there is nothing in the Fourth Gospel itself that could corroborate this later tradition. Even if Jesus' disciple John was the founder of the community, he was not the author of the Fourth Gospel in any form. In the circles of his own friends, the founder of the community was probably known as "the disciple whom Jesus loved." Perhaps this was the same John whom Paul met in Jerusalem at the occasion of the Apostles' Council (48/49 CE) as one of the "Three Pillars" (Gal 2:1-10). It is interesting that, like Peter, he is no longer mentioned at Paul's final visit to Jerusalem (56 or 58 CE); then it is only James, the brother of Jesus, with whom Paul negotiates about the acceptance of the collection from the Gentile churches (Acts 21:18). What had happened to Peter and John by this time?

We have some information about Peter and what he did after leaving Jerusalem. I am not referring to the tradition that connects Peter with the Roman church, although it may be true that Peter finally went to Rome where he was martyred, and indeed the

---

1. I ask the reader's indulgence that the following notes refer repeatedly to some of my own previous publications: the current chapter is an attempt to tell the whole "story" of the Johannine tradition as it seemed to emerge on the basis of some of my previous, more analytical attempts.

2. A different view of the history of the Johannine tradition was presented by Raymond E. Brown, *The Community of the Beloved Disciple* (New York: Paulist Press, 1979). I am nevertheless indebted to this work. Some of my arguments have been presented in my book, *Ancient Christian Gospels: Their History and Development* (Philadelphia: Trinity Press International, 1991) 250–71.

3. Irenaeus is the first author who says that this gospel was written by "John the disciple of the Lord . . . when he was living in Ephesus" (*Haer.* 3.11 = Eusebius *Hist. eccl.* 5.8.4).

First Epistle of Peter and the *Acts of Peter* claim that Peter was present in Rome. An older and more persistent tradition, however, connects Peter with Western Syria. Paul met Peter in Antioch shortly after the Apostles' Council (Gal. 2:11); the Gospel of Mark—in my opinion a writing from Syria[4]—locates the confession of Peter in Caesarea Philippi, north of Galilee (Mark 8:27–33). Matthew, certainly at home in Western Syria, adds to this Markan pericope a local tradition about the "power of the keys" that were entrusted to Peter (Matt 16:17–19). The *Gospel of Thomas*, also at home in Syria, preserves a tradition that juxtaposes Peter, Matthew, and Thomas (*Gos. Thom.* 13)— immediately after mentioning James of Jerusalem (*Gos. Thom.* 12). There are additional witnesses from the second century. Several writings from Syria claim Peter as their author: the *Kerygma of Peter*, the *Gospel of Peter*, and the *Revelation of Peter*. Moreover, the Jewish-Christian tradition of Syria has preserved a very close connection between Peter and Jesus' brother James.

When we turn to John, we find no traces of a comparable tradition. The connection of John the son of Zebedee with Ephesus is certainly secondary, just like the tradition that connects Peter to Rome. Although Irenaeus claims that Polycarp, bishop of Smyrna, knew this John in Ephesus, one looks in vain for any trace of knowledge of the Johannine writings in Polycarp's own letter. We are thus totally dependent upon internal evidence from the Fourth Gospel itself, and here all relevant data point to the realm of Southern Syria/Palestine.

1. The regions of this area, especially Galilee, Samaria, and the country east of the Jordan are frequently named in this gospel; individual place names, moreover, show that at least the traditions behind the Fourth Gospel, and perhaps even the author himself, were well acquainted with this geographical area.[5]

2. John 4 speaks not only about the conversion of the Samaritans (John 4:39–42) but also reports that the "Galileans had accepted Jesus" (John 4:45). The inhabitants of Judea, however, are normally depicted as hostile throughout the gospel. Note that οἱ Ἰουδαῖοι in this gospel should not be translated as "the Jews" but as "the Judeans," that is, the people from Judea and Jerusalem. To be sure, at the time of the writing of the gospel at the end of the first century, these "Judeans" were no longer in Jerusalem but had become the leaders of the newly forming, rabbinic Judaism in Galilee.

3. "Excommunication from the synagogue" (being made ἀποσυναγωγός) is mentioned in the New Testament exclusively in the Gospel of John (John 9:22; 12:42; 16:2). This technical term was developed during the reorganization of rabbinic Judaism after the fall of Jerusalem; that is, in the last decades of the first century. At this early time, however, it was hardly known outside Galilee and its environs

---

4. See my *Ancient Christian Gospels*, 289–92.

5. See the relevant commentaries on the passages in John in which place names occur; e.g., John 1:28 (Bethania beyond the Jordan), 1:44 (Bethsaida), 2:1 (Cana), 4:5 (Sychar in Samaria), 5:2 (Bethzatha in Jerusalem), and 11:54 (Ephraim).

because the influence of the rabbinic synagogue had not yet spread into other areas, even though it must have been strong in Galilee itself. If all the passages of the gospel in which excommunication from the synagogue is mentioned come from the hand of the final author of the Fourth Gospel; the author himself, as well as the tradition of his church, must have been at home in the northern regions of Palestine, if not in Galilee itself.

4. In John 1:47, Nathanael is called "a true Israelite in whom there is no deceit."[6] No doubt, the claim that Jesus' followers were the true Israelites was made outside Palestine (Gal 6:16), and recourse to the authority of Moses (John 5:45–46; 9:28–29) could also appear among Christians anywhere. Only in the Gospel of John, however, are these claims explicitly connected with an attempt to reconcile the two most important groups of Israel in Palestine itself, namely, the Judeans and the Samaritans (see especially John 4:20–23). The reconciliation of Jews and Gentiles, although not absent,[7] plays only a minor role. The author of the gospel also knows that this reconciliation was successful to a certain degree only between the Galileans and the Samaritans, while the Judeans and their leaders reestablished themselves in an explicit rejection of Jesus' followers, whom they even excommunicated from their synagogues.

The Tradition of the Words of Jesus

What was it that enabled these followers of Jesus to offer an alternative through which the seemingly irreconcilable enmity between the two major heirs of Israel's tradition, the Judeans and the Samaritans, could be overcome?

Four different types of traditions appear in the Fourth Gospel: (1) the miracle stories from the Semeia Source, (2) the passion narrative, (3) some Gnostic materials, and (4) discourses and dialogues that were developed on the basis of the sayings of Jesus.[8] I presuppose the observation that each of these traditions or sources at first had its own history and was developed independently, but there must have been crossovers and connections among them before the Gospel of John was composed in the form that we know. No doubt these different traditions and sources played a role in the Johannine community before the gospel was composed. I shall begin the discussion of these tra-

---

6. That Jesus is subsequently addressed as "King of Israel" (John 1:49) and that the following statement (John 1:51) alludes to the dream of Jacob's ladder suggests that Jesus as "the Son of Man" is indeed himself "Israel."

7. It is not clear whether the "Greeks" (Ἕλληνες) of John 12:20 are Gentiles or Greek-speaking Israelites from the diaspora.

8. On the question of sources in the Gospel of John, see the extensive discussion by Raymond E. Brown, *The Gospel According to John* (2 vols.; AB 29–30; Garden City, N.J.: Doubleday, 1966–1970) 1. xxiv–xl; Dwight Moody Smith, *The Composition and Order of the Fourth Gospel* (New Haven: Yale University Press, 1965); idem, "The Sources of the Gospel of John: An Assessment of the Present State of the Problem," *NTS* 10 (1963/64) 336–51.

ditions with the complex of the sayings of Jesus and the development of dialogues and discourses.

Individual sayings of Jesus that appear in the Johannine discourses sometimes have parallels in the Synoptic Sayings Source and, more frequently, in the *Gospel of Thomas*. As a whole, however, the Johannine tradition of Jesus' sayings is more closely related to the *Gospel of Thomas* in so far as it is dominated by an interpretation that considers Jesus' words as the only and fully sufficient source of eternal life. Thus, the saying in John 8:51 and its variant in 8:52:

Whoever keeps my word will not see death in eternity,

Whoever keeps my word will not taste death in eternity,

has a parallel in the *Gospel of Thomas* (Logion 1):

Whoever finds the interpretation of these words will not taste death.

Discipleship is also described in very similar words:

If you remain in my word, you will truly be my disciples and you will recognize the truth . . . (John 8:31)

If you become my disciples and listen to my words, these stones will serve you . . . *(Gos. Thom.* 19b)

The most important problem in the interpretation of these words is the question of their connection with the person of Jesus. In John, in the Synoptic Sayings Source, and in the *Gospel of Thomas,* wherever this question appears, it is answered without recourse either to Jesus' works or to his death and resurrection.

In the Synoptic Sayings Source, Jesus represents the eschatological appearance of heavenly wisdom, and as the disciples listen to his words, they are requested to make this wisdom present in their own conduct. Such conduct is opposed to the existing norms of the society; it therefore also includes freedom from the Law. The later redaction of the Synoptic Sayings Source,[9] which added the Son of Man sayings, explained the relationship to Jesus in a different way: Jesus is now also the Son of Man who will return in the near future for judgment over "this generation."[10] In both recensions of the Synoptic Sayings Source, it is not the individual who is addressed and called, but a group of people who understand themselves as a community that is opposed to the social and moral norms of the society in which they live.

In the *Gospel of Thomas,* Jesus is not only the "Living One," who speaks these words

---

9. With respect to the distinction between the earliest composition of Q and its later redaction, I agree with John S. Kloppenborg, *The Formation of Q: Trajectories in Ancient Wisdom Collections* (SAC; Philadelphia: Fortress Press, 1987); see also my *Ancient Christian Gospels*, 128–71.

10. See especially Q/Luke 12:42–46; 17:22–35.

that grant salvation and freedom from death; he also represents in his own person the way of return to the heavenly home—a way in which the disciples are invited to follow. Unlike the Synoptic Sayings Source, the question "Who are you?" is explicitly addressed to Jesus (*Gos. Thom.* 43, 91). To be sure, seeking Jesus means inquiring after his words (*Gos. Thom.* 43, 92), but Jesus can also say of himself that he is of divine origin and shares the divine dignity of the Father (*Gos. Thom.* 61,77), just as the disciples are taught that they come from the light and are "the chosen of the living Father" (*Gos. Thom.* 50, cf. 24b, 111). Consequently, the conduct of the disciples is described as radical encratism, which not only detests the human body as the burdensome garment of the true human self (*Gos. Thom.* 21, 37, 56, 80, 112) and abstains from the business activities of the world (*Gos. Thom.* 64, 95), but also rejects the traditional norms of piety, namely, prayer, fasting, and almsgiving (*Gos. Thom.* 6, 14a). It is therefore difficult to identify a sociologically tangible community of Thomas. The aim of the interpretation of these words of Jesus is the formation, not of a community, but of the individual (*Gos. Thom.* 23, 49). The rule of the Father cannot be defined in visible forms of community structures, but only in the recognition of the individual's divine self (*Gos. Thom.* 3). The ultimate mystery of the words of Jesus therefore cannot be taught or communicated (*Gos. Thom.* 13b). Disciples must find it in themselves.

In the sayings tradition that was incorporated into the Gospel of John, it is possible to identify a theological tendency that is analogous to that of the *Gospel of Thomas*. In John 3, the saying about rebirth is at first interpreted in a spiritualizing fashion:

> What is born by the flesh is flesh, and what is born by the spirit (πνεῦμα) is spirit (πνεῦμα). . . . The wind (πνεῦμα) blows where it wills, and you hear its sound, but you do not know whence it comes and where it goes. Thus is everyone who is born by the spirit (πνεῦμα). (John 3:6, 8)

Similarly, existing religious institutions, such as the temple in Jerusalem and the sanctuary on Mount Gerizim, are replaced by a spiritualized understanding of piety and worship:

> The time is coming and is already when those who truly worship the Father will worship him in the spirit and the truth. . . . God is spirit, and those who worship him must worship him in the spirit and in the truth. (John 4:23–24)

The saying about the light that is quoted in John 11:9–10 implies that one must seek the light *in oneself*:

> Whoever walks in the day does not stumble, because he sees the light of this world. But whoever walks in the night stumbles, because the light is not *in him*. (cf. also John 12:35–36)

The relationship of the disciple to Jesus is also defined in the Johannine tradition of the sayings in a way similar to the *Gospel of Thomas*. Jesus is the archetype of those who come from the Father or from the light; to seek Jesus here also seems to mean that one should seek in his words the way into the heavenly home. To be sure, the Judeans seem to be excluded:

> A little while, I am still with you, and then I go to the one who has sent me. You will seek me and not find me; and where I am, you cannot come. (John 7:33–34)

This saying suggests that the disciples, of course, would be asked to follow Jesus, as it is said explicitly in the *Apocryphon of James* (2.25-27):

> I shall go to the place from which I came; if you want to come with me, come!

Parallels to John 8 in the *Gospel of Thomas* (Logia 19, 24, 38, 43) demonstrate that this dialogue originally spoke about the conduct of the disciples of Jesus (John 8:12), knowledge of one's heavenly origin and one's return to heaven (John 8:14, cf. 21), the presence of Jesus in his words (John 8:25), and about the finding of one's true self through the words of Jesus (John 8:31).

Even more explicit is the tendentious and Gnostic interpretation of Jesus' sayings in the dialogue of John 14:2–12, to which there is a close parallel in the *Dialogue of the Savior* (25–30 = 131.19–132.19).[11] Originally this dialogue must have spoken about the "way" into the heavenly mansions and the vision of the Father as the recognition of one's true self, although the author of the Gospel of John interprets this Gnostic dialogue critically.[12] An almost completely Gnostic understanding of Jesus as the revealer appears in the sayings incorporated into John 17, the so-called "high-priestly" prayer of Jesus. Here, Jesus speaks openly about himself as the Gnostic revealer, who gathers together those who belong to him according to their divine destiny. If Jesus' departure, namely, his return to the Father—here nothing is said about death and resurrection[13]—means that now he will be temporarily separated from those who belong to him, the prayer affirms for them the abiding presence of eternal life in the knowledge of God and of the one whom he has sent. They are of the same divine essence as Jesus because, like him, they are not "from the world." Nevertheless, they must remain in the world for a time to continue his work.

Interpretation of the Gospel of John as a whole will show that the author rejects or modifies such Gnostic interpretation of the sayings of Jesus. In their original use by the Johannine community, however, these dialogues were shaped by a theological interpretation of Jesus' sayings that is comparable to that of the *Gospel of Thomas*, a theology that emphasized the recognition of one's divine self and the return to one's heavenly origin.

---

11. For a more detailed comparison of this passage from the *Dialogue of the Savior* with John 14, see "Dialogue and the Tradition of Sayings in the Gnostic Texts of Nag Hammadi," pp. 148–73 in this volume. See also my *Ancient Christian Gospels*, 179–80, and for the comparison of a similar passage from the *Apocryphon of James* with John 14, see 191.

12. I shall return to a discussion of this passage later in this chapter.

13. Only by placing this chapter just before the account of Jesus' arrest did the author of the Fourth Gospel establish a relationship of "Jesus' departure" to his death.

Gnostic Traditions

The materials used by the author of the Gospel of John not only reveal the existence of an earlier Gnostic interpretation of Jesus' sayings, they also include other traditions that have been shaped by a Gnostic view of salvation.[14] In this context, the prologue of the gospel, John 1:1-14, is most significant. Its Gnostic character has long been debated, and it has been suggested that it was not the myth of the Gnostic redeemer but rather the Jewish myth of Wisdom/Sophia that influenced the prologue.[15] This very well may be the case. The influence of the Wisdom myth is most evident in the presentation of the Logos as God's agent in the creation of the world. In the Wisdom of Solomon, however, a Gnostic understanding of salvation is already implicit—located precisely in the notion of redemption through the hidden presence of divine Wisdom.

In John 1:1–5 and 9–13, this Gnostic version of the Sophia myth is still visible. Verses 9–10 speak about the coming of the Logos into the world and say that the world knew him not. Verses 12–13 state explicitly that those who accept the Logos have a divine origin, that is, "those who are not born from blood nor from the will of the flesh nor from the will of a man, but who are born from God." That vv. 6–8, which refer to the coming of John the Baptist, and v. 14, which announces that the "Word became flesh," interpret this Gnostic myth critically, is another matter. Through these interpolations by the hand of the author of the Fourth Gospel,[16] the myth is bound to the subsequent narrative of the revelation in Jesus of Nazareth whose coming was to be announced by John the Baptist.

The Miracle Stories

It is one of the most widely accepted hypotheses of scholarship that the author of the Fourth Gospel used a written source, namely, the Signs or Semeia Source, from which he drew his miracle stories. Because this source reflects "Johannine" language through-out, it can be assumed that it was composed and used in the Johannine community.[17] A community that uses and transmits miracle stories is most likely a missionary com-munity. The controversy of Paul with his opponents in 2 Corinthians shows clearly the

---

14. Among many publications that deal with this issue, here I want to mention only the insightful essay of George W. MacRae, "Gnosticism and the Church of John's Gospel," in Charles W. Hedrick and Robert Hodgson Jr., eds., *Nag Hammadi, Gnosticism, and Early Christianity* (Peabody, Mass.: Hendrickson, 1986) 89–96.

15. It should not be doubted that John 1:1–5, 9–13 constitutes a pre-Christian hymnic fragment. For a discussion of the theories pertaining to the interpretation and background of the prologue, see Brown, *Gospel of John*, 1. 3–37.

16. John 1:14 may have been part of an earlier Christian adaptation of this Gnostic hymn to the beliefs of the Johannine community.

17. On the character of this source and its use by the author of the gospel, see especially James M. Robin-son, "The Johannine Trajectory," in Robinson and Helmut Koester, *Trajectories through Early Christianity* (Philadelphia: Fortress Press, 1971) 232–68.

purpose and function of such stories. It also demonstrates the significance of possession of the divine spirit and its powerful demonstration for successful missionary activity.[18] Moreover, the Lukan Acts of the Apostles illuminates how the miracles of the missionaries emphasize the supernatural power of the Jesus whom they proclaim. That the story of the wine miracle at Cana (John 2) is the adaptation of a pagan legend of Dionysus also points to the missionary activity among Gentiles of the Johannine community.

These miracle stories received a special orientation in the Johannine tradition. Jesus' role as the "Divine Man" (θεῖος ἀνήρ) has been heightened in such a way that his humanity almost disappears. Jesus indeed is depicted as the God who is walking on earth. As they are accomplished publicly, the miracles demand faith in Jesus as a matter of course. More important, they call forth a faith that gathers the many into the new people of God.

This orientation also demonstrates that, unlike the sayings in the *Gospel of Thomas*, these miracle stories are not addressed to individuals but to the people as a whole. This is especially evident in the story of the feeding of the five thousand (John 6:1–15). How much has been added by the author of the gospel in the present form of the story is difficult to say. A Johannine ritual of the Eucharistic meal, however, must be presupposed even for the older version of the story, and parts of the interpretation that follows (John 6:26–33) may have belonged to the traditional story, especially the Exodus motif: the Eucharistic bread is the manna that Moses gave that now grants eternal life. There is a close parallel to the Eucharistic prayers of the *Teaching of the Twelve Apostles* (*Didache* 9–10) insofar as in both instances only the Eucharistic bread is emphasized, and eating the bread is presented as a partaking of spiritual food for "Life" and "Gnosis." Moreover, neither in the Fourth Gospel nor in the *Didache* do we find a connection with the last meal of Jesus before his death. A reference to the blood of Jesus, however, and thus implicitly to his death, has been introduced by a later redactor in the interpolation at John 6:52–59.[19]

We may therefore conclude that, well before the composition of the gospel, the Johannine community pointed to the significance of the person of Jesus in two analogous ways: (1) Jesus is not only the giver of words of life but also the archetype of the one who is going the way into the heavenly home; (2) Jesus is not only the miracle worker but at the same time the giver of a sacrament that provides life for the participants. In both functions, Jesus is understood as a divine being; there is no reflection about the appearance of the divine revealer in the person of a real human being. The question of the humanity of Jesus of Nazareth became urgent only through the introduction of the final complex of materials that was incorporated into the tradition of the Johannine church, namely, the passion narrative.

---

18. On the opponents of Paul in 2 Corinthians, see Dieter Georgi, *The Opponents of Paul in 2 Corinthians: A Study in Religious Propaganda in Late Antiquity* (Philadelphia: Fortress Press, 1985) passim.

19. The full discussion is reported in Brown, *Gospel of John*, 1. 281–94, 303–4. The most convincing arguments against the integrity of the text have been presented by Günther Bornkamm, "Die eucharistische Rede im Johannesevangelium," *ZNW* 47 (1956) 161–69.

The Passion Narrative

The roots of the traditions of the Johannine community seem to lie in an understanding of Jesus in which the sayings of Jesus played a primary if not exclusive role. At some time during its history, however, this community also must have become aware of the existence of a narrative of Jesus' suffering and death. The story that was later incorporated into the Johannine gospel is closely related to the passion narrative used in the Synoptic Gospels and in the *Gospel of Peter*. It is not possible here to investigate the origin and development of this story.[20] I would like to emphasize only one aspect. The passion narrative did not have its origin in the historical memory of the witnesses, but was formed in analogy to the story of the suffering righteous. Liturgical use of the Psalms, Prophets, and Wisdom books must have given rise to the formation of an analogous story about the suffering of Jesus. This may have happened in the regular services of the community and/or in the context of the annual memorial celebration of Jesus' death and resurrection at the time of the Jewish Passover. All existing versions of the passion narrative include some reference to the date of the Jewish Passover. That may argue for the second alternative. It is not necessary that a common meal was connected with the memorial service at which the story of Jesus' suffering was told. The Quartodeciman practice of Asia Minor, with which the Johannine tradition was later connected, emphasized the fast that remembered Jesus' death at the time at which the Passover lambs were slaughtered and the sorrow of Jesus' disciples at the time at which the Jews were eating the Passover lamb. This dating of Jesus' death, that is, on the day before the Jewish Passover, is also evident in the Johannine calendar, and it is perhaps no accident that the Fourth Gospel does not connect the institution of the Eucharist with the last meal of Jesus with his disciples.

While the interpretation of the words of Jesus and the elaboration of the miracle stories did not originally show any relation to Jesus' death, the acceptance of the passion narrative by the Johannine community must have caused a major reorientation of its theology. Why, one may ask, would such a community have chosen to accept this story that was so clearly at variance with other traditions that this community had cultivated?

The reasons for the Johannine community's acceptance of the passion narrative must be sought in a more general development in the early Christian churches, namely, in their conscious attempt to create a worldwide network that could function politically and socially as a new Christian commonwealth. This development sometimes has been called "early catholicism." This term is misleading, however, because it has been used and abused to characterize the disappearance of so-called "primitive" Christian enthusiasm, the replacement of inspiration by the creation of ecclesiastical offices, and the introduction of a traditional Jewish morality—in other words, it has been used in the service of what is clearly a prejudiced picture of the development from Christian beginnings to the worldwide community. I suggest that we use the term Panchristianity.[21] This

---

20. See on this question my *Ancient Christian Gospels*, 216–40.

21. The possible usefulness of this term occurred to me after reading Gregory Nagy, *Pindar's Homer: The Lyric Possession of an Epic Past* (Baltimore/London: Johns Hopkins University Press, 1990) especially 52–53.

term is more appropriate for the characterization of the attempt to create a political and cultural entity in the context of an increasing super-regional intercommunication.[22] Crucial for such an effort was the introduction of a common ritual and a common story. These were the two most important elements in the building and maintenance of a community in antiquity.

This development began very early, long before the appearance of what has been called "early catholicism," namely in the church-political efforts of the apostle Paul. Paul's correspondence had no other purpose than to bind together the communities he had founded into the one Christian commonwealth. More than that, by means of the collection for Jerusalem, he also attempted, albeit with little success, to include the Jewish-Christian community of Jerusalem into this Panchristian development. Although the Pauline churches possessed a common ritual meal and also the beginnings of a narrative about Jesus' suffering, death, burial, and resurrection,[23] Paul based his attempt on the offering of a grant of money, a joint effort of all the Gentiles that was designed to call Jerusalem into the bond of ecumenical fellowship. Only the next generations would succeed in uniting many of the special communities and their traditions in a Panchristian movement that was based upon a common ritual and a common cult legend, namely, the passion narrative. Those groups who remained outside of these common symbols, the Gnostics and the Jewish Christians, were eventually excluded as "heretical."

The acceptance of the passion narrative by the Johannine community was identical with its entrance into the Panchristian network. This was first of all a political event, but it would have its theological consequences. Integrating the earlier, special Johannine Jesus traditions into the passion narrative was the theological achievement of the author of the Fourth Gospel. To be sure, different solutions would have been possible, and such solutions were probably discussed in the Johannine community before the composition of the Fourth Gospel. The passion narrative did not necessarily imply a conflict between the earlier gnosticizing tendencies of the Johannine traditions and the story of Jesus' death. That Jesus came from another world and that his kingdom was not of this world could also be expressed within the passion narrative itself; the discussion between Jesus and Pilate (John 18:36–37) proves the point. It also was not necessary to understand the traditional celebration of the Eucharist in the light of the sacrificial death of Jesus on the cross. However, the annual memorial celebration at the date of the Jewish Passover did indeed become constitutive for the Johannine festal calendar as well. Since this date of Jesus' death has been incorporated into the Johannine version of the passion narrative,

---

Nagy describes how, in the seventh and sixth centuries BCE, the increasing intercommunication of the originally isolated Greek cities resulted in the creation of a common story (the Homeric Epic) and a common ritual (the national Greek festivals of Olympia, Nemea, Isthmia, and Delphi).

22. For the communications of early Christian churches with each other through mutual visits and especially through the exchange of letters, see my article "Writings and the Spirit: Authority and Politics in Ancient Christianity," *HTR* 84 (1991) 353–72 = pp. 207–23 in Helmut Koester, *Paul and His World* (Minneapolis: Fortress Press, 2007).

23. The phrase "in the night in which he was handed over" (1 Cor 11:23), used by Paul in the introduction to his quotation of the words of institution, suggests that there was a narrative context in which this reference would be meaningful.

where it is mentioned four times,[24] one must assume that in the Johannine community this narrative also was connected with an annual memorial celebration. It may have been a simple meal before the day of Jesus' death, in which the foot-washing ritual was practiced (John 13:4–12).

The Theology of the Fourth Evangelist

The independence of the Fourth Evangelist from the Synoptic Gospels does not necessarily imply that he did not know anything about them. It only means that these gospels were of no concern to him. Instead, he understood his task to be the fresh interpretation of the Jesus traditions current in his own church in the light of the passion narrative. His question was how the gnosticizing interpretations of Jesus' words and the narratives of the epiphany miracles of the Divine Man Jesus could be understood if this same Jesus suffered and died on the cross. In his entire reinterpretation of these older traditions, the Fourth Evangelist moved the story of Jesus' suffering and death into the center of his reflections.

It is evident, moreover, that the integration of the interpretation of the sayings and of the miracle stories into the perspective of the passion narrative is not the work of one single theological genius, but consists of a number of insights and efforts that grew out of preaching, instruction, and discussions within the life of the community. This explains the many inconsistencies and doublets in several chapters of the gospel, especially in the farewell discourses (John 13–17).

The consistent purpose of the author is most clearly visible in the overall composition of the gospel: the tripartite introduction, consisting of the prologue (John 1:1–18), the narrative about John the Baptist (John 1:19–34), and the calling of the disciples (John 1:35–51); the tripartite conclusion with appearances of Jesus to Mary Magdalene (John 20:1–18), to the eleven disciples (John 20:19–23), and to Thomas (John 20:24–29).[25] Within this general frame, the two main parts of the gospel are clearly marked: the public activity of Jesus, beginning with the wine miracle (John 2:1–11) and ending with the raising of Lazarus (John 11:1–44); and the passion narrative, beginning with the anointing of Jesus in Bethany (John 12:1–7) and ending with his burial (John 19:38–42). The two main sections are closely connected in such a way that the last and most powerful miracle of Jesus, the raising of Lazarus, leads directly to the council of his death (John 11:45–53). The close connection of the greatest epiphany miracle of Jesus with the council of his death fundamentally called into question any belief in Jesus that was nothing but a belief in the epiphanies of the Divine Man.

Within the individual pericopes, it is often possible to see how difficult it was to integrate the traditional materials into the new orientation. This cannot be treated here in detail. I can, however, examine briefly two important features of this new orienta-

---

24. John 11:55–56; 18:28; 19:31; 20:1.

25. With the majority of exegetes, I consider John 21 to be a later addition; for a review of the discussion, see Brown, *Gospel of John*, 2. 1077–85 and bibliography at 2. 1131–32.

tion that have been introduced into the originally Gnostic and aretalogical materials: (1) a fresh understanding of the sayings about "seeking and finding," and (2) the reformulation of traditional wisdom sayings as statements in which Jesus speaks about himself, introduced by the characteristic Johannine "I am . . ." (ἐγώ εἰμι).

The interpretation of sayings about "seeking and finding" belongs to the most characteristic Gnostic understanding of the sayings of Jesus. The concern is always with seeking after the human self and its heavenly destiny. If there is talk about seeking Jesus, it is directed toward the inquiry into Jesus' life-giving words or toward Jesus as the archetype of the origin and destiny of the human self.

In the Fourth Gospel, however, sayings about "seeking and finding" have become an essential element in the total composition.[26] Jesus asks the first two disciples, who want to follow him, "Whom do you *seek*?" (John 1:38). One of the two, Andrew, *finds* his brother Simon and says to him, "We have *found* the Messiah" (John 1:41). Afterwards Jesus *finds* Philip (1:43) who in turn *finds* Nathanael and says to him, "We have *found* the one, about whom Moses in the Law and the prophets have written" (John 1:45). The one who has thus been found, however, is not characterized as a divine being but emphatically as a human person, "Jesus, Joseph's son from Nazareth." The author of the gospel certainly could have used different words to describe these encounters; for a good literary style he should have varied his vocabulary by the use of such terms as "to meet," "to see," and so forth. That he repeatedly uses the single term "to find" demonstrates his anti-Gnostic purpose. It is also evident in the almost banal identification of the one who has been found as "Jesus, Joseph's son from Nazareth" (John 1:45).

The counterpoint appears at the end of the gospel in the scene of Jesus' arrest, where Jesus repeats the question from the first chapter, "Whom do you *seek*?"—this time addressed twice to those who have come to arrest him (John 18:4, 7). Again the one they seek is said to be "Jesus of Nazareth" (John 18:5, 7). The same "Jesus of Nazareth" appears once more in the inscription on the cross; note that only in John's gospel is the inscription on the cross reported as "Jesus *of Nazareth* the king of the Judeans" (John 19:19).[27] In the encounter of the risen Lord with Mary Magdalene (John 20:15), Jesus once more asks the question, "Whom do you *seek*?"

In the course of the gospel itself, moreover, this saying of Jesus is employed several times. The people *seek* Jesus because of the works he has done, but in vain (John 6:24, 26; 7:11). Those who *seek* their own honor will die in their sins (John 5:44; 7:18; 8:50). Most striking is the often-repeated statement that those who *seek* Jesus most eagerly are the ones who want to arrest him.[28] Finally the mystery of *seeking* is laid open in the saying, "You will *seek* me and not *find* me" (John 7:34, 36). Since this word is directed to the Judeans, one might conclude that their unbelief is responsible for the failure of their search, but the beginning of the farewell discourses reveals that the disciples are in the same position:

---

26. I have treated this theme and its use in the Gospel of John on pp. 174–83.

27. Cf. Mark 14:26: "the king of the Judeans"; Matt 27:37: "this is Jesus the king of the Judeans"; Luke 23:38: "the king of the Judeans is this one"; *Gos. Pet.* 4.11: "this is the king of Israel."

28. John 5:18; 7:1, 19–20, 25, 30; 8:37, 40; 10:39; 11:8, 56.

I shall be with you for a little while longer. You will *seek* me, and as I have said to the Judeans: "Where I am going you cannot come," so I say now also to you. (John 13:33)

This is an outright rejection of the Gnostic claim that seeking Jesus will lead to the recognition of one's own divine self and enable the disciple to follow Jesus into the heavenly home. Instead, the earthly Jesus of Nazareth remains the one upon whom the disciples also must rely after his departure. They will indeed be able to do so, because he will return and remain with them as the Spirit of Truth and as their "Counselor" in their life in the world, reminding them of everything that Jesus had said (John 14:26; 15:26; 16:7–15).

The second characteristically Johannine feature in the new interpretation of these sayings of Jesus, in the light of the theology of the cross, is evident in the use of the self-designation of Jesus with "I am" (ἐγώ εἰμι).[29] It has been suggested that these ἐγώ εἰμι sayings are typical expressions of a Gnostic understanding of revelation. It is striking, however, that traditional words of Jesus appear in this particular formulation only in the Gospel of John.[30] Gnostic writings offer very few examples of this kind of self-designation of Jesus.[31] In Gnostic writings, equivalent sayings of Jesus are normally formulated in such a way that they describe the divine origin of the disciples as well. In the *Gospel of Thomas* Jesus does not designate himself as the light; rather the saying about the light is formulated as follows:

There is light in a person of light, and it illuminates the whole world; if he does not shine, there is darkness. (*Gos. Thom.* 24)

If this is the more traditional form, one must assume that the reformulation of the saying in John 8:12 is the work of the author of this gospel:

I am the light of the world. Whoever follows after me, will not walk in darkness but will have the light of life.

The presence of the light in Jesus is therefore not a prototype that can be repeated in the being of the disciples so that they become persons of light in the same way as he is. They remain dependent upon the presence of light in the earthly Jesus of Nazareth.

This relationship of the disciples to Jesus is especially clear in the dialogue of John 14, in its present form a Johannine redaction of an originally Gnostic dialogue that is

---

29. The best discussion of the various types of this formula of divine self-identification can be found in Rudolf Bultmann, *The Gospel of John: A Commentary* (Philadelphia: Westminster, 1971) 225–26 n. 3. See also Brown, *Gospel of John*, 1. 533–38.

30. Bultmann, *The Gospel of John*, 225–26 n. 3., has called this type the "recognition formula," which does not answer the question "Who are you?" but presupposes the search for the one who will bring life and salvation, e.g., "Who is the bread of life!" to which Jesus answers, "I am the bread of life that you seek."

31. Where the "I am" formula appears, e.g., in *Gos. Thom.* 77 ("I am the light that is above the All"), it belongs to a different type, namely, the identification formula.

preserved in the *Dialogue of the Savior* (25–30).[32] In this document the request for an explanation of the heavenly destiny of the human self is answered by a reference to the Gnosis of one's own divine self. In John 14, however, Thomas's request for an explanation of the way to the heavenly mansions (14:5) is answered by an ἐγώ εἰμι saying of Jesus:

> I am the way and the truth and the life; no one comes to the Father but through me. If you know me, you also know the Father. (John 14:6–7)

As the dialogue continues, the search for mystical vision, represented by Philip's request ("Show us the Father," John 14:8), is rejected in Jesus' statement:

> For so long have I been with you, and you do not know me, Philip? Whoever has seen me, has seen the Father. How can you say, "Show us the Father!" Do you not believe that I am in the Father and that the Father is in me? (John 14:9–10)

In John 8:28, it becomes clear what this ἐγώ εἰμι ultimately expresses:

> When you will raise up the Son of Man, then you will recognize that it is I (ὅτι ἐγώ εἰμι) and that I am not doing anything by myself, but as the Father has taught me thus I speak.

"Raising up of the Son of Man" is nothing but a reference to the crucifixion of Jesus (cf. John 3:14; 8:58). Thus the statement ἐγώ εἰμι makes its appearance once more, repeated three times and without any titles of dignity, in the scene describing Jesus' arrest. Jesus asks those who have come to carry out the arrest, "Whom do you *seek*?"; they answer, "Jesus of Nazareth," and Jesus answers, "It is I" (ἐγώ εἰμι, John 18:5, 6, 8).

Just as the Johannine interpretation of the miracle stories has demonstrated that Jesus' most spectacular miracle has no other result than his condemnation, so John's Gospel also protects Jesus' sayings against a Gnostic interpretation. The sayings become statements about a faith that remains bound to the earthly Jesus of Nazareth who was raised up on the cross. In this way the author of the Fourth Gospel has used the passion narrative to interpret the gnosticizing traditions of his own community and has brought this community and its special heritage into the movement of Panchristianity.

---

32. See above, n. 11.

11

DIALOGUE AND THE TRADITION OF SAYINGS IN THE GNOSTIC TEXTS OF NAG HAMMADI

In the scholarly discussion, the first three gospels of the canon of the New Testament have long been considered as source and criterion for the older tradition of sayings and therefore also for whatever Jesus said or might have said. The canon for the tradition about Jesus, which once had been established in the fight against Marcion and against Gnosticism, is thus confirmed at least in part by scholarly works. It is quite irrelevant here whether the sayings and speeches of Jesus transmitted in these three gospels are considered to be on the whole historical or whether this material is critically evaluated and only a relatively small portion is assigned to the historical Jesus. The problem among the canonical gospels in this respect is, of course, the Gospel of John. The relationship of the extensive speeches of Jesus in this gospel to the tradition of Jesus' sayings awaits clarification. As a result, there are no references to the Gospel of John in critical presentations of the preaching of Jesus. Rather, the character of the Synoptic tradition of sayings determines the reconstruction of the message of Jesus, as well as the conception of the transmission of Jesus' sayings in the earliest period of Christianity.

It must be admitted that—apart from the Gospel of John—dissimilar materials of sayings and speeches of Jesus were accessible only to a very limited degree. The possible sources that were available were deemed to be of too late a date and too speculative and esoteric, and therefore not fit to shake the consensus of New Testament scholarship with respect to the character of the earliest transmission of Jesus' sayings. However, two writings with sayings, dialogues, and speeches of Jesus, found in the fourth-century Codex Askewianus, have been known since 1851: the *Pistis Sophia* and the *Writing Without out Title*.[1] Then, a writing called *The Two Books of Jeu* came from the somewhat younger Codex Brucianus.[2] These Christian writings, preserved in Coptic translation, are

---

1. They were first published by G. M. Schwartze and J. E. Petermann in 1851. The authoritative translation was published by Carl Schmidt, *Pistis Sophia: Ein gnostisches Originalwerk des dritten Jahrhunderts aus dem Koptischen übersetzt* (Leipzig: Hinrichs, 1925).

2. First edition by E. Amélineau, 1891. A new edition of the Coptic text and a German translation was published by Carl Schmidt, *Gnostische Schriften in Koptischer Sprache aus dem Codex Brucianus* (TU 8; Leipzig: Hinrichs, 1892). The date of the manuscript is not certain; but the *Two Books of Jeu* must have been written earlier than the *Pistis Sophia* because the latter writing refers to them several times.

"gospels in the form of dialogues," although they cannot be dated any earlier than the first half of the third century CE. In 1919 when Carl Schmidt published one more "gospel in the form of dialogues," the *Epistula Apostolorum,* he entitled that writing "Dialogues of Jesus with His Disciples after the Resurrection."[3] This document was certainly written as early as the second century CE—some scholars want to date it early in that century—and is therefore not far away from the date of the writing of the canonical gospels; moreover, it cannot be designated, like the writings of the Codex Askewianus and Codex Brucianus, as heretical or Gnostic. The phrase "After the Resurrection" in the title, however, eliminated for the time being the task to consider the dialogues of this writing on the same level as the sayings and discourses of Jesus in the canonical gospels.[4]

In the year 1945, a Christian library of thirteen volumes in the Coptic language was discovered near Nag Hammadi in Upper Egypt. The approximately fifty writings of this library are now accessible in a complete facsimile edition of the Coptic manuscripts[5] and in English translation.[6] Appended to this library are the four writings of a closely related nature from the Coptic Papyrus Berolinensis 8502.[7] In this way, a large number of writings with new material including sayings, discourses, and dialogues of Jesus have come to light. This makes it necessary to open the question of the relationship of these dialogues and discourses of Jesus to the canonical gospels.

All writings of the Nag Hammadi Library are translations from Greek originals. The codices, in which they appear in Coptic language, must have been written shortly after the middle of the fourth century CE. Therefore the date for the composition of the Greek originals must be before or shortly after the year 300 CE. There are, however, good reasons to assume that almost all of these writings must be dated into the second or third century CE; in some instances one might even consider a date before the end of the first century CE. It will be necessary, of course, to corroborate in the scholarly discussion more exact dates for each of these writings. It is precisely among the earliest writings of the Nag Hammadi Library that one finds several "gospels in the form of a dialogue." I enumerate in the following such earlier writings in the sequence in which they appear in these 13 codices, adding also those preserved in the Codex Berolinensis (BG 8502):

---

3. Carl Schmidt, *Gespräche Jesu mit seinen Jüngern nach der Auferstehung* (TU 43, Leipzig: J. C. Hinrichs 1919).

4. Also in vol. 1 of the edition of the *New Testament Apocrypha* by E. Hennecke and Edgar Schneemelcher that appeared in 1959 [an English edition appeared in 1963], the chapter entitled "Dialogues of Jesus with His Disciples After the Resurrection" includes the *Freer Logion,* the *Epistula Apostolorum,* and the *Strasbourg Coptic Papyrus.* On the other hand, the *Sophia of Jesus Christ,* the *Dialogue of the Savior* (more about these two writings later in this chapter), the *Pistis Sophia,* and the *Two Books of Jeu* are assigned to a section entitled "Gospels current, directly or indirectly, under the name of Jesus, and similar works."

5. *The Facsimile Edition of the Nag Hammadi Codices,* published under the Department of Antiquities of the Arab Republic of Egypt, vols. I–XIII (Leiden: E. J. Brill), 1972–1977.

6. J. M. Robinson, ed., *The Nag Hammadi Library in English* (New York: Harper & Row, 1977).

7. W. Till, ed., *Die gnostischen Schriften des koptischen Papyrus Berolinensis 8502* (TU 60, Berlin: Akademie-Verl., 1955; 2nd ed. revised by Hans-Martin Schenke, Berlin: Akademie-Verl., 1972).

Apocryphon of James (I,2)
Book of Thomas (II,7)
Sophia of Jesus Christ (III,4 and BG 8502)
Dialogue of the Savior (III,5)
First Apocalypse of James (V,3)
Acts of Peter and the Twelve Apostles (VI,1)
Apocalypse of Peter (VII,3)
Letter of Peter to Philip (VIII,2)
Gospel of Mary (BG 8502, 1)

In the form of extensive discourses of revelation, the following appear:

Apocryphon of John (II,1; III,1; IV 1; BG 8502, 2)
Second Treatise of the Great Seth (VII,2)

Furthermore, there are dialogues in which a different redeemer figure appears, not Jesus himself, as the speaker. In the Hermetic tractates Hermes Trismegistus appears: *Discourse on the Eighth and the Ninth* (VI,6), *Asclepius* (VI,8). In the second part of *Hypostasis of the Archons* (II,4) the angel Eleleth appears.[8] Important for our discussion is *The Gospel of Thomas* (II,2). It is a collection of sayings of Jesus that occasionally has dialogic character.[9]

This is just a general survey. For a critical assessment, I consider some characteristic examples under the following subdivisions:

I. Gospel and dialogue as a secondary literary form.
II. Dialogue as instruction and as liturgy for initiation.
III. Dialogue as interpretation of traditional sayings.

I. Gospel and Dialogue as a Secondary Literary Form

The *Apocryphon of John* appears in its external form as a typical example of a dialogue-gospel. It begins with a scene that presents John in great doubt after Jesus has gone away; then the risen Jesus appears to John, coming from heaven, and addresses him:

---

8. Because of their close affinity to the dialogues and discourses of Jesus, the latter writings also are considered in the discussion.

9. There are a number of other writings in the Nag Hammadi corpus that bear the title "Gospel" (*Gospel of Truth, Gospel of Philip, Gospel of the Egyptians*) but are works of a very different character that bear no relationship to gospel traditions and literature of whatever form. Ph. Perkins ("Studies in the Origins and Development of the Gnostic revelation Dialogue" [diss., Harvard University, 1971]) treats the Gnostic dialogues as a genre that clearly differs from the genre of the gospel; on this question see also K. Rudolph ("Der gnostische Dialog als literarisches Genus," in P. Nagel, ed., *Probleme der koptischen Literatur* [Wissenschaftliche Beiträge, Halle: Saale, 1968] 85–107) who considers the possible relationship of the Gnostic dialogue to the ancient Erotapokrisis literature. Both contributions are important for the further discussion of the dialogues discussed previously under subdivision I.

"John, John, why do you doubt, or why are your afraid?"[10]

What follows is the self-presentation of the revealer:

"I am the one who is with you always. I am the Father, I am the Mother, I am the Son."[11]

But then John's question[12] leads directly into Jesus' instruction about the Pleroma, the cosmogony, and the work of the redeemer. Sometimes the discourse of Jesus is interrupted by John's questions. Such questions, however, are nothing but exegetical signals that are established especially for problems in the interpretation of Genesis, for example:

And I said, "Lord, what does it mean that she moved to and fro?" But he smiled and said, "Do not think it is, as Moses said, 'above the waters.' No, but when she had seen the wickedness which had happened, and the theft her son had committed, she (the Sophia) repented. And she was overcome by forgetfulness in the darkness of ignorance and she began to be ashamed. And she did not dare to return, but she was moving about. And the moving is the going to and fro."[13]

The problem here is the interpretation of Gen 1:2. In another instance, a question of John quotes an interpretation of the serpent (Genesis 2) that the author rejects:

And I said to the Savior, "Lord, was it not the serpent that taught Adam to eat?" The savior smiled and said, "The serpent taught them to eat from wickedness of begetting, lust and destruction...."[14]

All this is completely unrelated to the gospel tradition. First of all, Christian elements are missing completely in this mythical narrative and these interpretations of Genesis. Second, the dialogical element is entirely secondary; in most instances, such tractates are written without being cast in the form of a dialogue gospel; in fact, Irenaeus[15] apparently knew this same mythological tractate in a non-dialogical form. The dialogical form of the *Apocryphon of John* is therefore a secondary version of a probably pre-Christian mythological interpretation of Genesis.

The secondary dialogical reconstitution of a pre-Christian treatise is glaringly evident in the case of the *Sophia of Jesus Christ*[16] and the *Letter of Eugnostos.*[17] The *Letter of*

---

10. NHC II,1, 2.9–11. The translations are taken from F. Wisse, "The Apocryphon of John," in Robinson, *The Nag Hammadi Library in English*.

11. Ibid., 2.12–14.

12. Ibid., 2.25–26.

13. Ibid., 13.17–26; cf. NHC IV,1 21.13–15.

14. Ibid., 22.9–14. Other questions of John inserted by the author solicit comments on the fate of the soul; see ibid., 25.16–18; 26.7–10; etc.

15. *Haer.* 1.29.

16. NHC III,3 and V,1.

17. NHC III,4 and BG 8502, 3. Very instructive is the synopsis of the *Letter of Eugnostos* and the *Sophia of Jesus Christ* by Douglas M. Parrot in Robinson, *The Nag Hammadi Library in English,* 207–23.

Eugnostos is a treatise about the invisible divine world beyond the spheres of the visible heaven. It was written in the second century CE as a religious-philosophical essay, shows no Christian elements, and is closely related to Middle Platonism.[18] For the most part, this treatise has been used by a Christian author word-for-word and sentence-for-sentence to construct a dialogue of Jesus with his disciples, only occasionally with some additions. The product of this effort is the *Sophia of Jesus Christ,* which appears in the Nag Hammadi Library and also directly after the *Letter of Eugnostos.*[19]

The methodology of this dialogical transformation of the older treatise in the *Sophia of Jesus Christ* is apparent. The author begins with a scenario of the appearance of Jesus before his disciples.[20] He says that the twelve disciples and the seven women were perplexed about the true being of the underlying reality of the universe and the plan and the holy providence and the power of the authorities. Then Jesus appears and asks about their doubts:

> "What are you thinking about? Why are you perplexed? What are you searching for?"[21]

So far, the framework corresponds exactly to that of the *Apocryphon of John.* A question of Philipp for "the underlying reality of the universe and the plan"[22] introduces the reproduction of the first part of the philosophical treatise. In the following, however, the dialogue form is more strongly pressed upon the older writing than in the *Apocryphon of John;* the disciples' questions, often spun out of catchwords of the philosophical treatise, disrupt the original text frequently. For example, where the *Letter of Eugnostos* has mentioned "the God of truth,"[23] Matthew asks in the *Sophia of Jesus Christ:*

> "Lord, no one can find the truth except through you. Therefore teach us the truth."[24]

---

18. On the philosophy of the *Letter of Eugnostos,* see Demetrios Trakatellis, *The Transcendent God of Eugnostos* (Brookline, Mass.: 1991 [in the German publication of the article on which this chapter is based, my reference was to the original Greek version of this book]).

19. On the question of the dependence of the *Sophia of Jesus Christ* upon the *Letter of Eugnostos,* see M. Krause, "Das literarische Verhältnis des Eugnostosbriefes zur Sophia Jesus Christi," in *Zur Auseinandersetzung der Gnosis mit dem Christentum: Mullus; Festschrift für Th. Klauser* (JbAC. Ergänzungsband 1; 1964). H.-M. Schenke argued for the reverse relationship of dependence ("Nag Hammadi Studies II: The System of the Sophia Jesus Christi," *ZRGG* 14 [1962] 263–78). At that time he did not yet have access to the entire text of the *Letter of Eugnostos.* The Berlin Papyrus 8502 was known as early as the year 1896. Eduard Norden (*Agnostos Theos* [1913; 5th ed. 1971–72]) already quoted the *Sophia of Jesus Christ* (BG 8502, 83, 1–15). At that time he could not have known that this writing was but a secondary form of an originally non-Christian document.

20. BG 8502. 77.9–79.13 = NHC III,4 90.14–91.24.

21. BG 8502. 79.15–17; cf. NHC III,4 92.1–3.

22. BG 8502. 80.1–3 = NHC III,4 92.4–5.

23. NHC III,3 71.10.

24. NHC III,4 94.1–4.

Sometimes a question of a disciple introduces an excursus and thus provides the Christian redactor the opportunity to discuss a topic that the source does not treat.[25]

The *First Apocalypse of James* (NHC V,3) belongs to the same genre of dialogues. It is composed mainly of an instruction about cosmology and soteriology, beginning with God, the One-who-is, the relationship of the redeemer to female power in the cosmos,[26] the number and measure of the heavens, the weapons of the powers, and the function of the redeemer, especially with respect to his suffering.[27] The transformation of these instructions into a dialogue of Jesus with James, his brother, serves among other things to elucidate this material as prediction and interpretation of the martyrdom of James. In addition to the mythological discourses, other material also is included that seems to have been drawn from preaching, liturgy, and catechesis of a Gnostic community. Quite clearly recognizable is a hymn to the redeemer that shows a close affinity to the hymns of the *Odes of Solomon*, a Christian hymnbook of the second century:

> You have come with knowledge,
> that you might rebuke their forgetfulness.
> You have come with recollection,
> that you might rebuke their ignorance.
>
> . . . .
>
> For you descended into a great ignorance,
> But you have not been defiled by anything in it.
> For you descended into a great mindlessness,
> and your recollection remained.
> You walked in mud,
> but your garments were not soiled,
> and you have not been buried in their filth,
> and you have not been caught.[28]

The hymn concludes with the confession of the singer:

> And I was not like them, but I clothed myself with everything of theirs. There is in me forgetfulness, but I remember things that are not theirs. . . .[29]

In the description of the expected suffering and of the liberation of the soul, the author used a Gnostic catechism:

> When you are seized, and when you undergo these sufferings, a multitude will arm themselves against you that they may seize you. And in particular three of

---

25. NHC III,4 96.14–97.16. The conclusion added by the author of *Sophia of Jesus Christ* then is introduced by a question of Mary (NHC III,4 114.8–119.17).

26. NHC V,3 24.18–25.5.

27. NHC V,3 25.26–27.12; 27.18–29.3; 31.15–32.12.

28. NHC V,3 28,7–20. Translation by William R. Schoedel in Robinson, *The Nag Hammadi Library in English*, 263–64.

29. NHC V,3 28,20–25.

them will seize you—they who sit their as toll collectors . . . one of them, who is their guard, will say to you,
"Who are you or where are you from?"
you are to say to him,
"I am a son, and I am from the Father."
He will say to you,
"What sort of son are you and to what father do you belong?"
you are to say to him,
"I am from the Pre-existent Father and a son in the Pre-existent One." . . .
When he also says to you,
"Where will you go?"
you are to say to him,
"To the place, from which I have come, there I shall return."[30]

That this is older catechetical material is evident from *Gospel of Thomas* 50, where a similar catechism is quoted as a saying of Jesus:

Jesus said,
If they say to you,
"Where do you come from?"
say to them,
"We came from the light, the place where the light came into being . . ."
If they say to you,
"Is it you?"
say,
"We are its children, and we are the elect of the living Father."
If they ask you,
"What is the sign of your father in you?"
say to them,
"It is a movement and a repose."[31]

That traditions and teachings of a community are presented in the form of a dialogue gospel is by no means limited to Gnostic writings. The same is evident in the above mentioned *Epistula Apostolorum*, which Carl Schmidt had published under the title "Dialogues of Jesus with His Disciples after the Resurrection." Following the external frame (a letter of the apostles, chaps. 1–2), at first the writing presents a statement about God the creator in a creedal form (chap. 3) and then an enumeration of the lines of the christological confession, which are illustrated with brief narratives about Jesus' coming, ministry, suffering, and death. Only after the narrative about the resurrection—the motif of the doubt of the disciples is found here once again—(chaps. 10–11) do the revelation discourses of the risen Jesus begin (chaps. 12–50). These

---

30. NHC V,3 33.11–24 and 34.15–18. The secondary interpolation, 33.25–34.15, into this catechism has been omitted here.

31. Translation by Thomas O. Lambdin in Robinson, *The Nag Hammadi Library in English*, 132.

discourses and dialogues follow the schema of the Christian creed: the first coming of Jesus (chaps. 13–14); the second coming (chaps. 16–20); the resurrection of the flesh (chap. 21) together with the soul and the spirit (chap. 22); the last judgment (chap. 26); Christ's descent into the underworld (chap. 27); proclamation to the nations (chap. 30) with an excursus about Paul, the apostle to the nations (chaps. 31–33); and additional eschatological questions (chaps. 34–40). All these topics can be authenticated in other Christian writers of the second century as constitutive parts of the Christian creed. At the end of this dialogue gospel, the author has added church order material and parenetic traditions (chaps. 41–50).

A comparison of the *Epistula Apostolorum* with the writings of Justin Martyr is instructive. Justin presents numerous parallels in structure and content. Also in Justin, the Christian creed serves as the principle for the arrangement of his arguments. In both cases, material drawn from the gospels is employed; in both instances, the anti-Gnostic position is evident. The time of the composition of the *Epistula Apostolorum* is therefore most likely the same as the time of Justin Martyr, that is, about the year 150 or a bit later. The choice of the genre of the dialogue of Jesus with his disciples can be understood as answer-and-attack upon the already widespread Gnostic dialogue gospels.

To be sure, Justin also offers a parallel for the choice of the dialogue as a means of composition. Justin has presented his critical discussion of Judaism in his *Dialogue with Trypho* in the same literary form. Of course, it is not Jesus who is here the dialogue partner of the disciples; Justin himself assumes the role of the teacher and allows his opponent to ask the relevant questions. All this has little relationship to an actual disputation of Justin with a Jewish opponent. The material used by Justin, the topics of the discussion, the sequence in which they appear, and the individual proofs from Scripture are largely paralleled in his *First Apology*. Some originally independent pieces have been inserted as, for example, the interpretation of Psalm 22 in *Dial.* 96-107. Thus the form of the dialogue is secondary. Moreover, writings like Tertullian's *Adversus Judaeos* demonstrate that it was quite possible to compose a polemical writing against the Jews without such a secondary framework.

There are among the orthodox writers of the second and third centuries only very few examples for the use of the dialogue as a literary form. Apart from Justin's *Dialogue with Trypho,* one could refer the Latin apology of Minucius Felix, who also uses the form of the dialogue. But neither Irenaeus nor Clement of Alexandria, Tertullian, Origin, and Cyprian have utilized this genre. Justin's choice of this genre is perhaps due to by the fact that he belongs to the Middle Platonism and consciously presented himself as a philosopher, especially in his *Dialogue with Trypho.* As is well known, Justin's pagan contemporary, Lucian of Samosata, turned to the dialogue as his only means of literary expression after his conversion from rhetoric to philosophy. The renewed interest among the Platonists in the dialogues of Plato in the second century is likely to have contributed to this high estimation of the dialogue among the philosophers. I would question, however, whether the preference of the Gnostics for the dialogue is related—although a section of Plato's *Republic* has been found among the writings of Nag Hammadi (NHC VI,5). It is perhaps more the case that the occasion for the literary dialogues of the Gnostics must be sought in the two forms of the dialogue that will be discussed in the next two sections.

II. Dialogue as Initiation Instruction and Initiation Liturgy

The writing entitled the *Hypostasis of the Archons* (NHC II,4, also known as *The Reality of the Rulers*)[32] appears to be based in part upon a dialogue of instructions. In its external form, it is an instructional letter:"I have sent you this because you (sg.) inquire about the reality of the authorities."[33] The reference to the "great apostle," namely Paul, and the quotations of Col 1:3 and Eph 6:11-12 at the beginning[34] serve to present the entire book as a Christian writing. But there ends the contribution of the Christian editor. The first part of the writing provides an interpretation of Genesis 1–6.[35] As in other Gnostic writings of this kind, the style of exegetical and cosmological instruction dominates; there is not dialogical structure. The interpretation of Genesis 6—command of the archon to Noah to build an ark[36]—forms the transition to a second part that differs notably in terms of genre and content from the first part. The boundary between the two parts is marked by the appearance of Norea, the daughter of Eve,"the virgin whom the forces did not defile."[37] She is not a biblical figure, although her name has been formulated on the basis of the Hebrew name Naema.[38] Norea destroys the ark that had been built upon the command of the archon with fire. The archons want to lay hands on her and defile her. In distress Norea calls upon the holy one, the god of the entirety, and asks to be rescued.[39]

The fiction of Norea crying for help is upheld only at the beginning of the second part that now follows,[40] although even here elements appear that belong to the genre of instruction and liturgy of initiation. Norea's call for help is answered by the epiphany of the angel Eleleth. The self-presentation of the revealer follows Norea's question, which is asked in the proper style of the response to an epiphany:

"Who are you?"

"It is I who am Eleleth, sagacity, the great angel, who stands in the presence of the holy spirit. . . . and I shall teach you about your root."[41]

---

32. This document was translated into German by H.-M. Schenke (*ThLZ* 83 [1958] 661–70). However, this translation rests, like all subsequent German translations, on the inadequate photographic edition of P. Labib (1956). This also applies to the translation of P. Nagel, "Das Wesen der Archonten aus Codex II der gnostischen Bibliothek von Nag Hammadi" (*Wissenschaftliche Beiträge der Martin-Luther-Universität Halle* [Wittenberg, 1970]). A critical edition of the Coptic text with English translation was published by B. Layton, "The Hypostasis of the Archons or the Reality of the Rulers," *HTR* 67 (1974) 351–425. The translation quoted here is that of Bentley Layton in Robinson, *The Nag Hammadi Library in English*, 162–69.

33. NHC II,4 86.26–27.

34. NHC II,4 86.21–25.

35. NHC II,4 86.27–92.32.

36. NHC II,4 92.10–14.

37. NHC II,4 92.2–3.

38. See B. Pearson, "The Figure of Norea in Gnostic Literature," *Proceedings of the International Congress on Gnosticism at Stockholm 1973* (1977) 143–52.

39. NHC II,4 92.14–93.2.

40. Cf. the remark here that "the rulers of unrighteousness had withdrawn from her"; NHC II,4 93.8–9.

41. NHC II,4 93.8–14.

Part of the epiphany is also the description of the marvelous appearance of the heavenly figure:

> . . . like fine gold, and his raiment is like snow . . .[42]

For all that, Norea is forgotten. Instead, the author now speaks in the I-style; he has taken the place of Norea, who up to this point has been described using the third person:

> And I said:

> Sir, teach me about the faculties of these authorities—how did they come into being and by what kind of genesis, and of what material, and who created them and their force.[43]

Responding to this question, Eleleth presents a summary of the cosmogony, in which the element of Genesis interpretation is missing.[44] The next question, again in the I-style, refers to the soteriology:

> Sir, am I also from their matter?[45]

What follows is an anthropological instruction, which is addressed directly to the person asking the question:

> You, together with your offspring, are from the primeval father; from above, out of the imperishable light their souls are come . . . and all those who have become acquainted with this way exist deathless in the midst of dying mankind. Still that sown element (*sperma*) will not become known now.[46]

The third question concerns the eschatology:

> Then I said, "Sir, how much longer?"[47]

Here, the answer of Eleleth becomes a hymnic praise:

> Until the moment, when the true man reveals the existence of (?) the spirit of truth, which the father has sent.

> Then he will teach them about everything. And he will anoint them with the unction of the life eternal, giving him from the undominated generation.

---

42. NHC II,4 93.14–15.
43. NHC II,4 93.32–94.2.
44. NHC II,4 94.4–96.19.
45. NHC II,4 96.19.
46. NHC II,4 96.19–28.
47. NHC II,4 96.31–32.

Then they will be freed of blind thought: And they will trample under foot death, which is of the authorities: And they will ascend into the limitless light, were this sown element belongs.

Then the authorities will relinquish their ages: and their angles will weep over their destruction: And their demons will lament their death.

Then all the children of the light will be truly acquainted with the truth and their root, and the father of the entirety and the holy spirit.

They will say with a single voice, "The father's truth is just, and the son presides over the entirety": And from everyone unto the ages of ages, "Holy—holy—holy! Amen!"[48]

The appearance of an angel and the subsequent dialogue recall analogous dialogues in Jewish and Christian apocalypses. Certainly, there is the interpretation of whatever the seer has seen, whereas this element is missing in the *Hypostasis of the Archons*. More-over, in those apocalypses the dialogues are often secondary arrangements of theolog-ical statements. I would ask, however, whether the *Hypostasis of the Archons* is perhaps more closely related to the initiation dialogue of the Hermetic writings. In that case, its original form could have been such a dialogue, which has later been appended to an interpretation of Genesis, until finally a Christian redactor provided an introduction in order to legitimize the entire composition as a Christian writing by a reference to Paul's statements about the powers. In this case, the dialogue is not secondary but character-izes the genre of the underlying original in which the instruction for initiation of pre-Christian (Jewish?) sect is preserved.

The Hermetic writings of Codex VI demonstrate that pre-Christian initiation dia-logues were known in the circles that produced the Nag Hammadi Library. They con-sist of the Hermetic treatise *Asclepius* (already known in a Latin translation),[49] a *Prayer of Thanksgiving* (also already known from the Corpus Hermeticum),[50] and a hitherto unknown treatise, *Discourse on the Eighth and the Ninth*.[51] This latter Hermetic writing reveals very clearly the features of an initiation dialogue. The mystagogue represents at the same time the revealing deity. He is at first addressed as "My Father,"[52] but in the course of the dialogue he becomes "Hermes" and "Trismegistos."[53]

The initiate is not only instructed, he also receives from the mystagogue powers and is finally guided to pray and to call ecstatically the hidden name of the deity.[54] In the ritual of the holy kiss, the vision of the mystagogue is transferred to the initiate.[55] In this

---

48. NHC II,4 96.33–97.20.

49. NHC VI,8 = Corp. Herm. II (Nock-Festugiere) 322–52.

50. NHC VI,7 = Corp. Herm. II (Nock-Festugiere) 353–54; its Greek text is known as *Pap. Minaut*; cf. Corp. Herm. II, 353.

51. NHC VI,6.

52. NHC VI,6 52.2, 21; 53.16; etc.

53. NHC VI,6 59.10–11: "My Father, Hermes"; 59.15: "Trismegistos"; 59.24–25: "Father Trismegistos."

54. NHC VI,6 55.10–21; 61.8–9.

55. NHC VI,6 57.26–27.

written form, the dialogue is intended to be a reading mystery. That is demonstrated by the instruction at the end of the writing to deposit what has been written in the Temple of Hermes in Diospolis and to make it accessible only to those who have made the required progress.[56] The reader is expected to identify with the initiate, who speaks in the book, and with his experience and thus enter into the dialogue with the mystagogue and revealing deity to arrive at the same experience of initiation.

It is apparent that liturgical traditions of the community also have been incorporated in the *Discourse on the Eighth and the Ninth*. In the prayer of the initiate that begins with the singular "I," the "we" of the praying community later appears:

I call upon you, who rules over the kingdom of power,[57]
... [predications of the deity follow] ...
Lord, grant us wisdom from your power that reaches us, so that we may describe to ourselves the vision of the eighth and the ninth. We have already advanced to the seventh since we are pious and walk in your law. And we fulfill your will always.

. . . .

The birth of the self-begotten one is through you, the birth of all begotten things that exist. Receive from us these spiritual sacrifices, which we send to you with all our heart and our soul and all our strength. Save that which is in us and grant us immortal wisdom.[58]

The *Prayer of Thanksgiving*,[59] which follows in Codex VI and was understood by the scribe or collector of the materials for this Codex as the immediate continuation of the initiation dialogue, also provides evidence for the liturgical practice of the community, in which this literature was used:

We give thanks to You!

Every soul and heart is lifted up to You, undisturbed name, honored with the name "God" and praised with the name "Father," for to everyone and everything comes the fatherly kindness and affection and love, and any teaching that is sweet and plain, giving us mind, speech, and knowledge.[60]

After the prayer, the writing says:

When they had said these things in the prayer, they embraced each other and they went to eat their holy food, which has no blood in it.[61]

----

56. NHC VI,6 61.18–63.32.
57. NHC VI,6 55.24–26.
58. NHC VI,6 56.22–25.
59. NHC VI,7.
60. NHC VI,7 63.34–64.6
61. NHC VI,7 65.3–7.

The dialogue is thus oriented towards ritual and liturgy and reflects dialogical pieces of an actually existing practice of initiation as well as of a celebration of a worship service. The dialogue is not a secondary literary device used to present any kind of theological or philosophical writing. Analogies could be demonstrated from other parts of the Corpus Hermeticum, certainly for the treatise *Poimandres*. It would be worthwhile to investigate also other Christian-Gnostic dialogues with respect to their liturgical structure and materials.

III. Dialogue as an Interpretation of Sayings

In a third genre of the dialogue gospel one finds a close connection of these writings with the transmission and interpretation of the tradition of sayings of Jesus. The concept "sayings of Jesus" must be understood here very broadly; moreover, the question of authenticity of any of these sayings should not intrude in the investigation. As "sayings of Jesus," I include all sayings traditions that could have been transmitted orally as "words of the Lord," were eventually fixed in written form, and could also subsequently be referred to as sayings of the Lord. With respect to the form of such sayings, one can find proverbs, wisdom sayings, parables, also Logia (or "logoi") in the narrower sense, prophetic and apocalyptic sayings, revelatory sayings—often formulated in the I-style—and rules of the community and liturgical materials.

To this genre of sayings dialogue belong the following: The *Apocryphon of James* (*Epistula Jacobi*),[62] the *Dialogue of the Savior*,[63] and in some sense also the *Gospel of Thomas*,[64] which stands at the beginning of the development with its short dialogues of Jesus with his disciples. To this early state of development one also must add, of course, the Synoptic Gospels and their sources. I shall, however, restrict my discussion here to examples from the newly discovered writings from Nag Hammadi. Later it also will be necessary to discuss the Gospel of John. The analysis of these dialogues of sayings is difficult because they use not only sayings of Jesus that are known from other sources but also sayings that have no parallels in the gospels known to us. That is especially problematic in the face of the fact that these dialogues in their interpretation of sayings often allude only to them and dispense with a full quotation of the saying in question. Often traditional sayings are already modified as soon as they are introduced, or a question of the disciples refers to them. It is therefore necessary to begin with examples, for which parallels, variants, or analogies are known from other sources. It also is probable that more traditional sayings of Jesus are hidden in these dialogues. Further critical investigation may unearth more such materials.

---

62. NHC I,2. In the following, it is quoted according to the translation by Francis E. Williams, in Harold W. Attridge, ed., *Nag Hammadi Codex I (The Jung Codex)* (NHS 22; Leiden: Brill, 1985).

63. NHC III,5. In the following, it is quoted according to the translation by Stephen Emmel in Emmel, Helmut Koester, and Elaine Pagels, *Nag Hammadi Codex III, 5: The Dialogue of the Savior* (NHS 26; Leiden: Brill, 1984).

64. NHC II,2; In the following, it is quoted according to the translation by Thomas O. Lambdin, in Bentley Layton, ed., *Nag Hammadi Writings of Codex II, 2-7* (2 vols.; NHS 20; Leiden: Brill, 1989).

In a number of instances, such dialogues consist only of a question of the disciple and an answer of Jesus in the form of a traditional saying; the next question may already lead to another saying. An example for this is found in the *Dialogue of the Savior*:

Judas said,
"Tell me, Lord, what the beginning of the path is."
He (Jesus) said,
"Love and goodness. For if one of these existed among the governors, wickedness would never have come into existence."[65]

The basis apparently is a traditional proverb:

The beginning of the path is love and goodness.

This is a wisdom saying that is analogous to Sir 1.14:

The beginning of wisdom is love and goodness.

The traditional proverb has been transferred into dialogical form, and an explanatory statement about the archons has been added to it.

Another example from the same writing reveals a combination of several traditional sayings:

Matthew said,
"Tell me, Lord, how the dead die and how the living live."
The Lord said,
"[. . .] ask me about a saying [. . .] which I have not seen, nor have I heard it except from you. But I say to you that when that what invigorates a man is removed, he will be called 'dead.' And when what is alive leaves what is dead, what is alive will be called upon."[66]

It appears that two different traditional sayings are utilized here. One of these is also in *Gos. Thom.* 17, used as the beginning of the answer of Jesus; this saying has also been quoted by Paul in 1 Cor 2:9 and has a parallel in Matt 13:16–17 (Luke 10:23–24):

Jesus said,
"I shall give you what no eye has seen
and what no ear has heard
and what no hand has touched
and what has never occurred to the human mind."

---

65. NHC III,5 142.4–8.
66. NHC III,5 139.20–140.9.

But a second saying that is preserved in *Gos. Thom.* 11 is hidden in the question of Matthew:

> Jesus said,
> "This heaven will pass away,
> And the one above it will pass away.
> The dead are not alive,
> And the living will not die."

It is to this apocalyptic saying which also the answer of Jesus in the *Dialogue of the Savior* alludes and expands with an anthropological statement perhaps in reference to Genesis 2, according to which it is the soul that provides life to the body: is she free, then the body is the "dead," and the soul now becomes even more alive. That the question of the disciple rests on a traditional saying can only be proven by reference to the isolated transmission of this saying in the *Gospel of Thomas.*

In other instances, one can only surmise that a traditional saying has been employed. *Gos. Thom.* 24 preserves the following:

> His disciples said,
> "Show us the place where you are, since it is necessary for us to seek it."
> He said to them,
> "Whoever has ears, let him hear.
> There is light within a man of light,
> And he lights up the whole world.
> If he does not shine, there is darkness."

In addition to the frequently used sentence "Whoever has ears, let him hear!" (Mark 4:9, etc.), Jesus' answer contains an exegesis of the saying about the "Light that should not be placed under a bushel basket" (Matt 5:15); already Matt 5:16 had expanded this saying:

> Therefore let your light shine among human beings.

But also the question of the disciples for the "place" possibly alludes to a traditional saying of Jesus, because this topic frequently appears in these dialogues, for example, in *Dialogue of the Savior:*

> They said to him,
> "What is the place to which we are going?"
> The Lord said,
> "The place you can reach ... [...] stand there!"[67]

---

67. NHC III,5 142.16–19.

At another passage of the same writing appears what seems to have been a traditional saying of Jesus:

... to come [forth ...] and enter [into the place of life] so that they might not (be) held ... [in] this impoverished cosmos.[68]

Sayings about the "place" seem to have been known also in the Gospel of John (see below).

The examples presented here about the manner of forming dialogues on the basis of traditional sayings must suffice here. They can be easily multiplied. The richness of the underlying wealth of traditional sayings in such dialogue gospels can be demonstrated in the *Apocryphon of James* (NHC I,2). In its external form it pretends to be a secret book in the form of a letter (*Epistula Jacobi*) that reports revelation of Jesus to Peter and James. The situation described in this letter's introduction depicts the twelve disciples "all sitting together and remembering what the savior had said to each one of them, whether in secret or openly, and putting it in books."[69] This terminology is typical for the citation of sayings of Jesus in a rather early stage of the tradition, when written gospels do not necessarily have to be presupposed. The Acts of the Apostles (20:35), adducing a saying of Jesus, speaks about "remembering" the words of the Lord; this term also appears in *1 Clement* (13.2; 46.8); in the *Letter of Polycarp* (2.3); and is especially evident in Papias of Hierapolis, the eager collector of pieces of Jesus' sayings from the oral tradition.[70] Thus the *Apocryphon of James* indicates right at the beginning of the work that it is concerned with traditional sayings of Jesus. It can remain an open question here whether the source for these sayings was the oral tradition or a written gospel. The latter seems to me very unlikely; but this still must be demonstrated in a detailed investigation.

The dialog is introduced by a saying of Jesus:

I shall go to the place from where I came.[71]

This sentence reproduces an older wisdom saying in which Wisdom speaks about her coming into the world and her return into her heavenly abode. This wisdom saying has entered the tradition of Jesus' sayings very early; the Gospel of John alludes to this saying several times, for example John 7:33:

Only a brief time I shall be with you,
I am going back to the one who has sent me.

The continuation of the speech of Jesus in the *Apocryphon of James* may have belonged to the same saying of Jesus:

---

68. NHC III,5 132.2–5.

69. NHC I,2 2.9–15.

70. See Helmut Koester, *Synoptische Überlieferung bei den Apostolischen Vätern* (TU 65; Berlin: Akademie-Verlag, 1957) 4–6.

71. NHC I,2 2.23–24.

If you wish to come with me, come![72]

Compare John 14:2–3:

> In my Father's house are many mansions.
> I am going to prepare a place for you;
> I come again in order to take you with me,
> so that where I am you will be also.

The topic of the interpretation that follows is introduced by another saying of Jesus that is not explicitly quoted but only alluded to. Jesus is now addressing James and Peter specifically, whom he has drawn aside:

> Do you not, then, desire to be filled?
> And your heart is drunken;
> do you not then want to be sober?
> Therefore, be ashamed! Henceforth, waking or sleeping,
> remember that you have seen the Son of Man.[73]

The exact wording of the saying that is used here is preserved in the *Gos. Thom.* 28:

> Jesus said,
> "I took my place in the midst of the world,
> and I appeared to them in the flesh.
> I found all of them intoxicated.
> I found none of them thirsty.
> And my soul became afflicted for the sons of men,
> because they are blind in their hearts and do not have sight;
> for empty they came into the world and empty do they seek to leave the world.

Although many of terms that the two passages share appear frequently in Gnostic writings, the common terms "empty," "drunken/intoxicated," "thirsty," "heart," and "blind/see" suggest that the saying from the *Gospel of Thomas* was the basis for this address to Peter and James in the *Apocryphon of James*. Once again, this is a wisdom saying, in which Jesus speaks like Wisdom in the style of a revelation discourse about his own mission. The *Apocryphon of James* has transformed this revelation discourse into an admonition.

After a brief interpretation, the next topic is introduced by James in an allusion to two synoptic sayings:

> But I answered and said to him,
> "Lord, we can obey you if you wish, for we have forsaken our fathers and our villages and followed you. Grant us therefore not to be tempted by the devil, the evil one."[74]

---

72. NHC I,2 2.24–25.
73. NHC I,2 3.8–14; the preceding lines (2.40–3.7) of the address of Jesus are untranslatable fragments.
74. NHC I,2 4.23–30.

Cf. Luke 18:29–30; Matt 10:27–29:

> Peter said:
> "Behold, we have left everything and followed you."
> But he said,
> "Truly, I say to you, there is no one who has left his house or wife or brothers or parents or children for the sake of the dominion of God who will not receive back manifold in this world, and in the other world life eternal."

In addition, there is an allusion to Matt 6:13:

> And lead us not into temptation
> but deliver us from the evil one.

In his answer, Jesus says among other things:

> Or do you not know that you have yet to be abused and to be accused unjustly, and have yet to be shut up in prison and condemned unlawfully and crucified without reason, and buried shamefully, as I myself by the evil one.[75]

The prediction of the discipleship of Jesus in suffering is clearly present here; cf. Mark 13:9–13, etc. A traditional saying of Jesus that has been cited in the question of a disciple is thus interpreted by another traditional saying in Jesus' answer.

In the following discussions of the *Apocryphon of James,* parables are repeatedly quoted and interpreted, among them also parables of Jesus that are not attested in the Synoptic Gospels, for example, the parable of the palm shoot:

> Do not allow the kingdom of heaven to wither; for it is like a palm shoot, whose fruit has dropped down around it. They (i.e., the fallen fruit) put forth leaves, and after they had sprouted, they caused their womb to dry up.[76]

Or:

> For the word is like a grain of wheat; when someone had sown it, he had faith in it; and when it had sprouted, he loved it because he had seen many grains in place of one. And when he had worked, he was saved because he had prepared it for food, and again he left some to sow. So also can you yourselves receive the kingdom of heaven.[77]

Closely related, and also corresponding to the style of synoptic parables, is the following parable:

---

75. NHC I,2 5.9–20.
76. NHC I,2 7.22–27.
77. NHC I,2 8.16–25.

For the kingdom of heaven is like an ear of grain after it had sprouted in a field. And when it had ripened, it scattered its fruit and again filled the field with ears for another year.[78]

There is also an allusion to those who live as foreigners in a city,[79] which is told in the *Shepherd of Hermas (Sim. 1),* although there it is not identified as parable of Jesus.

It is typical for a dialogue gospel to progress to a longer discourse of Jesus that is not interrupted by questions of the disciples, but which nevertheless is based upon sayings and their interpretation. In this respect, the *Apocryphon of James* is closely related to the Gospel of John in which also dialogical sections alternate with longer discourses of Jesus.

Longer discourses can also be found in the other dialogue gospel, the *Dialogue of the Savior* (NHC III, 5). But they have a different origin. The analysis of this book is complex, because it is apparently a compilation of materials of a different character.[80] The beginning is a lengthy discourse of the savior describing the path of the soul through the hostile powers, including also a prayer.[81] These pieces have to be ascribed to the compiler of the document, whose language is closely related to that of the New Testament letters to the Colossians and Ephesians and the Epistle to the Hebrews. There are no dialogical elements. Following this introduction is a dialogue that is based on sayings of Jesus.[82] This dialogue, however, is interrupted twice, once by a myth of creation based upon an interpretation of Genesis 1–2,[83] and for a second time by a wisdom-type explanation of a cosmological list (darkness, light, fire, water, wind).[84] In both instances, these pieces have been inserted into the older dialogue by the compiler. A short apocalyptic vision that shows some relationship to *Enoch* 17[85] already may have been part of the older dialogue. After the introduction and these secondary materials have been eliminated, a dialogue between Jesus and Judas, Matthew, and Miryam remains, comprising about 60 percent of the preserved writing. Longer speeches are missing in this dialogue; rather, questions and answers alternate in rapid succession. Sayings of Jesus are introduced, questioned, sometimes repeated, varied or expanded, and then interpreted briefly. In other words, this is an expanded sayings collection, in some respects comparable to the *Gospel of Thomas* and to the synoptic sayings collection Q—only somewhat further developed. This dialogue can thus be assessed as standing in between a simple

---

78. NHC I,2 12.22–27.

79. NHC I,2 11.17–27.

80. My literary-critical analysis of the document has meanwhile been published in Emmel, Koester, and Pagels, *Nag Hammadi Codex III, 5,* pp. 2–15.

81. NHC III,5 120.2–124.22.

82. NHC III,5 124.23

83. NHC III,5 127.33–131.15. This myth of creation is also presented in the form of a dialogue. But it is not based on sayings of Jesus; the dialogical form is here a secondary feature.

84. NHC III,5 133.16–134.24. The compiler has expanded this list by Christian interpretations; e.g., regarding "water" he remarks: "For what use is there for him to be baptized in it" (sc. if he does not understand water; 134.14–15). In 134.14–15 he remarks: "And how will someone, who does not know [the son?], know the [father?]."

85. NHC III,5 134.24–137.3.

collection of sayings and an expanded dialogue gospel like the *Apocryphon of James* and the Gospel of John. As far as parallels to the sayings that appear elsewhere are concerned, ten are found in the Gospel of Matthew (most of them also in Luke), two in the Gospel of John, sixteen in the *Gospel of Thomas*, and one in the Epistle of James. On the other hand, redactional elements in the form of the sayings as they occur in the canonical gospels are missing completely. In view of the numerous parallels in the *Gospel of Thomas,* it is probably more likely to assume that the source for this dialogue gospel was a collection of sayings that resembled the synoptic sayings source but had been further developed analogously to the development that is visible in the *Gospel of Thomas*.

The intended interpretation often enters into the quotation of a saying. For example, the saying about the eye as the light of the body appears in Matthew 6:22 in this form:

The eye is the lamp of the body.
So if your eye is healthy,
Your whole body will be full of light;
but if your eye is unhealthy,
your whole body will be full of darkness.

In the *Dialogue of the Savior,* this saying appears in modified wording:

The lamp of the body is the mind.
As long as the things inside you are set in order,
that is . . . your bodies are luminous.
As long as your hearts are dark,
the luminosity you anticipate
[. . .].[86]

It is perhaps possible to describe the *Dialogue of the Savior* as an interpretation of sayings also in a different perspective: the writing is not just interested in the interpretation of sayings but also in the exploration of specific topics, which are indicated by some eminent sayings of Jesus. At the beginning of the *Gospel of Thomas* appears the saying about seeking and finding that is also attested elsewhere; the following quote is a translation of its more original form attested in the Greek fragments of the *Gospel of Thomas:*

Let him who seeks continue seeking until he finds.
When he finds, he will be amazed.
And when he becomes amazed, he will rule.
And once he has ruled, he will attain rest.[87]

---

86. NHC III,5 125.18–126.1; the final line of the saying is lost due to the corruption of the manuscript.
87. *Pap. Oxy. 654,* 5–9 = *Gos. Thom.* 2. Reconstruction and translation by Harold Attridge in Layton, *Nag Hammadi Codex II, 2–7,* pp. 113 and 126.

In the dialogue that forms the basis of the extant writing, sayings about seeking and finding are dominating in the first part.[88] The next section reports an apocalyptic vision that fills the disciples with amazement.[89] Following this section are sayings about ruling, and the final part of the dialogue—as far as the very poorly preserved text permits a judgment—deals with sayings about the place and the path to the heavenly resting place.[90] In this context the dialogue emphasizes that the disciples have not yet reached the status of ruling and resting because they still must carry the burden of earthly labor and toil, in which even Jesus himself still has a part.[91] This makes clear that the dialogue does not presuppose a situation of an appearance of Jesus after his resurrection. To be sure, the dialogue also emphasizes what is said at the beginning of the *Gospel of Thomas*:

Whoever finds the interpretation of these sayings will not experience death.

At the end of the *Dialogue of the Savior* the phrase "the one who has understood" appears, and after some very fragmentary lines the words "he will live."[92] Both writings therefore may show a relationship to the Gospel of John;[93] cf. John 6:63:

The words I have spoken to you are spirit and are life.

And John 8:52:

Whoever keeps my word will not taste death.

In the *Dialogue of the Savior* short dialogues with sayings are sometimes expanded to longer dialogue units. The saying of Jesus about entering into the place of life that has been mentioned above is, in fact, the beginning of a larger unit which ends with another saying of Jesus that is a variant of the well-known maxim about knowing oneself:

The Lord said, ...
". . . to come [forth . . .] and enter [into the place of life] so that they might not (be) held . . . [in] this impoverished cosmos."
Matthew said,
"Lord, I want to see that place of life . . . where there is no wickedness but rather there is pure light."

---

88. NHC III,5 125.11–17; 126.6–10; 128.2–5; 129.14–16.

89. NHC III,5 134.24–137.3; cf. 136.2–4: "Then the disciples were amazed at all the things he had said to them."

90. NHC III,5 138.7–21; 141.3–12; 142.4–8, 16–19.

91. NHC III,5 139.6–7; cf. 141.5–6.

92. NHC III,5 146.18–19; 147.19.

93. [As I look at the translation of the critical edition of the text, which was not available at the time of the original publication of this chapter as an article, I should warn that this is very hypothetical as far as the *Dialogue of the Savior* is concerned; HK].

The Lord said,
"Brother Matthew, you will not be able to see it as long as you are carrying this flesh around."
Matthew said:
"Lord, [if I cannot] see it, let me [know it]."
The Lord said,
"Everyone who has known himself has seen it . . . everything given to him to do . . . and has come to . . . in his goodness."[94]

With respect to structure and topic, and perhaps also with respect to the sayings that appear here, this dialogue is analogous to John 14:2–12, except for that fact that the Johannine dialogue is further developed and expanded. For better comparison, I am reproducing the Johannine dialogue here in a shortened form:

Jesus said,
"And if I go and prepare a place for you, I will come again and take you to myself, so that where I am, you may be also."
Thomas said to him,
"Lord, we do not know where you are going. How do we know the way?"
Jesus said to him,
"I am the way and the truth and the life. No one comes to the Father except through me."
Philip said to him,
"Lord, show us the Father, and we will be satisfied."
Jesus said to him,
"Whoever has seen me has seen the Father. . . . Very truly I tell you, the one who believes in me will also do the works that I do."

The sequence of the topics is the same in both cases: the place (of life)—to get there and to see—to know—to do. But in the Gospel of John, the decisive answer of Jesus is christological ("Who has seen me"), while in the *Dialogue of the Savior,* it is turned into an anthropological direction ("Whoever has known himself"). The typical Johannine features are missing in the *Dialogue of the Savior* here as also elsewhere (only the compiler of the extant document seems to have known the Gospel of John). It is therefore advisable not to speak of literary dependence but rather of a parallel development of the same material of sayings. The question arises whether traditional sayings are embedded in such dialogues, which the author of the Gospel of John has used to compose his dialogues and discourses of Jesus. It seems to me that this is in fact the case. An example for this may be the following section of the Gospel of John 16. In this discourse the following statements appear in John 16:23–24 and 16:30:

---

94. NHC III,5 132.2–19.

"On that day you will ask nothing of me. . . . Ask and you will receive, so that your joy may be complete."
His disciples said,
". . . Now we know that you know all things, and do not have need that anyone question you."

Compare here the *Dialogue of the Savior:*

And let him who [. . .] seek and find and rejoice.[95]

Gos. Thom. 92:

Seek and you will find.
Yet what you asked me about in former times, but which I did not tell you then, I do desire to tell, but you do not inquire after it.

Acts of John 98:

There must be one man to hear those things from me;
for I need one who is ready to hear.

It is not possible at this point to draw final conclusions. But a few working hypotheses can be suggested:

1. The discourses and dialogues of the Gospel of John are built upon traditional sayings of Jesus to a larger degree than has been assumed heretofore.

2. The sayings dialogue from the writings found at Nag Hammadi, as well as other apocryphal gospel materials that were already known, may have preserved such sayings independently of the Gospel of John and thus provide a handle to recognize the sayings that are the basis for the Johannine discourses and dialogues.

To make further progress with these working hypotheses, however, I must open the question of the dating of non-canonical writings again. Wherever synoptic sayings material is found in non-canonical writings, one is more prepared to admit possible dependence upon independent transmission. Such writings may not necessarily have come into existence later than the canonical gospels. This independence has been questioned with respect to the *Gospel of Thomas,* which contains many synoptic sayings, but in my opinion is evident. A date in the latter half of the first century for the original composition of this gospel is quite plausible. But whenever so-called Johannine sayings appear in apocryphal writings, one is hastily tempted to assume dependence upon the Gospel of John. Such dependence, however, is difficult to prove for the *Apocryphon of James* and for the *Dialogue of the Savior*—not to speak of the *Gospel of Thomas,* which presents many

---

95. NHC III,5 129.15.

of those Johannine sayings. But also for the *Dialogue of the Savior*, that is, for the older sayings dialogue, on which this writing is based, I would assume a date in the last decades of the first century. The genre of the dialogue here is not as much developed as in the Gospel of John and the use of written sources cannot be demonstrated. The final compilation of the extant document must be dated in the first half of the second century; it presupposes knowledge of the corpus of the Pauline writings—although any influence of the Synoptic Gospels is difficult to establish even here.

In this context, it is advisable to draw into the discussion another gospel fragment that has been known for some time, the Papyrus Egerton 2. In the translation in the Hennecke-Schneemelcher edition of the *New Testament Apocrypha*, this gospel is categorized as "an unknown gospel with Johannine features." The fragment was first published in 1935.[96] The widespread assessment that this document is a compilation from the four canonical gospels is problematic, especially in view of the paleographical dating by the editors: the hand of the manuscript agrees with the style of writing that appears in datable papyri up to the beginning of the second century. This implies that Papyrus Egerton 2 competes for the rank of the oldest Christian document with the oldest manuscript of a canonical gospel, the fragment of the Gospel of John in the Rylands Papyrus 457 (𝔭 52). Several parallels to the Gospel of John correspond to one of the assumed sources of the Fourth Gospel. This is most obvious with respect to a passage of Papyrus Egerton 2 that may have been the basis for a longer discourse of Jesus in John 5:39–47:

> To the rulers of the people he said this word:
> "You search the Scriptures in which you think you have life. These are they which bear witness of me. Do not think that I came to accuse before my Father! There is one that accuses you, even Moses, on whom you have set your hope. . . . Because if you had believed Moses, you would have believed me; because concerning me he wrote to your fathers.[97]

John has added to the first part of this saying:

> Yet you refuse to come to me that you may have life.

The second part was expanded by John with a juxtaposition of "Scriptures" and "Word":

> But if you do not believe his writings, how will you believe my words?

In addition, the Fourth Evangelist inserted between the parts of the saying a longer discourse about "taking honor from each other" (John 5:42–44). Also in this respect, the text of John 5 proves to be secondary in comparison with the saying attested in Papyrus Egerton 2.

It is not my intention here to renew the search for the written sources of the Gospel

---

96. H. I. Bell and T. C. Skeat, *Fragments of an Unknown Gospel* (London: Published by the Trustees [of the British Museum], 1935).

97. Fragment I; translation, J. Jeremias in Schneemelcher, *New Testament Apocrypha* (1991) 1. 98.

of John. Rather, Papyrus Egerton 2 should serve as an example for the possible preservation of older material in extracanonical writings. Further investigation of the newly discovered dialogue gospels could prove to be fruitful especially for the Gospel of John and for the clarification of the development of the traditions that have been utilized in its discourses and dialogues. That supposes, however, that the treatment of these newly found writings is not a priori burdened by unfounded all-inclusive judgments of their literary dependence upon canonical writings. W. Schneemelcher's verdict in his introduction to the edition of the apocryphal gospels is characteristic for such an assessment of this literature. In all the gospels in which visions and dialogues of Jesus with his disciples are reported, he sees tendentious works of Gnostics, who are dependent upon the canonical gospels. Their peculiarities of style (the form of a dialogue) are for him not just formal features but intrinsically are connected to their content, that is, to their theological intentions. He explicitly includes the *Dialogue of the Savior* and the *Gospel of Thomas* in this category of writings and says about the latter that the tendency of this entire collection of sayings was nothing other than to communicate "Gnosis" and thus "life."[98] One should, of course, not readily deprive the canonical gospels of their intention to communicate knowledge and life—whether or not these words are set in quotation marks. But most of all, it is necessary, as we have seen, to differentiate between the various types of dialogue gospels. And it is questionable whether it is possible to juxtapose apocryphal and canonical gospels as clearly distinguishable in terms of both form and content.

The genre of the dialogue gospels that I discussed in the last part of this chapter is not characterized by freely invented revelation discourses, but by a continuation of the tradition of Jesus' sayings and an endeavor to illuminate their meaning. In this respect, these writings are one with the gospels of the New Testament canon. Even if here the sayings often are different from the forms typical for the synoptic tradition, their close relationship with the Gospel of John should be a warning signal. Moreover, even the Synoptic Gospels present several sayings of a "Johannine" character. I recall the following passages only:

Everything has been handed over to me by my Father;
and no one knows the Son except the Father,
and no one knows the Father except the Son
and to whom the Son wants to reveal.[99]

I praise you, Father, . . . that you have hidden this from the wise and understanding. . . .[100]

I shall bring forth what has been hidden from the beginning of the world.[101]

---

98. W. Schneemelcher in Hennecke-Schneemelcher, *Neutestamentliche Apocryphen* (Tübingen: J. C. B. Mohr [Paul Siebeck], 1958) 1. 50–51. [It is appropriate to note here that Schneemelcher has substantially altered this negative judgment in a more recent edition of the this work; English translation 1991. HK]

99. Matt 11:27.

100. Matt 11:25–26.

101. Matt 13:35.

Parallels to such synoptic sayings appear not only in the Gospel of John, in the *Gospel of Thomas*, and in the *Dialogue of the Savior* but already in the writings of Paul, especially in 1 Corinthians 1–4.[102] This also should be considered whenever the question of the date of such sayings traditions is under consideration.

The newly discovered documents, like the well-known older apocryphal materials, have a right to be questioned, whether they could provide information for the investigation of the earliest history of Christianity. The perception of that history, specifically our understanding of the tradition of the sayings of Jesus, might then change substantially. It cannot be expected that several dozen hitherto unknown writings from the first three centuries can be easily incorporated into the established image of historical developments that scholarship had constructed without the knowledge if these writings. It may turn out that even the Johannine dialogues and discourses are based upon very old material from the tradition of the sayings of Jesus and that even apocryphal dialogues of Jesus with his disciples use such old sayings material. Then this branch of the tradition and its witness deserves, in addition to the synoptic sayings, more weight in the reconstruction of the earliest history of the tradition.

102. H. Koester, "Gnostic Writings as witnesses for the Development of the Sayings Tradition," in Bentley Layton, ed., *The Rediscovery of Gnosticism* (Numen Supp. 41; Leiden: Brill, 1980) 1. 238-62.

12

THE FAREWELL DISCOURSES
OF THE GOSPEL OF JOHN

Their Trajectory in the First and Second Centuries

I. The Sayings of Jesus about "Seeking and Finding"

The sayings of Jesus on the theme, "seek and find" or "ask and receive," are well known and recur several times in variant forms in the gospels of the New Testament. The following variant appears among a number of these familiar sayings; it is preserved in Matthew and in Luke:

> Ask and it will be given to you; seek and you will find; knock and it will be opened to you. For everyone who asks, receives; and the one who seeks, finds; and to the one who knocks, it will be opened. (Matt 7:7–8)

In the Christian tradition, these sayings always have been understood as words related to the granting of things asked in prayer. Whether they be our wishes or our requests, we can present them before God, because God responds to the prayers of his people.

In the *Gospel of Thomas*, however, this same saying is interpreted in another way. There Jesus does not exhort the disciples to ask in prayer for everything of which they might have need; instead, he invites them, insistently, to seek the sayings that he wishes to give them and to ask the meaning of these sayings in order to obtain life. Thus, the *Gospel of Thomas* is introduced by these urgent words:

> These are the secret sayings that the living Jesus spoke and Didymos Judas Thomas recorded. And he said, "Whoever discovers the interpretation of these sayings will not taste death."

The saying which immediately follows (2) describes the process thanks to which this "seeking" attains its outcome:

> "Let the one who seeks not stop seeking until he finds and, when he finds, he will be amazed, and when he is amazed, he will rule, and when he rules, he will rest."[1]

---

1. This translation is based on the Greek version cited by Clement of Alexandria *Strom.* 5.14 § 96 and

174

The author of the Fourth Gospel has made these sayings concerning "seeking life" one of the principal themes of all his work. In this gospel, moreover, the words of Jesus procure eternal life:

"The words that I have spoken to you are spirit and life." (John 6:63)

Or again,

Simon Peter answered him: "Lord, to whom can we go? You have the words of eternal life." (John 6:68)

But the disciples, in the Gospel, are invited to seek not wisdom but Jesus himself above all, and only afterwards to inquire of his words. Thus, the first meeting of Jesus with other persons that is reported in the Gospel begins with this question addressed to two disciples of John the Baptist, who have begun to follow Jesus: "What do you seek?" (John 1:38). A little while afterwards, Andrew is going to find his brother Simon and says to him, "We have found the Messiah" (John 1:41). And when Philip wishes to make Jesus known to Nathaniel, he says to him, "We have found him of whom Moses in the Law and also the Prophets wrote" (John 1:45). Just as these meetings with Jesus are inaugurated by the question, "What do you seek?" so after the discovery of the empty tomb Jesus meets Mary Magdalene and asks of her, "Woman, why are you weeping? Whom do you seek?" (John 20:15).

This "seeking Jesus" is put on stage dramatically in the Fourth Gospel. The crowd *seeks* Jesus because of the miracles that he has accomplished (John 6:24–26; 7:11); but this seeking leads to nothing. Those who *seek* their own glory, and not the glory of God, will die in their sins (5:44; 7:18; 8:50). But the people who *seek* Jesus with the greatest zeal are those who wish to arrest him and want him to perish (5:18; 7:1, 19–20, 25, 30; 8:37, 40; 10:39; 11:8, 56). When they later arrive to arrest Jesus, they find that he advances towards them, asking them, "Whom do you seek?" (John 18:4, 7; cf. also 18:8).

For the crowd as well as for the disciples, the mystery linked to this "seeking Jesus" is expressed in this affirmation of John 7:34 and 36:

"You will seek me and you will not find me. Where I am, you cannot come."

In John 13:33, the disciples are placed before the same mystery:

"Little children, yet a little while I am with you. You will seek me; and as I said to the Jews so now I say to you: Where I am going you cannot come."

The incapacity of the hostile crowd to find Jesus can be explained simply as a consequence of its incredulity. But what about the disciples? For those who would continue to believe in Jesus, the central matter is this: whether to be with Jesus after his departure and to attain the place to which he goes. If the Farewell Discourses of the Gospel of John are dominated by this question, this may be explained by the fact that a Gnostic response existed already as a prerequisite.

---

attributed by him to the *Gospel of the Hebrews* (*Strom.* 2.9 § 45). I believe that this is the original text of the saying found in the *Gospel of Thomas*.

II. The Gnostic Understanding of
the Theme "Seek and Find"

The clearest example of this Gnostic response is furnished by two sayings in the *Gospel of Thomas* (49 and 50):

> Jesus said, "Blessed are those who are alone and chosen, for you will find the kingdom. For you have come from it and you will return there again." Jesus said, "If they say to you, 'Where have you come from?' say to them, 'We have come from the light, from the place where the light came into being by itself'. . . . If they say to you, 'Is it you?', say, 'We are its children and we are the chosen of the living Father.' If they ask you, 'What is the evidence of your Father in you?' say to them, 'It is motion and rest.'"

To recognize one's origin is here the only thing that is necessary. One finds a variant of this solution in the *Apocryphon of James*. In this text, Jesus appears to his disciples 550 days after his resurrection (NHC I,2, pp. 2, 22–33):

> We [the disciples] said to him, "Have you departed and removed yourself from us?" But Jesus said, "No, but I shall go to the place from which I came. If you wish to come with me, come!" They all answered and said, "If you bid us, we come!" He said, "Verily, I say unto you, no one will ever enter the kingdom of heaven at my bidding, but (only) because you yourselves are full."[2]

The sense is clear. The disciples must find that which they seek within themselves, in order to know that their being is full of the divinity that constitutes their real self. The *Dialogue of the Savior*[3] expresses the same idea, in a passage which appears close to the dialogue of John 14.[4] In the *Dialogue of the Savior* (27–30), a similar question is posed to Jesus:

> [Matthew] said, "Lord, I wish [to see] this place of life [. . .] where there is no wickedness, but rather there is pure [light]."

---

2. The English translation of the citations from this Nag Hammadi writing is from Frederick Wisse in James Robinson, ed., *The Nag Hammadi Library in English* (San Francisco: Harper, 1990).

3. One finds in this writing certain sections in the form of dialogue belonging to a more ancient gospel, which itself does not depend on any of the canonical gospels; see on this subject Helmut Koester and Elaine Pagels, "Report on the Dialogue of the Savior (CG III, 5)," in R. McL. Wilson, ed., *Nag Hammadi and Gnosis: Papers Read at the First International Congress of Coptology* (Cairo: December, 1976; NHS 14; Leiden: Brill, 1987) 66–74, as well as the introduction to the edition of Stephen Emmel, *Nag Hammadi Codex III, 5: The Dialogue of the Savior* (NHS 26; Leiden: Brill, 1984) 1–16.

4. For a more detailed comparison between this passage of the *Dialogue of the Savior* and John 14, see chapter 11, "Dialogue and the Tradition of Sayings in the Gnostic Texts of Nag Hammadi."

The Lord [said], "Brother [Matthew], you will not be able to see it [as long as you are] carrying the flesh around."

[Matthew] said, "Lord, [. . .] not see it, let me [know it]."

The Lord [said], "[Everyone] who has known himself has seen [it, . . .] every thing given to him to do [. . .] and he has come to [. . .] it in his [goodness]."[5]

The progression of the dialogue between Jesus and Matthew presupposes that as a human being, one has need neither of a physical ascension nor of a visionary experience; rather, the encounter with oneself leads one to accomplish the works that are in accord with the goodness of one's divine being.

III. "To Seek the Way" in the Farewell Discourses

This Gnostic solution is explicitly rejected in the Farewell Discourses of the Gospel of John. As in the passages quoted of the *Apocryphal Letter of James* and of the *Dialogue of the Savior,* John 14 begins with an affirmation of Jesus concerning the place to which he returns:

"In my Father's house are many rooms; if it were not so, would I have told you that I go to prepare a place for you. . . . And you know the way where I am going." Thomas said to him, "Lord, we do not know where you are going; how can we know the way?" Jesus said to him, "I am the way, and the truth, and the life; no one comes to the Father, but by me." (John 14:2, 4-6)

This declaration of Jesus has the air of being a direct refutation of the affirmation of the *Apocryphon of James*: "No one will ever enter the kingdom of heaven at my bidding" (NHC I, 2, p. 2,29–34). In John 14, the believers are totally dependent upon Jesus in their seeking the way that leads to the Kingdom. In John 14, as in the *Dialogue of the Savior,* Jesus rejects the request of the one who aspires to a visionary experience:

Philip said to him, "Lord, show us the Father, and we will be satisfied." Jesus said to him, "Have I been with you so long and yet you do not know me, Philip? Whoever has seen me has seen the Father. . . . I am in the Father and the Father is in me." (John 14:8–10)

But, in contrast to the *Dialogue of the Savior,* John 14 does not reject the vision in order that the disciple may better discover true knowledge within himself. On the contrary, John points the disciple back to Jesus inasmuch as Jesus is the presence of the Father. To believe in Jesus becomes thus identical to finding eternal life. Equally, the works that

---

5. NHC III,5, p. 132, 6–19 = 27–30. Translation adapted from Stephen Emmel, *Dialogue of the Savior.*

are accomplished by those who find life in Jesus are not works that issue from their own goodness; they are rather the works of Jesus himself:

Amen, amen, I say to you, whoever believes in me will do the works that I do, and will do greater ones than these, because I am going to the Father. (John 14:12)

Once again, the theme "seek and find/ask and receive" is then taken up in this saying of Jesus:

And whatever you ask in my name, I will do it. (John 14:13)

Although the disciples continue to be presented as those who seek and who request, the accent is different. The accent falls no longer upon the fact that they *receive* that which they request, but rather upon the fact that Jesus *accomplishes* for them that which they have requested.

There is no doubt that the affirmations of the Johannine Farewell Discourses are formulated in the context of a controversy with already existing Gnostic solutions. John wants to show that there can be no other answer to the quest outside of faith in Jesus. In the Gnostic discourse, the disciples must go to find in themselves their true dwelling place in the divine world. According to John, on the contrary, Jesus will come back to his disciples; he and his Father will establish their dwelling place within and among those who love him (John 14:18–24). Thus the text no longer insists on the fact that Jesus comes from the Father and returns to the Father, but rather on the fact that he goes to the Father and will return to the disciples. There is a reversal of the Gnostic sequence linked to the scheme of descent/ascent. Jesus will return and be always with his disciples, in the form of the Paraclete, the Spirit of Truth, which will remind all what he has said to them (John 14:26).

The theme "seek and find" returns again in another way. In the *Dialogue of the Savior*, a new variant of this saying appears in the following form:

And [let] him who [knows] seek and find and [rejoice]. (NHC II,5, p. 129, 14–16 = 20)

The *Apocryphon of James* uses this same sentence in a discourse that presents near parallels with certain themes of the Johannine Farewell Discourses:

Behold, I shall depart from and go away and do not wish to remain with you any longer, just as you yourselves have not wished it. Now, therefore, follow me quickly. This is why I say unto you, 'for your sakes I came down.' You are the beloved; you are they who will be the cause of life in many. Invoke the Father, implore God often and he will give to you. Blessed is he who has seen you with him when he was proclaimed among the angels, and glorified among the saints; yours (pl.) is life. Rejoice and be glad as sons of God. Keep his will that you may be saved. I intercede on your behalf with the Father.[6]

---

6. NHC I,2, 10,22–11,5.

Perhaps one may attempt to regard this passage as a Gnostic commentary on John 16. However, Ron Cameron has demonstrated the improbability of such a derivation; it is very improbable, according to Cameron, that the discourse in the *Apocryphon of James* is based upon the Gospel of John.[7] Rather, it is necessary to assume that the two writings depend upon a common source, of which the Gnostic version is preserved in the *Apocryphon of James*. At issue in this text is that Jesus goes away after having descended here below for his disciples, that the disciples request to follow, that Jesus invites them to pray to the Father and promises to intercede for them, and that the vision of God is the source of life, and indeed, the joy of the disciples.

The author of the Fourth Gospel has reinterpreted his source, by inverting again the Gnostic scheme. It is not at the vision of the Father but at the time of the return of Jesus that the disciples will rejoice:

> So you have sorrow now, but I will see you again, and your hearts will rejoice, and no one will take your joy from you. (John 16:22)

In the Gospel of John, the disciples also must pray to the Father, but Jesus will not intercede for them with the Father:

> "Until now you have not asked anything in my name; ask and you will receive, so that your joy may be complete.... On that day you will ask in my name, and I do not tell you that I will ask the Father for you. For the Father himself loves you, because you have loved me and have come to believe that I came from God." (John 16:24, 26–27)

That which procures the assurance of salvation is no longer the religious experience of the vision of God. Rather, love of the Father, the love of Jesus, and the love of the disciples for one another delimit the domain in which salvation is present.

IV. The Continuation of the Gnostic Trajectory of John

The *Gospel of Thomas* provides evidence that at the beginning of the Johannine trajectory stands a very early Gnostic interpretation of the words of Jesus. Discourses that are preserved in the *Dialogue of the Savior* and the *Apocryphon of James* developed these themes more fully. The coming of Jesus from the Father and his return to him are symbols of a religion of the other world; those who belong to Jesus "know the way" that leads outside of this world, and they can thus follow Jesus and attain their celestial dwelling place. The author of the Fourth Gospel reinterprets this scheme in a critical way. Jesus himself becomes "the way," and the vision of God becomes identical with seeing Jesus. The disciples remain in this world because they are those whom the Father

---

7. Ron Cameron, *Sayings Traditions in the Apocryphon of James* (HTS 34; Philadelphia: Fortress Press, 1984) especially 116–20.

loves and with whom Jesus remains, after returning to them in the form of the Spirit of Truth.

The "Johannine Trajectory," however, does not end there. The Johannine farewell discourses contain a radical and paradoxical affirmation—salvation is totally present among the disciples and in their love of each other. This paradoxical affirmation has had a double effect: a rejection of the Fourth Gospel, on the one hand, and attempts at a new interpretation, on the other hand. As we know, the Fourth Gospel was not accepted easily, especially during the second century. As far as Justin Martyr is concerned, the Gospel of John was either unknown to him or he avoided making use of it.[8] In Rome, a strong opposition to the theology of John arose and remained until the end of the second century, and some uncertainty remained as to whether this gospel should be accepted.[9]

From another perspective, the Montanists in Phrygia connected their account of the promises of Jesus in the Farewell Discourses with the prophesy of the John of the Apocalypse. A new prophetic message emerged. Montanus claimed to be the Paraclete, the coming of which had been announced in the Gospel of John. He announced, furthermore, the manifestation of the New Jerusalem that the visionary of Patmos had described. Although the new prophetic message of the Phrygians certainly aroused numerous debates and controversies, it did not make any direct contribution to the interpretation of the Farewell Discourses of John.

During the second century, the theological interpretation of the Fourth Gospel became an almost exclusive endeavor of the Gnostics. The Gnostic authors of the *Apocryphon of John* and of the *Acts of John* claimed the authority of the Fourth Gospel in favor of their Gnostic interpretation of the message of Jesus. In the *Acts of John*, the "discourse on the polymorphy of the Lord" (chaps. 87–93) describes the diverse forms of the apparition of the earthly Christ. While the manner of description often has been interpreted as a phenomenon of docetism, it also can be understood as an expression of the superhuman or divine nature of Jesus:[10]

> For when he had chosen Peter and Andrew, who were brothers, he came to me and my brother James, saying, "I need you, come to me!" And my brother when he heard this said, "John, what does he want, this child upon the shore who called us?" And I said, "What child?" And he answered me, "The one who is beckoning to us." And I replied, "Because of the long watch we have kept at sea, you are not seeing well, brother James. Do you not see the man standing there who is handsome, fair and cheerful-looking?" (*Acts of John* 88.10–17)[11]

---

8. For the saying on baptism, cited by Justin *1 Apol.* 61.4, and used in John 3:3–5, see Arthur Bellinzoni, *The Sayings of Jesus in the Writings of Justin Martyr* (NovTSup 17; Leiden: Brill, 1967) 134–38. See also the discussion of the problem in Hans von Campenhausen, *The Formation of the Christian Bible* (Philadelphia: Fortress Press, 1972) 169. There is no doubt that this saying came to Justin by way of liturgical tradition.

9. Cf. von Campenhausen, *Formation of the Christian Bible*, 238–40.

10. On the interpretation of the discourse of polymorphy of chaps. 87–93, 103–5, and its relation to chaps. 94–102 of the *Acts of John*, see Eric Junod and Jean-Daniel Kaestli, *Acta Iohannis* (CChr Series Apocryphorum 1–2; Turnhout: Brepols, 1983) 466–93 and 581ff. The citations that follow refer to the chapters and lines of the edition of Junod-Kaestli and generally reproduce their translation.

11. Translation Knut Schäferdick in Wilhelm Schneemelcher, ed., *New Testament Apocrypha* (2 vols.; Louisville: Westminster/John Knox, 1992) 2. 180.

When they reach the shore, Jesus helps them to secure the boat. Then he manifests himself anew: in the eyes of John, he has the aspect of a bald man, with a thick beard spread out, while in the eyes of James, he appears as a young man with a beard just beginning. The disciples report also that Jesus never closes his eyes and that his gaze is always directed towards the sky. When John rests on the breast of Jesus, he perceives this Jesus alternately as soft and tender or hard like rock (chap. 89). His body is sometimes material, but other times immaterial and as if totally nonexistent. As for his feet, they leave no imprint upon the soil (chap. 93).

The author of these chapters certainly knows the Gospel of John, but he refers only incidentally to it and uses equally the other canonical gospels. However, one question remains open: is it not necessary to understand the insistence placed here upon the super-human aspect of the forms of the apparition of the earthly Jesus as a polemic against the Fourth Gospel and its affirmation that "the Word has become flesh" (John 1:14)?

For the following section of the *Acts of John* (chaps. 94–102), Jean-Daniel Kaestli has shown convincingly that there is not only a literary dependence upon the Gospel of John but also a conscious continuation of the tradition and the Johannine inheritance.[12] These chapters are the expression of a Johannine circle that does not accept, in the same sense as the evangelist, the departure of Jesus to the Father and his return to the disciples in the form of the Paraclete. On the contrary, they emphasize the Gnostic scheme—that Jesus returns to the Father and invites his disciples to follow—and the way in which the Fourth Gospel has understood the Johannine tradition is consciously rejected. Possibly this Gnostic scheme may have been ritualized, here, in the sacrament of dance; Jesus' invitation to the disciples is put on stage here by the singing of a hymn. In this hymn, Jesus, who has never truly assumed a real human body and who is in fact an angelic being, invites his disciples to participate with him in a dance that will transport them to another world:

"I will pipe, dance all of you!"—"Amen."
"I will mourn, beat you all your breasts!"—"Amen."
"(The) one Ogdoad sing praise with us."—"Amen."
"The twelfth number dances on high."—"Amen."
"To the All it belongs to dance in the height"—"Amen."
. . . .
"Being moved towards wisdom,
    you have me as a support; rest in me.
What now I am seen to be
    that I am not
What I am you shall know
    When you come."[13]

---

12. Jean-Daniel Kaestli, "Le mystère de la Croix de lumière et le johannisme. Actes de Jean chs. 94–102," *Foi et Vie* 86. *Cahier biblique* 26 (1987) 35–46; see also Junod and Kaestli (n. 10 above) 589–632, esp. 595–600.

13. *Acts of John* 95 and 96, excerpts; translation Schäferdick in Schneemelcher, *New Testament Apocrypha*, 2. 182–85.

In the face of this docetic interpretation and this spiritualization of Christian existence, the *First Letter of John* not only underlines that only those who confess "Jesus come in the flesh" (1 John 4:2) are truly his disciples; it speaks also of the presence of God in the love of the disciples.

> My beloved, let us love one another, because love comes from God. And whoever loves is born of God and knows God . . . because God is love. (1 John 4:7–8)

A docetic understanding of Jesus, which is explicitly rejected by the *First Letter of John,* reappears emphatically in the *Apocryphon of John.* Here Jesus comes back, as he had promised. John, son of Zebedee, meets, on the road from the Temple, a Pharisee who asks him where his Lord is. John replies, "He has gone to the [place] from which he came."[14] The apostle leaves then for a desert place, while asking himself:

> How then was the savior appointed and why was he sent into the world by his Father, and who is his Father who sent him and of what sort is that aeon to which we shall go?[15]

Jesus appears to him then, at first under the aspect of a child, then under that of an old man, then under a multiplicity of forms.[16] He says to John:

> John, John, why do you doubt or why are you afraid? You are not unfamiliar with this image, are you? . . . I am the Father, I am the Mother, I am the Son. I am the undefiled and incorruptible one. Now I have come to teach you what is and what was and what will come to pass.[17]

The following text is a secret teaching on the subject of this world here, from the perspective of the spiritual world, and the way of salvation that is open to all those who belong to the race which comes from on high.

V. The Presence of the Father in the Love of the Disciples

In the writings discussed above, just as in the first commentaries on the Gospel of John redacted by the Valentinian authors,[18] the Fourth Gospel's paradoxical affirmation of

---

14. NHC II,1, p. 1, 5–12; translation Wisse in Robinson, *Nag Hammadi Library,* 105.

15. NHC II,1, p. 1, 21–25; translation ibid.

16. NHC II,1, p. 2, 1-9; translation ibid.

17. NHC II,1, p. 2, 9-18; translation ibid.

18. Such is the Valentinian interpretation of the prologue of John cited by Ireneaus, *Adv. Haer.* 1.8.5–6 and the commentary of Heracleon, preserved in fragments in Origen, *Comm. in Ioh.,* passim. On these texts, see Elaine H. Pagels, *The Johannine Gospel in Gnostic Exegesis* (SBLM 17; Nashville: Abingdon, 1973). See also

the presence of life in the love of the disciples has disappeared in favor of a cosmological theory of salvation. There exists, however, a document that strives to maintain this
paradox, while presenting a new interpretation of the Johannine Jesus. This occurs in
the *Gospel of Truth*, preserved in the Library of Nag Hammadi and probably written by
Valentinus himself. Certainly, also here, Jesus is not truly human:

> When he appeared, instructing them about the Father, the incomprehensible one,
> when he had breathed into them what is in the thought, doing his will, when
> many had received the light, they turned to him. For the material ones were
> strangers and did not see his likeness and had not known him. For he came by
> means of fleshly form, while nothing blocked his course because incorruptibil-
> ity is irresistible, since he, again, spoke new things, still speaking about what is in
> the heart of the Father. . . .[19]

What Jesus taught to his disciples, however, through his words and his example, is that
it is love acting effectively and beneficently in the disciples' earthly existence while they
accomplish their mission:

> Say, then, from the heart that you are the perfect day and in you dwells the light
> that does not fail. Speak of the truth with those who search for it and of knowl-
> edge with those who have committed sin in their error. . . . Make firm the foot
> of those who have stumbled and stretch out your hands to those who are ill. Feed
> those who are hungry and give repose to those who are weary. . . . So you do the
> will of the Father, for you are from him. For the Father is sweet and in his will is
> what is good. He has taken cognizance of the things which are yours, that you
> might find rest in them.[20]

At the end of this writing, a passage describing the disciples recalls certain themes
of the Johannine Farewell Discourses and mentions the mysterious presence of eternity
in the midst of their human existence:

> But they themselves are the truth; and the Father is within them and they are in
> the Father, being perfect, being undivided in the truly good one, being in no way
> deficient in anything, but they are set at rest, refreshed in the Spirit. . . . But it is
> in [the place of rest] that I shall come to be, and (it is fitting) to be concerned at
> all times with the Father of the all and the true brothers, those upon whom the
> love of the Father is poured out and in whose midst there is no lack of him.[21]

Jean-Michel Poffet, "Indices de réception de l'évangile de Jean au IIe siècle, avant Irénée," in Jean-Daniel
Kaestli et al., eds, *La communauté johannique et son histoire* (Genève: Labor et Fides, 1990) 305–21; and Jean-
Daniel Kaestli, "L'exégèse valentinienne du quatrième évangile," ibid., 323–50.

   19. NHC I,3, pp. 30,32–31,11; translation Harold W. Attridge and George W. MacRae in Robinson, *Nag
Hammadi Library*, 46.

   20. NHC I,3, pp. 32,31–37; 33,1–5 and 30–37; translation ibid, p. 47.

   21. NHC I,3, pp. 42,25–33; 43, 2–8; translation ibid., p. 51.

13

GNOSTIC SAYINGS AND CONTROVERSY TRADITIONS IN JOHN 8:12–59

Preface

The origin and composition of the Johannine discourses and dialogues are still among the major unsolved problems of New Testament scholarship. Rudolf Bultmann had argued for a major written source of revelation discourses that was used by the author of the Fourth Gospel.[1] This theory was almost unanimously rejected by subsequent scholarship. Later commentators usually acquiesce in describing the elements of the characteristic style of these discourses and treat them as a whole as compositions of the author.[2] The effort to identify traditional sayings of Jesus incorporated in these discourses so far has provided very limited results because the Synoptic Gospels were used as the primary criterion in this search.[3] As I have argued elsewhere,[4] it seems to me that comparison with apocryphal gospels, such as Papyrus Egerton 2, the *Gospel of Thomas*,[5] the *Dialogue of the Savior*, and the *Apocryphon of James* can give us some clues for understanding the process of composition of the Johannine discourses and for identifying the traditional sayings utilized in their composition.

In this study, I propose to use John 8:12–59 as a test case for two reasons: (1) Parallels to this chapter frequently occur in gospels of the Nag Hammadi corpus, especially in the *Gospel of Thomas*. (2) This Johannine section contains controversies of Jesus with his Jewish opponents. These controversies are of the same type as those of John 5:39–47, which are paralleled by a section of the "Unknown Gospel" of Papyrus

---

1. *The Gospel of John: A Commentary* (Philadelphia: Westminster, 1971) passim.

2. Raymond E. Brown, *The Gospel according to John* (2 vols.; AB 28–29; Garden City, N.Y.: Doubleday, 1966–1970) 1. cxxxii–cxxxvii (with literature).

3. C. H. Dodd, *Historical Tradition in the Fourth Gospel* (Cambridge: Cambridge University Press, 1963) 335–420.

4. Helmut Koester, *History and Literature of Early Christianity (Introduction to the New Testament,* vol. 2) (2nd ed.; New York: de Gruyter, 2000) 182–87; Koester, "Dialogue and the Tradition of Sayings in the Gnostic Texts of Nag Hammadi," included in this volume, pp. 148–73.

5. Raymond E. Brown ("The Gospel of Thomas and the Fourth Gospel," *NTS* 9 [1962/63] 155–77) investigated in detail the parallels to the Gospel of John in the *Gospel of Thomas*, but he simply assigned these parallels to Johannine influence upon the second, i.e., Gnostic source of the latter Gospel. In his commentary, Brown repeatedly refers to these parallels in the *Gospel of Thomas* but does not draw any consequences for the analysis of the Johannine discourses.

Egerton 2, that is, they could possibly be identified as materials drawn from a written source.[6]

I. Composition of the Passage

Traditionally, the unit John 8:12–59 has been viewed as highly problematical and disjointed. Bultmann split this section into nine disparate smaller units that he assigned to different sections in his attempt to reconstruct the original order of John's gospel.[7] Brown says, "An analysis of the structure of chapter viii (12ff.) is perhaps more difficult than that of any other chapter or discourse in the first part of the Gospel."[8] One may wonder, however, whether the interpreters have asked the right question. Well-organized discourses, such as the discourse on the bread that has come down from heaven in John 6, have led to the assumption that the primary criteria of organization must be cohesion and the logical progress of an argument. The author may have achieved that in some of the Johannine discourses, but the first stage of the process of composition was the collection of originally independent smaller units that did not necessarily have the same thematic orientation. Different sections of the Gospel of John indeed represent different stages of development along the trajectory from the collection of oral materials to the composition of coherent literary units.[9] John 8:12–59 may belong to a comparatively early stage in this process. If this is the case, the more original units will be more clearly recognizable in this chapter. Its disjointed appearance, then, is simply an indication of a more original stage in the development of this literature. It is, therefore, not surprising that materials used here for the composition are still more easily recognizable than in other chapters of the Gospel.

The section begins with the characteristic "I am" (ἐγώ εἰμι) self-predications of Jesus, followed by a promise:

I am the light of the world.
He who follows after me will not walk in darkness,
but will have the light of life. (8:12)

The structure of the self-predication [recognition formula][10] and the promise are exactly the same as in John 6:35:[11]

---

6. See the chapter, "Apocryphal and Canonical Gospels," included in this volume, pp. 3–23.

7. Cf. Bultmann, *The Gospel of John*, passim. The various segments of John 8:12–59 (together with sections from other chapters) appear in the following order and context: 7:19–24; 8:13–20; 6:60–7:14; 7:25–29; 8:48–50; 8:54–55; 7:37–44; 7:31–36; 7:45–52; 8:41–47; 8:51–53; 8:56–59; 9:1–41; 8:12; 12:44–50; 10:1–12:32; 8:30–40.

8. Brown, *The Gospel according to John*, 1. 342. Cf. his comment on the first part of this section (p. 343): "Yet, within 12–20 the thought skips and jumps."

9. I am referring to the model of composition in several stages, suggested by Brown. Cf. his *John*, 1. xxxiv–xxxix; Brown, *The Community of the Beloved Disciple* (New York: Paulist Press, 1979) 17–24.

10. Bultmann, *Gospel of John*, on John 6:35.

11. Cf. also 10:9; 11:25; 16:5. There are several modifications of this formula: 6:51; 10:7, 11, 14; 14:6; 15:1. All these are products of the author of the Gospel of John.

I am the bread of life.
He who comes to me will not hunger
And he who believes in me will never thirst.

It has not been possible to demonstrate that sayings with the "I am" formula in the Gospel of John are traditional.[12] Rather one must assume that the author of the Fourth Gospel employs the formula in order to reshape, as self-predications of Jesus, materials that were available to him in a different form. In John 6:35, such materials are at his disposal in the form of a midrash on the manna from heaven. But for the metaphor of the light used in the self-predication of 8:12, no such biblical materials were available. The fundamental contrast between light and darkness that appears here has parallels in the literature from Qumran,[13] but it is missing in the sayings of Jesus in the Synoptic Gospels.[14] It can be found, however, in sayings of Jesus preserved in writings from Nag Hammadi. Compare the following:

Dial. Sav. III,5, 127, 1–6
If one does not [. . . the] darkness he will [not] be able to see [the light]. Therefore [I] tell you [. . . of the] light is the darkness. [And if one does not] stand in [the darkness, he will not be able] to see the light.

Gos. Thom. 24
The light is within a man of light,
And he lights up the whole world.
If he does not shine, he is darkness.

We know that such sayings were known to the author of the Fourth Gospel, as is evident from John 11:9–10:

If someone walks in the day, he does not stumble,
because he sees the light of this world.
But if someone walks in the night, he stumbles,
because the light is not in him.[15]

In John 8:12 the fundamental contrast ["not walk in the darkness"—"have the light of life"] corresponds to the contrast expressed in these sayings. One can therefore assume

---

12. Heinz Becker (*Die Reden des Johannesevangeliums und der Stil der gnostischen Offenbarungsrede* [FRLANT 68; Göttingen: Vandenhoeck & Ruprecht, 1956]) has demonstrated that the form of the "promise" is clearly traditional. But he is less convincing in his attempt to show the traditional character of the "I am" formula—notwithstanding the fact that self-predications are, of course, widespread in the religions of the time. See on the whole question Brown, *John*, 1. 535–38.

13. Brown, *John*, 1. 340.

14. "You are the light of world" (Matt 5:14) uses the word "light" only as image, but lacks the contrast of light and darkness as metaphors for the realms of good and evil.

15. Variants of this saying are present in John 12:34–36; cf. 9:4–5. It is typical for the style of such sayings that they play with the ambiguity of the metaphor and shift from its use as an "image" to its understanding as a principal metaphysical designation. Cf. also 1 Thess 5:4–6.

that the "I am" saying, together with the promise, is a Johannine reformulation of a traditional saying about light and darkness.

The following discussion about Jesus' "testimony" (μαρτυρία) continues earlier debates of Jesus with his opponents in the Gospel of John, in particular the debate of John 5:35–47.[16] It seems to me that all the discussions about the "testimony" ultimately rely upon traditions originating in the debates of the early Johannine community with its Palestinian Jewish opponents. References to Scripture, Moses, the Law, and John the Baptist dominate these traditions.[17] The close relationship to these traditions also is evident in the formulation of John 8:14a ("And even if I testify to myself, my testimony is true")—a deliberate contradiction to John 5:31 ("If I testified to myself, my testimony would not be true"). For one portion of the debate about "testimony" in John 5:31–47, there is external confirmation for the hypothesis that the author of John was using older, and indeed written, materials. Papyrus Egerton 2, the fragment of an "Unknown Gospel," published in 1935,[18] reproduces a debate between Jesus and the lawyers and rulers of the people about the testimony of the Scriptures and Moses that was most probably the source for John 5:39 and 45.[19]

John 8:14b ("because I know whence I came and where I am going, but you do not know whence I came and where I am going") cannot be ascribed to the same source. Rather it is an adaptation of a traditional saying of Jesus. Its character is patently Gnostic, and while it is used elsewhere in John with respect to Jesus,[20] it can also be used of the believers who share his origin and destiny.

Compare the following:

Gospel of Thomas 49:
Blessed are the solitary and the elect
for you will find the kingdom.
For you are from it,
and to it you will return.

Gospel of Thomas 50:
If they say to you, "where do you come from?"
say to them, "We came from the light. . . ."

John 8:15–16 resumes the discussion of the realized eschatology of 5:22–24. These verses belong to the author's own interpretation of the expectation of the future

---

16. Bultmann (*Gospel of John,* on 8:13–20) considers the section beginning with 8:13 as the conclusion of the complex comprising John 5:1–47 and 7:15–24.

17. On the Midrashic structure of these traditions, cf. J. Louis Martyn, *History and Theology in the Fourth Gospel* (2nd ed.; Nashville: Abingdon, 1979) passim. Although the term μαρτυρία is typically Johannine, it is hardly a creation of the author of the Gospel. It also occurs in this context in Papyrus Egerton 2; see below.

18. H. I. Bell and T. C. Skeat, *Fragments of an Unknown Gospel and Other Early Christian Materials* (London: British Museum, 1935); for further literature see chapter 1, "Apocryphal and Canonical Gospels," included in this volume, pp. 3–23.

19. For further discussion of the relationship of Papyrus Egerton 2 to the Gospel of John, see ibid., pp. 13–17 of this volume.

20. Cf. John 16:28: "I have gone out from the Father and I have come into the world; again I leave the world and I am going to the Father."

judgment of God (or of Jesus) that was widely held in early Christian circles.[21] The purpose of this "flashback" to 5:22–24 is perhaps only to introduce a statement about the unity of Jesus and the Father. The preparation for this statement is further supplemented by another fragment from the tradition of earlier debates with Judaism from which John had already drawn 8:13–14a. The reference to the Law is explicit in 8:17 ("and it is written in your law") and there is no doubt about the conscious reference to the legal rule of two witnesses (Deut 17:6; 19:15). That John 8:18 (where Jesus is pointing to himself and to the Father as the two witnesses) contradicts this rule that requires two witnesses in addition to the person concerned, should not lead to the surprise question why Jesus "does not mention John the Baptist who was sent to testify to the light," nor can it be explained by references to exceptions in rabbinic jurisprudence.[22] Rather, this sentence is formulated by the author to provoke the question "where is your father?" (8:19a), which in turn gives the opportunity to quote once more a traditional saying that concludes this section.

John 8:19b ("You do not know me or the Father; if you knew me, you would also know the Father") reflects the saying that is most fully preserved in Matt 11:27 and Luke10:22:

No one knows the Son except the Father,
and no one knows the Father except the Son
and anyone to whom the Son chooses to reveal him.

This saying is cited in several other passages of the Gospel of John, all of them certainly independent of the Synoptic Gospels (cf. especially John 14:7–10),[23] and it also appears in *Dial. Sav.* III,5: 134, 14–15:

And if he does not know the Son,
How will he know the [Father]?

Cf. *Gos. Thom.* 69:
Blessed are those who have been persecuted within themselves.
It is they who have truly come to know the Father.

John 8:20 seems to be entirely redactional.[24] Although 8:21 introduces a new theme, the explicit remark "no one arrested him, because his hour had not yet come" interrupts

---

21. On John's critical interpretation of traditional Christian eschatology, see Bultmann, *Gospel of John,* on John 3:19 and 5:21.

22. Brown, *John,* on John 8:18.

23. Cf. Helmut Koester, "Gnostic Writings as Witnesses for the Development of the Sayings Tradition," in Bentley Layton, ed., *The Rediscovery of Gnosticism: Proceedings of the International Conference at Yale, New Haven, Conn. March 28–31, 1978* (Supplement to Numen 41. Studies in the History of Religions 41; 2 vols.; Leiden: Brill, 1980–1981) 238–61.

24. Bultmann (*Gospel of John,* on John 8:20) finds in this verse the conclusion of the entire section that began in John 5:1 (see n. 16).

the context more than necessary. I would suggest that at this point the author returned to his source from which he had drawn the debates of Jesus with his Jewish opponents. Papyrus Egerton 2 confirms this. In this fragmentary papyrus, the first preserved section, containing parallels to John 5:39 and 45 (see above), was followed—after a lacuna of uncertain length—by a fragment that begins as follows:

> [to gather] stones together to stone him, and the rulers laid their hands on him that they might arrest him and [deliver] him to the multitude. But they [were not able] to arrest him because the hour of his betrayal [was] not yet [come]. But he himself, the Lord, escaped out of [their hands] and turned away from them.

This was obviously the conclusion of the debate with the lawyers and rulers preserved in the first fragment of the papyrus. In John 8:20, the author of the Fourth Gospel used only a part of this conclusion. Other sentences from this report of an attempted arrest of Jesus appear in John 7:30, 44; 10:31, 39.[25]

II. Tradition History

Rather than proceeding with a detailed analysis of the subsequent sections of John 8, I shall present a brief survey of John 8:21–59, indicating those instances in which one can assume either the utilization of traditional sayings or the dependence upon other source materials.

John 8:21–22: A traditional saying:
I am going away and you will seek me . . .
Where I go, you cannot come.[26]

Cf. *Gos. Thom.* 38:
There will be days when you look for me and not find me.

Ap. Jas. I,2: 2,22–27:
"Have you departed and removed yourself from us?"
But Jesus said: "No, but I shall go to the place whence I came.
If you wish to come with me, come.[27]

John 8:21b, 23–24: "You will die in your sins," and the discussion about "being from below/the world" and "being from above/not from the world," is the interpretation by the author of the Gospel.

---

25. It is far more likely that John used this report repeatedly (to create the impression of an increasing hostility) than that the passage in Papyrus Egerton 2 was pieced together from passages in three different chapters of the Gospel of John.

26. The same saying is used in John 7:34, 36 ("You will seek me and not find me, and where I am you will not be able to come") and John 13:33 ("You will seek me, and as I said to the Jews, where I am going you will not be able to come").

27. Cf. *Ap. Jas.* I,2: 14,20–21: "I shall ascend to the place whence I came."

John 8:25–26a:
They said to him:
"Who are you?"
Jesus said to them:
"First of all, what I say to you.[28]
I have many things to say and to judge about you."[29]

Cf. *Gos. Thom.* 43:
His disciples said to him:
"Who are you that you should say these things to us?"
[Jesus said to them:]
"You do not realize who I am from what I say to you,
But you are like the Jews. . . ."

John 8:26b–29 is the interpretation of the author of the Fourth Gospel using the typical Johannine motif of the "I am" in relation to the "raising up of the Son of Man," that is, the crucifixion of Jesus (cf. John 3:14; 18:5, 6, 8). It is clear from this interpretation that the author understands very well the identity of Jesus person with his speaking: "You will recognize that it is I (ἐγώ εἰμι) and that I do nothing from myself, but that I speak as my father has taught me" (8:28).

John 8:30: A composition of the Evangelist.

John 8:31–32: A traditional saying:
If you remain in my word,
you will truly become my disciples,
and you will know the truth,
and the truth will make you free.

Gos. Thom. 19:
If you become my disciples,
and listen to my words,
these stones will minister to you.
There are five trees in paradise . . .
Whoever becomes acquainted with them
will not experience death.

John 8:33–36: This section could be assigned to the same source from which John drew other materials of debates of Jesus with his Jewish opponents. C. H.

---

28. On the notorious difficulties to translate this sentence, cf. Brown, *John*, note on 8:25. The point seems to be the same as the one of the parallel in *Gos. Thom.* 43, i.e., that whatever Jesus says represents his identity.

29. How difficult this passage is, if one does not recognize the dependence upon a traditional saying, is clearly expressed in Bultmann's (*Gospel of John*, on 8:25–27) statement that a decision is not possible.

Dodd[30] has argued that John 8:35 ("The slave does not remain in the house for-ever") is a traditional saying. He also points to the fact that "The truth will make you free" of John 8:32 and "He who commits sin is a slave" of 8:34 are Stoic maxims.[31] This suggests that the final phrase of the saying of John 8:31–32 may have been added by the author of John in view of his interpretation here. Indeed, this final phrase has no parallel in the possibly more original form of the saying as quoted in *Gos. Thom.* 19.

John 8:37–50: The analysis of this section is difficult, and I am not able to present a convincing solution. It seems to me, however, that further efforts in isolating more traditional sayings in the gospel literature of the Nag Hammadi writings would result in further clarification. The problem in this section is twofold. (1) Traditional sayings are modified by the author of the Gospel of John. (2) They are closely interwoven with fragments of the Fourth Gospel's source, relating debates of Jesus with his Jewish opponents. What follows are just a few sugges-tions, all of them questionable.

John 8:37: Reference to John's source reporting attempts to arrest Jesus.

John 8:38: "What I have seen from my Father, that I speak." Possibly a variation of the saying quoted in 8:26–27.

John 8:39–41: Comments on the source containing debates of Jesus with his opponents.

John 8:42: "I have come from God . . ."; traditional saying.

John 8:43: Johannine expansion of the discourse.

John 8:44: Quote of a tradition about the devil as murderer.[32]

John 8:45–46: Johannine expansion of the discourse.

John 8:47: "He who is from God hears God's words"; variation of a traditional say-ing.

John 8:48–50: "You are a Samaritan and you have a demon"; from a source con-taining Jesus' debates with opponents; cf. Mark 3:20–22.

The last section is more easily recognizable with respect to its components.

---

30. *Historical Tradition,* 379–82.

31. Ibid., 380; cf. 330.

32. Bultmann's investigations (*Gospel of John,* 320–21) showed that it was very likely that such a tradition is used here in John 8:44 as well as 1 John 3:8, 15.

John 8:51: A traditional saying:
Truly, truly I say to you:
"Whoever keeps my word,
Will not see death into eternity."[33]

Cf. *Gos. Thom.* 1:
Whoever finds the interpretation of these sayings
will not experience death.

Dial. Sav. III,5:147, 18–20:
[. . .] understands this
[. . .] will live for[ever].

John 8:52–59: The interpretation uses the same source of Jesus' debates with Jewish opponents that I posited for several preceding sections. This is confirmed by 8:59, "They took up stones to throw at him, but Jesus hid himself and went out of the temple"; cf. the passage from Papyrus Egerton 2 quoted above.

In conclusion, let me reiterate that the disjointed appearance of this chapter of the Gospel of John seems to result from the use of two types of traditional materials that have not been fully developed into a logical discourse: (1) traditional sayings of Jesus, most of which have parallels in gospels that usually are called "Gnostic," although there are a number of parallels in the Synoptic Gospels. The history of these sayings, however, still must be integrated into the history of the sayings of the Synoptic tradition; (2) a (written) source of debates of Jesus with his Jewish opponents, of which a sample has been preserved in Papyrus Egerton 2. The character of these debates and their relationship to the Synoptic controversy stories still requires further clarification.

III. Nag Hammadi Parallels to John

Future analysis of the discourses of the Gospel of John will profit from the search for further additional sayings in Nag Hammadi writings. I simply will list some of the Johannine passages to which striking parallels exist in the *Gospel of Thomas,* the *Dialogue of the Savior,* and the *Apocryphon of James.* The list does not claim to be complete,[34] and traditional sayings of John documented from other sources have not been included.[35]

John 3:35:
The Father loves the Son and has given everything into his hand.[36]

---

33. Cf. John 6:33: "The words which I have spoken to you are spirit and life."

34. I am not listing all possible parallels between John and the *Gospel of Thomas* which Brown assembled in his article (see n. 5) but only those instances in which the same traditional saying seems to be used.

35. E.g., the saying of John 3:3, 5 that is also quoted in Justin *1 Apol.* 61.4. On other synoptic materials, see Dodd, *Historical Traditions,* 335–65.

36. Cf. also John 10:28–29; 13:3.

Cf. *Gos. Thom.* 61:
I am he who exists from the Undivided.
I was given some of the things of my Father.

John 4:14:
He who drinks from the water that I give him
will never thirst into eternity.
But the water that I will give him
will become in him a spring of bubbling water to eternal life.[37]

Cf. *Gos. Thom.* 13:
You have drunk, you have become intoxicated
from the bubbling spring that I have measured out.

John 6:63: See above, on John 8:31.

John 7:33–34: See above, on John 8:21–22:
I am going to the one who sent me.
You will seek me and not find me,
And where I am you cannot come.

John 7:37–38: See above, on John 4:14.

John 9:4: See above, on John 8:12.

John 10:29: See above, on John 3:35.

John 11:9–10: See above, on John 8:12.

John 12:35–36: See above, on John 8:12.

John 13:33: See above, on John 8:21–22.

John 14:2–3 (2–12): A close parallel to this discourse, probably a more original
variant is preserved in *Dial. Sav.* III,5: 132,2–19;[38] cf. also *Ap. Jas.* I,2: 2,24–26.

John 14:9:
Such a long time I have been with you,
and you have not known me, Philip?

Cf. *Ap. Jas.* I,2: 13,39–14,2:
I have revealed myself to you (sg.), James,
and you (pl.) have not known me.

---

37. Cf. also John 7:38–39.
38. For a more detailed analysis, see my article "Gnostic Writings as Witnesses for the Sayings Tradition"
(see n. 23).

John 16:23–24:
Truly, truly I say to you,
whatever you ask the Father
he shall give you in my name . . .
Ask and you will receive
so that your joy will be full.

Cf. *Gos. Thom.* 92 (cf. 94):
Seek and you will find.

Dial. Sav. III,5:129,14–16:
And he who [knows, let him] seek and find and [rejoice].

Ap. Jas. 1,2:10,32–34 and 10,39–11,1:
Invoke the Father,
implore God often,
and he will give to you. . . .
Rejoice and be glad as sons of God.

John 16:23a, 30 (in the form of a question of the disciples):
23: And on that day you will not ask me anything.
30: Now we know that you know everything,
and have no need that someone ask you.

Cf. *Gospel of Thomas* logion 92:
Yet what you asked me about in former times
and which I did not tell you then,
now I do desire to tell,
but you do not inquire after it.[39]

John 16:25 (cf. 16:29):
Those things I have spoken to you in parables.
The hour is coming, when I shall no longer speak
to you in parables,
but I shall speak to you about the Father openly.

Cf. *Ap. Jas.* I,2:7,1–6:
At first I spoke to you in parables,
and you did not understand;
now I speak to you openly,
and you do not perceive.[40]

---

39. Cf. also *Dial. Sav.* III,5:128,1–5; *Acts of John*, 98.
40. This version of the saying resembles Mark 4:10–12 more closely than John 16:25.

John 16:28: See above, on John 8:14.

John 17: There are numerous parallels to passages in Gnostic gospels and dis-courses[41] as well as to sayings already quoted above. In its genre and style, how-ever, John 17 resembles literary Gnostic discourses much more closely than other parts of this gospel. Therefore, this chapter would require an investigation involv-ing different methodological criteria.

John 20:29:
Blessed are those who have not seen
and yet believe.

Cf. *Ap. Jas.* I,2:12,38–13,1:
Blessed will they be who have known me;
woe to those who have heard and have not believed.
Blessed will they be who have not seen yet [have believed].[42]

IV. Conclusion

In conclusion, let me point out a few challenging problems concerning my hypothesis.

1. In most of the Gnostic texts, traditional sayings already are embedded in dialogue and discourse. It is difficult to isolate them, and the exegete's eyes are not suffi-ciently trained for this task.

2. The type of sayings tradition that confronts us here is fundamentally different from the one that we are accustomed to in the Synoptic Gospels, because inter-pretations are not *added to* traditional sayings. Rather, they are expressed in the transformation of the sayings themselves. For example, *Dial. Sav.* III,5:125,19, "The light of the body is the mind," has replaced the traditional term "eye" with the interpretive term "mind." Thus, original metaphors can disappear in favor of their new epexegetical equivalents.

3. There seems to be little respect for the original "form" of a saying; that is, basic formulations ("There is light within a man of light, and he lights up the whole world") can be transformed into I-sayings ("I am the light of the world").

4. Compared to the Synoptic tradition, there is an ever-increased tendency to attract materials that are not true "sayings," but rather creedal statements, catechisms, wisdom lists, and formulations of biblical exegesis.

---

41. E.g., John 17:9–10; cf. *Gospel of Thomas* logion 100; John 17:23; cf. *Ap. Jas.* I,2:4,40–5,5.
42. Cf. also *Ap. Jas.* I,2:7,17–25.

5. We know too little about "Gnostic hermeneutics." What are the rules and criteria of interpretation, and how have they been applied in the process of transmission and exegesis of traditional materials?

Success in solving at least some of these problems will certainly lead to the realiza-
tion that there was a much broader base to the first-century sayings tradition than the
Synoptic Gospels would suggest.

III

JESUS, HIS SAYINGS, AND HIS STORY

14

JESUS THE VICTIM

I. The Original Quest of the Historical Jesus

In the second half of the nineteenth century, Albrecht Ritschl, the influential theologian who taught for many decades at the University of Göttingen, defined the kingdom of God as the achievement of the universal moral community. This, he proposed, is the goal of the divine action in the world and the purpose of the ministry of Jesus. As God's action is motivated by his love, Jesus incorporates this love in his teaching as well as in his suffering and death. Jesus indeed *is* God, but only insofar as he represents fully God's moral purpose for humankind. Nothing in the ministry of Jesus documents Jesus' divinity in metaphysical or supernatural terms. Rather, this divinity is revealed because Jesus as a human being remained faithful to his vocation to the very end, in spite of the resistance and hatred of the world. What Jesus demands of us is to make the kingdom of God a reality in this world; we can fulfill this demand if we live the life of love and patience that has been revealed in Jesus. The goal of the kingdom of God is the uniting of the entire world as a community, in which the love of God is realized by all as the moral purpose of God's creation and of all human life.

It was this understanding of Jesus' divinity, as wholly defined by Jesus' faithfulness to God's moral purpose, that was called into question by the rebellious young scholars of the Göttingen history-of-religions school: Johannes Weiss, William Wrede, Hermann Gunkel, Wilhelm Bousset, Ernst Troeltsch, and later also Hugo Gressmann, Wilhelm Heitmüller, and Rudolf Otto. Hermann Gunkel's dissertation, "The Activities of the Holy Spirit," published in 1888,[1] ended once and for all an understanding of the Holy Spirit as the guiding principle of institutionalized religion and secularized moral action—an understanding that dominated, as Gunkel stated, "exegetes who are influenced by unhistorical and rationalistic thinking."[2] On the contrary, he argued, the Bible understands "spirit" as the uncontrollable and supernatural power of miracle, irrational inspiration, and divine action.

Johannes Weiss's book *The Preaching of Jesus about the Kingdom of God* appeared a few years later in 1892.[3] Its publication had been delayed for a few years until the death of his father-in-law, Albrecht Ritschl, so as not to offend him. This book, as well as those

---

1. Hermann Gunkel, *Die Wirkungen des heiligen Geistes nach der populären Anschauung der apostolischen Zeit und der Lehre des Apostels Paulus* (3rd ed.; Göttingen: Vandenhoeck & Ruprecht, 1909).

2. Ibid., iii.

3. Johannes Weiss, *Die Predigt Jesu vom Reiche Gottes* (Göttingen: Vandenhoeck & Ruprecht, 1892; 2nd ed. 1900; 3rd ed. 1964).

of his other Göttingen friends, advertised the discovery that the rationalistic and moral-
istic categories of their time were not capable of comprehending the early Christian
concept of the kingdom of God. Whereas these categories had their roots, as Johannes
Weiss states, in Kant's philosophy and in the theology of enlightenment, Jesus' concept
of the kingdom of God was informed by the apocalyptic mythology of ancient Judaism
and was thoroughly eschatological, messianic, and supernatural.

Albert Schweitzer characterized Johannes Weiss's work as the beginning of a new era
in the life-of-Jesus research. Recognizing its significance, he asks why the book did not
have an immediate impact:

> Perhaps . . . according to the usual canons of theological authorship, the book
> was much too short—only sixty-seven pages—and too simple to allow its full
> significance to be realized. And yet it is precisely this simplicity which makes it
> one of the most important works in historical theology. It seems to break a spell.
> It closes one epoch and begins another.[4]

What was characteristic for this new epoch of the view of Jesus? Albert Schweitzer
described this well at the conclusion of his *Quest of the Historical Jesus*:

> The study of the Life of Jesus . . . set out in quest of the historical Jesus, believ-
> ing that when it had found Him it could bring Him straight into our own time
> as a Teacher and Savior. . . . The historical Jesus of whom the criticism of the
> future . . . will draw the portrait, can never render modern theology the services
> which it claimed from its own half-historical, half-modern Jesus. He will be a
> Jesus who was Messiah, and lived as such, either on the ground of literary fiction
> of the earliest Evangelist, or on the ground of a purely eschatological Messianic
> conception.[5]

II. The New Quest of the Historical Jesus

The insights of the history-of-religions school dominated the interpretation of the
preaching of Jesus and his ministry for the first half of the twentieth century in critical
New Testament scholarship.[6] What has come to be known as "a new quest of the historical Jesus" was well aware of the danger of modernizing Jesus. Ernst Käsemann, who
opened the "new quest" with his lecture of 1953,[7] vehemently rejected the continua-

---

4. Albert Schweitzer, *The Quest of the Historical Jesus: A Critical Study of Its Progress from Reimarus to Wrede*
(New York: Macmillan, 1959). This work was first published in the year 1906 under the title *Von Reimarus zu
Wrede: Eine Geschichte der Leben-Jesu-Forschung* (Tübingen: Mohr). The first English translation of the second
edition of Schweitzer's work (now entitled *Geschichte der Leben-Jesu-Forschung*) appeared in 1910 (London:
Black).

5. Ibid., 398–99.

6. For a general survey of the influence of the work of Johannes Weiss, see Dieter Georgi, "Leben-Jesu
Theologie/Leben-Jesu Forschung," *TRE* 20. 570–72 (bibliography pp. 573–75).

7. Ernst Käsemann, "Die Frage nach dem historischen Jesus," *ZThK* 51 (1954) 125–53; Eng. trans. "The

tion of the old type of life-of-Jesus study.[8] The new quest of the historical Jesus was informed by the search for the historical foundation of the Christian kerygma. It had no interest in bypassing the proclamation of the early Christian community in order to get uninhibited access to a real and original historical Jesus. On the contrary, James M. Robinson, who has coined the formulation "a new quest of the historical Jesus,"[9] had titled his original lecture "The Kerygma and the Quest of the Historical Jesus."[10] What was at stake here was the validity of the Christian kerygma. Is this kerygma bound to a myth, a mere legend? Or is it formed as a response to the life and death of a human being and to his words and actions?

Like Albert Schweitzer's "(old) quest of the historical Jesus," the "new quest" also rejected unequivocally life-of-Jesus study. Käsemann insisted that Christian faith can never rest on such knowledge; it remains bound to the proclamation of the kerygma, in whatever form.[11] For those who are inclined to disregard the Christian kerygma and who want to go directly to the historical Jesus, the search will never produce anything but an artificial justification for their cause, however worthy.

Nevertheless, almost exactly one hundred years after the first publication of the discoveries of the history-of-religions school, the renaissance of the quest of the historical Jesus has returned full circle to a position that is not unlike that of Albrecht Ritschl and of the portraits of Jesus drawn by the nineteenth-century authors of a "life of Jesus." In a recent article, Marcus Borg describes two fundamental features of this renaissance: (1) "The eschatological consensus that dominated much of this century's Jesus research . . . had seriously eroded" and (2) "We . . . not only know more 'facts' about first-century Palestine, but we also understand the dynamics of that social world better."[12] To be sure, the degree to which eschatology is seen as informing Jesus' ministry is different in these portraits discussed by Marcus Borg.[13] But all

---

Problem of the Historical Jesus," in Ernst Käsemann, *Essays on New Testament Themes* (SBT 41; London: SCM, 1964) 15–47.

8. See his critical discussion of Joachim Jeremias's call for a return to the Jesus of history: "The 'Jesus of History' Controversy," in Ernst Käsemann, *New Testament Questions of Today* (Philadelphia: Fortress Press, 1969) 24–35.

9. This is the title of James M. Robinson's book in its English edition (SBT 25; London: SCM, 1960).

10. The German edition of his book retains the original title: *Kerygma und historischer Jesus* (2nd ed.; Zürich/Stuttgart: Zwingli, 1967).

11. Käsemann, "The 'Jesus of History' Controversy," 24–35.

12. Marcus J. Borg, "Portraits of Jesus in Contemporary North American Scholarship," *HTR* 84 (1991) 1–22. The book by Dale Allison (*The End of the Ages Has Come: An Early Interpretation of the Passion and Resurrection of Jesus* [Philadelphia: Fortress Press, 1985, esp. 101–14), again arguing for the eschatological character of Jesus' preaching of the kingdom of God, seems to be incompatible with a new consensus that has emerged from the current renaissance of scholarship concerning Jesus' preaching and ministry.

13. E. P. Sanders depicts a historical Jesus who is entirely in agreement with certain eschatological and messianic concepts of the Judaism of his time (*Jesus and Judaism* [Philadelphia: Fortress Press, 1985]). For Richard Horsley, Jesus belongs firmly to the radical prophetic, and in this sense "eschatological," tradition of Israel; see his *Bandits, Prophets and Messiahs: Popular Movements at the Time of Jesus* (with John S. Hanson; Minneapolis: Winston-Salem, 1985); Horsley, *Jesus and the Spiral of Violence* (San Francisco: Harper & Row, 1987); Horsley, *Sociology and the Jesus Movement* (New York: Crossroad, 1989). Burton Mack denies any relationship of Jesus' ministry to Judaism and its apocalyptic mythology (*A Myth of Innocence: Mark and Christian Origins*

later attempts want to reconstruct a historical Jesus while bypassing the early Christian kerygma.

Such moves are consistent with the primary methodological approaches to those materials that can be assigned to the historical Jesus. The various portraits of Jesus that have come to us in ancient Christian materials are the result of the theologizing of the early Christian churches. It seems a matter of course that one isolates those units of the tradition that are not completely altered, or even altogether created, by eschatological and other theological interpretations, which later were put forward by the early church. What must be stripped away are early attempts at gnosticizing or catholicizing Jesus' message; adherence to patriarchal, anti-feminist, and hierarchical structures of society; and the desire to establish rule and order in religious communities with their worship, liturgy, creeds, and systems of subordination. What emerges in all instances is a portrait of Jesus, drawn as scientifically verifiable history, which is free of these secondary accretions and alterations. It makes little difference here whether one ascribes the new found insights just to Jesus himself or to Jesus *and* to the earliest group of his followers, no longer called "the early church" but "the Jesus movement."[14] The latter approach is certainly more judicious. However, in each case one is dealing with phenomena that are assigned to dates earlier than the first Christian texts, both the Pauline letters and the earliest gospels, because it is evident that the deterioration into an ecclesiastical establishment and organized religion was a very early process. Thus the very brief period of the ministry of Jesus and an equally brief period after Jesus' death emerge as the only enlightened times, which might have been extended for a few more decades only in the isolation of the rural areas of Galilee among followers of Jesus who ultimately composed the Synoptic Sayings Source. In any case, the "new quest" was concerned with the discontinuity between Jesus the preacher and the kerygma in which Jesus had become the object of the proclamation, but later portraits of Jesus find a continuity between Jesus' historical sayings and the use of these sayings among his followers—and ultimately between Jesus and ourselves.

The tendency in scholarship toward a non-eschatological Jesus is, of course, closely related to the discovery of the *Gospel of Thomas* and to the hypothesis of an earlier stage of the Synoptic Sayings Source (Q), in which the apocalyptic expectation of the coming Son of Man was still absent[15]—a hypothesis that I myself have supported. It is

---

[Philadelphia: Fortress Press, 1988]). For Elisabeth Schüssler Fiorenza, whatever could be called eschatological in the earliest Jesus movement is integrated in Jesus' understanding of himself as the prophet and messenger of Sophia (*In Memory of Her: A Feminist Theological Reconstruction of Christian Origins* [New York: Crossroad, 1983]). Marcus J. Borg, although he depicts Jesus as part of the charismatic-prophetic tradition of Israel, also denies the essential significance of eschatology in Jesus' message and ministry; see his *Conflict, Holiness and Politics in the Teachings of Jesus* (New York/Toronto: Mellon, 1984); Borg, *Jesus: A New Vision* (San Francisco: Harper & Row, 1987).

14. The word "church" seems to have very negative connotations; "movement'" seems to be preferable today. I cannot help but remember that Hitler and the National Socialists called their own endeavor a "movement" (*Die national-sozialistische Bewegung*).

15. John S. Kloppenborg, *The Formation of Q: Trajectories in Ancient Wisdom Collections* (Studies in Antiquity and Ancient Christianity; Philadelphia: Fortress Press, 1987); see also my *Ancient Christian Gospels* (Philadelphia: Trinity Press International, 1990) 133–49.

questionable, however, whether this early stage of Q can really be defined as non-eschatological,[16] and even more doubtful whether one can draw from such observations the conclusion that the preaching of the historical Jesus had no relation to eschatology.[17]

Other factors that contribute to the portrait of a non-eschatological preaching of the historical Jesus are the terms of our own view of the world that leaves little room for reckoning with supernatural powers such as God and Satan, not to mention apocalyptic mythologies. We again are on the way toward a human Jesus who is just like one of us; one who holds values that are very close to our ideological commitments; a Jesus who is a social reformer and who attacks patriarchal orders; a Jesus who, as a real human person, can stand as an example and inspiration for worthy causes. This view stands in stark contrast to the view of scholars such as Johannes Weiss and Albert Schweitzer. Their worldview did not include an eschatological orientation either, but they acknowledged that Jesus' mythical and eschatological worldview was an utterly strange feature that left them bewildered and did not allow the development of an image of Jesus that would fit their categories.

Of the Jesus of Paul and of the gospels, Albert Schweitzer knew that he is a life-giving power, but at the same time one who "Himself destroys again the truth and goodness which His Spirit creates in us, so that it cannot rule the world."[18] However, of the historical Jesus he remarks: "We can . . . scarcely imagine the long agony in which the historical view of the life of Jesus came to birth. And even when He was once more recalled to life, He was still, like Lazarus of old, bound hand and foot with graveclothes."[19] And Albert Schweitzer had enough courage and honesty to design his personal moral and religious commitment without the blessings of the Jesus of history.

III. The Historical Jesus and the Christian Proclamation

For whatever reason, there is no question that the true historical Jesus, that extraordinary human person, remains a very intriguing and attractive topic even today. The widespread interest in the newly discovered *Gospel of Thomas* proves the point. Perhaps this gospel reveals the real and uncontaminated Jesus as well as his most original words. Be it simple curiosity, be it in the service of a serious religious search, or be it in the interest of a vital ideological commitment, to have Jesus on one's side is evidently important even today. The general public's interest in, and sometimes very hostile reaction to, the findings of the "Jesus Seminar" illustrates the point. On the other hand, one might refer to the continuing claim of evangelical Christians that it is Jesus himself, and he alone, who provides the foundation for their religious commitment. Whether it is the

---

16. The myth of Wisdom is in itself eschatological. The Wisdom of Solomon speaks of a future or transcendental vindication of the rejected righteous people.

17. Even the *Gospel of Thomas* presupposes and criticizes a tradition of eschatological sayings of Jesus.

18. Schweitzer, *Quest of the Historical Jesus*, 2.

19. Ibid., 4.

Jesus one seeks as a personal savior—or a historical Jesus who might respond to a cherished cause—the question is still the same. The only difference is that critical scholars might claim that, as historians, they have some advantages over the more simple-minded believers in Jesus as their savior: a more accurate knowledge of the historical and social situation in first-century Palestine, a better critical ability to identify sources, and a more learned approach to the reconstruction of past history. But is the fundamental question really different?

The problem of the historical Jesus has been short-circuited here, because access to the historical Jesus as a person has become the *first* item on the agenda. Such an approach has its pitfalls. It isolates persons of the past from their historical context and from the situation in which those who transmitted all available information were called into a departure for new shores. Isolation from the historical context is especially hazardous in the case of Jesus, as it also is in the case of Socrates or of Julius Caesar. All three, Socrates, Caesar, and Jesus, were either executed or murdered. This was experienced by their followers as an event that radicalized their critical interpretation of that world. For Plato, the historical Socrates could no longer explain the world that had radically changed because of his death. For Augustus, what mattered was Caesar's testament that gave him the legitimation and the vision to create a new world. For the disciples of Jesus, his execution implied a denial of all values of a world order that had made Jesus its victim. In Plato's dialogues, Socrates speaks as one who already has experienced that the soul is immortal. In Augustus's politics, the murdered dictator became the *divus Julius,* the god Caesar. Jesus' followers endeavored to write paradoxical biographies of a Jesus whose words and works are those of a being who already had died and had risen to a new life.

While a reflection about Jesus' death plays no central role in the more recent portraits of Jesus, all early Christian traditions are acutely aware of this fact. All sources—and this includes the tradition of the wisdom sayings and its theology—agree that the tradition about Jesus must be seen in this light: his rejection, suffering, and death. Whatever the personal aspirations and hopes of Jesus of Nazareth were, his message of the coming of God's kingdom did not leave him as the victor, but as the victim. The entire tradition about the historical Jesus is bound into the testimony of his followers, who were charged to design a new order of the world in which the victim was vindicated.

To be sure, some went out to imitate the great Jesus in their own performance of miracles and religious demonstrations. Jesus as a great person became the standard for following him. This portrait of Jesus as the divine human being has especially haunted the spirit of Western culture ever since. It became important and frightening in the nineteenth-century idea of the genius, from Goethe to Nietzsche and Adolf Hitler,[20] a development that was not unrelated to the life-of-Jesus research.

In another instance, the message of Jesus the victim was spelled out in more metaphysical terms. Jesus was seen as Wisdom/Sophia, who had come into this world but was despised and rejected and so returned to her heavenly abode (John 1:5, 9–13; *Gos. Thom,*

---

20. See my article "The Divine Human Being," *HTR* 78 (1985) 243–52; reprinted in Koester, *Paul and His World* (Minneapolis: Fortress Press, 2007) 118–25.

28). The response of the believer here is the development of realized eschatology and wisdom mysticism as we find it in the *Gospel of Thomas* and among the opponents of Paul in 1 Corinthians.[21] Such belief has its social consequences; the regular bonds of patriarchal family structures and economic dependence were broken down in favor of freedom and equality. In this understanding, the followers of Jesus competed with other messages of nonpolitical and sometimes non-eschatological views of salvation, for example, those propagated by Neopythagorean philosophers and Cynic preachers, or by Jewish mystics and apologists like Philo of Alexandria.

However, Jesus as a victim was also understood as a political message in which the early Christian proclamation was confronting the political eschatology of the Roman imperial period, both in its pagan and Jewish forms. The components are explicitly eschatological and political, with all their social, communal, and revolutionary implications. It is decisive that the core of the message of these Christian missionaries was the proclamation of a ruler of the new age who was the victim of the established authoritarian political order. As this order was in turn based on an ideology of realized eschatology, it was impossible for Jesus' followers to ignore the realized eschatology of imperial Rome.

One could discuss the confrontation of early Christian communities with several variants of ancient Jewish eschatology and apocalyptic theology; however, the confrontation with the eschatology of Rome was decisive for the formation of the message of Jesus the victim. Indeed, the dying Jesus is explicitly confronted with the Roman order of realized eschatology in the inscription on his cross: "Jesus of Nazareth, King of the Jews" (John 19:19; cf. Mark 15:26 par.). His death was a political execution by Roman authorities—it must be remembered that only at a later time did the Christians assign the responsibility for Jesus' death to the Jewish authorities. The name Pontius Pilate remained the symbol for the confrontation with Rome and its political order. The proclamation of Jesus' vindication was as eschatological as Rome's ideology. It should be considered within the general framework of the Roman imperial propaganda of a realized eschatology.

IV. The Age of Augustus as Realized Eschatology

Hellenistic utopian concepts played an important role as early as the founding of Heliopolis by the slave Andronicus, when the last king of Pergamum gave his country to Rome by testament in 135 BCE. Also the slave insurrections of Eunus of Apamea (136–132 BCE) and Spartacus (73–71 BCE) seem to have been inspired by utopian revolutionary ideas. The strong influence of Hellenistic utopian concepts on the eschatology and organization of the Essenes has been demonstrated by Doron Mendels.[22] To be sure, Jewish apocalypticism had its special roots and its special features. But, in the Roman imperial period, it was nevertheless part and parcel of the general eschatolog-

---

21. See Koester, *Ancient Christian Gospels,* 55–62, 124–28.
22. Doron Mendels, "Hellenistic Utopia and the Essenes," *HTR* 72 (1979) 207–22.

ical spirit of the time,[23] and it was even present in the spiritualized eschatology of Jewish Gnosticism that rejected the entire this-worldly reality as bondage to evil powers. After Augustan Rome had adopted these eschatological and utopian ideals and domesticated them for its own purposes, every movement of liberation would naturally confront the state-sponsored realized eschatology of the Caesar.

Rome's political eschatology grew out of the announcement of doom that had come over the entire political and natural world:

Already the second generation is destroyed in the civil war, Rome falls into ruin through its own power.

With these words, Horace begins his *16th Epode*, written in the midst of the civil wars that ravaged Rome during the first century BCE. In the verses that follow, Horace calls for the emigration by ship over the high seas, like the boat people who fled from the horrors of Vietnam, for all those who still have a vision of a blessed future and who have the courage of hope. They will return only after a cosmic catastrophe and not until the establishment of a new paradise will signal the beginning of an eschatological restitution. The Appenine Mountains will plunge into the ocean; then the paradise will come when the tiger mates with the deer and the falcon with the dove, when the earth grows fruit without the hurt of the plow, and when honey flows from the bark of the oak.

Dieter Georgi has called attention to the prophetic eschatology of the Roman poets.[24] Indeed, from the time of Caesar to the false Neros of the time of Domitian, the Roman world was dominated by prophetic eschatology. It was an eschatology that was political, revolutionary, and saturated with the sense of doom and the expectation of paradise. The vision of paradise appears in Virgil's famous *Fourth Eclogue*:

Of themselves, untended, will the she-goats then bring home their udders swollen with milk, while flocks afield shall of the monstrous lion have no fear.... No more shall mariner sail, nor pine-tree bark ply traffic on the sea, but every land shall all things bear alike.... The sturdy ploughman shall loose yoke from steer ...

Virgil adds two other elements to the eschatological vision: first, the birth of the divine child shall usher in "the last age by Cumae's Sibyl sung:" "the child of gods, great progeny of Jove"; and second, the end-time will fulfill the promises and the righteousness of the primordial time—Virgil accomplished this vision in his great epic, the *Aeneid*, in which he connects the destiny of Rome to the mythic origins described in Homer's *Iliad*. Eduard Norden argued that these Roman eschatological expectations had their

---

23. See also the *Jewish Sibylline Oracles*; see John J. Collins, "Sibylline Oracles," in *OTP* 1. 317–417. A significant collection of relevant essays was edited by David Hellholm, *Apocalypticism in the Mediterranean World and the Near East* (Tübingen: Mohr/Siebeck, 1979).

24. Dieter Georgi, "Who is the True Prophet?" in *Christians among Jews and Gentiles: Essays in Honor of Krister Stendahl* (eds. George MacRae, George Nickelsberg, and Albert Sundberg; Philadelphia: Fortress Press, 1986) 100–26; reprinted in Georgi, *The City in the Valley: Biblical Interpretation and Urban Theology* (Atlanta: Society of Biblical Literature, 2005) 25–51.

origins in the same Egyptian prophecies that also influenced Isaiah 9–11 and in turn, Jewish and Christian eschatology.[25]

Augustus not only was aware of these prophetic eschatological poems; he consciously announced his new order of peace as their fulfillment. Horace, two decades after the writing of his prophecies of doom, commissioned by Augustus to compose the festive ode[26] for the secular celebrations in the year 17 BCE, summarizes the themes of the prophecy in the form of a realized eschatology: the new age is beginning right now. The references to Troy and to Aeneas indicate that the promises of the story of Rome's foundation are now fulfilled. Apollo (Phoebus), as the god of the new age, is addressed in the very beginning and several times throughout the ode. Fruitfulness of the earth and fertility of the womb will characterize the new *saeculum*, as peace, honor, and respect already have begun to return.

The Ara Pacis, erected by Augustus in the year 9 BCE to commemorate the new age of peace, repeats in its sculpture the same eschatological topics. On the western side, the most exquisitely executed relief sculptures show Aeneas sacrificing to the *penates publici*, the "Great Gods," whom he had brought from Samothrace to Rome. On the eastern side, *Terra* is depicted set in a paradisiac idyll.

Realized eschatology also appears in the inscriptions that record the introduction of the new Julian calendar. The following is a quotation from the inscription of Priene from the year 9 BCE, celebrating the introduction of the new solar calendar:

> Because providence that has ordered our life in a divine way . . . and since the Caesar through his appearance (ἐπιφανείς) has exceeded the hopes of all former good messages (εὐαγγέλια), surpassing not only the benefactors who came before him, but also leaving no hope that anyone in the future would surpass him, and since for the world the birthday of the god was the beginning of his good messages (Ἦρξεν δὲ τῷ κόσμῳ τῶν δι' αὐτὸν (sc. τὸν Σεβαστὸν) εὐαγγελίων ἡ γενέθλιος ἡμέρα τοῦ θεοῦ) [may it therefore be decided that . . .].[27]

There are several characteristic features of this Roman imperial eschatology: (1) The new age is the fulfillment of prophecy, and it corresponds to the promises given in the primordial age. (2) The new age includes this earth as well as the world of the heavens: Apollo as Helios is the god of the new age; the zodiac sign of the month of Augustus's birth appears on the shields of the soldiers. (3) The new age is universal; it includes all

---

25. Eduard Norden, *Die Geburt des Kindes: Die Geschichte einer religiösen Idee* (Leipzig: Teubner, 1924; reprint, Darmstadt: Wissenschaftliche Buchgesellschaft, 1958). Georgi suggests that Horace was directly influenced by Jewish missionary theology ("Who is the True Prophet?" 110).

26. The *Carmen saeculare* (Hans Färber and Wilhelm Schöne, eds., *Horaz: Sämtliche Werke* [Darmstadt: Wissenschaftliche Buchgesellschaft, 1982]).

27. For the entire Greek text of the inscription, see Wilhelm Dittenberger. *Orientis Graeci inscriptiones selectae* (2 vols.; Hildesheim: Olms, 1960) #458, vol. 2. pp. 48–60. The text quoted above is found in lines 40–42. The Greek text of the portion of the inscription quoted above is conveniently reprinted with a brief commentary in *Griechische Inschriften als Zeugnisse des privaten und öffentlichen Lebens* (ed. Gerhard Pfohl; Tusculum; Munich: Heimeran, 1966) 134–35.

nations: the new solar calendar is introduced by the vote of the people of the cities all over the empire. (4) There is an enactment of the new age through the official celebrations of the empire, like the secular festivities of the year 17 BCE, mirrored by the subsequent introduction of Caesarean games in many places. (5) The new age has a savior figure, the greatest benefactor of all times, the *divi filius*, usually translated into Greek as υἱὸς τοῦ θεοῦ—"Son of God"—the victorious Augustus.

V. Jesus and Eschatology

After Jesus' death, his followers had to answer the question, Who was this, whose cross had borne the inscription "Jesus of Nazareth, King of the Jews"? Their answer was unanimous: he was the victim of the world and the age, whose end he had announced. That he was proclaimed now as the one who was living, who had been raised from the dead, and who was present in the power of the Spirit, does not mean that he was victorious after all. The mythical symbolism in which such beliefs about Jesus' vindication are described is a secondary question. It does not matter whether it was the pouring out of the Spirit, the appearances of the living Jesus, the witness of his resurrection, or the recognition that his words remained as a life-giving power—in every instance Jesus' followers believed that the new world and the new age had arrived, or could be obtained, through the one who was rejected, who suffered, who did not find a home in this world, and who had been put to death.

Therefore, the proclamation was thoroughly eschatological. It pointed to a future that was radically different from that promised by any of the ideologies and realities of which Jesus had become a victim. As a victim of this world and of its political powers, Jesus could not be resurrected, as it were, as a great human being, an insightful preacher, and an example of moral and religious virtues. The message—though founded in an actual event within human history, in a real human life, and in words spoken by this human being—could no longer rely on the memory of the life, words, and deeds of a human individual—no matter how great and powerful. On the contrary, the portrait of the great human or even super-human personality itself belonged to the world that had killed Jesus.

This proclamation has found its most radical expression in Paul, who insists that we no longer know Christ according to the flesh,[28] and for whom "imitation of Christ" is identical with becoming nothing oneself and everything for all people (see 1 Cor 10:32–11:1; Phil 3:17–19). Moreover, the gospels of the New Testament make clear that discipleship, following after Jesus, is identical with taking one's cross and giving away one's life (Mark 8:34–38 par.).[29] Even in the *Gospel of Thomas*, Jesus the Living One cannot be understood by his disciples as someone who is just like them. On the con-

---

28. For a discussion of this paradoxical statement in 2 Cor 5:16, see Dieter Georgi, *The Opponents of Paul in Second Corinthians* (Philadelphia: Fortress Press, 1986).

29. The Gospel of Luke is the only exception; here Jesus indeed appears as an example of piety and in his death as the exemplary martyr.

trary, Jesus is always beyond their grasp, part of a new world that the disciples want to measure with the yardstick of a world that has passed: "His disciples said to him, 'Twenty-four prophets spoke in Israel, and all of them spoke in you.' He said to them, 'You have omitted the one living in your presence and have spoken (only) of the dead'" (*Gos. Thom.* 52).[30]

But were the life and words of Jesus of Nazareth indeed eschatological? Or were the eschatological schemata of his early followers subsequently assigned to a Jesus whose original ministry and message did not contain any eschatological elements? That seems very unlikely. Within a year or two of Jesus' death, Paul persecuted the followers of Jesus because of their eschatological proclamation. That leaves precious little time in which the followers of a non-eschatological Jesus could have developed an entirely new eschatological perspective without a precedent in the preaching and actions of Jesus.[31] The problem is not whether Jesus of Nazareth preached an eschatological message. Rather, the difficulty arises from the fact that the shape and the details of Jesus' eschatology can be discerned only insofar as they are refracted in the eschatological imagery of Jesus' followers.[32] What one finds in the relevant sources is a bewildering variety of traditional eschatology, used as the framework for the Christian message, ranging from the Messiah, Wisdom/Sophia, and the coming Son of Man to Temple ideology and to the Pauline proclamation of Jesus' resurrection as the turning point of the ages. How can one decide which of these refractions represents most legitimately what Jesus himself had preached?

This question cannot be answered by choosing one of these eschatologies and assigning it to the historical Jesus. The church had to respond to political and metaphysical systems based on ideologies of eschatological fulfillment. This response had to be given in the terms of whatever these ideologies proclaimed and could not simply be informed by whatever Jesus had said and done. After Jesus' death, continuity was no longer possible.

The coming of the new age through "Jesus the victim" implied a complete reversal of all political, social, and religious values that were held sacred and holy in the world of ancient Judaism as well as in the Roman system of realized eschatology. How did the reversal of traditionally accepted values, which became the very basis of the founding of communities of the new age and the new world, correspond to the ministry of Jesus of Nazareth?[33] If that correspondence cannot be established, "we may be," as Käsemann

---

30. Trans. Thomas O. Lambdin, in Ron Cameron, *The Other Gospels: Non-Canonical Gospel Texts* (Philadelphia: Westminster, 1982).

31. Paul was called within not more than five years of Jesus' death, probably within two or three years, and he was called to proclaim an eschatological message that he had previously persecuted (Gal 1:13–16), namely, that the new age had begun with the resurrection of Jesus.

32. The only eschatological term that can be assigned to Jesus with certainty is "rule of God" (βασιλεία τοῦ θεοῦ); see esp. Luke (Q) 6:20; 13:28–29. Perhaps also the term "this moment" (ὁ καιρὸς οὗτος) belongs to the eschatological terms of Jesus; see Luke (Q) 12:54–56.

33. James M. Robinson has demonstrated that Paul's description of the experiences of the ministry of the apostles in 2 Corinthians may correspond very closely to the preaching of Jesus, although there is no direct reference to any "historical" words of Jesus (*A New Quest*, 124–25).

warned, "superimposing the predicate 'Christian' on an understanding of existence and of the world, in which Jesus acts merely as occasioner and Christ merely as a mythological cipher:"[34] Were the new eschatological values proclaimed by the Christians true to the preaching of Jesus of Nazareth?

Critical historical inquiry may be able to establish that in the earliest tradition of Jesus' sayings, he himself proclaimed and lived such a reversal of values; that serving others rather than lording over them was the order of the rule of God,[35] that lending to those who cannot repay their loan was the way of the new age (Luke 6:34),[36] that loving one's enemy was the only possible response to hostility (Luke [Q] 6:27–28), that people from all the nations of the world would be invited to the feast of the kingdom (Luke [Q] 13:28–29), and that those who had nothing to lose—the poor, those who were hungry, and those who weep—would inherit it (Luke [Q] 6:20–21). Perhaps there is a vision of the community of the new age, of the rule of God, in whatever fragments of Jesus' preaching can be discerned. It is a vision that is eschatological, albeit often expressed in words that must be classified as wisdom sayings. It is a vision that reckons with God's coming, a coming that begins to be realized in the community of those who dare to follow him. And it is a universalistic vision of a banquet in which privileges of status, wealth, and religious heritage are no longer relevant. But there is no guarantee that such sayings or the inaugural sermon of Q (Luke [Q] 6:27–49) represent the preaching of the historical Jesus. Moreover, it is interesting that sayings of highly charged mythical content are rarely assigned to this Jesus by modern interpreters. In any case, the fragmentary character of these texts, even if some sayings originate with the historical Jesus, does not permit the writing of the story of his life and message—not to speak of a "reconstruction" of the historical Jesus. Such an attempt only reveals once more the preoccupation with the search for the great human personality. It may bypass the real challenge that arises from early Christian texts, namely, to understand our world on the basis of criteria that have their origin in the proclamation of Jesus the victim. We have enough talk about great personalities of religious traditions. After Jesus died, his followers recognized that Jesus as a great human person would mean nothing, but that the kingdom of God had to be proclaimed as the utopia of a new community, a new political order, and indeed a new world.

---

34. Käsemann, "The 'Jesus of History' Controversy," 44.

35. Mark 10:42–44 may be an original saying of Jesus; however, Mark 10:45 ("the Son of Man has come to give his life as a ransom for many") must be assigned to the later community.

36. If Jesus was a teacher of secular wisdom, this saying is an invitation to bankruptcy.

15

THE MEMORY OF JESUS' DEATH AND THE WORSHIP OF THE RISEN LORD

On the Ides of March of the year 44 BCE, the dictator of Rome, Julius Caesar, was assassinated. Nobody knew whether this event would reconstitute the Roman Republic of old, or whether it would usher in a new period of civil war, similar to the one that had devastated not only Rome and Italy, but also the provinces for many decades before Caesar's ascendancy to sole power. The young poet Horace, in a poem that is preserved as his *Sixteenth Epode*, lamented at that time that Rome's ruin was finally at hand:

> Already the second generation perishes in the war of the parties,
> Rome is ruined through its own power. . . .
> We, the impious devotees of an age of blood, are perishing,
> And wild animals again occupy our soil. . . .
> If you ask what all of us, or only the good ones among us,
> May do to escape these woes,
> Well, no better advice can be given than that of the Phokien state of old,
> who fled with curses the state of their fathers,
> fields and hearths and hollowed dwellings
> they left to wild boars and predatory wolves.[1]

Horace calls his fellow citizens to go aboard ship to flee to the far lands of the blessed isles, not to return until the land is renewed and the lion and the tiger live in peace with the cow and the fawn and the falcon with the dove.

The Age of Augustus: Story and Cult

Caesar was dead. No one, not even the mighty Marc Antony, general and consul of the year, dared to come forward to honor the memory of Rome's murdered leader, who had settled the veterans, given benefits to the poor, and guarded the peace of the land. No one dared except one young man, who had been named as the heir in the testa-

---

1. My translation from Hans Färber, ed., "Carmina, Oden und Epoden," in *Horaz Sämtliche Werke* (Tusculum; Zürich: Artemis, and Darmstadt: Wissenschaftliche Buchgesellschaft, 1982), abbreviated.

ment of the murdered dictator: Octavian. Out of his own funds—nobody knew where he got the money, but, after all, he was the son of a banker—he financed the games in honor of Julius Caesar. As fate or providence willed it, when the games were celebrated, a comet appeared in the skies, the *sidus Iulium* ("star of Julius Caesar"), to proclaim Caesar's ascension to the realms of the immortal gods and the beginning of a new age. Two years later, Caesar was officially elevated to become one of the gods of the Roman people, and the worship of the dead dictator was established in Rome itself as well as in many Italian cities.

The tribulations of the people, however, had not yet come to an end. The fight of the parties continued, as Octavian and Marc Antony with Lepidus made an alliance (the Second Triumvirate) against the self-styled defenders of the old Republic. Several hundred senators were killed in the "proscriptions" and their property confiscated. Among those killed was the venerable Cicero. Indeed, the civil war ignited again three years after Caesar's death. Yet, the ancient prophecy of the birth of the child who would rule over a new age of peace, ultimately derived from Egyptian sources and still alive in the late Hellenistic period, had not been forgotten.[2] Hundreds of years earlier, it had appeared in Israel, where it had been sung by the prophet Isaiah:

The people who walked in darkness have seen a great light,
And those who lived in a land of great darkness—on them light has shined. . . .
For the yoke of their burden, and the bar across their shoulders,
The rod of their oppressor, you have broken. . . .

For a child has been born for us, a son given to us.
Authority rests upon his shoulders, and he is named
Wonderful Counselor, Mighty God,
Everlasting Father, Prince of Peace.

His authority shall grow continually, and there shall be endless peace
For the throne of David and his Kingdom.
He will establish and uphold it with justice and with righteousness
from this time onward and for evermore.[3]

Now in Rome, another prophet and poet arose,[4] renewing hope with the words of the same ancient prophecy. In the year 40 BCE, during the consulate of Asinius Pollio, in the midst of all fears, Virgil wrote his famous *Fourth Eclogue*:[5]

2. On the question of the revival of this prophecy in the first century BCE, see especially Eduard Norden, *Die Geburt des Kindes: Geschichte einer religiösen Idee* (Leipzig: Teubner, 1924; reprinted, Darmstadt: Wissenschaftliche Buchgesellschaft, 1958).

3. Isaiah 9:2–3, 6–7 (NRSV). On the reliance of Isaiah 7, 9, and 11 upon ancient Egyptian traditions, see Norden, *Geburt des Kindes,* 51–52; Hans Wildberger, *Jesaja* (BKANT 10; Neukirchen: Neukirchener Verlag, 1972) 1. 363–89.

4. Dieter Georgi ("Who is the True Prophet?" in George MacRae, George Nickelsberg, Albert Sundberg, eds., *Christians among Jews and Gentiles: Essays in Honor of Krister Stendahl* [Philadelphia: Fortress Press, 1986] 100–126) has convincingly demonstrated the appearance of eschatological prophecy in the works of Virgil and Horace.

5. For the relationship of the appearance of the comet (the *Sidus Iulium*) to the composition of the

Now the last age of the Cumaean (Sibyl's) song has come.
Great from pure beginnings grows the order of ages.
Now the Virgin returns, and also returns the rule of Saturn,
Now the new scion is sent down from high heaven.
Only do you, at the boy's birth in whom the iron age
Shall cease and the golden age shall arise,
favor him, chaste Lucina; already reigns your Apollo.

This glorious age shall begin with you the Consul,
O Pollio, and the courses of the great months will commence
Under your guidance, whatever remains of our old wickedness
is done away and the earth will be free from never-ceasing dread.
He will receive the life of a god, and will see with the gods
Mingling the heroes, will himself appear among them,
And will rule a peaceful earth's orbit with the virtues of the fathers.[6]

It would take another decade, however, before this peace became a reality. During those years and after Marc Antony's defeat in the battle at Actium in the year 31 BCE, when the shape of the new rule of Augustus's peace became more clearly discernible, Virgil wrote his *Aeneid,* the great poem that would become the new Roman national epic for many generations. This work reaches back in story and genre to the ancient Greek national epic, Homer's *Iliad.* During the formative centuries of the Greek nation, the *Iliad* had been the story that made all the Greek cities and tribes one people. As it was sung again and again at the great Greek festivals at Delphi, Olympia, Isthmia, and Nemea, the *Iliad* was the story that told the truth for all Hellenes, while the cultic sacrifices to the gods confirmed the covenant with the gods and secured their protection. Cult and story together had thus been the bond for all Hellenes. The cult, rituals, and athletic competitions of the Panhellenic sanctuaries, especially Olympia and Delphi, where closely connected with the performance of the Homeric epic by lyric poets like Pindar. Gregory Nagy has analyzed this pattern masterfully and instructively in a chapter on "Panhellenism" in his book *Pindar's Homer.*[7] As these poets reached back to the mythical past of the Homeric story, their recasting of this story, in contrast to local versions, were aimed at creating a statement of truth (ἀλήθεια) "in the overarching process of achieving a convergent version acceptable to all Hellenes."[8] This process remains fluid "to the point where the latest version becomes the last version, a canonization

---

Fourth Eclogue, see Dietmar Kienast, *Augustus: Princeps and Monarch* (Darmstadt: Wissenschaftliche Buchgesellschaft, 1982) 188. Norden (*Geburt des Kindes,* 152–54) points out that in the year 40 BCE the new moon fell on December 25, the assumed day of the winter solstice, and that there is evidence that such an occurence was then considered to be very significant. This may explain why Virgil issued this poem in that particular year.

6. My translation from Johannes and Maria Götte, eds., *Virgil: Landleben* (Tusculum; Zürich: Artemis, and Darmstadt: Wissenschaftliche Buchgesellschaft, 1995).

7. Gregory Nagy, *Pindar's Homer: The Lyric Possession of an Epic Past* (Baltimore: Johns Hopkins University Press, 1990) 52–81.

8. Ibid., 61.

that brings to a final state of crystallization what had been becoming an ever less-fluid state of variation in performance."[9]

Virgil allows his story of the founding of a new people to begin with Troy at the moment of its destruction: the Trojan hero Aeneas, son of Aphrodite, flees with his father Anchises on his shoulders, who is holding the sacred Palladium. The epic describes Aeneas's travel to his final destiny, the shores of Italy and the founding of Rome. Julius Caesar already had used the motif of Aeneas fleeing from Troy on a denarius of the year 46 BCE;[10] since he belonged to the house of the Julians, he could claim to be an off-spring of Aeneas and thus ultimately of the goddess Aphrodite/Venus herself. Augustus, the adopted son of the divinized Caesar, who had early called himself *Divi filius* ("son of God"), was not only the son of the god Caesar but likewise the offspring of Venus, who thus becomes *Venus genetrix,* soon worshiped as the divine ancestor of the emperor in many places of the Roman world and depicted on numerous coin issues of Augustus.[11]

In Virgil's epic, the story of Aeneas is at the same time a prophetic anticipation of Augustus. He is explicitly named in the prophecy that promises Aeneas an offspring, who will rule the whole inhabited world.[12] On the shield that Aeneas receives from Venus, the entire battle of Actium and Augustus's and Agrippa's victory over Marc Antony and Cleopatra is depicted in great detail.[13] The words of the ancient story describe the new age, predict the appearance of its founding hero Augustus again and again, and intimately connect it with the renewal of cult and ritual that will confirm the legitimacy of the new age of the savior Augustus. In the central niche of one of the large exedras of the Forum of Augustus, a sculpture group of Aeneas shows the hero flee-ing from Troy with his father Anchises on his shoulders and his little son Ascanius by the hand; the household gods, the Penates, are held by Anchises.[14] These Penates, the household gods rescued from Troy and mighty divine companions and advisors of Aeneas, would then be worshiped in the Temple of Vesta, together with the Palladium, as guarantors of the permanence of the house of Augustus. Next to the Penates is *Venus genetrix* as the divine progenitor of the new ruler. Apollo as the god of the new age outshines Jupiter, the god of the old Republic; accordingly, the grandiose Temple of Apollo is built next to the house of Augustus. Finally, the cult of the divinized Caesar prefigures the arrival of the cult of the emperor.

Apollo/Phoebus, together with his sister Artemis/Diana, especially are celebrated, when Augustus orders the Secular Games for the year 17 BCE.[15] Once again the appear-

---

9. Ibid.

10. See Paul Zanker, *The Power of Images in the Age of Augustus* (Ann Arbor: The University of Michigan Press, 1988) p. 35, fig. 27a.

11. Ibid., fig. 27c; p. 54, fig. 41.

12. *Aeneid* 6.788–804.

13. Ibid., 8.675–713.

14. The original is lost but can be reconstructed from a wall painting on a house facade in Pompeii; see Zanker, *Power of Images,* 201–2. Zanker (p. 202) points out that "the young Trojan hero, barely out of Troy, is depicted as a future Roman, wearing not only Roman armor, but, as ancestor of the Julian clan, even patri-cian footwear."

15. The Secular Games were introduced during the First Punic War in the year 249 BCE and repeated in

ance of a comet, understood as the reappearance of the *Sidus Iulium,* confirmed the chosen date.[16] The poet Horace, who once wrote the apocalyptic poem that predicted Rome's inevitable destruction through the civil war, was commissioned to write the official hymn for this celebration. The hymn, which proclaims the beginning of the golden age, was performed before the Temple of Apollo by a chorus of children in festive dress:

> Phoebus and Diana in woodlands regent,
> Glories of the sky, to be held in future
> Honor as in past: we entreat you on this
> sacred occasion.

> When the Sibyl's chanted instructions call for
> Chosen maidens chaste and unwedded youth to
> sing this hymn to gods in whose sight our seven
> hills have known favor.

> Sun of bounty who, with your shining chariot,
> Bring and close the day, ever new yet changeless,
> May no greater thing than this Rome, our City,
> rise in your prospect.

> Goddess, rear our children, uphold the laws our
> Leaders have enacted to govern wedlock,
> Laws we pray may yield generations also
> fruitful in offspring.

> Destinies you uttered proved true, O Parcae;
> What you so ordained, may the fixed and changeless
> End of time preserve, and let blessings past be
> ever continued.

> May our Earth, abundant in fruit and cattle
> Yield the headed grain as a crown for Ceres;
> May our crops be nurtured with wholesome rains and
> Jupiter's breezes.

> If the gods willed Rome into being when they
> Bade the walls of Troy win Etruscan shores and
> Bade the nation's remnant transplant its hearths by
> rescuing voyage.

---

149 BCE, but not held in 49 BCE during the Civil War. They were originally dedicated to the chthonic deities. Augustus, however, recalculated the chronology according to a 110-year cycle and rededicated the games to the goddesses of Fate (Parcae), the birth goddess Ilythiya, Mother Earth, Jupiter, Phoebus (Apollo) and Diana. See Färber, ed., "Carmina, Oden und Epoden," 286–87.

16. Cf. Kienast, *Augustus,* 99.

If unscathed from Ilian flames, Aeneas,
Blameless chief survivor of perished homeland
Led the way, predestined to found a city
greater than ever:

Then, O gods, give young people taintless morals,
And, O gods, to tranquil old men give peace, and
To the race of Romulus give all glory,
riches and offspring.

Grant the pleas submitted with votive bulls by
Venus' and Anchises' exalted scion,
He who first wars enemies down, then lets them
live in his mercy.

Sea and land acknowledge his hand of power,
By the Alban axes the Medes are daunted,
Scyths and Hindus, haughty not long ago, now
seek his pronouncements.

Homewards now I carry my trust that Jove and
All the gods have heard these entreaties; I am
Phoebus' and Diana's chorus,
hymning their praises.

Trust and Peace and Honor and ancient Manners
Venture back among us, and long-neglected
Upright Conduct; Plenty comes too, and brings her
horn of abundance.[17]

The time of the end of the civil war and of the rise of Augustus was an age of anxiety and of realized eschatology. Prophecy and fulfillment and the experience of a new beginning initiated a new formation of story and cult as the basis for a new order of peace and the creation of a new people. Virgil's epic was closely tied to the renewal of the religious foundation of Rome and its rituals, now seen not just as the story and ritual of the old city but as the charter of a new community of all nations. While the old Republic had exploited the conquered nations, for the sole benefit of Rome's upper classes, the new order, legitimized by story and cult, was designed to transform Rome into the benefactor of all humankind. Thus it is not surprising to find in the inscriptions that announce the introduction by Augustus of the solar calendar (the "Julian Calendar")—itself an eschatological symbol—in the cities of the provinces the praise for the immeasurable benefactions received through the "appearance" (ἐπι-

---

17. Excerpts from the translation by Charles E. Passage, *The Complete Works of Horace* (New York: Ungar, 1983).

φανεία) of the "Savior" (σωτήρ) Augustus. The messages that announced the birth-day of the savior and benefactor were celebrated in these inscriptions as "good news," "gospels" (εὐαγγέλια).[18]

Christian Beginnings: Passion Story and Eucharist

The close connection of story and ritual was fundamental also in Israel. As the covenant was renewed in Israel's major festivals, such as the Day of Atonement and Passover, the story of the exodus from Egypt and of the leader and lawgiver Moses was told again. It is indeed preserved in written form in the Bible of Israel in more than one version and is commemorated in numerous Psalms. It is this story of the exodus, through which the various tribes of Israel became one nation. Just as the Greek people found themselves united into one nation in the great story of the war on Troy, to which all tribes, king-doms, and cities had sent their contingent, so was also the nation of Israel created by the story that made the people of all its tribes descendants of Jacob/Israel: all could claim ancestors—the children of Jacob and their offspring—who had been miracu-lously led out of Egypt and through the sea and the desert into the promised land. This was the covenant that was reenacted in the rituals and offerings of the annual festivals, especially in the feast of Passover.

Throughout the centuries, however, the promises of the blessings of that covenant had been more a hope than a reality. Only for the brief period of the reigns of David and Solomon did those blessings seem to have been tangible. That time was remembered as the golden age of Israel. But afterwards, the northern kingdom of Israel was destroyed by the Assyrians, and much of its population was deported. The remaining southern kingdom of Judah fell to the Babylonians, and large numbers of its population were exiled to Babylon. To be sure, the Persians allowed the exiles to return and to rebuild their temple in Jerusalem and, apparently, also permitted a reorganization of the rem-nants of the north under the leadership of the priests of Samaria. Two small temple states existed, first as Persian vassals, later under the domination of Hellenistic kings after the conquest by Alexander. Then, after less than a century of independence under the Hasmonean rulers, they were conquered by Rome and incorporated into the Roman province of Syria.

Yet, prophecy had not died, and hope was alive and was constantly renewed. It took numerous forms: as the vision of Deutero-Isaiah (who envisaged a return of Moses as the servant who was to suffer and then be exalted by God); as the hope of the creation of a new heaven and earth (in which the elect of Israel would ascend to rule the world as in the apocalyptic literature like Daniel and Enoch and others); or as the withdrawal of the people of the covenant to Qumran at the Dead Sea (where they celebrated their

---

18. The most famous of these "gospel" inscriptions comes from Priene and is dated to the year 9 BCE. The full text of this inscription can be found in p. 207 above.

meals in anticipation of the coming of the messianic meal with the anointed priest and the anointed king). The Jewish historian Josephus tells of numerous messianic prophets appearing in Palestine during the first decades of the first century CE, who attempted to re-enact or to prepare for the messianic liberation of Israel. One of these persons was the prophet who is remembered in the New Testament gospels as John the Baptist. Offering a final opportunity of repentance, he proclaimed the coming judgment of God that would usher in God's reign.

A student of the prophet John, baptized by him and evidently continuing his proclamation of the imminent coming of the reign of God, was a certain Jesus. In the year 30 CE, on the day when the celebration of Passover was to begin at sundown,[19] this Jesus was crucified in Jerusalem by the Roman governor Pontius Pilate as a political criminal. The inscription on his cross proclaimed that he was "Jesus of Nazareth, the king of the Jews."[20]

What happened then? This is the most difficult and puzzling question. The gospel writings of the New Testament are not a reliable guide. All of them were written many decades or even more than half a century after the event. Their authors belong to the second and third generation after Jesus. It is possible, to be sure, to discover in these writings earlier materials and traditions. The value of such traditions and their relationship to Jesus, however, is a complex question. Historical methodology requires the investigation of the earliest available sources. There are such earliest sources, namely, the letters of Paul. All of these letters are written roughly two decades after the death of Jesus and two decades or more before the first extant gospel literature. Moreover, their author must be considered a contemporary of Jesus. In the Letter to Philemon, written probably in the year 54 CE, he calls himself an "elderly man" (πρεσβύτης), which according to traditional Greek usage designates a man in his fifties.[21] This puts Paul in the generation of Jesus. Moreover, according to Paul's own account of the years of his previous ministry in his letter to the Galatians 1:13–2:1, his calling as an apostle must be dated no later than the year 35 CE, possibly earlier.[22] Paul thus clearly belongs to the first generation and is the sole contemporary witness to the earliest developments.

His writings preserve a number of traditional formulae. If Paul became an apostle no later than in the year 35, these traditional formulae may be dated to the very first years of the new Jesus communities. Some of these formulae refer to the proclamation, that is, the "gospel" (εὐαγγέλιον); others refer to the ritual of the earliest communities. It

---

19. The question of the day of Jesus' crucifixion—on the day before Passover (according to the Gospel of John) or on the first day of Passover (according to the Synoptic Gospels)—cannot be discussed here. I am convinced that the Johannine dating preserves the original date; cf. John 18:28.

20. John 19:19; cf. Mark 15:26 and parallels.

21. See Eduard Lohse, *Colossians and Philemon: A Commentary on the Epistles to the Colossians and Philemon* (Hermeneia; Philadelphia: Fortress Press, 1971) 198–99.

22. See Helmut Koester, *History and Literature of Early Christianity* (Introduction to the New Testament vol. 2; 2nd ed.; New York: de Gruyter, 2000) 107–9; for the date of Galatians and Paul's chronology, see also Hans Dieter Betz, *Galatians: A Commentary on Paul's Letter to the Churches in Galatia* (Hermeneia; Philadelphia: Fortress Press, 1979) 9–12.

is necessary to investigate these formulae not only with respect to the earliest proclamation and its relationship to Jesus.[23] In that case, the result tends to establish an irreconcilable contrast between the historical Jesus as the proclaimer of a message of salvation and the community's proclamation of the person of Jesus as the savior. The result is quite different, however, if one also examines the relationship of the ritual of the community to Jesus.

The two most important traditional formulae appear in the First Letter to the Corinthians. In both instances, Paul states that he had "received" them (παρέλαβεν). The first of these, in 1 Cor 11:23–25, explicitly quotes traditions concerning the ritual of the community, namely, the celebration of the Eucharist. In the quotation formula, Paul says that he received this tradition "from the Lord" (ἀπὸ τοῦ κυρίου, 1 Cor 11:23). This is intriguing. It cannot mean that it was Jesus himself who communicated this formula to Paul.[24] Rather, Paul thus designates the Lord as the creator of this tradition. One cannot, however, draw the conclusion that therefore the words of institution, in the form in which they are quoted by Paul, were created by the historical Jesus. The alternative historical Jesus or risen Christ is non-existent for the apostle, who received this tradition from the community of followers of Jesus before him and assigns its origin to Jesus Christ the Lord, who is both the earthly and the heavenly Christ.[25] Yet, Paul anchors this tradition in the historical situation of the last meal of Jesus with his disciples. He claims a continuity between the meal celebrated by the community with the meal celebrated by Jesus "in the night in which he was handed over."

Is it possible to infer that the Christian community meal—not necessarily the exact words of its institution—had its origin in Jesus? There is indeed good evidence that Jesus celebrated common meals with his disciples and friends. What is told in the reports about Jesus' last meal,[26] as well as in other information,[27] indicates that these common meals were understood as anticipation of the messianic banquet.[28] The information,

---

23. In the investigation of traditional materials in Paul's letters, scholars have emphasized the search for the earliest "kerygma." See especially the headings of the subdivisions in Rudolf Bultmann, *Theology of the New Testament* (New York: Scribner's, 1951): "The Kerygma of the Earliest Church" (pp. 33–62) and "The Kerygma of the Hellenistic Church Aside from Paul" (pp. 63–189). However, this almost exclusive focus on the proclaimed word, deeply rooted in the emphasis upon word and faith in the dialectic theology of the time after World War I, is a poor hermeneutical instrument. The scholars of the history-of-religions school from the time before World War I knew better when they emphasized cult and ritual as constitutive parts of the formation of religious community. To such ritual belong the narrative of remembrance and the recourse to the language of tradition and scripture.

24. In that case one would expect the preposition παρά rather than ἀπό.

25. For the understanding of the Eucharist in 1 Corinthians I am especially indebted to the groundbreaking essay of Günther Bornkamm, "Lord's Supper and Church in Paul," in Bornkamm, *Early Christian Experience* (ed. and trans. Paul L. Hammer; New York: Harper & Row, 1969) 123–59; for the question of the understanding of ἀπὸ τοῦ κυρίου, see ibid., 130–32.

26. Mark 14:22–25 par.; 1 Cor 11:23–26. Nothing in these traditions indicates that Jesus' last meal was a Passover meal.

27. See the stories about the feeding of the multitudes, Mark 6:30–44 par.; Mark 8:1–10; John 6:1–14.

28. The closest parallel can be found in the common meals of the Essenic community. But also the Jewish meal prayers used by the author of the Teaching of the Twelve Apostles (*Didache* 9–10) indicates that eschatological expectations could be expressed in regular Jewish meal prayers.

however, comes from two different Eucharistic traditions. Their similarities and differences can best be explained if it is assumed that both ultimately derive from the meals that Jesus celebrated with his disciples and friends: (1) the tradition of the *Didache,* in which the Eucharistic prayers express the eschatological consciousness of the congregation,[29] and (2) the tradition that is preserved in 1 Corinthians 10 and 11 and in Mark 14, in which the religious significance of the meal is expressed in the words of institution. In both traditions, the eschatological orientation is predominant. There can be little doubt that this eschatological component derives directly from Jesus himself.

The Eucharistic prayers of the *Didache* as well as the words of institution belong to the earliest period of the formation of Christian communities and may well predate the first collections of Jesus' sayings. For Paul, the words of institution are already a fixed tradition that he has received.[30] The formulation of this tradition belongs to the very first years after Jesus' death and probably to the Hellenistic community of Antioch. The tradition preserved in the *Didache* also must have been at home early in the area of Syria and Palestine.[31] Three constituent parts of this ritual tradition are significant.

First, in Mark 14:25, the words of institution conclude with a sentence anticipating Jesus' return in the future: "I shall not drink again from the fruit of the vine until I drink it new in the kingdom of God"; a close correspondence can be found in Paul's command in 1 Cor 11:25: "As often as you eat this bread and drink this cup, you shall proclaim the death of the Lord until he comes." It is paralleled in the *Didache* in the Aramaic words concluding the Eucharistic liturgy: "Maranatha!" = "Our Lord come!" (*Did.* 10.6.).[32]

Second, the bread appears as the symbol of the eschatological community. This is expressed in 1 Cor 10:16–17: "The bread that we break, is it not a sharing in the body of Christ? Because there is one bread, we who are many are one body." Likewise in 1 Corinthians 11, the bread as the symbol of the "body of Christ" designates the community, not the corpse of Jesus: "For all those who eat and drink without discerning the body, eat and drink judgment against themselves." The "body" that must be recognized is the community. Similarly, the Eucharistic prayers of the *Didache* understand the bread as the symbol of the community: "As this broken bread was scattered upon the mountains, but was brought together and became one, so let your church be gathered together from the ends of the earth into your kingdom."[33]

Third, the cup (in the oldest form it is not the wine!) is understood as the symbol of the new covenant. There is no reason to doubt that all three elements, the eschatological outlook, the understanding of the bread as symbol of the community,

---

29. The best detailed analysis of the Eucharistic prayers of the *Didache* has been presented by Kurt Niederwimmer, *The Didache: A Commentary* (Hermeneia; Minneapolis: Fortress Press, 1998) 139–54.

30. This is clearly stated in 1 Cor 11:23. For a discussion of the significance of the terminology of transmission, see Klaus Wegenast, *Das Verständnis der Tradition bei Paulus und in den Deuteropaulinen* (WMANT 8; Neukirchen: Neukirchener Verlag, 1962) 52–70, 111–13.

31. The close connection of the *Didache's* Eucharistic prayers with Jewish meal prayers points to a Jewish Christian community in Jerusalem or in Galilee.

32. That Paul also knew this liturgical call (cf. 1 Cor 16:22) confirms that the formulation of these Eucharistic liturgies took place in a bilingual community, in which Greek as well as Aramaic was spoken.

33. *Did.* 9.4.

and the cup as a symbol of the new covenant, have their origin in meals that Jesus celebrated, in particular in his last meal before his death. The *Didache* refers to the cup as the "holy vine of your servant David, that was made known through your servant Jesus,"[34] without a reference to Jesus' death or to the outpouring of his blood. In 1 Cor 11:25, however, the cup speaks of Jesus' death as a sacrifice for the new covenant. The words, "Do this in remembrance of me," clearly connect this cultic ritual to the death of Jesus.

This cultic meal, however, though standing in continuity with meals during Jesus' lifetime, does not stand alone as an extension of a ritual that had its origin in Jesus' life. It must be interpreted together with a story that appears in Paul's letters as the "gospel" (εὐαγγέλιον). In 1 Cor 15:1–7, Paul again explicitly appeals to a tradition that he has received in his quotation of the gospel. Both quotations of a received tradition are closely connected to the death of Jesus, in the first instance through the dating of the words of institution to "the night in which he was handed over"—note that the translation "in which he was betrayed" is certainly wrong—in the second instance by the quotation of a short formula that speaks of Jesus' death, burial, resurrection, and appearances after his death.

In both instances, what is quoted is a formula, that is, a kind of shorthand reference to a larger context. It is inconceivable that only such formulae existed at the beginning, while larger narrative contexts were developed at a later time.[35] Who this Jesus was, that is, who celebrated a last meal, then died, was buried and raised, would have been told and spelled out in more detail. The words of institution were hardly the only words that accompanied the celebration of the Eucharist, nor is it conceivable that Paul's sermons consisted of nothing but the gospel formula of 1 Cor 15:3–7. The formulations quoted by Paul as tradition already presuppose not only an institutionalized ritual but also larger contexts of narrative and interpretation. There are clear references to this context in both instances. In 1 Cor 15:3–7 this context is indicated in the statement that Christ "died for our sins according to the scriptures" and that he was raised "according to the scriptures." Two things are said here: first, Christ's death was a vicarious offering for sins; second, this death took place according to the stories of the death for others that were told in the scriptures of Israel. References to the same scriptures are also evident in 1 Cor 11:23–25: the formulation "the body of Christ [given] for you" indicates the vicarious nature of this death, and the reference to the new covenant establishes a close connection to the ancient covenant of Israel.

These references are not apologetic notes that try to prove the truth of the Christian gospel according to the pattern of prophecy and fulfillment. "He died for our sins according to the scriptures" points to a number of scriptural passages that tell stories of

---

34. *Did.* 9.2.

35. Bultmann (*The History of the Synoptic Tradition* [trans. John Marsh; Oxford: Blackwell, 1968] 152 n. 1, 371) refers to the kerygma as it is present in the predictions of Jesus' suffering and resurrection in Mark 8:31; 9:31; 10:33–34 and in the speeches of the Book of Acts. But it is not possible to assume that these formulae existed while a narrative of the passion was not yet in existence.

the servant who suffered and died on behalf of others.[36] They are the foundation for the interpretation of the death of Jesus and they provide the language for the telling of the story of Jesus.Very close linguistic parallels to 1 Corinthians 11 and 15 appear, especially in the scriptural passage about the suffering servant of Isaiah 53. Compare 1 Cor 15:3 "he died for our sins" (ἀπέθανεν ὑπὲρ τῶν ἁμαρτιῶν ἡμῶν) with "Surely he has borne our sins" (οὗτος τὰς ἁμαρτίας ἡμῶν φέρει) in Isa 53:4, and "he was wounded for our sins and crushed for our iniquities" (μεμαλάκισται διὰ τὰς ἁμαρτίας ἡμῶν) in Isa 53:5. Especially significant is Isa 53:6:"The Lord handed him over because of our sins" (καὶ ὁ κύριος παρέδωκεν αὐτὸν ταῖς ἁμαρτίαις ἡμῶν), which reappears in 1 Cor 11:23:"In the night in which he was handed over" (ἐν τῇ νυκτὶ ἐν ᾗ παρεδίδοτο).[37] This close affinity of language demonstrates that the reading of such scriptures as Isaiah 53 was part of the liturgy of the Eucharist. Paul's reference to "the night in which he was handed over" also reveals that both the apostle and the Corinthian community knew an entire story about Jesus' death and suffering—otherwise the mention of a specific time would not make sense. The story did not narrate the events of Jesus' suffering and death as a report derived from historical memory but in the language of the prophets and psalms of Scripture. That is borne out by the later passion narratives of the canonical gospels and of the *Gospel of Peter,* which utilize repeatedly the stories of the suffering righteous in the Scriptures of Israel[38] and detail the events in Jesus' story and their sequence accordingly.[39]

The earliest tangible presence of Jesus must therefore have been the story of his suffering and death. It utilized the tradition and language of the ancient scriptures of Israel in order to narrate an eschatological event in the context of a cultic action that was rooted in a ritual practice instituted by Jesus himself. It was in this ritual and story that the earliest Christian communities established their relationship to the history of Jesus.

The pattern that we have observed, namely, the close connection of story and ritual, do not belong to the domain of religious history in the narrower sense. The parallels from Greece, Rome, and Israel demonstrate that one is dealing here with the establishment of a political community and the formation of its religious foundation. In the case of Augustus and Rome, story and ritual signify the creation of a new era of peace for all nations in terms of an eschatological perspective. The founding of early Christian communities, from Jerusalem to Antioch and then to the Pauline churches in Asia Minor and Greece, is not simply a feeble attempt to establish a new religious sect, however modest the beginnings may have been. Much more is at stake. The designations that these new communities used for themselves demonstrate the political dimension of this venture. Typical terms for religious communities, such as "synagogue" or

---

36. References to Scripture in the letters of Paul usually point to larger contexts, even if only one or two verses are quoted. This is especially evident in 1 Cor 10:1–11; 2 Cor 3; and Gal 4:21–31.

37. See also Gal 1:3–4: ἀπὸ . . . κυρίου ἡμῶν Ἰησοῦ Χριστοῦ τοῦ δόντος ἑαυτὸν ὑπὲρ τῶν ἁμαρτιῶν ἡμῶν, and the discussion and the literature cited in Betz, *Galatians,* 37–43.

38. Psalm 22 (21 LXX) has been used in particular. Other psalms of lament, such as Ps. 68 (69 LXX), also have been used.

39. George W. E. Nickelsburg, "The Genre and Function of the Markan Passion Narrative," *HTR* 73 (1980) 153–84.

thiasos or *koinon* (the Greek terms for a religious associations) are missing. Instead, the term *ekklesia* (the Greek term designating the democratic assembly of all free citizens) predominates.[40] Also the term "Israel of God" appears as the designation for the new Christian community[41]—claiming that this is the creation of the promised eschatological Israel as a nation for all people. Moreover, the term "gospel" for the Christian proclamation is also drawn from the political realm: it was used for the messages issuing from the emperor in the announcement of the new age of peace.[42]

Like the stories of Greece and Rome, also the new Christian story is rooted in a venerable ancient tradition, from which it draws its images and language. But as Virgil's epic develops its story from ancient Troy and relegates the older story of the founding of Rome by Romulus and Remus to a secondary position, so the Christian cult narrative is developed in a recourse to Israel's story of the suffering righteous, thus replacing Israel's story of the Exodus and also claiming to end the validity of the law of Moses. At the same time, the death of Jesus and his vindication is remembered in the ritual of the Eucharist as the founding sacrifice of a new covenant, that is, of a new political order. The cult of the Kyrios Christ and the story that seeks to legitimize the new Israel as an eschatological event are anchored in the traditional language of Israel and at the same time in the actual suffering and death of the historical Jesus of Nazareth.

According to early Christianity, the law of Moses was set aside because of its demand that Israel separate itself from the Gentile world. Therefore, the founding of the new nation—now consisting of both Jews and Gentiles[43]—required new legislation. As Augustus had made recourse to the legislation of Caesar, the new community reaches back to the words of Jesus as part of this legislation, especially the commandment of love, in which all the law and the prophets are summarized. This recourse to Jesus' sayings, as evident, for example, in 1 Corinthians 7 and in Romans 12, and later in the Sermon on the Mount of the Gospel of Matthew, is an important element of historical continuity; but it also reveals the same freedom as Augustus's resumption of the legislation of Caesar. In the earliest understanding of the continuity with the historical Jesus, neither the report of Jesus' miracles nor the transmission of his sayings was constitutive. Rather, the new understanding of the significance of Jesus' celebration of common meals in anticipation of the "messianic banquet" and the story of his suffering and death provided the constitutive elements for the self-definition of the community as a new nation and of its claims to eschatological fulfillment of the hopes of all people.

---

40. For the political meaning of the term ἐκκλησία, see Karl Ludwig Schmidt, "ἐκκλησία," *TDNT* 3 (1965) 513–17; see also Dieter Georgi, *Theocracy in Paul's Praxis and Theology* (trans. David Geen; Minneapolis: Fortress Press, 1991).

41. Compare Gal 6:16; see also the reference to "Israel according to the flesh" (1 Cor 10:18), implying that the Christian community is the true Israel according to the Spirit.

42. See also the gospel inscription from Priene, quoted on p. 209 above. On the attempt to derive the term εὐαγγέλιον from Deutero-Isaiah, see Gerhard Friedrich, "εὐαγγελίζομαι," *TDNT* 2 (1964) 709–10. See also Helmut Koester, *Ancient Christian Gospels* (Philadelphia: Trinity, 1990) 2–3.

43. See the new charter for this community, apparently a baptismal formula, that demolishes the ethnic, social, and gender differentiations: "There is no longer Jew or Greek, there is no longer slave or free, there is no longer male and female; for all of you are one in Christ" (Gal 3:28).

Conclusion

In the early church, the story of Jesus' suffering and death remained fluid for a long time. Evidence for this are the different versions of the passion narrative in the gospel literature, owing to the oral performances of the story in the ritual celebrations, ever enriched by new references to the scriptures of Israel. This process of oral performances intended to establish an inclusive statement of truth in the establishment of a new nation—Pan-Christianity. Canonization did not freeze just the latest version of this story. Instead, the four-gospel canon allowed different versions to stand side by side. On the other hand, gospels that did not include the narrative of Jesus' suffering and death were excluded from the canon of the New Testament—although many gospels of this kind existed at that time. The new community could only be nourished by the Pan-Christian versions of a story told in the context of the performance of the ritual.

16

THE HISTORICAL JESUS AND THE CULT OF THE KYRIOS

I. The Beginnings of the New Quest for the Historical Jesus

Albert Schweitzer's critical assessment of the nineteenth-century attempts to reconstruct the life and message of the historical Jesus appeared at the beginning of the twentieth century and was published in the year 1910 in an English translation under the title *The Quest of the Historical Jesus.*[1] At that time, it effectively silenced attempts to reconstruct the life of Jesus. The subsequent form-critical investigation of the gospel tradition deepened the skepticism about the reliability of available biographical data. Moreover, the intellectual shock of the two world wars undermined the value of an exemplary biography of the founder of the Christian faith. In Rudolf Bultmann's *Theology of the New Testament,* published in the years after World War II, Jesus appeared only as a presupposition of New Testament theology.[2]

In the year 1953, Ernst Käsemann initiated a new phase of the inquiry into the historical Jesus with his lecture on "The Historical Jesus and the Christ of the Kerygma" that was presented at the annual meeting of the "Old Marburg Students," the circle of Rudolf Bultmann's friends and former students.[3] When the Heidelberg New Testament scholar Günther Bornkamm published his *Jesus von Nazareth* in 1956,[4] it became the landmark of a new period of interest in the historical Jesus. The book was immediately

---

"The Annual Faculty Research Lecture at Harvard Divinity School," *Harvard Divinity School Bulletin* 24:3 (1995) 13–18. This lecture is not the documentation of a lonely individual effort but owes much to colleagues and students at Harvard. I am especially indebted to our former students Dr. Marianne Bonz and Prof. Ellen Aitken and to my colleague in the Classics department, Gregory Nagy. The reading of their scholarly work and numerous discussions have provided fresh insights that have been invaluable for my own reflections on this subject.

1. Albert Schweitzer, *The Quest of the Historical Jesus: A Critical Study of its Progress from Reimarus to Wrede* (New York: Macmillan, 1959). This work was first published in the year 1906 under the title *Von Reimarus zu Wrede: Eine Geschichte der Leben-Jesu-Forschung* (Tübingen: Mohr). The first English translation of the second edition of Schweitzer's work (now entitled *Geschichte der Leben-Jesu-Forschung*) appeared in 1910 (London: Black).

2. Rudolf Bultmann, *Theology of the New Testament* (2 vols.; New York: Scribner's, 1951–55) 1. 3–32.

3. Published in *ZThK* 51 (1954) 125–53; reprinted in Käsemann, *Exegetische Versuche und Besinnungen* (2 vols.; Göttingen: Vandenhoeck & Ruprecht, 1960–1964) 1. 184–214; English translation: "The Problem of the Historical Jesus," in Käsemann, *Essays on New Testament Themes* (SBT 41; London: SCM, 1964) 15–47.

4. Günther Bornkamm, *Jesus von Nazareth* (Urban Taschenbücher; Stuttgart: Kohlhammer, 1956).

successful; was republished in as many as eleven new German editions; and translated into English,[5] Dutch, Japanese, Danish, Italian, French, Portuguese, and Spanish. Soon after its first publication, this new interest in Jesus was hailed and discussed programmatically by James M. Robinson under the title "The New Quest for the Historical Jesus," published 1959.[6]

Bornkamm's book about Jesus of Nazareth eschews any and every attempt to write a "life" of Jesus. The work begins with the sentence, "No one is any longer in the position to write a life of Jesus." What is central for the writing of a biography and what had dominated the original quest for the historical Jesus, namely, the inquiry into the social conditions and psychological motivations of the work, life, and fate of the historical person Jesus, did not play any role in the beginning of this New Quest. Rather, the New Quest was motivated by a theological problem, namely, the search for the historical foundation of the Christian proclamation, the kerygma of the early church. In this proclamation Jesus' coming and fate was announced as the event of salvation that made God and his kingdom a present reality among the believers.

Was this proclamation related simply to the naked historical fact of Jesus' death and resurrection? Or was there an essential connection between the intention of Jesus' works and words on the one hand and the preaching of the church on the other hand? Only if this question could be answered positively could the historical foundation of the kerygma seem to be secure. What Jesus of Nazareth had done and said and suffered should have some continuity with the Jesus Christ who became the object of Christian faith and the content of the Christian proclamation—despite all the misunderstandings and reinterpretations of the tradition about him. Bornkamm endeavored to demonstrate that Jesus of Nazareth and the kerygma of the early church were constituent parts of one and the same historical process.

The same caution was voiced in Rudolf Bultmann's reaction to the beginnings of the new quest. In 1960 in a lecture delivered before the Academy of Arts and Sciences at Heidelberg,[7] Bultmann characterized these beginnings of the New Quest as follows:

> In the time of the life-of-Jesus research (that is in the so-called liberal theology [of the 19th century]) the question was inspired by the attempt to liberate the historical Jesus from the secondary layer of theological interpretation, through which he had been obscured by means of the proclamation of the early church. . . . Today the direction of the inquiry has been reversed: the new quest is interested in the demonstration of the unity of the historical Jesus with the Christ of the kerygma.[8]

---

5. *Jesus of Nazareth* (London: Hodder and Stoughton, 1960), with a brief translator's preface by James M. Robinson.

6. James M. Robinson, *A New Quest for the Historical Jesus* (SBT 25; London: SCM, 1960); cf. Robinson, *Kerygma und historischer Jesus* (Zürich: Zwingli, 1967).

7. "Das Verhältnis der urchristlichen Botschaft zum historischen Jesus," *SHAW.PH* 1960.3, 5–27 = Rudolf Bultmann, *Exegetica* (Tübingen: Mohr/Siebeck, 1967) 445–69 [translation mine].

8. *Exegetica,* 445–46.

II. The Recent Search for the Historical Jesus

Beginning in the 1970s, numerous new books on the historical Jesus were published[9] beginning with such works as Morton Smith's *Jesus the Magician*[10] and epitomized in recent years by—to name only a few—the works of Richard Horsley (Jesus, as a Galilean social revolutionary),[11] Burton Mack (Jesus, as a Cynic preacher),[12] John P. Meier (Jesus, as a marginal Jew),[13] and finally, John Dominic Crossan's presentation of Jesus as a Galilean peasant.[14] All these works have in common the concept that the concern for a historical and theological continuity that correlated the historical Jesus to the proclamation of the church has all but been dropped completely. Instead, the interest has turned toward the person of Jesus as such, regardless of any resulting continuity or discontinuity between Jesus and the belief and proclamation of the early church. Moreover, parallel to the old quest of the nineteenth century, these investigations again have turned to recovery of the person of Jesus, his conditioning by his social environment, and his psychological motivations and intentions.

In a critical assessment of this veritable flood of publications on the historical Jesus, Dieter Georgi observed in an article[15] that the cessation of interest in the historical Jesus just before World War I had been closely tied to what he calls the "Burgher-Dämmerung"[16] that characterized this period and that was confirmed in the subsequent catastrophes of the two world wars that seemed to end the mercantile world of the bourgeois establishment. Therefore, the return of interest in the life of Jesus after World War II can be seen as the consequence of the restoration of the bourgeois establishment, in which the life of an important individual provides the role model for either its moral justification or its—albeit revolutionary—criticism. At the conclusion of his essay, Georgi writes:

> I observe the main cause in the continuous social and historical situation of the whole quest for the historical Jesus, that is, its location within the evolution of the bourgeois consciousness, not just as an ideal but as an expression of a socioeconomic and political momentum. The contemporaneity of the New Quest with the end of the New Deal and the restoration of the bourgeoisie in the United

---

9. For a survey with extensive comprehensive bibliographies, see John Telford, "Major Trends and Interpretive Issues in the Study of Jesus," in Bruce Chilton and Craig A. Evans, *Studying the Historical Jesus: Evaluations of the State of Current Research* (Leiden; New York: E. J. Brill, 1994) 33–74.

10. Morton Smith, *Jesus the Magician* (New York: Harper and Row, 1978).

11. *Bandits, Prophets and Messiahs: Popular Movements at the Time of Jesus* (with John S. Hanson; Minneapolis: Winston-Salem, 1985); Horsley, *Jesus and the Spiral of Violence* (San Francisco: Harper & Row, 1987); Horsley, *Sociology and the Jesus Movement* (New York: Crossroad, 1989).

12. *A Myth of Innocence: Mark and Christian Origins* (Philadelphia: Fortress Press, 1988); Mack, *The Lost Gospel: The Book of Q and Christian Origins* (San Francisco: HarperCollins, 1993).

13. *A Marginal Jew: Rethinking the Historical Jesus* (2 vols.; The AB Reference Library; New York: Doubleday, 1991–1994).

14. John Dominic Crossan, *Jesus: A Revolutionary Biography* (San Francisco: HarperCollins, 1994).

15. Dieter Georgi, "The Interest in Life of Jesus Theology as a Paradigm for the Social History of Biblical Criticism," *HTR* 85 (1992) 51–83.

16. Ibid., 79.

States and Germany after World War II and within the confines of a burgeoning market-centered Atlantic community is not accidental.[17]

Indeed, it seems that the attempt to recover the historical person of Jesus of Nazareth unwittingly mirrored a movement that reached its apex in Newt Gingrich's "Contract with America." There is a considerable movement from the very guarded steps, taken by German scholars in the first two decades after World War II, to the confidence of the last fifteen years, especially in the United States, the victorious leader of the capitalist world. It is perhaps no accident that almost all the major recent works on the historical Jesus have been produced by American scholars.

These American works on the historical Jesus took advantage of a breakthrough in scholarly research in the investigation of a particular early-Christian tradition about Jesus, namely, the transmission of his sayings. A consensus has emerged in scholarship that Matthew's and Luke's gospels, in addition to their dependence upon the narrative of the Gospel of Mark, used a second common source, the so-called Synoptic Sayings Source (Q), that contained only sayings of Jesus. Some newly discovered non-canonical materials, especially the *Gospel of Thomas,* also may be closely related to this sayings tradition.[18] A number of investigations have tried to clarify the development of this Synoptic Sayings Source, concluding that it must have developed in two stages.[19] In its earlier stage, it was primarily a collection of wisdom and prophetic sayings of Jesus. At the second stage, sayings about the coming judgment and about the appearance of Jesus as coming Son of Man were added. Therefore only the earlier stage of the composition of Jesus' sayings in this document appears to reflect more or less directly the preaching of Jesus himself.

III. The Synoptic Sayings Source and the Historical Jesus

How should the sayings in this earliest stage of the Sayings Source be understood and what is their context and, by implication, what is the context to which the historical Jesus belongs? Moreover, is this context related in any way to the tradition of Israel? Some dimension of this tradition is preserved in Elisabeth Schüssler Fiorenza's attempt to interpret Jesus' message and ministry as a theological continuation of Israel's wisdom movement. She sees Jesus as the child and prophet of the goddess "Wisdom" (Sophia), who proclaimed to the people marginalized by society that God was on their side.[20]

---

17. Ibid., 83.

18. Helmut Koester, *Ancient Christian Gospels: Their History and Development* (London: SCM, and Philadelphia: Trinity Press International, 1990) 86–95.

19. This thesis has been most presuasively presented by John Kloppenborg, *The Formation of Q. Trajectories in Ancient Wisdom Tradition* (SAC; Philadelphia: Fortress Press, 1987). Kloppenborg is partly dependent upon the work of Dieter Lührmann, *Die Redaktion der Logienquelle* (WMANT 33; Neukirchen-Vluyn: Neukirchener Verlag: 1969). See also Koester, *Ancient Christian Gospels,* 128–171.

20. Elisabeth Schüssler Fiorenza, *In Memory of Her: A Feminist Theological Reconstruction of Christian Ori-*

Richard Horsley reconstructs the historical context for Jesus' social-revolutionary Galilean ministry primarily on the basis of information from the Jewish historian Josephus and also admits a certain relationship of Jesus' message to the political and social criticism that is present in Jewish apocalyptic materials.[21]

Much more problematic is the thesis that Jesus was simply a wandering Cynic philosopher in the tradition of the social criticism of Greek Cynicism—a thesis that is by no means new[22] but was forcefully presented by Burton Mack.[23] Mack completely separates the historical Jesus not only from the tradition of Israel but also from the process of the formation of early Christian communities. According to him, the narrative of the passion and resurrection of Jesus is a much later artificial product, invented by some disciples of Jesus decades after the event in order to find an answer to the persecutions that they experienced. Jesus' message, reconstructed exclusively on the basis of the wisdom materials of the Sayings Source, therefore becomes a phenomenon that has no relationship whatsoever with either the religion of Israel or the theology of the early church. To find any relationship of Jesus to the world of antiquity, Mack must make recourse to the questionable assumption of the presence of secular Greek Cynic preachers in Galilee in the first century CE.

Mack's work also epitomizes the general tendency that denies any eschatological elements in Jesus message. The reconstruction of a Jesus who is purified of all eschatological elements finally would make the beginnings of Christianity as a movement with a pervasive eschatological message a complete conundrum.

Three decades ago, James M. Robinson had stated emphatically:

The recourse to an event that marked the turning point of the ages must not be constructed as a criterion of differentiation between the situation of the church and the situation of Jesus. The early Christian community as well as Jesus understood their own situation as one that was created by God's intervention in the course of history.[24]

Can the historical Jesus really be separated from the pervasive eschatological orientation of early Judaism?

---

gins (New York: Crossroad, 1984) 135 and passim. Although mostly Q-materials are used in her reconstruction of Jesus' message, Schüssler Fiorenza also relies on other information from the synoptic tradition.

21. See n. 12.

22. The thesis of "Jesus the Cynic" was first proposed more than a hundred years ago and was also advocated by Friedrich Nietzsche; see Hans-Dieter Betz, "Jesus and the Cynics: Survey and Analysis of a Hypothesis," *JR* 74 (1994) 453–75. In more recent times, it was proposed first by F. G. Downing, "Cynics and Christians," *NTS* 30 (1984) 584–93, and several subsequent publications. In the United States, it was further elaborated by Leif E. Vaage, "The Ethos of an Itinerant Intelligence" (Ph.D. diss., Claremont Graduate School, 1987).

23. Mack, *A Myth of Innocence*, 63–77; see also his *The Lost Gospel*. For a critical assessment of Mack's work, see James M. Robinson, "The History-of-Religions Taxonomy of Q: The Cynic Hypothesis," in Holger Preißler und Hubert Seiwert, *Gnosisforschung und Religionsgeschichte: Festschrift für Kurt Rudolph zum 65. Geburtstag* (Marburg: diagonal-Verlag, 1994) 247–65.

24. *Kerygma und historischer Jesus,* 213.

IV. The Eschatological Trajectory of Jesus' Sayings

Although it did not contain the expectation of the coming of the Son of Man on the clouds of heaven, even the earliest stage of the Sayings Source must be understood as the eschatological interpretation of prophetic sayings of Jesus. The beatitudes, which were originally the opening lines of the inaugural speech of Jesus in the Sayings Source, cannot be classified as wisdom beatitudes. Wisdom beatitudes always bless wise action and behavior. Psalm 1:1 is typical: "Blessed are those who do not follow the advice of the wicked." It is a prophet who calls those blessed who are poor, hungry, and weeping (Luke 6:20–22). Other sayings from the earliest form of the Sayings Source also must be understood as prophetic announcements of the turning of the ages. To love one's enemies and bless the persecutors, and to lend to those who will not repay are not commendations of wise behavior; they announce an eschatological moment (Luke 6:27–28, 34). John the Baptist is praised as the greatest among those who were born by women because he called for the final repentance before the coming of God's kingdom (Luke 7:28). And Jesus calls himself the one who has come to light a fire on earth (Luke 12:29). Those who can interpret the signs of the time will recognize that the kingdom of God has already come upon them (Luke 17:20–21).[25]

Even those sayings of the oldest form of the Sayings Source that cannot be claimed as genuine sayings of Jesus clearly show that the community that fashioned them understood itself as the bearer of an eschatological message. The speech of the sending of the disciples speaks of the harvest at the turning point of the ages: "The harvest is plentiful but the laborers are few" (Luke 10:2). To announce that those who come from east and west and north and south will eat at the table of the kingdom of God (Luke 13:29) presupposes a prophetic authority that even transcends the boundaries of Israel as the heir of God's promise.

This earliest form of the sayings collection may have been composed somewhere in Palestine in the forties or fifties of the first century, that is, about twenty years after the death of Jesus. The further development of this tradition took two different routes. Both are probably caused by the increasingly revolutionary temperament of Palestinian Judaism in the seventh decade of the first century that fatefully resulted in the insurrection against Rome in the Jewish War of 66–70 CE. One of these two routes is visible in the apocalyptic redaction of the Sayings Source, while the other can be observed in the formation of the *Gospel of Thomas*. Both developments result from an attempt to answer the question of how Jesus' eschatological message was related to the political messianic fervor of the revolutionaries.

The second stage of the Sayings Source opened with a challenge to the political revolution. The commandment to love one's enemies was reconfirmed. The judgment will come from God, not from a victory of the revolutionaries. Jesus as Son of Man will come soon to rescue the faithful and to destroy those who have been disobedient:

---

25. One could argue that this saying, because it lacks a parallel in the Gospel of Matthew, does not belong to the Synoptic Sayings Source. However, the parallel in *Gos. Thom.* 113 demonstrates that it was part of the earliest stages of the sayings tradition.

The days are coming when you will long to see one of the days of the Son of Man and you will not see it. They will say to you, "Look there!" or "Look here!" Do not go, do not set off in pursuit. For as the lightning flashes and lights up the sky from one side to the other, so will the Son of Man be in his day (Luke 17:22–24).

These followers of Jesus in Palestine thus rejected the revolution of the Jewish War in favor of an apocalyptic expectation. This agrees with the information that the Jerusalem community left the city and emigrated to Pella east of the Jordan before the beginnings of open hostilities.

A very different development of the early eschatological tradition of the sayings of Jesus can be observed in the *Gospel of Thomas.* There are no apocalyptic elements, and there is no expectation of the Son of Man and of the coming judgment. Rather, the eschatological outlook of the sayings of Jesus has been understood under a new perspective, which may be called "Gnostic": the kingdom of God does not lie in the future but in the recognition of the divine origin of the human self:

If those who lead you say to you, "See the kingdom is in the heavens," then the birds of the heavens will precede you. If they say to you, "It is in the sea," then the fish will precede you. Rather the kingdom is in you and outside of you. When you know yourselves, then you will become known, and you will realize that is you who are the sons of the living Father (*Gos. Thom.* 3).

In both instances, in the second stage of the Sayings Source as well as in the *Gospel of Thomas,* the new interpretations presuppose that the earlier words of Jesus were oriented eschatologically. One might speak of a continuity that reaches from the genuine sayings of Jesus to the apocalyptic and Gnostic versions of eschatology. Pealing layer after layer of the later accretions and interpretations one might thus reach the message of the historical Jesus. However, continuity is very problematic when one deals with a tradition of sayings. First of all, the creator of a tradition of sayings, be it sapiential or prophetic, does not have any control over his own role in the interpretation. Indeed, in this trajectory of the transmission of sayings, the prophet Jesus of Nazareth was transformed into the coming Son of Man or into the Gnostic revealer. Second, a tradition of sayings is not bound to specific social and political structures of a community and its institutions; it is symptomatic that all attempts to reconstruct the community of the Sayings Source have met with failure. Third, the historical context to which Jesus, the creator of the tradition, belongs no longer obligates the interpreter; Scripture and tradition of Israel play at best a marginal role in the later redaction of the Sayings Source and is even rejected in the *Gospel of Thomas.*

Historians are therefore treading on very thin ice if they try to recover the historical person of Jesus through a critical analysis of the sayings tradition. A person of past history can only be understood if the extant sources reveal the traditions to which such a person belongs as well as the subsequent structures, practices, and institutions of a community in which the memory of this person is preserved. The investigation of the sayings tradition is ultimately a dead-end in the endeavor to understand the historical Jesus and, at the same time, the historical effects of his ministry.

V. Eschatology, Community, and Ritual

It is well known that the tradition from and about Jesus did result in the creation of religious communities with tangible social structures in the earliest Christian churches outside of Palestine. These Hellenistic communities before Paul have been primarily understood from the perspective of their kerygma, that is, their proclamation of the death and resurrection of Jesus as the turning point of the ages. This has produced the famous dichotomy between Jesus as the proclaimer of the coming kingdom of God and the Christ who was now the object of Christian faith. No path seemed to lead from this kerygma of the early church to the Jesus of history.

However, this almost exclusive focus on the proclaimed word, deeply rooted in the emphasis upon word and faith in the dialectic theology of the time after World War I, is a poor hermeneutical instrument. The scholars of the history-of-religions school from the time before World War I knew better when they emphasized cult and ritual as constitutive parts of the formation of religious community. To such ritual belongs the narrative of remembrance and the recourse to the language of tradition and Scripture.

When the relationship of the Jesus of Nazareth to the early Christian communities is seen in this perspective, the continuity becomes immediately apparent. The common meals that Jesus celebrated with his disciples and friends were understood as anticipations of the messianic banquet. These meals resulted in two different cultic meal traditions, which were developed independently of each other: (1) a tradition (represented in the *Didache*) in which the Eucharistic prayers express the eschatological consciousness of the congregation and (2) a tradition (preserved in 1 Corinthians 10 and 11 and in Mark 14) in which the religious significance of the meal is expressed in the words of institution. Both traditions belong to the earliest period of the formation of Christian communities and may well predate the first collections of Jesus' sayings. Further, in the case of the words of institution that for Paul are already a fixed tradition, it is clear that the cultic meal must be interpreted together with a story that appears in Paul's letters as the "gospel" (εὐαγγέλιον). Paul's use of brief formulas in 1 Cor 11:23–26 and 1 Cor 15:1–7 already presuppose not only an institutionalized ritual but also larger contexts of narrative and interpretation. The earliest tangible presence of Jesus in the Christian communities must therefore have been the story of his suffering and death, narrated as an eschatological event in the context of a cultic action that was rooted in a ritual practice instituted by Jesus himself. It was in this ritual and story that the earliest Christian communities established their relationship to the history of Jesus.[26]

The close connection of ritual with a story that reaches back into the venerable tradition of the past corresponds to an important pattern of the constitution of religious and political community in antiquity.

---

26. See the more extensive discussion in "The Memory of Jesus' Death and the Worship of the Risen Lord," chapter 15.

VI. Narrative, Ritual, and Tradition in Antiquity

In antiquity, the primary constituents of community were widely accepted cults and rituals connected with the telling of a story that restated the tradition in ever new versions until it finally reached the stage of canonization. Professor Nagy of Harvard University has analyzed this pattern masterfully and instructively in a chapter on "Panhellenism" in his book *Pindar's Homer.*[27] The cult, rituals, and athletic competitions of the Panhellenistic sanctuaries, especially Olympia and Delphi, where closely connected with performance of the Homeric epic by the lyric poets. As these poets reached back to the mythical past of the Homeric story, their recasting of this story, in contrast to local versions, were aimed at creating a statement of truth (ἀλήθεια) "in the overarching process of achieving a convergent version acceptable to all Hellenes."[28] This process remained fluid "to the point where the latest version becomes the last version, a canonization that brings to a final state of crystallization what had been becoming an ever less-fluid state of variation in performance."[29]

An analogous process can be observed in the creation of a new ritual and narrative in Rome at the time of Augustus through which the beginning of a new age was proclaimed and celebrated. After Julius Caesar was assassinated, a cult for the Divus Julius was immediately established. After the consolidation of his power, Caesar's heir Augustus took advantage of the existence of this cult that honored a person who had died as a god, and refashioned it into a comprehensive cult that could be renewed with the deification of every succeeding emperor. At the same time, Virgil created in his *Aeneid* the story that would become the new national epic of Rome. It is a new story, but at the same time it is a story that reaches back to the oldest Greek myth and epic tradition by connecting the founder of Rome to the story of Troy from Homer's *Iliad.* The celebration of the beginning of a new era in the secular festival of the year 17 BCE again was accompanied by the words of a poet in Horace's *Carmen saeculare.* A decade later, Augustus consecrated the new Altar of Peace, the *Ara Pacis,* with a festive procession and sacrifices. Among the preserved reliefs of this monument appears not only a symbolization of a peaceful and fruitful mother earth but also a depiction of the Trojan hero Aeneas's sacrifice at the founding of Rome. It would be interesting to investigate the subsequent establishments of the cult of Caesar and Dea Roma or of Augustus and Rome in other cities of the empire. As in Virgil's epic, there is clear evidence for attempts to relate the new imperial cult to time-honored religious rituals and stories of traditional deities. For example, in Athens, the new cult of the city goddess Roma and of Augustus, the founding hero of a new state, was set up as an analogy to the cult of the city goddess Athena and to Athens' founding hero Erechtheus. There is also evidence that Virgil's epic was by no means an unalterable canonical text. Under Domitian, who

---

27. Gregory Nagy, *Pindar's Homer: The Lyric Possession of an Epic Past* (Baltimore: Johns Hopkins University Press, 1990) 52–81.

28. Ibid., 61.

29. Ibid.

attempted to renew the eschatological spirit of the time of Augustus, several new versions of a new epic narrative appeared.

The same pattern is evident in the history of Israel. If the exact relationship of the narrative of the exodus to the festival and ritual of the renewal of the covenant is still debated, there can be no question that the retelling of the exodus story and the reformulation of the giving of the law was intimately related to the creation of Pan-Israel, the new nation consisting of the twelve tribes, until canonization finally took place in the establishment of the five books of Moses as scripture. With respect to Passover, the close connection between the ritual and the remembering of the exodus is evident. Here, as in Greece with its several national festivals (in addition to Olympia and Delphi also Nemea and Isthmia), the narrative need not be limited to one particular ritual. It can be observed that the story of Jesus' suffering, death, and resurrection accompanies not only the celebration of the Eucharist but also can be connected with the ritual of baptism.[30]

The cult of the Kyrios Christ and the story that legitimizes the "New Israel" as an eschatological event are anchored in the traditional language of Israel and, at the same time, in the actual suffering and death of the historical Jesus of Nazareth. The recourse to Jesus' sayings evident, for example, in 1 Corinthians 7, in Romans 12, and later in the Sermon on the Mount of the Gospel of Matthew, is another important element of historical continuity. On the other hand, the gnosticizing interpretation of the sayings of Jesus that appears in the wisdom tradition of the Sayings Source and in the *Gospel of Thomas* must have appeared as illegitimate because it was concerned only with the timeless religious dimensions of individual salvation and ignored the application of Jesus' preaching for the building up of the political and social order of the new nation and the eschatological dimension of its consciousness. The conflict between these two traditions and interpretations of the sayings of Jesus is as old as Paul's controversy with the wisdom teachings in Corinth in 1 Corinthians 1–4.

Of course, the wisdom teachers in Corinth, the Synoptic Sayings Source, and the *Gospel of Thomas* also belong to the history of the effects of the ministry of Jesus of Nazareth. But the tradition of the wisdom sayings did not include the political and eschatological dimensions of Jesus' announcement of the coming of the new age. Similarly, the modern discovery of the historical Jesus as a wisdom teacher, or even as a philosopher in the tradition of Cynicism, may serve the economic and religious advancement of the chosen individual for whom an eschatological message can only appear as a threat. Moreover, it is doubtful that the claim of such historical continuity is hermeneutically justifiable, because it neglects the categories by which antiquity understood the political dimensions of historical continuity. Cult and story, both fashioned in the language of ancient, albeit mythical, traditions, were—and perhaps still are—more powerful constituents of the historical continuity that incorporates the eschatological vision of its founder as well as of a new people and a new political and social order.

---

30. See especially Romans 6.

17

THE STORY OF JESUS
AND THE GOSPELS

In the following I intend to sketch three different trajectories for the development of traditions from and about Jesus from their beginnings to the final tangible literary end products. I have entitled these trajectories (1) "From Jesus' Death to the Gospel of Mark," (2) "From Jesus the Prophet to the Gospel of Matthew," and (3) "From Jesus as Wisdom from Heaven to the Gospel of John." At the end I shall discuss the work of Luke as the new epic for the Christian nation.

I. From Jesus' Death to the Gospel of Mark

Thanks to the letters of Paul, we have at least some fragmentary knowledge of the events that produced an explosive expansion of the earliest church into the Gentile world. The Book of Acts is a much less reliable source because it tries to establish an idealized picture of the beginning of the church; however, some of the information used by Luke supplies additional useful data.

The situation of the Israelites in Judea, Samaria, and Galilee in the first half of the first century CE is well known. The country had been under Roman rule for nearly a century, first governed by a Roman vassal king, Herod the Great, who was an Idumean; then by some of his sons, two of whom were still holding on to their small fiefdoms: Antipas ruled Galilee and Peraea, and his brother Philipp ruled the areas north and east of the Sea of Galilee. Judea and Samaria, however, had been under direct Roman administration since the year 6 CE, although the Roman governor, who normally resided in Caesarea Maritima, largely left the administration of the internal affairs of Judea to the high priest and the Sanhedrin in Jerusalem. We know little about the interior organization of the Israelites living in Samaria. The arrangement of 6 CE that put Samaria and Judea into one administrative district resulted in numerous hostilities because of the enmity between Judeans and Samaritans. The enmity had its ultimate cause in the destruction of the Samaritan Temple on Mt. Gerizim by the Hasmonean rulers of Palestine two centuries earlier. One should not forget, however, that the Samaritans were law-abiding Israelites.

There was a considerable non-Jewish population in Palestine. A special district of ten cities south and east of the Sea of Galilee, known as the Decapolis, including such cities as Gerasa, Pella, and Scythopolis, was essentially Greek. The city of Samaria had been reorganized as a Greek city by Herod the Great and named "Sebaste" in honor of Augustus. Herod also founded the port city of Caesarea as a Greek city, although it had a substantial Jewish population. The northern capitals of Sepphoris and Tiberias in Galilee, as well as Philipp's capital Caesarea Philippi, were probably more Greek than Jewish.

There was a wealthy upper class, especially the Sadducees in Jerusalem and some people connected to the courts of the northern vassal kings. But in most of Israel very few, if any, people in the country considered this as the situation promised to Israel by God's covenant. Josephus later described the four "philosophical" parties among the Jews as the Pharisees, Sadducees, Essenes, and Zealots. This categorization is misleading, *pace* the designation "philosophical." It is evident that there was no unanimity among the people with respect to the path to freedom and to the fulfillment of the promises of the covenant. Although most of the people seemed to have gone about their daily business more or less peacefully, there is good evidence to indicate that the appeal of prophets or would-be revolutionaries could stir up a lot of unrest at any moment. It is unlikely that the Zealots were a unified movement at the time. Smaller groups of bandits or guerrillas, however, seem to have existed throughout the period. Though their aspirations may have been rather nebulous, it is likely that they pretended to be liberators, who wanted to fulfill the messianic prophecies of freedom. The Zealots later became the core group of those who rose up against Roman rule in the Jewish War of 66–70 (73) CE.

Only two movements had a clear agenda for the restoration of the freedom and glory of Israel. The first were the Essenes, apparently mostly Palestinian but not limited to the Essene establishment at Qumran. They were a sect that was deeply influenced by Hellenistic utopian ideas combined with ancient Israelite concepts of the holy war ideology. The conflict with the Hasmonean rulers resulted in the founding of a sectarian movement and the establishment of an ideal society, based at Qumran. Its members were obligated to fulfill the covenant of Moses according to their special interpretation and to be prepared to participate in the final eschatological battle in which the angels of God would be victorious against the forces of Belial, the prince of darkness. The Essenes considered the ruling high priests of Jerusalem as illegitimate, and there is good evidence that they saw in the Romans the representatives of Belial. On the other hand, it is not clear that they were actively preparing a revolutionary war against Rome, though they seemed eventually to have participated in the uprising against Rome.

The second group with a clear agenda were the Pharisees. The problems of our understanding of the Pharisees at the time of Jesus are well known because the gospels of the New Testament are the earliest extant written sources, and they are clearly biased. There should be no doubt, however, that the Pharisees at that time were an international movement that was not limited to Palestine. The famous Pharisee Hillel came from Babylonia, and Paul—a Pharisee according to his self-presentation—came from the Greek-speaking diaspora (Damascus or Tarsus). Their aim must have been to bring Israel to a complete and acceptable fulfillment of the law as the precondition for the coming of the Messiah or of God's kingdom. Paul understood his own commitment in this way, and the later Pharisaic *4th Book of Ezra* written shortly after the Jewish War, emphasizes once more the necessity for all of Israel to fulfill the law, lamenting that Israel's failure to do so was the cause for the disaster of the Jewish War and the destruction of the Temple and of Jerusalem.

In the late twenties of the first century CE, a prophet with the name of John appeared, who preached a baptism of repentance for protection in the coming final judgment of God. He was apprehended by king Herod Antipas and executed. The Jewish historian Josephus confirms what is evident from the reports preserved about him in the gospel tradition that try to present him as a forerunner of Jesus. The one, whom John was announcing to come after him, was originally not Jesus but God, coming for the final judgment. In the tradition of Christianity, that Jesus had been baptized by John is one of the erratic blocks that can be seen as reliable historical information. As the disciples of John constituted a rival sect, the followers of Jesus were not all too eager to preserve this memory.

I shall resist the temptation here to reconstruct the story of Jesus as the successor of John. All that is known for certain is that Jesus was baptized by John, that he must have continued his ministry in some way, however modified, and that he was executed a few years later. It is impossible to tell in detail what happened immediately after Jesus' crucifixion and death. We do not know whether Jesus' disciples stayed in Jerusalem or fled to Galilee. There are, however, some events that triggered the beginnings of a new congregation: (1) Jesus, who had been condemned, appeared after his death to many people who had known him during his life, and probably also to others, like Paul; (2) a gathering of followers of Jesus experienced an outpouring of the spirit that was traumatic as well as creative. Both occurrences are unusual.

First, there are numerous reports in antiquity of the appearance of a deity or some dead human being. All of these, however, are appearances to one or a few individuals. There are no stories of such appearances to a large number of people as they are reported in 1 Corinthians 15:5–8: "(he appeared) first to Peter, then to the Twelve, then to more than five hundred brothers and sisters at the same time, . . . then to James, then to all apostles," and finally to Paul himself. The list could be enlarged because there is good evidence that several women, foremost Mary of Magdala, were also witnesses of such appearances of Jesus after his death. Paul received this report a few years after the death of Jesus, and he did not doubt it because he himself also was a witness of such an appearance of Jesus.

The account of the pouring out of the Holy Spirit at Pentecost, as it appears in Acts 2, is highly stylized and suffers from secondary interpretations. At its basis, however, is an older report of what we would call a "Pentecostal" experience—inspiration and speaking in tongues—that must have been overwhelming. To those present, it signaled an eschatological event. Even if the reference to the prophecy of Joel in Acts 2 is a secondary literary explanation, there can be no doubt that the original event was indeed understood in terms of the arrival of the divine spirit of the last times that would bring visions to the old and the young and give male and female slaves a share of this spirit. This event resulted in the creation of a new community that understood itself as the true Israel of the end of the times.

The people who had seen Jesus and who had experienced the arrival of the spirit were all Israelites. All of them knew that Jesus had been raised from the dead—because of these visions and the experience of the spirit, not because the tomb of Jesus was empty! That is another story, and it was most likely told later because Jesus' followers knew that Jesus was alive and that there was no need to return to the tomb in order to worship him there like a dead hero. The question was: why did he have to suffer and to die? To answer this question, the disciples did not try to recall the events that had befallen Jesus during his trial, suffering, and death. Rather, as believing people of Israel, they returned to the Scriptures. From the respective remarks of Paul in 1 Corinthians 11 and 15 and from the later passion narrative, it is safe to conclude that among these Scriptures, especially in Isaiah 53, they found the answer to the question of Jesus' suffering and death:

> He was despised, and forsook human beings,
> a man of suffering and familiar with sickness;
> and like one before whom one covers one's face.
> Despised—so we held him of no account. . . .

> Truly he bore *our* sickness, and *our* sufferings—
> he took them upon himself
> . . . but he was desecrated for *our* sin,
> smitten because of *our* transgressions. . . .

> And he gave him his grave among criminals,
> and his grave beside a rich man,
> although he had not committed any act of violence,
> and there was no deceit in his mouth. . . .

> After the anguish of his life he shall see light and be satisfied.
> Through the knowledge he, the one who is just,
> my Servant, will make the many just,
> and their debts he will take upon himself. . . .

> Therefore I will give him a share with the many
> and with the powerful he will share spoil;
> because he surrendered his life to death,
> and let himself be numbered among sinners.
> He was the one who bore the crimes of many
> and he will intercede for their sins.[1]

This reading of Scripture is the wellspring of the passion narrative. Other passages from Scripture, like Psalm 22, also played a role in its formation. In fact, there is very little in this story that has not been developed on a scriptural basis, while perhaps the only historical information that was remembered was Pontius Pilate, the judge who sentenced him, and the inscription he put on the cross: "Jesus of Nazareth, king of the Jews."[2]

At the same time, the reading of these Scriptures and the telling of the story belonged to a particular life situation, namely, the celebration of the common meal. To be sure,

---

1. Excerpts from Isa 53:3–12; *Deutero-Isaiah* (trans. Klaus Baltzer; Hermeneia; Minneapolis: Fortress Press, 2001) 392–93.

2. This inscription is not a Christian invention proclaiming the true dignity of Jesus. Rather, Pilate wanted to make clear with this proclamation how he intended to deal with every messianic pretender.

the story of the Emmaus disciples[3] is a rather late novelistic account of the events. However, it seems to me that it captures well the primary elements of the founding events of the new community. While these two nameless disciples are on the way, Jesus joins them and listens to their laments about the death of the one whom they had hoped "was the one to redeem Israel" (v. 21). In his answer, Jesus says:

> Was it not necessary that the Messiah should suffer these things and then enter into his glory? Then beginning with Moses and all the prophets, he interpreted to them all the things about himself in all the scriptures. (vv. 26–27)

> When he was at the table with them, he took bread, blessed it and broke it, and gave it to them. Then their eyes were opened and they recognized him; and he vanished from their sight. (vv. 30–31)

From what we learn from the first two chapters of Galatians, it is certain that there was unanimity about the content of the gospel and about the celebration of the common meal between Paul and Barnabas and others from Antioch on the one side, and Peter, John, and Jesus' brother James in Jerusalem on the other side. What Paul had received "from the beginning"[4] was not the special tradition of Antioch; it also was the tradition of Jerusalem. What was controversial according to Galatians 2 was the question of the circumcision of Gentiles who had joined the community. Furthermore, the conflict that arose in Antioch afterwards concerned the question of the common meal; when "certain people from James" (Gal 2:12) arrived, Peter and Barnabas turned away from the common meal with the uncircumcised Gentile members. Clearly, for Paul the common meal, the Eucharist, was the symbol of the unity of the New Israel of Jews and Gentiles. Thus, he accused Peter and Barnabas of being hypocrites because they had formerly participated in this common meal of Jews and Gentiles (Gal 2:11–14). But the common meal as well as the "gospel," that is, also the story of Jesus' suffering and death, was shared by Antioch and Jerusalem.

This story of Jesus' suffering and death, however, was told, and it was told in varying forms. The Gospel of Mark, the Gospel of John, and the *Gospel of Peter* preserve written forms of this story that exhibit many similarities, especially in the transformation of a number of scriptural passages about the suffering servant or the persecuted righteous into narrative about Jesus. But, at the same time, they are also sufficiently different to warrant the conclusion that the story circulated orally in a number of versions. However, the author of the Gospel of Mark and to some degree also the author of the Gospel of John,

---

3. Luke 24:13–32.

4. That Paul is dependent upon tradition is confirmed by the quotation formula he uses in 1 Cor 15:1–3. This should not be questioned on the basis of Gal 1:11–12, where Paul says that he "did not receive [the gospel] from a human source, . . . but through a revelation of Jesus Christ." Since Paul persecuted the Christians before his call, he must have known quite well what these Christians were proclaiming. Moreover, Galatians 1–2 presupposes that he and Jerusalem proclaim the same gospel; the divine authorization for the gospel that he is preaching refers primarily to the fact that his gospel is directed to the Gentiles. That is also meant by "the gospel that I proclaim among the Gentiles" (Gal 2:2).

as they wrote down the story that was told in their communities, meanwhile also revealed that the question "who was this Jesus?" had found different answers. The author of the Gospel of Mark is confronting the claim that Jesus was not the suffering servant but primarily a messianic figure, who worked great miracles, a "divine man."

It is futile to ask whether this tradition of Jesus' miracle working had its origin in historical reports about Jesus' activity. This cannot be known because all these stories are formed according to typical patterns of Hellenistic propaganda on behalf of great religious leaders, for example, the first-century CE Neo-Pythagorean, Apollonius of Tyana. In the Christian missionary propaganda, aretologies, that is, strings of miracle stories of Jesus had been developed that sometimes paralleled stories of the missionaries' own miracles that they might use as "letters of recommendation." Paul confronted such miracle-working apostles in Corinth and refuted their claims in his Second Letter to the Corinthians. That these rival missionaries also told miracle stories of Jesus is indicated in Paul's polemical remark that he no longer recognizes a "Christ according to the flesh" (2 Cor 5:16), that is, a miracle-working Messiah, but only the suffering and dying Jesus, whose image is present in the suffering and dying of the apostle.[5]

Mark's gospel has been characterized as a passion narrative with a lengthy introduction. This gospel is indeed written in order to confirm that the superiority of the Christian message cannot be established in competition with rival political and religious claims for greatness in this world. To be sure, Jesus is presented as a great miracle worker[6] in the first part of his gospel. As a witness of these great deeds of Jesus, Peter confesses at Caesarea Philippi, "You are the Messiah" (Mark 8:29). But then Mark inserts the gospel reformulated as a prediction of the Son of Man's suffering, death, and resurrection (Mark 8:31). Peter, who objects to this understanding of Jesus, is rebuked, "Get behind me, Satan!" (Mark 8:33). The disciples must learn from now on that:

> . . . among the Gentiles those whom they recognize as their rulers lord it over them, and their great ones are tyrants over them. But it is not so among you; but whoever wishes to become great among you must be your servant, and whoever wishes to be first among you must be the slave of all. For the Son of Man came not to be served but to serve, and to give his life a ransom for many. (Mark 10:42–45)

The allusions to the suffering servant of Deutero-Isaiah are evident in the final sentence that is not a historically verifiable word of Jesus at all but an affirmation by the community that the only legitimate presence of God's power in this world is visible in humiliation and suffering and in the abrogation of all power and greatness. The tradition of the great miracle worker Jesus has thus been subordinated to the story of the passion. The passion narrative is validated by placing the last meal of Jesus right before the story of Jesus' arrest and trial (Mark 14:17–31).

---

5. I am dependent here on the work of Dieter Georgi, *The Opponents of Paul in Second Corinthians* (Philadelphia: Fortress Press, 1986).

6. Morton Smith, *Jesus the Magician* (San Francisco: Harper & Row, 1978).

II. From Jesus the Prophet to the *Gospel of Thomas*

It is most striking that a very different recourse to Jesus was developed at the same time that was in no way related to the understanding of Jesus as the suffering servant. When Jesus had been executed, some of his followers established a memory of him as the great teacher that they found documented in his words. The people who began the collection of these words may or may not have been personally acquainted with Jesus' ministry during the time of his life. What they preserved were not extensive records of Jesus' teaching, but reformulated summaries of what they had learned—reformulated in such a way that it could be remembered and be used for the instruction of the followers. What is preserved in the earliest composition of the Synoptic Sayings Gospel Q is mostly prophetic sayings and instructions for the community, its organization, and its missionary activity. There is no recourse to Jesus' suffering, death, and resurrection; no reflection on the understanding of Jesus' ministry and fate as an eschatological event according to the Scriptures of Israel;[7] and no effort of understanding Jesus' ministry and fate as an eschatological event. The programmatic statements at the beginning of the oldest form of the Sayings Gospel Q, however, reveal some unusual features. The poor are blessed (Q/Luke 6:20), and the hungry are promised to be filled (Q/Luke 6:21). The disciples are told that they should love their enemies and should do good to those who hate them (Q/Luke 6:27). They should not lend money to those from whom they expect a repayment (Q/Luke 6:34). The implications are clear: the members of the community of the followers of Jesus are asked to distance themselves from the revolutionary hatred of the foreign overlords, namely, the Romans, and to sever their ties with the money-driven selfishness of the economy. The formulation of these materials corresponds to the form of wisdom speech. Their intention, however, stands in stark contrast to the tradition of wisdom instruction, because the latter is designed to encourage moral, albeit clever, conduct in order to earn rewards and blessing: economic, social, and political in the course of one's life in this world. Blessings for those who fear the Lord and obey the commands of wisdom, as well as curses upon the fools, are a commonplace in wisdom speech.[8] John Kloppenborg[9] quotes Proverbs 3:33 as an example:

> The Lord's curse is on the house of the wicked;
> but he blesses the abode of the righteous.

In the inaugural sermon of Q, however, it is neither righteousness that is praised nor wickedness that is condemned. Rather, blessings refer to social status and to human conditions: the poor are blessed, not because they have done something that deserves a

---

7. In the earliest strata of the collection of these sayings, scriptural references and quotations were apparently absent.

8. Hans Dieter Betz (*The Sermon on the Mount* [Hermeneia; Minneapolis: Fortress Press, 1995] 586) notes that "series of beatitudes and 'woes' are found in prophetic, apocalyptic, and wisdom literature."

9. *The Formation of Q. Trajectories in Ancient Wisdom Tradition* (Studies in Antiquity and Christianity; Philadelphia: Fortress Press, 1987) 190.

reward, but simply because they are poor. The features of these blessings have been described as typical for "sapiential beatitudes, in particular, serialization and placement at the beginning of an instruction."[10] It must remain questionable, however, whether the designation of these beatitudes as sapiential can be upheld. The beatitudes of the inaugural sermon of Q (= Luke 6:20–21) promise blessings that are fulfilled in the future of God's kingdom.[11] As far as the content of these beatitudes is concerned, parallels are not found in wisdom literature but in eschatological materials, for example, in the eschatological hymn[12] that is preserved as the "Magnificat" (Luke 1:52–53):

> He has brought down the powerful from their thrones
> and lifted up the lowly.
> He has filled the hungry with good things
> and sent the rich away empty.

The beatitudes announce an eschatological moment that calls for a decision on behalf of the kingdom of God.[13] That the followers of Jesus, who remembered the blessings of the poor, the hungry, and those who weep, made this decision and paid a price for it is formulated in the fourth beatitude that blesses Jesus' disciples because of their experience of hatred and rejection (Q/Luke 6:22–23b).[14] Whoever gave these beatitudes the form in which they appear in the inaugural sermon, the community of the Sayings Gospel, remembered in these sayings that the proclamation of Jesus was prophetic and that it called the community into a new existence that required its members to reject the revolutionary messianism of the time, to honor the poor, and to refrain from their exploitation in the practice of loaning money for interest.

The further development of the earliest collections of these sayings went in two different directions. One development of the tradition of the sayings of Jesus that was very closely related to the original version of the Sayings Gospel Q is visible very early, namely, in Paul's controversy with the Corinthians that is evident in 1 Corinthians 1–4.[15] Paul argues here against the claim of some Corinthians that they possess words of saving wisdom. That several phrases and one quotation have close parallels in the *Gospel*

---

10. *Formation of Q*, 188; the placement of beatitudes at the beginning of a variety of documents corresponds to ancient tradition; see Betz, *Sermon on the Mount*, 97–105.

11. They are also paralleled in a venerable Greek genre of blessings that are specifically concerned with the future and afterlife.

12. Perhaps this hymn was inherited from the disciples of John the Baptist. See Rudolf Bultmann (*The History of the Synoptic Tradition* [Rev. ed.; New York: Harper & Row, 1976] 296). For the eschatological character of this hymn, see François Bovon (*Luke 1: A Commentary on the Gospel of Luke 1:1–9:50* [Hermeneia; Minneapolis: Fortress Press, 2002] 64).

13. Bultmann (*History of the Synoptic Tradition*, 109–110) has therefore identified the beatitudes as prophetic sayings.

14. 6:23c ("for so their fathers did to the prophets") is most certainly a later addition to Q because none of the parallels to this fourth beatitude (1 Pet 4:14; *Gos. Thom.* 68, 69a) present this clause; cf. Kloppenborg, *Formation of Q*, 173.

15. For an analysis of these chapters and the sayings to which they allude, see Helmut Koester, "Gnostic Writings as Witnesses for the Development of the Sayings Tradition," in Bentley Layton, ed., *The Rediscovery of Gnosticism*, vol. 1: *The School of Valentinus* (NumenSup. 41; Leiden: Brill, 1980) 238–61.

of Thomas indicates that sayings of Jesus were here understood as revelations of divine secrets. This interpretation of sayings would eventually lead to their esoteric understanding that is fully present in the *Gospel of Thomas*. Jesus thus becomes the messenger of words of hidden truth that give eternal life and immortality. I shall return to this interpretation of Jesus' sayings later in the context of the discussion of the Gospel of John.

The second development of the earliest sayings collections appears in the redaction of the Sayings Gospel that is dominated by the addition of sayings about the future judgment and the announcement of the sudden and unexpected coming of the Son of Man. The first characteristic of this redaction of Q is the expectation of the sudden revelation (ἀποκαλύπτεται, Q/Luke 17:30) of the Son of Man "in his day" (ἐν τῇ ἡμέρᾳ αὐτοῦ, Q/Luke 17:24) or "in that day" (ἐν τῇ ἡμέρᾳ ἐκείνῃ, Q/Luke 17:31). The coming is unexpected and there will be no time to escape (Q/Luke 17:31). The same apocalyptic expectation is found in some materials of Q/Luke 12:39–59; cf. the conclusion of the parable of the thief: "because the Son of Man will come in an hour that you do not expect" (ὅτι ᾗ ὥρᾳ οὐ δοκεῖτε ὁ υἱὸς τοῦ ἀνθρώπου ἔρχεται, Q/Luke 12:40). The following parable of the faithful and unfaithful servants (Q/Luke 12:41–46) also illustrates the suddenness of the coming (Q/Luke 12:46), although the title Son of Man has not been introduced into the allegorizing conclusion of this parable.

A second element that is typical for the redactor is the announcement of the judgment over "this generation" (γενεὰ αὕτη, Q/Luke 11:29–32, 50–51). Closely related is Q/Luke 10:12–15 with the announcement of judgment over Chorazin, Bethsaida, and Kaphernaum.[16] The hand of the same redactor is recognizable furthermore in the parable that compares the people "of this generation" (τῆς γενεᾶς ταύτης) to children playing in the market place (Q 7:31–32). Furthermore, the redactor of the Sayings Gospel also provided a new introduction with the judgment sayings of John the Baptist (Q/Luke 3:7–9, 16–17).[17] The tone for the new judgment orientation of the book was thus clearly set.

These apocalyptic sayings come from a tradition that also furnished the apocalyptic Son of Man sayings to the Gospel of Mark. The Markan apocalypse (chapter 13) culminates in the prediction of the coming of the Son of Man (Mark 13:26) and in the statement that "this generation" (ἡ γενεὰ αὕτη) shall not pass away until all this has happened (Mark 13:30). Although "this generation" here is referred to without any negative predicates, it is explicitly called "adulterous and sinful" in the Son of Man saying in Mark 8:38. There are good reasons to assume that these sayings shared by Mark and the redactor of Q were coined by Christian prophets in Palestine during the turmoil of the sixties of the first century that resulted in the Jewish War, perhaps even as late as during the war itself. It was the answer of the followers of Jesus to the rise of anti-Roman revolutionary messianism in Palestine. The apocalypse of Mark 13 reveals the

---

16. The formulation "that city" (ἡ πόλις ἐκείνη) corresponds to "this generation" (γενεὰ αὕτη), and the distinctive phrase "in that day" (ἐν τῇ ἡμέρᾳ ἐκείνῃ) is also used (Q 10:12).

17. Kloppenborg, *Formation of Q*, 102–7. It is not likely that a description of the Baptist's appearance also was added.

political position of this group. They are warned not to believe any false prophets who proclaimed, "Behold, the Messiah is here" (Mark 13:21–22). The relationship of these followers of Jesus to the Temple of Jerusalem was fundamentally positive, since the threat of its destruction is seen as a sacrilege (Mark 13:11). The group, however, had suffered persecution from their fellow Israelites (Mark 13:9); divisions ran deep even in families (Mark 13:12). The prophets do not explicitly condemn the Romans but rather advise the followers of Jesus to separate and seek refuge elsewhere (Mark 13:14b–16).

The prophets who shaped the materials of the Markan apocalypse belong to Judea (Mark 13:14b), perhaps to the community of Jerusalem.[18] On the other hand, the Son of Man and judgment sayings of the Q community, located outside of Judea,[19] do not reveal the same degree of tribulation; they reflect a different and less urgent experience of persecution and resistance to their mission (cf. the addition of Q 10:12–15 to Q 10:10–11[20]) and should therefore be located outside of Galilee. Both the Jerusalem group and their Q counterparts share the desire to establish an alternative to the two dominating political options of the time: messianic war against Rome or collaboration with the Roman authorities. The community of the Sayings Gospel, now in a new political situation, is advised by its prophets that faithfulness to Jesus' command to love one's enemies requires it to withdraw from the beginning hostilities of the war and to increase its watchfulness for the coming of the Son of Man.

It is in this later form of the Sayings Gospel that the Gospels of Matthew and Luke used it for their composition. I shall leave the discussion of the use of Q in the Gospel of Luke aside here and make only a few comments about its use in the Gospel of Matthew. The primary source of Matthew, of course, was the Gospel of Mark. But the tradition of the sayings of Jesus, and especially the Sayings Gospel Q, made an enormous impact upon the shaping of Matthew's gospel, which was to become the most popular and widely used gospel of the early church. While the Markan narrative of Jesus' ministry is totally dominated by the passion narrative, this narrative, though retained by Matthew as an important part of his gospel, is no longer the formative element of his book. Rather, the teachings of Jesus now dominate the composition. Most of these teachings are arranged in five major speeches, beginning with the Sermon on the Mount (Matthew 5–7) that incorporates most of the materials of the inaugural speech of Q and ending with the eschatological speech (Matthew 24–25) that combines Q's apocalyptic prophecies with those of the Markan apocalypse. The arrangement into five speeches recalls the five Books of Moses, and it is evident that Matthew thus presents Jesus as the new Moses. Although the name of Moses never appears, Matthew wants to tell the reader that Jesus is the one who restores the law of Moses and that therefore the followers of Jesus, who abide by the teaching of Jesus, are the legitimate community of Israel. They constitute, however, the eschatological Israel that expects the final return of Jesus as the Son of Man, and that anticipates the meal in the king-

---

18. Egon Brandenburger (*Markus 13 und die Apokalyptik* [Göttingen: Vandenhoeck & Ruprecht, 1984]) has presented a cogent analysis of the apocalyptic source used by Mark and about the position of its author.

19. I hesitate therefore to locate the Q redaction in Galilee because the messianic fervor at the beginning of the Jewish War was no less intense there than it was in Judea.

20. Dieter Lührmann, *Die Redaktion der Logienquelle* (WMANT 33; Neukirchen-Vluyn: Neukirchener Verlag, 1969) 62–63; Kloppenborg, *Formation of Q,* 196–97.

dom of God in its Eucharistic celebrations. By combining the Sayings Gospel and the Gospel of Mark into a new document, Matthew has also reconciled the once separate community of Q with the Pauline tradition of the story of the suffering servant as the foundational epic of the new Israel. Matthew completes the trajectory that begins with the eschatological preaching of John the Baptist and runs through Jesus' proclamation of the kingdom for the poor through the renewal of the apocalyptic prophecy of Q's redaction into the church's expectation of the return of Jesus as the judge of the last times. In this way, Matthew's gospel became the charter for Israel, for which Jesus was both Moses the legislator and Moses the suffering servant.

III. From Jesus as Wisdom from Heaven to the Gospel of John

Ever since the discovery of the *Gospel of Thomas,* scholars have been surprised by the close affinity of some of its sayings not only to the synoptic tradition but also to the Gospel of John.[21] I have argued this case in detail,[22] and it seems to me that the author of the Gospel of John is by no means dependent upon the *Gospel of Thomas* but presupposes an understanding of Jesus' sayings as saving wisdom that was further developed in the *Gospel of Thomas.* Not only were Jesus' words interpreted in this way, also Jesus himself was seen as the pre-existent figure of Wisdom, who had come down from heaven and then returned to her heavenly abode. This wisdom myth had been developed in the Jewish wisdom movement and has found expression in some passages of the Book of Proverbs, in the Book of Sirach, and in the Wisdom of Solomon. Also, the Alexandrian Jewish philosopher Philo repeatedly elaborates this myth of Wisdom. Wisdom was created before the beginning of the world; she is enthroned next to God, and the world was created through her. She reveals herself on earth but is rejected and returns to her heavenly abode. However, to those who seek her diligently, she reveals herself and provides life and immortality.

Early Christian understanding of Jesus has applied this Jewish myth of Wisdom to Jesus at a very early time. Paul already knows a hymn about Christ as this pre-existent heavenly figure, which he quotes in Philippians 2. A similar hymn about Christ as "first-born of creation" is quoted in Colossians 1. There also are passages in the synoptic tradition of Jesus' sayings in which Jesus speaks in the role of wisdom, for example, the famous invitation to those who are weary and are carrying heavy burdens, to whom Jesus promises rest (Matt 11:28–30). The *Gospel of Thomas* (28) also presents a speech of Jesus in which Jesus reveals himself as heavenly Wisdom, who has come into the world but is not understood by human beings.

The Gospel of John begins with such a wisdom hymn, in which Hellenistic influence is visible insofar as "Wisdom" now has been replaced by the Greek term "Logos":

---

21. See especially Raymond E. Brown, "The Gospel of Thomas and St. John's Gospel," *NTS* 9 (1962/63) 155–77, who argues, however, for a dependence of the *Gospel of Thomas* upon the Gospel of John; cf. also Brown, *The Gospel according to John* (2 vols.; AB 29–30; Garden City, N.J.: Doubleday, 1966–70) lxxxii.

22. Helmut Koester, *Ancient Christian Gospels: Their History and Development* (Philadelphia: Trinity Press International, 1990) 113–24.

"In the beginning was the Word, and the Word was God. . . . All things were created through the Word" (John 1:1–2). As in the Jewish Wisdom myth, also the hymn quoted in John 1 speaks about the coming of the Logos: "The Logos was in the world, and the world came into being through him; yet the world did not know him" (John 1:10).

At the same time, John uses a number of sayings in which Jesus speaks words of revelation that communicate life:

John 8:51:
Whoever keeps my word will not see death in eternity.

cf. *Gos. Thom.* 1:
Whoever finds the interpretation of these sayings will not taste death.

John 4:14:
Whoever drinks from the water that I shall give him will not thirst in eternity, but the water that I shall give him will become in him a spring of bubbling water unto eternal life.

cf. *Gos. Thom.* 13:
Because you have drunk, you have become intoxicated from the bubbling spring that I have measured out.

John 11:9–10:
If someone walks in the day, he does not stumble, because he sees the light of the day. But if someone walks in the night, he stumbles because the light is not in him.

cf. *Gos. Thom.* 24b:
There is light within a man of light and he lights up the whole world. If he does not shine, he is darkness.

John 16:4b–5:
Those things I did not tell you from the beginning when I was with you. Now I am going to the one who sent me, and none of you asks me, "where are you going?"

cf. *Gos. Thom.* 92:
Yet what you asked me about in former times and which I did not tell you then, now I desire to tell, but you do not inquire after it.

The number of such parallels can easily be enlarged. All these sayings are grouped around the topic of recognizing the light in Jesus and in oneself and thus to gain knowledge and to gain eternal life. They are closely related to the use of the Wisdom myth about Jesus, who came from heaven to communicate saving knowledge to those who are willing to hear and to learn that they themselves can discover the saving light, life, and truth in themselves. Both the Gospel of John and the *Gospel of Thomas* utilize the same wisdom understanding of a tradition of Jesus' sayings. It is a tradition that appears, as I indicated previously, as early as Paul's Corinthian correspondence, that is, almost half a century before the composition of the Gospel of John. It may have grown out of the application of the Jewish Wisdom mythology to Jesus, which must also be dated in the time of Paul, that is, in the first two decades of the mission of the followers of Jesus after his death. That sayings of the historical Jesus are the origin of this tradition is not likely, because it is apparent that these sayings are a secondary development of older prophetic sayings that spoke about the coming kingdom of God. Such transformation of older sayings about the future kingdom into sayings that speak about the presence of the kingdom in the self-knowledge of the disciples is evident in a number of sayings of the *Gospel of Thomas*. Compare, for example, *Gos. Thom.* 3, which explicitly rejects the understanding of the kingdom in an eschatological sense:

> Jesus said: If those who lead you say, "See the kingdom is in the sky," then the birds of the sky will precede you. If they say to you, "it is in the sea," then the fish will precede you. Rather, the kingdom is inside of you. When you come to know yourselves, then you will become known, and you will realize that you are the sons of the living Father. But if you will not know yourselves, you dwell in poverty, and it is you who are that poverty.

While the *Gospel of Thomas* further developed and expanded the mystical or Gnostic reinterpretation of this tradition of sayings, the Gospel of John endeavored to limit and criticize the evidently Gnostic tendency of these sayings. This is done in the Gospel of John in two ways: (1) John adds commentaries to these sayings that indicate that their meaning cannot be understood if one seeks the truth and the light in oneself; rather, the truth and the light and the life are found only in Jesus. The disciples are thus challenged to believe in Jesus and not to seek knowledge in their own divine selves, and (2) belief in Jesus is, to be sure, believing that Jesus is the revealer, who has come down from heaven, but he is also the one who died on the cross and whose suffering and death was his glorification.

The understanding of these sayings in terms of belief in Jesus rather than in terms of the knowledge of self is especially evident in some of the secondary expansions of sayings into larger dialogues and discourses that are so characteristic of much of the Gospel of John. There is a dialogue of Jesus with his disciples, preserved in the *Dialogue of the Savior* (25–30), another newly discovered writing from the Coptic-Gnostic Library of Nag Hammadi,[23] where Mary asks Jesus about the way to the heavenly places. In the answer, which is, unfortunately, a bit fragmentary, Jesus seems to speak about finding that place in one's own heart. When Matthew requests "to see that place of life where there is no wickedness, but rather there is pure light," Jesus answers, "Brother Matthew, you will not be able to see it, as long as you are carrying flesh around," implying that only after death, when the soul is freed from the burden of the flesh, is it possible to see the place of light. When Matthew further requests to know that place, even though he cannot see it, Jesus answers: "Everyone who has known himself has seen it, and everything that is given to him, he will do in his goodness."[24] The Gospel of John has apparently used and reinterpreted this same or a similar dialogue in chapter 14:

---

23. Stephen Emmels, Helmut Koester, and Elaine Pagels, *Nag Hammadi Codex III, 5: The Dialogue of the Savior* (NHS 26; Leiden: Brill, 1984).
24. The text is very uncertain at this point.

(Jesus said:) "In my Father's house there are many dwellings; if not, I would have told you, because I go to prepare a place for you. . . . And I come again to take you to myself, so that where I am you also will be. And where I go, you know the way." Thomas said to him, "Lord, we do not know where you are going; how can we know the way?" Jesus said to him, "I am the way and the truth and the life; no one comes to the Father except through me." Philip said to him, "Show us the Father, and it will be sufficient for us." Jesus said to him, ". . . Who has seen me has seen the Father. How do you say, 'Show us the Father'? Do you not know that I am in the Father and the Father in me? . . . The Father who dwells in me does his works. . . . He who believes in me will also do the works I do, and will do greater ones than these."[25]

What is emphasized here instead of the Gnostic concept of knowing oneself and recognizing ultimate divinity in oneself is the binding of the disciple to Jesus by seeing Jesus and believing in Jesus, in whom the Father is present, and doing the works that Jesus is doing.

This belief in Jesus as the foundation of the disciples' existence is not just belief in the appearance of a heavenly revealer, whom one must seek in order to gain knowledge, but belief in a Jesus who is a real human being, who has suffered and died on the cross. In the beginning of his gospel, John uses the often-cited wisdom saying about seeking and finding—namely seeking and finding the kingdom and ultimately one's true self (*Gos. Thom.* 1, 92, 94). The author presents Jesus as asking the disciples, who come to him, "Whom do you seek?" (John 1:38). It seems that it is indeed Jesus, the revealer, the Messiah, the Son of Man, whom they are seeking and whom they now have found. The Gospel of John, however, raises the question repeatedly, of who this Jesus really is. Yes, he is the one who has come down from heaven, who says of himself that he is the light of the world, the true bread from heaven, the way, the truth, and the life. But the question, "Whom do you seek?" appears once more at the end of the gospel, when the soldiers with Judas come to arrest Jesus. Here Jesus asks again twice, "Whom do you seek?" and when they say each time "Jesus, from Nazareth!" Jesus answers twice, "I am" (John 18:4–9). Who is this Jesus? He is the human being from Nazareth, who has come to suffer and to be crucified. Thus the mysterious word of Jesus of John 8:28 is finally explained. There Jesus had said to those who questioned him, "When you see the Son of Man raised up (that is, on the cross), then you will know who I am (ὅτι ἐγώ εἰμι)." In this way the author of the Gospel of John has made the tradition about Jesus, the Logos from heaven, the Wisdom of creation, the revealer of truth and eternal life, subject to the tradition of the suffering servant. The narrative of Jesus' trial, suffering, and death on the cross reveals his ultimate and true identity, and the disciples are asked to believe in this Jesus of Nazareth. Thus John presents the dying Jesus with his last words, "It has been accomplished" (John 19:30).

---

25. For a more detailed comparison of the sayings of Jesus in the Gospel of John and in the *Dialogue of the Savior* and in other Gnostic gospels, see Koester, *Ancient Christian Gospels,* 259–66.

IV. The Work of Luke as the Epic for the Christian Nation

It is more difficult to understand what happened to the tradition of Jesus in the Gospel of Luke. It is probably the latest of the Four Gospels, written at the very end of the first century and looking back over two generations of Christian churches. Today Luke's gospel is one of four gospels of the canon of the New Testament. Luke, however, did not write a gospel but a much larger work that also included what we now call the Acts of the Apostles. These two books were originally parts of one single work that was later divided into two separate writings. To understand what the author wanted to accomplish with his work, it is necessary to look at the whole of his work.[26]

Evidently, this is not just a work about Jesus, and in his preface Luke neither presents it as a work about Jesus nor calls it a gospel. Rather, he says that he wants to write an orderly account of the things that have been fulfilled among us (Luke 1:1–4). Overlooking the entire work, it is striking that the book does not begin with the birth of Jesus, like the Gospel of Matthew, but with the birth of a prophet of Israel, John the Baptist, and it ends with the arrival of the apostle Paul in Rome and his activity in the capital. The announcement of the birth of John the Baptist is explicitly dated in the reign of Herod the Great (Luke 1:5), who ruled until the year 4 BCE, and the work ends more than half a century later around the year 60 CE. It begins in Jerusalem, and Luke's work ends in Rome. It is thus deliberately designed to cover not just a few years but a longer period, and it wants to cover the entire geographical region from a venerable ancient city of the East, that now lies in ruins, to the current capital of the world. The age-old prophecies of the people of this ancient city guide the course of the entire story from its beginning to the end.

All this reminds us of the epic of Virgil, whose main protagonist, Aeneas, flees the burning city of Troy and finally arrives at the Italian shore to become the founder of the new nation of the Romans. What the author of Luke-Acts endeavors to accomplish is no less than what Virgil has achieved in his work, namely, to write an epic that symbolizes the founding of a new nation, albeit it an epic written in prose rather than in hexameters. Scholars have long debated whether Luke's work is history or legend or romance. Each of these hypotheses is burdened with difficulties; these difficulties, however, disappear if one recognizes that epic defines the genre of Luke's work.

John the Baptist is the divinely ordained forerunner, the last of the prophets of Israel, whose mission binds the coming of the Savior to the ancient promises. The Savior himself is born in the city of the David, and from here he is guided by the Spirit of God throughout his ministry, endowed with divine power and victorious over Satan. His death in Jerusalem only seems to be the tragic ending. In reality, it is part of the fulfillment of Israel's prophecy that required the Messiah to go into his glory through suffering. It is once more the Spirit of God, now poured out over all the people, who

---

26. For the understanding of Luke-Acts as an epic, I am especially dependent here on the challenging work of Marianne Palmer Bonze, *The Past as Legacy: Luke-Acts and Ancient Epic* (Minneapolis: Fortress Press, 2000); at the time of the writing of this lecture, her work was available to me in the form of a Harvard University doctoral dissertation.

guides the increase of the new nation from Jerusalem through all adversities to the final arrival in the city of Rome.

This framework gave Luke the opportunity to weave written sources and other traditions exquisitely into a rich tapestry in which the dominant thread is divine guidance that rescues the hero repeatedly from adversity and regularly turns apparent calamity into another step towards final victory. Legend and miracle are as welcome for this story as are references to historical events. What is especially striking is the fact that this epic framework allowed Luke to preserve his sources and materials quite faithfully in their original form. While Mark, and especially Matthew, often change the form and wording of their sources, to impress their visions upon these materials, Luke uses primarily the framework of his writing to express his purpose. Were Luke a historian, he could be reprimanded for his uncritical use of legendary materials, even by ancient standards for the writing of history. But since he is writing an epic story, legends illustrating divine guidance and purpose are most welcome and can be told uncritically, often embellished and artistically arranged, as in the birth stories of John the Baptist and Jesus. Sayings of Jesus drawn from the Sayings Gospel Q as well as from Luke's special source seem more faithfully preserved than elsewhere. These materials also include many of the most important parables of Jesus. The wording of these materials often seems archaic; they did not have to be altered and theologically updated because the literary purpose of the entire narrative provides their meaning.

Luke's work was not well understood and appreciated in the ancient church. It was rarely quoted in the second century—only Marcion used it towards the middle of the second century for the composition of his gospel, purified of all references to the Bible and thus stripped of all the epic thrust of the narrative. By the time of Marcion, however, what has survived as the Gospel of Luke had already been severed from its continuation, now transmitted as the "Acts of the Apostles." The latter was soon considered as a historical record of the oldest period of Christianity, used extensively as a historical source by the fourth-century church historian Eusebius of Caesarea and others after him—and alas, by numerous modern scholars.

The first part of Luke's work, though often judged inferior to the Gospel of Matthew, was eventually incorporated at the end of the second century by bishop Irenaeus into the four-gospel canon of the New Testament. It was fitting for Irenaeus's new creation because, like Matthew, Mark, and John, it also included a passion narrative. The story of Jesus had originally been developed as the cult narrative for the celebration of the Eucharist. In the attempt to forge a unity of the many Christian communities, the primary bond was the Eucharist as the ritual of the new Christian nation. If the story of Jesus, now in its written form, also was to be a unifying element in this effort, the canon of a new scripture could include only those gospels that told the story of his suffering and death. However important the Sayings Gospel Q had been in the preservation of Jesus' words, and however deep the secret wisdom of the *Gospel of Thomas* might appear, their lack of a passion narrative would certainly disqualify them. It is significant, on the other hand, that the four-gospel canon was not exclusive but rather inclusive. Originally, each of these four gospels had been the special book of particular communities. As their gospels were included in the canon, the communities that had created and transmitted them also were incorporated into the unity of the church universal.

18

THE SAYINGS OF Q AND
THEIR IMAGE OF JESUS

I. The Present Situation in Q Research and Its Problems

The synoptic Sayings Gospel (Q) has been the object of intense efforts of scholarship
during the last decades, beginning with James M. Robinson's seminal essay "ΛΟΓΟΙ
ΣΟΦΩΝ" in the Bultmann Festschrift of 1964[1] and culminating in the International Q
Project that published its last installment of the reconstructed Greek text of Q in the
Journal of Biblical Literature in the fall of 1995[2] and a few years later, the full critical edition of Q.[3] Contrary to the earlier view that the synoptic Sayings Gospel Q grew out
of Jesus' eschatological or apocalyptic proclamation,[4] a different perspective recently
evolved primarily among some American scholars, most of whom had participated in
the International Q project.[5] These scholars agree with most earlier works in assuming

1. James M. Robinson, "ΛΟΓΟΙ ΣΟΦΩΝ. Zur Gattung der Spruchquelle Q," in Erich Dinkler, ed., *Zeit
und Geschichte: Dankesgabe an Rudolf Bultmann zum 80. Geburtstag* (Tübingen: Mohr/Siebeck, 1964) 77–96;
an expanded English translation was published in Robinson, ed., *The Future of Our Religious Past: Essays in
Honor of Rudolf Bultmann* (New York: Harper & Row, 1971) 84–130, and republished in Robinson and Helmut Koester, *Trajectories through Early Christianity* (Philadelphia: Fortress Press, 1971) 71–113.

2. Milton C. Moreland and James M. Robinson, "The International Q Project: Work Sessions 23–27
May, 22–26 August, 17–18 November 1994," *JBL* 114 (1995) 475–85. The results of previous work sessions
were published in *JBL* 109 (1990) 499–501; 110 (1991) 494–98; 111 (1992) 500–508; 112 (1993) 500–506;
113 (1994) 495–500.

3. James M. Robinson, Paul Hoffmann, and John S. Kloppenborg, *The Critical Edition of Q* (Hermeneia
Supplement; Minneapolis: Fortress Press, 2000).

4. Characteristic of this view is Siegfried Schulz, *Q: Die Spruchquelle der Evangelisten* (Zurich: Theologischer Verlag, 1972), who assumes an enthusiastic-apocalyptic orientation as the matrix of Q. Other studies,
however, also maintain that eschatology is the primary element in the composition and redaction of Q; see
Dieter Lührmann, *Die Redaktion der Logienquelle* (WMANT 33; Neukirchen-Vluyn; Neukirchener Verlag,
1969) 93–104; Paul Hoffmann, *Studien zur Theologie der Logienquelle* (NTA NF 8; Münster: Aschendorff, 1972);
also Helmut Koester, *Ancient Christian Gospels: Their History and Development* (Philadelphia: Trinity Press International, 1990) 129–71. For a comprehensive survey of scholarship on Q until 1982, see Frans Neirynck,
"Recent Developments in the Study of Q," in Joël Delobel, ed., *Logia: Les paroles de Jésus: Mémorial Joseph Cop-
pens* (BETL 59; Leuven: Peeters, 1982) 29–75; reprinted with additional notes in Frans Neirynck, *Evangelica
II* (BETL 99; Leuven: Peeters, 1991) 409–64.

5. This consensus is largely based upon John Kloppenborg, *The Formation of Q: Trajectories in Ancient Wisdom Tradition* (SAC; Philadelphia: Fortress Press, 1987), and it is typically represented in the essays of the
recently published work of John S. Kloppenborg, ed., *Conflict and Invention: Literary, Rhetorical, and Social Studies on the Sayings Gospel Q* (Valley Forge, PA: Trinity Press International, 1995).

that Q was originally composed in Greek[6] and that it exhibits in all its stages an orientation that is fundamentally different from that found in the Pauline churches.[7] In other respects, however, they differ from the previous consensus in several ways:

1. There is a good deal of confidence that it is possible to distinguish between an original composition of Q and one or several later redactions. In its original composition, the model for the genre of Q was the "wisdom book," and its orientation was sapiential; however, the redaction(s) of Q incorporated apocalyptic sayings and judgment sayings, thus introducing an apocalyptic perspective.

2. Q was composed in Galilee, both in its original form and in its second stage. It reflects the small-town and village social, economic, and political situation of Lower Galilee, and those who composed Q seem to have belonged to the literate class of the scribes of these communities.[8]

3. Some scholars in this group have argued that the original composition of Q lacks any eschatological orientation.[9] Rather, its "wisdom" is directed towards the social questions of its time and location. If one wants to reconstruct the teachings of Jesus on the basis of this original version of Q, the corresponding picture of the historical Jesus is that of a wisdom preacher or even of a social revolutionary.

The combination of these three assumptions, however, leads into a vicious circle. To restrict a Greek document to Galilee and to limit it to a single message does not leave room for the diversity of the tradition of Jesus' sayings and for their wide geographical distribution at an early formative stage. Sayings that were collected in the "Inaugural Sermon" of Q (6:20–46)[10] are also found in the letters of Paul.[11] James Robinson and I have argued that the Corinthians were familiar with sayings that have close parallels in the *Gospel of Thomas*.[12] These same sayings have also found their way into Q 10:21–24,[13]

---

6. Although Q apparently contains a number of sayings that were originally formulated and transmitted in Aramaic, even the oldest written version of Q was composed in Greek. There is, however, a new perspective in so far as attempts have been made to understand the literary and rhetorical structure of Q on the basis of parallels and analogies from the Greek world.

7. Only the sayings of Jesus matter, and the narrative of Jesus' passion and the stories of his appearance after his death are either unknown or ignored.

8. John S. Kloppenborg, "Conflict and Invention: Recent Studies on Q," in Kloppenborg, ed., *Conflict and Invention*, 3–6.

9. John S. Kloppenborg, however, ascribes an eschatological orientation also to the original composition of Q; see his "The Sayings Gospel Q and the Quest of the Historical Jesus," *HTR* 89 (1996) 337–39.

10. All references to chapter and verse of "Q" are identical to those numbers in the Gospel of Luke; instead of "Q/Luke" or "Luke," I have just used the short formula "Q + chapter and verse."

11. See my *Ancient Christian Gospels*, 52–55.

12. James M. Robinson, "Basic Shifts in German Theology," *Interpretation* 16 (1962) 82–86; Robinson, "ΛΟΓΟΙ ΣΟΦΩΝ," in Robinson and Koester, *Trajectories*, 87–88, n. 39; this footnote was not incorporated into the English translation of this essay, but see Robinson, "Kerygma and History in the New Testament," in Robinson and Koester, *Trajectories*, 30–34; see my *Ancient Christian Gospels*, 55–62.

13. For a parallel to the "hidden wisdom which God has predetermined before the ages" (1 Cor 2:7), see also Matt 13:35: "I will utter what has been hidden since the foundation of the world."

most likely into its earliest stage of composition. At the same time, the *Gospel of Thomas* itself is a witness to early collections of sayings that were also incorporated into the first composition of Q.[14] Evidence for such collections of sayings appears in 1 Peter, James, and *1 Clement*.[15] It is hardly possible to restrict the earliest collection and circulation of sayings to a geographically limited area, in which only one singular ideological perspective determined their selection and composition. It could be argued, however, that the author of Q, living in Galilee, had access only to a particular strand of the otherwise widely-distributed and diverse traditions of sayings and that his composition was more uniform than the sayings tradition in general. Yet, that the original composition of Q was in Greek and was based upon sayings circulating in Greek should caution against such a notion. The use of the Greek language cannot simply be explained by drawing a historically problematic image of a thoroughly Hellenized Galilee;[16] rather, the employment of Greek necessarily implied that those who transmitted these sayings participated in a wider cultural context.

The most problematic issue in the understanding of Q as a wisdom book is the question of its religious or philosophical orientation. John Kloppenborg had presented an impressive analysis of two (or even three) stages of the development of Q in which he identified the earliest stage as a wisdom book.[17] Kloppenborg himself, however, did not claim that the composition of Q as a wisdom book implies an absence of any eschatological orientation, and most scholars engaged in Q research have usually refrained from drawing conclusions from their work with respect to the historical Jesus.[18] Yet Kloppenborg's hypothesis has been used in some publications (Burton L. Mack,[19] Leif E. Vaage[20]) in order to argue that this first stage of Q presented not just wisdom teaching

---

14. See the documentation in my *Ancient Christian Gospels*, 133–62.

15. Ibid., 64–75. See also James M. Robinson, "Early Collections of Jesus' Sayings," in Delobel, *Logia: Les paroles de Jésus*, 389–94.

16. See, e.g., Burton Mack, *Who Wrote the New Testament? The Making of the Christian Myth* (San Francisco: HarperSanFrancisco, 1995) 38–39.

17. *The Formation of Q.* Kloppenborg's thesis is based upon some suggestions that James M. Robinson and I had made in earlier articles as well as on the work of Dieter Lührmann, *Redaktion der Logienquelle*.

18. Some critics of studies of Q have misunderstood scholars such as Kloppenborg and myself by advocating the image of a completely non-eschatological historical Jesus, who was nothing but a Cynic or semi-Gnostic wisdom teacher. See on such criticism Kloppenborg, "The Sayings Gospel Q and the Historical Jesus," 336, n. 120.

19. "Lord of the Logia: Savior or Sage," in James E. Goehring et al., eds., *Gospel Origins & Christian Beginnings: In Honor of James M. Robinson* (Sonoma, Calif.: Polebridge, 1990) 49–63; Burton Mack, *The Lost Gospel: The Book of Q and Christian Origins* (San Francisco: HarperSanFrancisco, 1993); see also Mack, *A Myth of Innocence: Mark and Christian Origins* (Philadelphia: Fortress Press, 1988). In his book, *Who Wrote the New Testament?*, Mack repeats the Cynic hypothesis regarding the earliest form of Q: "The lifestyle of the Jesus people bears remarkable resemblance to the Greek tradition of popular philosophy characteristic of the Cynics. Cynics also promoted an outrageous lifestyle as a way of criticizing conventional mores, and the themes of the two groups, the Cynics and the Jesus people, are largely overlapping" (p. 50). In this book, however, Mack does not claim that the Cynic lifestyle of this Jesus movement necessarily reflected the lifestyle of the historical Jesus (see pp. 45–46).

20. "The Ethos and Ethics of an Itinerant Intelligence" (Ph.D. diss., Claremont Graduate School, 1987). For further bibliography on the Cynic hypothesis, see James M. Robinson, "The History-of-Religions Tax-

in general, but reflected popular Cynicism. This resulted in the conclusion that Jesus himself must have understood his own mission as that of a social critic in the style of a Hellenistic Cynic preacher—a thesis that was questioned critically by Hans-Dieter Betz[21] and James M. Robinson.[22] At the same time, the redaction of Q appears as a secondary transformation of wisdom teaching into eschatological and apocalyptic prophecy and thus as a radical alteration of the view of Jesus from that of a Cynic sage into that of a prophet and apocalyptic visionary.

The reconstruction of the earlier stage of Q may even be influenced by this hypothesis. There is a temptation to relegate to the second stage of Q not only the obviously apocalyptic predictions of the coming of the Son of Man and the clearly secondary judgment sayings but also other sayings of an eschatological or prophetic character. Kloppenborg has doubtlessly furnished the foundation for this reconstruction of the stages of Q. He provided[23] a formal analysis of Q's wisdom instructions, listing all materials that would fit into this formative concept. The question is whether Kloppenborg's wisdom book should be understood as an ideal construct that helps to understand its formative literary genre or as the reconstruction of an actual wisdom document with a pure wisdom message that stood at the beginning of the redactional history of Q. The latter is extremely unlikely for two reasons: (1) even the inaugural sermon (Q 6:20–49) shows a tension between eschatological prophecy (as distinct from "radical wisdom") and the designs of wisdom instruction.[24] (2) as long as external controls are lacking, internal analysis alone is problematic, because it is hardly possible to assume that an ancient author—not to speak of one who is primarily a collector of traditional materials—would strictly adhere to a definition of a literary genre that is, after all, the product of modern scholarship. The merit of Kloppenborg's work is that he has been successful in isolating certain sections of Q that show how the original author has "inscribed" his materials in order to create a writing that presents the ethics of the community. The strategy of this author is "hortatory and deliberative," while the redactor's strategy is "epideictic, intent on defending a view of Jesus (and of John, and the Q people) and characterizing opponents in a negative way."[25] The question remains whether there are some Q materials that cannot be clearly identified as belonging either to the original purpose of the author or to the redactor's program. Such materials perhaps could be assigned to the original version of Q, although it may not be possible to detect their exact place in that composition.

onomy of Q: The Cynic Hypothesis," in Holger Preissler and Hubert Seiwert, eds., *Gnosisforschung und Religionsgeschichte: Festschrift für Kurt Rudolph zum 65. Geburtstag* (Marburg: Elwert, 1994) 247.

21. "Jesus and the Cynics: Survey and Analysis of a Hypothesis," *Journal of Religion* 74 (1994) 453–75.

22. "The History-of-Religions Taxonomy of Q," 247–65.

23. *The Formation of Q*, 342–45.

24. That the earlier stage of Q includes quite a few sayings that should be classified as prophetic rather than sapiential has been demonstrated by Richard Horsley, "Logoi Prophêtôn? Reflections on the Genre of Q," in Birger A. Pearson, ed., *The Future of Early Christianity: Essays in Honor of Helmut Koester* (Minneapolis: Fortress Press, 1991) 195–209.

25. Kloppenborg, "The Sayings Gospel Q and the Historical Jesus," 336.

II. The Gospel of Thomas and
the Stages of the Development of Q

I had been impressed by Dieter Lührmann's argument that the Q sayings about the judgment over this generation did not belong to the original Q materials but came from the hand of the redactor.[26] My own suggestion that there may have been an older edition of Q grew out of the observation that numerous sayings were shared by Q and the *Gospel of Thomas* but that the latter did not reveal any knowledge of the sayings about Jesus as the coming Son of Man.[27] Most of the sayings of Q with parallels in the *Gospel of Thomas* should therefore be assigned to Q's earliest stage of composition.[28] As a result, two fixed points appeared in the development of Q: (1) at the beginning a collection with many sayings that have parallels in the *Gospel of Thomas,* (2) a redaction that added the sayings about the coming of the Son of Man[29] and the judgment over this generation.[30]

Although the beginnings of Q are more difficult to determine with any precision, it is fairly easy to be certain about some features of Q's final redaction and its eschatology. It is dominated by sayings of the future judgment and the apocalyptic announcement of the coming of the Son of Man. The first characteristic of the redaction of Q is the expectation of the sudden revelation (ἀποκαλύπτεται, Q 17:30) of the Son of Man ἐν τῇ ἡμέρᾳ αὐτοῦ (Q 17:24) or ἐν τῇ ἡμέρᾳ ἐκείνῃ (Q 17:31). Since the coming is unexpected, there will be no time to escape (Q 17:31). The same apocalyptic expectation is found in some materials of Q 12:39–59; cf. the conclusion of the parable of the thief: ὅτι ᾗ ὥρᾳ οὐ δοκεῖτε ὁ υἱὸς τοῦ ἀνθρώπου ἔρχεται (Q 12:40). The following parable of the faithful and unfaithful servants (Q 12:41–46) also illustrates the suddenness of the coming (Q 12:46), although the title Son of Man has not been introduced into the allegorizing conclusion of this parable.

A second element that is typical for the redactor is the announcement of the judgment over "this generation" (γενεὰ αὕτη, Q 11:29–32, 50–51). Closely related is Q

---

26. *Redaktion der Logienquelle*, passim.

27. See "One Jesus and Four Primitive Gospels," in Robinson and Koester, *Trajectories*, 170–72; see also Helmut Koester, "Q and Its Relatives," in James E. Goehring et al., eds., *Gospel Origins & Christian Beginnings*, 49–63.

28. See my *Ancient Christian Gospels*, 138–39 and passim.

29. Lührmann (*Redaktion der Logienquelle*, 40–41, n. 6, cf. 74–75), however, did not include the sayings about the Son of Man in the final redaction but assigned them to the older layer of the Q materials. On the development of scholarship, see James M. Robinson, "The Q Trajectory: Between John and Matthew via Jesus," in Pearson, *The Future of Early Christianity*, 178–89.

30. Such a division of the two stages of Q is not in full agreement with Kloppenborg (*The Formation of Q*, 102–70), who had identified three different complexes of sayings that characterize this second stage of Q: (1) the announcements of judgment (including the Q materials of the preaching of John the Baptist in Q/Luke 3 and most of the materials of Q 7:1–35 and 16:16); (2) the controversies (materials in Q 11:14–52); (3) the "Logia Apocalypse" (most of Q 17:23–37); closely related to this section are the apocalyptic materials in Q 12:39–59. Kloppenborg, however, although arguing for their connection with the second stage of Q, does not include them in the "Logia Apocalypse" but considers this section as a separate entity.

10:12–15 with the announcement of judgment over Chorazin, Bethsaida, and Kapher-naum. ἡ πόλις ἐκείνη corresponds to γενεὰ αὕτη, and the distinctive phrase ἐν τῇ ἡμέρᾳ ἐκείνῃ also used (Q 10:12). The hand of the same redactor is recognizable fur-thermore in the parable that compares the people "of this generation" (τῆς γενεᾶς ταύ-της) to children playing in the market place (Q 7:31–32).

These apocalyptic sayings that were introduced into Q by the redactor come from the same tradition that also furnished the apocalyptic Son of Man sayings to the Gospel of Mark. The Markan apocalypse culminates in the prediction of the coming of the Son of Man (Mark 13:26) and in the statement that "this generation" (ἡ γενεὰ αὕτη) shall not pass away until all this has happened (Mark 13:30). While "this generation" is here referred to without any negative predicates, it is explicitly called "adulterous and sinful" in the Son of Man saying (Mark 8:38). There are good reasons to assume that these sayings, shared by Mark and the redaction of Q, were coined by Christian prophets in Palestine during the turmoil of the sixties of the first century that resulted in the Jew-ish War, perhaps even as late as during the war itself. It was the answer of the followers of Jesus to the rise of anti-Roman revolutionary messianism in Palestine. The apocalypse of Mark 13 reveals the political position of this group. They are warned not to believe any false prophets who proclaimed, "Behold, the Messiah is here" (Mark 13:21–22). Their relationship to the Temple of Jerusalem is fundamentally positive, since the threat of its destruction is seen as a sacrilege (Mark 13:11). The group, however, had suffered persecution from their fellow Israelites (Mark 13:9); divisions ran deep, even in fami-lies (Mark 13:12). The prophets do not explicitly condemn the Romans but advise the followers of Jesus to separate and seek refuge elsewhere (Mark 13:14b–16).

The prophets who shaped the materials of the Markan apocalypse belong to Judea (Mark 13:14b), perhaps to the community of Jerusalem.[31] On the other hand, the Son of Man and judgment sayings of the Q community, located outside of Judea,[32] do not reveal the same degree of tribulation; they reflect a different and less urgent experience of persecution and resistance to their mission (cf. the addition of Q 10:12–15 to Q 10:10–11[33]). Both the Jerusalem group and their Q counterparts share the desire to establish an alternative to the two dominating political options of the time: messianic war against Rome or collaboration with the Roman authorities.

III. Eschatology in the Earlier Stage of the Sayings Gospel Q

John Kloppenborg[34] assigned to the later stage not only the sayings about the judg-ment of this generation and about the coming of the Son of Man, but also the entire

---

31. Egon Brandenburger (*Markus 13 und die Apokalyptik* [FRLANT 134; Göttingen: Vandenhoeck & Ruprecht, 1984]) has presented a cogent analysis of the apocalyptic source used by Mark and the position of its author.

32. I hesitate therefore to locate the Q redaction in Galilee because the messianic fervor at the begin-ning of the Jewish War was no less intense there than it was in Judea.

33. Lührmann, *Redaktion der Logienquelle*, 62–63; Kloppenborg, *Formation of Q*, 196–97.

34. Kloppenborg, *Formation of Q*, passim.

sections in which they are embedded, namely Q 3:7–9, 16–17; 4:1–13; the Q materials in Luke 7:1–35 and in Luke 11:14–52; Q 12:39–59; 17:23–37.[35] Three observations, however, argue for a more explicit eschatological orientation of the earliest composition of Q: (1) sayings that are not characteristic for the theology of the redactor are found in these "secondary" sections; (2) sayings with parallels in the *Gospel of Thomas* appear not only in the sections assigned by Kloppenborg to the first stage of Q—where they are very frequent—but occasionally also in the sections assigned to the redactor. (3) a number of sayings in Kloppenborg's original wisdom book Q are in fact prophetic sayings.

(1) Eschatological sayings in redactorial passages of Q.

I shall discuss here only one example, namely Q 12:8–9 (ὅς ἂν ὁμολογήσῃ ἐν ἐμοὶ ἔμπροσθεν τῶν ἀνθρώπων, καὶ ὁ υἱὸς τοῦ ἀνθρώπου ὁμολογήσει κτλ.). It seems, at first glance, to be a secondary addition to a group of wisdom sayings (Q 12:2–7) and a most likely candidate for assignment to the redactor of Q because of the use of the title Son of Man and because of what may be called an "apocalyptic" notion of reward and punishment.[36] Q, however, does not identify the Son of Man with Jesus; Matthew achieves this identification by replacing "the Son of Man" with the first person singular.[37] In Q 12:8–9 the Son of Man is an angelic figure in the divine court who functions as the advocate for the faithful—a concept that is not specifically apocalyptic. If this saying can be assigned to the original version of Q, it would prove that "Son of Man" as a title for a figure of the divine court was indeed known at an early time in these circles of Jesus' followers and would later have served as a convenient foundation for prophets to announce that this Son of Man, now identified with Jesus, would return as the divinely appointed judge.

(2) Sayings of the early stage of Q with parallels in the Gospel of Thomas.

Most sayings about John the Baptist (Q 3:2b–4, 16–17, 21–22) and the account of the temptation of Jesus (Q 4:1–13), assigned to the secondary stage of Q, lack parallels in the *Gospel of Thomas*. Parallels are found, however, in the *Gospel of Thomas* to two sayings in the section that Kloppenborg entitles "John, Jesus, and This Generation" and assigns entirely to the redactor (Q 7:1–35)[38]: Q 7:24–26 ("What did you go out into the desert to see?" and so forth) has a parallel in *Gos. Thom.* 78, and Q 7:28 ("Among

---

35. Ibid., 102–70; moreover, a number of additional sayings in the remaining sections of Q also are assigned to the redactor. Some materials that lack parallels in Matthew are not considered as possibly deriving from Q; e.g., Luke 12:13–21; 17:20b–21; on the latter, see ibid., 154–55.

36. Ibid., 207–8.

37. Matt 10:32–33; also the variant in Mark 8:38 presents that (secondary) identification of the Son of Man with Jesus and includes a secondary reference to "this generation"; this reference is absent in Q 12:8–9.

38. Kloppenborg, *Formation of Q*, 107–21.

those born of a woman no one is greater than John") appears in _Gos. Thom._ 46. Although John the Baptist is not explicitly mentioned in the first of these two sayings, it is evident from the context in Q that he is the subject of the saying. Moreover, it is probable that these two sayings belonged together from the beginning. They were separated by the redactor of Q who inserted the reference to Mal 3:1 and Exod 23:20 (Q 7:27). Both sayings are eschatological insofar as they contrast the present time of the kingdom of God with the past, relegating John the Baptist to the past. They must have been formulated in the polemic of the early followers of Jesus with the disciples of John.

Most of Q 11:14–52 is excluded in Kloppenborg's reconstruction of the original composition of Q.[39] He allows as parts of the first stage only Q 11:2–4 (the Lord's Prayer) and Q 11:9–13 (the sayings about asking and receiving);[40] _Gos. Thom._ 92 and 94 provide parallels to the latter sayings. There are, moreover, several parallels in the _Gospel of Thomas_ to the remaining materials of Q 11:

Q 11:21–22 (The strong man's house)[41]   = _Gos. Thom._ 35.
Luke 11:27–28 (True blessedness)   = _Gos. Thom._ 79 (=Q?).[42]
Q 11:33 (Light not under a bushel)   = _Gos. Thom._ 33b.
Q 11:34–36 (The eye as the light of the body)   = _Gos. Thom._ 24.
Q 11:39b–41 (Wash outside of the cup)   = _Gos. Thom._ 89.
Q 11:52 (They took the key of knowledge)   = _Gos. Thom._ 39.[43]

Most of these sayings are wisdom sayings. The two sayings from the speech against the Pharisees, however, are classified as prophetic sayings by Bultmann.[44] To assign Q 11:52 to a later stratum of the tradition, because here "the kingdom is viewed as a present reality and as a realm into which one can enter even now"[45] is an odd judgment; on the contrary, one must ask whether it is not exactly this view of the kingdom that is characteristic of the earliest layer of the Q tradition.

Of Q 12:2–59, Kloppenborg assigns only two small sections to the original composition of Q, namely 12:2–12[46] and 12:22–34.[47] The _Gospel of Thomas_ presents parallels to Q 12:2 _(Gos. Thom._ 5 and 6b), 12:3 _(Gos. Thom._ 33), 12:22 _(Gos. Thom._ 36[48]), and 12:33 _(Gos. Thom._ 76b). There are, however, in this section of Q a number of further sayings that have parallels in the _Gospel of Thomas:_

---

39. Ibid., 141–47.

40. Ibid., 203–6.

41. On the question of the inclusion in Q of this saying, see Koester, _Ancient Christian Gospels,_ 142–43; Kloppenborg, _Formation of Q,_ 125.

42. There is no parallel in Matthew, but the parallel in the _Gospel of Thomas_ suggests that this pericope may have stood in Q; see Koester, _Ancient Christian Gospels,_ 143.

43. _Gos. Thom._ 102 has preserved another woe against the Pharisees ("Woe to the Pharisees, for they are like a dog sleeping in the food trough of cows: the dog neither eats nor lets the cows eat"). That smaller collections of such woes circulated very early is also evident in Mark 12:38–40.

44. Rudolf Bultmann, _The History of the Synoptic Tradition_ (2nd ed.; Oxford: Basil Blackwell, 1968) 113.

45. Kloppenborg, _Formation of Q,_ 143, referring to Schürmann.

46. From which he excludes 12:8–9 (see above) and 12:10.

47. _Formation of Q,_ 206–22.

48. Parallels to Q 12:25, 27a appear in the Greek version of the _Gospel of Thomas_ (Pap. Oxy. 655).

Q 12:10 (The blasphemy not forgiven)	= *Gos. Thom.* 44.[49]
Luke 12:13–14 (Dividing the inheritance)	= *Gos. Thom.* 72[50] (Q?).[51]
Luke 12:16–21 (Parable of the rich farmer)	= *Gos. Thom.* 72.
Q 12:39 (Parable of the thief)	= *Gos. Thom.* 103.[52]
Luke 12:49 (Fire on earth)	= *Gos. Thom.* 10 (Q?).[53]
Q 12:51–53 (Not peace, but the sword)	= *Gos. Thom.* 16.
Q 12:54–56 (Signs of the time)	= *Gos. Thom.* 91.

Also Q 17:21–35, mostly formulated by the redactor of Q, contains three sayings with parallels in the *Gospel of Thomas* that should be considered here:

Luke 17:20–21 (When will the kingdom come?)	= *Gos. Thom.* 113 (Q?).[54]
Luke 17:22 (Seeking and not finding)	= *Gos. Thom.* 38 (Q?).[55]
Q 17:34 (Two in one bed)	= *Gos. Thom.* 61a.

A surprising number of sayings in this group are eschatological. They reveal an eschatological perspective that is distinctly different from the one introduced by the redactor of Q because the emphasis here is on the presence of the kingdom in Jesus and in his words. In some instances, the version preserved by the *Gospel of Thomas* does not imply the element of watching for an event in the future. The parable of the thief rather emphasizes the *place* of the entry of the robber; it seems to have been reformulated by the redactor of Q so that it would point to the unknown future *time* and therefore motivate the admonition to watchfulness. The original question of the "where?" of the kingdom, which is also evident in Q 12:54–56 and 17:20–21, has been changed by the redactor into the question of "when?".[56] Another element in these sayings is the emphasis upon the urgency of the kingdom's presence (see especially Q 12:49, 51–53; 17:34). These sayings do not speak of judgment to be administered in the form of punishment and reward, but they call to grasp the present moment.

Can the sayings discussed previously be incorporated into the final section of the original version of Q? Kloppenborg[57] has singled out several sayings that he assigns to

---

49. For a discussion of the relationship of the several versions of this saying, see Koester, *Ancient Christian Gospels*, 92–93.

50. On the relationship of *Gos. Thom.* 72 to Luke 12:13–14, see Gregory J. Riley, "Influence of Thomas Christianity on Luke 12:14 and 5:39," *HTR* 88 (1995) 229–35.

51. On the question of whether this apophthegma and the following parable should be included in Q, see John S. Kloppenborg, *Q Parallels: Synopsis, Critical Notes, & Concordance* (Sonoma, Calif.: Polebridge, 1988) 128.

52. The same parable also is used in *Gos. Thom.* 21; see Koester, *Ancient Christian Gospels*, 146.

53. On the question of the inclusion of this saying in Q, see Kloppenborg, *Q Parallels*, 142; Kloppenborg, *Formation of Q*, 151, n. 213. The following saying, Luke 12:50 ("I must be baptized with a baptism . . ."), however, is certainly a Lukan addition.

54. On the question of the inclusion of this saying in Q, see Koester, *Ancient Christian Gospels*, 155–56.

55. Ibid., 149, n. 1.

56. Ibid., 153, 155–56.

57. Ibid., 223–37.

the final section of the original version: Q 13:24 ("Strive to enter through the narrow door"); Q 13:26–27 (a prophetic threat against those who say, "We ate and drank with you"); Q 13:28–29, 30 (a prophetic oracle about the participation of the Gentiles in the kingdom); Q 13:34–35 (lament over Jerusalem); Q 14:16–24 (parable of the Great Supper = *Gos. Thom.* 64); and Q 14:26–27 and 17:33 (three discipleship sayings). If the other sayings with parallels in the *Gospel of Thomas* that I discussed previously were incorporated into the final section of Q, the prophetic and eschatological character of this section would become even more evident. To call it the eschatological conclusion of Q in its original form would be more appropriate, while the "Logia Apocalypse" (Q 17:23–37) was composed as the final section of the redaction of Q—incorporating and reinterpreting some of the materials of the original eschatological conclusion of the Sayings Gospel.

(3) Prophetic sayings in Q's original composition

The thesis that the formative genre of Q was a wisdom book has great merit. Indeed, even individual sections of Q have been composed in close correspondence to this genre. Yet this insight can be deceptive. There is an inherent tension between the intent of the sayings incorporated into this wisdom genre and the objective of a wisdom book or speech. The inaugural sermon of Q (6:20b–49) demonstrates this tension.

On the eschatological character of the beatitudes (6:20b–23b) see above pp. 241–42. All the other materials in this section are admonitions and with respect to their formal structure, they can be classified as sapiential. Yet, to do what the first three admonitions (Q 6:27–35) mandate would in no way be very wise. To love one's enemies, not to retaliate, and to lend to those who will not pay back is decidedly foolish in terms of conventional wisdom. On the contrary, these admonitions state an eschatological alternative to political, social, and economic choices that differ radically from wise behavior. In accordance with the political expectations of Israel, hatred of the Roman occupation forces would seem a national duty. Those who would neither choose to become messianic fanatics nor collaborate with the Romans, but feared God and were willing to obey his commandments, might at least deserve wise counsel that could insure personal success and financial prosperity in spite of the political turmoil. To love the hated Roman occupiers would spell trouble with one's fellow Israelites. Only with the last admonition of this section, "Be merciful" (Q 6:36), the discourse enters the realm of general rules of wise behavior.

The following verses (Q 6:37–49) belong wholly to the world of conventional wisdom: not to judge in order not to be judged; a blind person cannot lead the blind; a disciple is not above the teacher; the tree is known by its fruit. The initial beatitudes as well as the admonitions to choose radically new political, social, and economic alternatives seem to have opened the possibility of adopting much of what conventional wisdom has taught. The acceptance of the prophecy of the new eschatological existence of the kingdom does not lead into foolishness but into a behavior that has guided people everywhere for centuries. All sapiential sayings in Q 6:37–49 are "international,"[58] while references to the law of Israel and to the fear of the God of Israel, typical for Jewish sapiential literature, are completely missing.

A statement about a fundamentally new eschatological attitude also stands at the beginning of the second "sapiential" speech of Q 9:57–62 and 10:2–16, 21–24. The introduction of this speech states the radical homelessness of human beings, that is, their separation from their normal social context (Q 9:57–58). This is underlined with the sayings about the dead burying their dead (Q 9:59–60) and the saying that the one who puts his hand to plow and looks back is not fit for the kingdom of God (Q 9:61–62).[59] The following instruction for the messengers of the arrival of the kingdom of God, however, are conventional wisdom: large harvest and few workers (10:2), the worker is worthy of his food (10:7), and other instructions are common sapiential sayings. A special feature is the conclusion of this speech, Q 10:21–24, comprising two sayings that present Jesus as the eschatological revealer and praise the disciples for what they see now. If these "Johannine" sayings belong to the first version of Q[60]—the latter may be a variant of *Gos. Thom.* 17 and 38—the original composition of Q makes a strong statement about the eschatological moment that the disciples have been requested to announce.

IV. The Original Version of Q and Its Image of Jesus

The composition of the Sayings Gospel Q and its redaction reflect a process in which the community develops a clearer definition of its purpose and identity. In doing so, the collection and composition of sayings puts forward an image of Jesus that mirrors the community's mission in a time that is highly charged with eschatological expectations. The original version of Q does not justify the view that the community of Q began as a rather innocuous wisdom association that only later developed an eschatological outlook because its members had experienced rejection and persecution.[61] The search for the earliest tradition will hardly lead us "to a social space for cultivating a sane and circumspect society made possible by the wisdom remembered in Jesus' name."[62] On the contrary, the original version of Q insists that the ways of the kingdom of God are

---

58. See Betz, *Sermon on the Mount*, especially his excursus on "Rules for Teachers and Students" (621–22).

59. There is no parallel in Matthew but this saying may have been part of Q. "Of all the Lukan *Sondergut*, this has the strongest possibility of deriving from Q since it is found in a Q context, the saying coheres with the preceding sayings formally, and it evinces the same theology of discipleship typical of other Q sayings" (Kloppenborg, *Q Parallels*, 64). Kloppenborg (*Formation of Q*, 190–92) assigns this saying to the original composition of Q.

60. Kloppenborg, ibid., 197–203.

61. This is how one can formulate the basic thesis of Mack, *A Myth of Innocence*.

62. Ron Cameron, "The Gospel of Thomas and Christian Origins," in Pearson, *The Future of Early Christianity*, 392.

becoming a reality in the conduct and experience of the disciples because they follow the voice of an eschatological prophet who announces the presence of the kingdom in their midst.

The image of Jesus that is accessible through the most original version of Q is that of an eschatological prophet. He announces the coming of the kingdom to those who have been excluded from the benefits that the society should provide—which most likely included the majority of the people at that time—and he praises the disciples because they are witnesses of events that generations before them have longed to see. This is not a tame and rational Jesus but a divine messenger who brings conflict and division even into the family. His preaching and teaching instructs the community to understand its own identity as a people who are realizing the eschatological moment in their existence and work, not as fanatics but as human beings who follow the guidance of wisdom in their common life. Jesus also demands that wisdom must govern the conduct of the missionaries, especially when they are not accepted. I can find no indication that the mission of the community has been a failure; on the contrary, the harvest is great and it requires more workers. It is possible that Jesus also was remembered in the common meals of the community. The petition of the Lord's prayer that God's kingdom come is linked to the petition for the daily bread (Q 11:2–4). There is also the eschatological outlook to the banquet, when people will come from everywhere to sit at table in the kingdom of God (Q 13:28–29). References to a liturgy for the common meal celebrations do not appear in Q; one can assume, however, that eschatologically interpreted Jewish meal prayers were used. *Didache* 9–10 has preserved such prayers— a witness for a Eucharist under eschatological auspices, albeit without any reference to the death of Jesus. Whether the earlier version of Q was the product of a community in Galilee depends upon the judgment sayings against Chorazin, Bethsaida, and Kaphernaum (Q 10:13–15). They may not have been part of the first stage of Q. It should also be remembered that Q 13:34–35 is a lament over Jerusalem. The question of the mission to the Gentiles may have been controversial within the community. This controversy, however, would have begun in the very first years of its existence, as it apparently did in Jerusalem itself and elsewhere, even before Paul began his ministry as a missionary in "Arabia," that is, no later than the year 35 CE and, moreover, in the immediate neighborhood of Galilee. The mention of Tyre and Sidon in Q 10:13–14 could well serve as evidence that the Gentile mission of this community had long since been carried into Greek-speaking cities of southern Syria several decades before the original version of Q was composed. The early decades of this community must have been dominated by an eschatological message that was carried to the Gentiles in areas outside of Galilee, although Palestinian connections are still visible in the later apocalyptic redaction of Q.

From the very beginning, the tradition of sayings preserved in the Sayings Gospel Q is dominated by an eschatological orientation. The earliest stage of Q's eschatology is not necessarily the only reflection of Jesus' preaching. It is also quite likely that other early materials of Jesus' sayings have survived outside of the trajectory of Q and have been incorporated into canonical and extra-canonical gospels independently of Q.[63]

---

63. Kloppenborg, "The Sayings Gospel Q and the Quest of the Historical Jesus," 329–31.

As far as Q is concerned, however, its trajectory belongs, from the very beginning, to the interpretation of an eschatological tradition of Jesus' sayings, mirroring an image of Jesus as an eschatological prophet in the tradition of Israel. The Jesus of the earliest formation of the Sayings Gospel Q proclaims the arrival of God's kingdom as a challenge to the disciples, who are asked to realize that their own existence belongs to a new eschatological moment. This may not be a direct and unbroken mirror of the preaching of the historical Jesus; but it certainly excludes any recourse to a Jesus who was but a social reformer or a philosopher in the tradition of the Cynic preacher.

19

THE HISTORICAL JESUS
AND HIS SAYINGS

I. Sayings and Narrative Materials in the
Old Quest for the Historical Jesus

It is characteristic of the more recent search for the historical Jesus that it is almost exclusively engaged in the investigation of Jesus' sayings. With the belief that only Jesus' sayings convey anything about the Jesus of history, the more recent "New Quest" returned to the very beginnings of this quest that was initiated by Samuel Hermann Reimarus (1694–1768).[1] Reimarus, a professor of classics at Hamburg and a deist, set the stage in a major work on the Bible that was, however, not published during his lifetime. After his death, Reimarus's children gave the manuscript of their father's work to Gotthold Ephraim Lessing (1729–1781), a friend of the famous Jewish philosopher Moses Mendelssohn, who was then the leading theologian and poet of the Enlightenment in Germany. Then the librarian of the Welf's Duke of Braunschweig in Wolfenbüttel, Lessing published parts of Reimarus's writings as the famous "Wolfenbüttel Fragments,"[2] claiming that he had accidentally found parts of such writing among the manuscripts in the Duke's library but not revealing the identity of the author in order to protect his children. Of the first six fragments, published in 1777, only the last, "On the Story of the Resurrection," deals with the gospels of the New Testament; the other essays deal with the Hebrew Bible.

Reimarus argues here without any attempt of a critical assessment of the sources, but with a very clever combination of various pieces of information, that the entire story of the resurrection of Jesus was manufactured by the apostles. The apostles had learned

---

1. For the so-called Old Quest for the historical Jesus, the most important critical assessment remains, of course, Albert Schweitzer, *The Quest of the Historical Jesus: A Critical Study of Its Progress from Reimarus to Wrede* (New York: Macmillan, 1959). This work was first published in German in the year 1906 under the title *Von Reimarus zu Wrede: Eine Geschichte der Leben-Jesu-Forschung* (Tübingen: Mohr). The first English translation of the second edition of Schweitzer's work (entitled *Geschichte der Leben-Jesu-Forschung*) appeared in 1910 (London: Black). Among recent discussions of the history of this quest, the most significant are Dieter Georgi, "The Interest in Life of Jesus Theology as a Paradigm for the Social History of Biblical Criticism," *HTR* 85 (1992) 51–83; Georgi, "Leben-Jesu-Theologie/Leben-Jesu-Forschung," *TRE* 20 (1990) 566–75 (with extensive bibliography). For the role of the sayings of Jesus in the quest of the historical Jesus, see John S. Kloppenborg, "The Sayings Gospel Q and the Quest of the Historical Jesus," *HTR* 89 (1996) 307–44.

2. The two fragments concerning the New Testament are now conveniently available in English translation: Charles H. Talbert, ed., *Reimarus: Fragments* (Philadelphia: Fortress Press, 1970).

comfortable living in the company of Jesus, how preaching and healing was rather lucra-
tive as long as they had a company of admiring women, who gave them sufficient
money to eat well. Now that Jesus was gone, they took counsel in secret behind closed
doors, waited for fifty days (the period to Pentecost) before stealing the body of Jesus.
They figured that the story of Jesus' resurrection would give them a chance to resume
the proclamation of the kingdom, to do miracles (which they had learned from Jesus),
and to create an organization in which they could become wealthy and powerful. Thus
the beginnings of Christianity rest on a fraud.

A final fragment was published by Lessing in 1778, "About the Purpose of Jesus and
of His Disciples." This is the most brilliant part of Reimarus's work. For the first time
in history, Reimarus sets out to distinguish between those parts of the canonical gospels
that report Jesus' original preaching, on the one hand, and the additions of the disciples, on the other hand. He ascribes to Jesus only sayings, and among these only those
that fit into the tradition and teachings of Judaism: the call to repentance, the criticism
of the Pharisees—Jesus preaches a better righteousness in the fulfillment of the law—
and the love of God and of neighbor:

> One need but examine the beautiful Sermon on the Mount, that most explicit
> of all Jesus' speeches, and he will be thoroughly convinced that Jesus' sole inten-
> tion is man's repentance, conversion and betterment, insofar as these consist of a
> true inner and upright love of God, of one's neighbor, and of all that is good.[3] . . .
> Thus the goal of Jesus' sermons and teachings was a proper, active character, a
> changing of the mind, a sincere love of God and of one's neighbor, humility, gen-
> tleness, denial of the self, and the suppression of all evil desires. These are not
> great mysteries or tenets of the faith that he explains, proves, and preaches; they
> are nothing other than moral teachings and duties intended to improve man
> inwardly and with all its heart, whereby Jesus naturally takes for granted a gen-
> eral knowledge of man's soul, of God and his perfection, [and] salvation after this
> life.[4]

Reimarus denies all and any intentions of Jesus to introduce anything new or hitherto unknown, or even to found a new religion, to teach mysteries, and to introduce
new articles of faith. In every way, Jesus remains a Jew, does not even reject the cere-
monial law but assigns only a secondary position to it, ranking behind the moral law.
When Jesus calls himself Son of God or Messiah, he remains fully with the world of
Judaism, believing that as the Messiah he is one who is especially loved by God, not one
who should be worshiped as if he were a God.

The original work of Reimarus, from which Lessing published these fragments, was
entitled "Apology for the Rational Worshipers of God." It was indeed meant as a defense
of the dignity of the religions of Judaism and Christianity in the face of the publication of a number of French pamphlets that attacked and ridiculed these religions. But

---

3. Quoted from Talbert's edition, pp. 67–68.
4. Ibid., pp. 69–70.

as a deist, Reimarus could not admit the possibility of any miracles, especially the report of the resurrection, which he considered as pure fraud and deliberate deception. It is also evident that Reimarus's deist convictions led him to present the teachings of "Jesus the Jew" as perfectly enlightened preaching of a purer worship of God and of a higher morality.

The ensuing controversies in the nineteenth century, however, quickly turned from the emphasis upon the sayings of Jesus to the discussion of the narrative materials, especially Jesus' miracles. In fact, the Wolfenbüttel Fragments were soon forgotten,[5] and an interest in Reimarus's work disappeared until David Friedrich Strauss two generations later. Reimarus, however, had a successor in the United States, namely, the third president of this country, Thomas Jefferson. Jefferson, who like Reimarus, was a deist, compiled a selection of the sayings of Jesus that followed the same principles. What has become known as the "Jefferson Bible"[6] was designed to present the pure rational and humanitarian thoughts of Jesus. As he wrote in a letter of 1813 to John Adams, Jefferson had long been occupied with a plan to extract

> . . . the very words only of Jesus, paring off the amphiboligisms into which [the Evangelists] have been led, by forgetting often, or not understanding, what had fallen from him, by giving their own misconceptions as his dicta, and expressing unintelligibly for others what they had not understood themselves.[7]

Jefferson first attempted an earlier work entitled "The Philosophy of Jesus of Nazareth"; this has not been preserved.[8] Jefferson then bought two copies each of a Greek New Testament, a Latin Bible, a French translation, and an English translation and cut and pasted on 82 facing pages in four parallel columns his selections of the Greek, Latin, French, and English texts, using all four canonical gospels. Of the narrative materials, he included only parts of the birth narratives and of the story of Jesus' trial and death; there

---

5. The only major refutation of Reimarus came from the leading liberal rationalist theologian and scholar in Germany, Johann Salomo Semler (1725–1791). Semler had spent all his life in the service of promoting a liberal and rational understanding of the Bible and Christianity, and he argued for the freedom of theological scholarship. Scripture should not be understood as the revelation of dogma and doctrine but as the human witness of the revelation of God. The purpose of the divine revelation is the communication of truths and moral values in order to establish a religious relationship of human beings with God. However, in his refutation of Reimarus, Semler (*Beantwortung der Fragmente eines Ungenannten insbesondere vom Zwecke Jesu und seiner Jünger* (Halle, 1779) moves to a more conservative position. He distinguishes two different modes of teaching: one that moves in images and pictures, accommodating the teaching to the common Jewish people, and another one that speaks directly about spiritual and moral truths. From this perspective he refutes Reimarus's work sentence by sentence without any real understanding of the problems that Reimarus had brought into the open.

6. Thomas Jefferson, *The Life and Morals of Jesus of Nazareth: Extracted textually from the Gospels in Greek, Latin, French, and English* (Washington: Government Printing Office, 1904). This is a facsimile edition of Jefferson's work that had been purchased by Congress in 1895 ("Jefferson Bible").

7. Quoted from the "Introduction" by Cyrus Adler to the "Jefferson Bible," p. 15 (see n. 6 above).

8. Apparently, Jefferson had at first thought that such an abridgment of the gospels might be useful "for the use of the Indians, unembarrassed with matters of fact or faith beyond the level of their comprehensions" (Quoted from Adler, "Introduction," 18).

are no reports of miracles and of appearances of the risen Jesus. The bulk of the work consists of sayings of Jesus. Of his work, he wrote on January 29, 1815 to Charles Clay:

> Probably you have heard me say I had taken the four Evangelists, had cut out from them every text they had recorded of the moral precepts of Jesus, and arranged them in a certain order, and although they appeared but as fragments, yet fragments of the most sublime edifice of morality which had ever been exhibited to man.[9]

Thus, among German as among American deists, the question of myth, miracle, and legend in the stories of the gospels is simply ignored and thrust aside with a sovereign grasp of Jesus' moral philosophy. On the other hand, among European New Testament scholars, the following period is dominated by either super-naturalist or rationalistic explanations of the miracles of Jesus. Often, both these perspectives are combined.[10] Many elements of both explanations are still current today, especially among many theologians and Christian believers less enlightened than Reimarus and Jefferson.

The super-naturalist explanation allows the view that God as the creator has the right to invalidate the laws of nature for his own purposes. Indeed, it is understood that this is the way in which divinity reveals itself. Thus miracles must be believed as they are described. The rationalistic interpretation also accepts the view that the reports of miracles in the gospels are believable. However, they can be explained rationally. Healing can be understood as due to the suggestive power of Jesus. When it appears that Jesus raised Lazarus from the dead, Lazarus was simply buried too early (usually within a day in the ancient world), that is, he was actually buried alive and Jesus knew that. He also realized immediately that the son of the widow and the daughter of Jairus were not actually dead but had only fallen into a deathlike faint. So he could "raise" them, and the bystanders, who saw what happened, reported that Jesus had raised them from the dead. Exorcisms are a common phenomenon because there are such things as diseases caused by mental conditions.

More problematic are the so-called nature miracles, like the Walking on the Water and the Stilling of the Tempest. But these also can be explained: there was a fog along the shores of the lake, and Jesus walked along the shore but appeared—because of the fog—to be walking on water. Peter did not realize that and tried to walk on the water; fortunately, as the boat was close to the shore, Jesus was able to stretch out his hand from the shore and save him. Also the Stilling of the Tempest has a rational explanation: Jesus knew that the water would be calm if they sailed around the nearest mountainous peninsula; so he grabbed the rudder and behold, they found themselves in quiet waters in no time.[11]

---

9. Ibid.; it seems that Jefferson here refers to the earlier lost work, but what he says here well illustrates the purpose also of the later work.

10. For the following survey see the respective chapters of Schweitzer, *The Quest of the Historical Jesus.*

11. These explanations are drawn from the work of the most prominent scholar of the rationalistic tradition, Heinrich Eberhard Gottlob Paulus (1761–1851). In his work (*Commentar über das Neue Testament,* Part 1: *Die drei ersten Evangelien* [3 vols.; Leipzig: Barth, 1812]), he rejected everything that understood religion as

The resurrection of Jesus presented the most formidable problem. Many rationalists here resort to a super-naturalist interpretation, or they are satisfied with stating that the disciples had visions or dreams—that is, perfectly natural phenomena that can be explained psychologically. Other more consistent rationalists like Paulus insisted that Jesus was not really dead when he was taken from the cross but was only in a trance. At this point, however, some presentations of the life of Jesus from the early nineteenth century begin a novelistic tradition in this genre—a tradition that was and remains purely rationalistic. It is interesting that, in these lives of Jesus, the secret society of the Essenes begins to play a role. Whatever was known about the Essenes at that time through the reports of Philo, Josephus, and Pliny the Elder—the Dead Sea Scrolls were not discovered until the middle of the 20th century—was used for novelistic accounts of Jesus' miracles, for example, that Jesus' friends, the Essenes, had prepared secretly a store of thousands of loaves in a cave just behind Jesus so that Jesus could feed the multitudes, or that the Essenes drugged Jesus before his crucifixion and then took him from the cross before he was completely dead and revived him.[12]

It was David Friedrich Strauss (1808–1874) who introduced a new perspective to the life-of-Jesus research.[13] In order to understand Strauss's work, it is necessary to discuss briefly the work of Johann Gottfried Herder (1744–1803).[14] Herder argues that

---

a matter of the intuition of the soul and as feeling. Pietism and mysticism had no place in true religion. Rather, religion was only and purely knowledge of what was true and what was right. It is therefore necessary to recognize the rational truth of everything that is reported in the biblical writings. However, "true" is only that which is "possible" from a philosophical and scientific perspective: miracles are "impossible." But because the Bible is "true," miracles must be explained rationally. What is really miraculous about Jesus are not his so-called miracles but the appearance of a perfect moral character in this extraordinary human being. The recognition of this high moral purpose and its rational acceptance are identical with true faith. Thus faith is nothing but rational thought in which one becomes one with the moral character of Jesus.

12. See chapter 12 of Schweitzer's *Quest.*

13. Strauss had studied philosophy and theology in Tübingen and Berlin. He wanted to attend the lectures of the famous philosopher Georg Wilhelm Friedrich Hegel (1770–1831) in Berlin, but Hegel died a month after the arrival of Strauss in that city. When Strauss was in high school, Ferdinand Christian Baur, who would later become professor in Tübingen and who is still famous as the founder of the "Tübingen School," had been one of his teachers. After his studies, Strauss for a short time was a Protestant minister; then, in 1832 at the age of twenty-four, he became the head tutor (*Repetent*) at the famous Tübingen Stift; this position also gave him the right to lecture at the university. At the beginning, his classes were devoted exclusively to philosophy, which he taught as an enthusiastic Hegelian. However, the envy of senior professors in the philosophy faculty prevented his promotion to a permanent teaching position in this field. So he sought to establish a career in theology and turned first to the question of the life of Jesus. Within three years, he completed his *The Life of Jesus Critically Examined*—a work of almost 1,000 pages that was published in its first edition in 1835. This work was a revolution in New Testament studies; but it also destroyed his academic career. He lost his position in Tübingen, and a call to a chair in Theology at the University of Zurich in 1839 was withdrawn because of the protest of conservative church leaders. Strauss spent the rest of his life as a private scholar, financed by a small inheritance from his father and a small salary that the University of Zurich was obliged to pay to him annually until the end of his life.

14. His important work, *Ideen zur Philosophie der Geschichte der Menschheit,* was first published in 1784–1791 (English translation: *Reflections on the Philosophy of the History of Mankind* [Chicago: University of Chicago Press, 1968]) and did not have any effect on the quest for the historical Jesus for almost half a century until David Friedrich Strauss. Later, Herder's insights were especially influential in the development of form criticism at the beginning of the twentieth century.

language is the medium through which human beings become themselves, become truly human. As human beings can exist only as historical beings, the memory and the re-creation of the past in language interpret the past for the present. In this process, however, no interest exists in investigating the past "as it really was." Rather, "history" is created insofar as the past informs the understanding of the present. The forms of language, through which the past becomes present, are not a matter of free individual choice, inasmuch as language is not something that an individual invents spontaneously in every new situation. On the contrary, language is already given as a social reality; it belongs to a people or community. Here, language lives in the forms of poetry, genuinely including song, legend, and myth, which are by definition oral, that is, not subject to the critical standards of publication in written form. This implies for the understanding of the gospels of the New Testament that the memory of Jesus in legend and myth is older and more genuine than the later historical and literary rationalization.[15]

It is this insight of Herder that Strauss utilizes in his *Life of Jesus,* taking a radical turn against both the super-naturalist and the rationalist interpretations by introducing the concept of myth. The life of Jesus in the gospels is not a historical report in any way, but a mythical description that wants to express the permanent and lasting foundation of the Christian religion. What is important about Jesus as the founder of a new religion for all humankind is not the historicity of the reports, but the way in which these reports about Jesus, that is, the gospels, express the eternal truth that in Jesus' life and ministry, the perfect union of the divine and the human has become a reality. Myth is therefore the legitimate vehicle for the proclamation of the unity of the divine and the human in Jesus. This is what the gospels proclaim, and those who understand this proclamation can share in the revelation of this truth insofar as they themselves become conscious of this idea for the conduct of their own lives. Therefore, no historical criticism can touch the foundations of the Christian religion.

This gave Strauss the freedom for a radical criticism of the story that the gospels report. The understanding of Jesus as Son of God is already part of the mythical presentation; therefore, it cannot be used as a foundation for the inquiry into the consciousness of the historical Jesus. An exorcism of an evil spirit may have been historical. But the form of the story in the gospels, where the demon addresses Jesus as Son of God, has no claim to historicity. The entire attempt to interpret Jesus' miracles rationally is thus discarded—not to speak of a super-naturalistic acceptance of a miracle, which a truly scientific worldview does not permit. The nature miracles are even more mythical; they mostly draw on materials from the Old Testament, like the feeding of the multitudes—a story that is modeled after the feeding of Israel in the wilderness. Finally, all reports of the resurrection of Jesus are completely mythical and have no historical foundation.

Strauss introduces another new element in his investigation of the story of Jesus. For both the rationalists and the super-naturalists, the Gospel of John had seemed to be the most historical of all gospels because John's miracles are fewer and told in more detail

---

15. See also Marcia Bunge, "Text and Reader in Herder's Interpretation of the New Testament," in Wulf Koepke, ed., *Johann Gottfried Herder: Language, History, and the Enlightenment* (Columbia, S.C.: Camden House, 1990) 138–50.

(which was understood as a sign of their historicity); also the three journeys of Jesus to Jerusalem in the Fourth Gospel were believed to be historical. At the same time, John seemed to give access to the deepest thoughts of Jesus in the long discourses of this gospel. Strauss, however, returns to the Synoptic Gospels as the more reliable historical sources. He did not, however, follow Herder's suggestion that the Gospel of Mark should be considered as the oldest gospel, but gave the crown to the Gospel of Matthew as the oldest and most historical.[16] Herder had argued that the original gospel must have been oral; only in the oral form is the genuine communication of a message alive. It is here that stories are freely told according to the social and religious milieu of the hearers. It was therefore necessary that the story of Jesus was told in different oral forms. The written gospels are reflections of this living oral narrative. The Gospel of Mark is seen as the oldest because it is closest to the early oral proclamation. Matthew and Luke, Herder thinks, used the notes that Mark had originally composed for his gospel. If, however, Matthew and Luke expanded the Markan story, they do not simply add to a written record; rather, the oral story was still alive and had expanded according to the laws of oral narrative. Thus Matthew and Luke now incorporate the fruits of the continuing life of the oral tradition.[17]

New arguments for the priority of Mark had been brought forward by Karl Lachmann,[18] Christian Gottlob Wilke (1786–1854),[19] and Christian Hermann Weisse (1801–1866).[20] This thesis, soon accepted by many scholars, gave the quest of the historical Jesus a new direction because it opened an opportunity of discovering in the Gospel of Mark's narrative the original course of the ministry of Jesus. The ministry of Jesus rather than his words became the focus of the quest. It was believed that Mark's description of Jesus' ministry in three parts was indeed the actual course of Jesus' career: he first went from town to village and from village to town in Galilee, preaching and healing; he never refers to himself as the Christ (only the demons know that, while the disciples do not understand); then Peter recognizes Jesus' true identity in the famous confession at Caesarea Philippi. From then on, Jesus reveals to the disciples the true meaning of his messianic identity on his way to Jerusalem. Finally, beginning with the triumphant entry into Jerusalem itself, Jesus acts out in full his messianic status, continuing with the cleansing of the temple and his masterful debates with the scribes and Pharisees and confirming his messianic mission in his trial and suffering. By the end of the nineteenth century, this "life of Jesus," presented in ever so many variations, was confidently established as the true historical picture, mirrored in Mark, the oldest of the gospels.

---

16. Strauss is here dependent upon the hypothesis developed by Johann Jacob Griesbach (1745–1812), who had published his arguments for the priority of Matthew in 1789 in his *Commentatio qua Marci evangelium totum e Mattthaei et Lucae commentariis decerptum esse demonstratur.* This "Griesbach hypothesis" was revived by William Farmer and some of his students. The discussion of the merits of this hypothesis leads beyond the scope of this chapter; but see Helmut Koester, *Ancient Christian Gospels: Their History and Development* (Philadelphia: Trinity Press International, 1990) 128–33.

17. Herder, *Christliche Schriften*, 1794–98.

18. "De ordine narrationum in evangeliis synopticis," *Theologische Studien und Kritiken* 8 (1835) 570–590.

19. *Der Urevangelist oder exegetisch-kritische Untersuchung über das Verwandtschaftsverhältnis der drei ersten Evangelien* (Dresden/Leipzig: Gerhard Fleischer, 1838).

20. *Die evangelische Geschichte kritisch und philosophisch bearbeitet* (2 vols.; Leipzig: Breitkopf & Härtel, 1838).

II. The Crisis of the Old Quest

This confidence was attacked in the first years of the twentieth century by Albert Schweitzer in his famous criticism of the life of Jesus research and by William Wrede. Just a few years before the first publication of Albert Schweitzer's work on the "Quest of the Historical Jesus," William Wrede, a member of the Göttingen circle that was called the history-of-religions school, published his work on the "Messianic Secret in the Gospels."[21] It was at a time when the thesis of the priority of the Gospel of Mark had been confidently defended by the suggestion that this gospel is still closer than the other gospels to the actual historical development of the ministry of Jesus. The framework of the Gospel of Mark, Wrede argued convincingly, was constructed by the author on the basis of his special theological concern; it has nothing to do with the sequence of events in the historical ministry of Jesus. Rather, Wrede argued, Mark deliberately constructed a schema according to which the messianic ministry of Jesus was not understood by the disciples during Jesus' Galilean ministry, then revealed in the confession of Peter but put under the veil of secrecy until the resurrection. Wrede's theory has been modified in subsequent research with the argument that the tradition previous to Mark did indeed present Jesus' ministry as messianic,[22] but that Mark shrouded the miracles, and Jesus' messianism in general, in secrecy because he wanted to argue that Jesus' true calling was the Son of Man who had to suffer and to die. In any case, since Wrede's work, it has been more generally recognized that the framework of the Gospel of Mark was not a reflection of the actual historical memory of Jesus' career but the result of a theological theory of the author of this gospel. It was a theological schema designed to provide a general outline into which older sources and traditions could be incorporated. Not Mark, and even less so any other gospel, can give us reliable information about the course of Jesus' ministry or tell us anything about Jesus' motivations, his experiences, or his self-consciousness. All of the possibly relevant information falls in the category of "redaction," that is, it belongs to the various frameworks created by the authors of the gospels to accommodate older traditional units. The subsequent development of the form-critical and redaction-critical methods by Karl Ludwig Schmidt,[23] Martin Dibelius,[24] and Rudolf Bultmann[25] confirmed this judgment and

---

21. William Wrede, *Das Messiasgeheimnis in den Evangelien: Zugleich ein Beitrag zum Verständnis des Markusevangeliums* (Göttingen: Vandenhouck & Ruprecht., 1901); English translation: *The Messianic Secret* (Library of Theological Translations; London: Clarke, 1971).

22. Wrede saw the reason for this Markan construction in the fact that Jesus' historical ministry was actually not messianic. The theory of the messianic secret was invented by the author of Mark to conceal this well-known fact. Mark suggests by the theory of the messianic secret, invented by him, that Jesus' miracles were done in secret and that Jesus had told his disciples and everyone else to keep silent about them until the resurrection, so nobody knew about the miracles.

23. *Der Rahmen der Geschichte Jesu* (Berlin: Trowitzsch, 1919).

24. *Die Formgeschichte des Evangeliums* (Tübingen: Mohr/Siebeck, 1919); English translation: *From Tradition to Gospel* (New York: Scribner's, 1934).

25. *Die Geschichte der synoptischen Tradition* (FRLANT 29; Göttingen: Vandenhoeck & Ruprecht, 1921); English translation: *The History of the Synoptic Tradition* (2nd ed.; New York: Harper & Row, 1968). For a dis-

deepened the scholarly skepticism, especially with respect to all narrative materials of the gospels.

Albert Schweitzer's work, first published in 1906,[26] though not agreeing with Wrede's arguments about the secondary character of the Markan framework,[27] brought this period of life-of-Jesus research to a definitive end. Yet, there was a discovery of a new source for the historical Jesus that had strangely been overlooked in the quest of the historical Jesus, even by the nineteenth-century scholar Heinrich Julius Holtzmann, who had most convincingly argued for the existence of this source, namely the Synoptic Sayings Gospel Q, the lost second common source for Matthew and Luke, containing mostly sayings of Jesus.[28] This Sayings Gospel had to wait for the beginning of the twentieth century to be taken seriously as a source for the historical Jesus. "It was in the loss of confidence in Mark (on the basis of Wrede's work) that von Harnack attempted to substitute Q as a source, not for the reconstruction of a life of Jesus, but at least for a reconstruction of Jesus' self-consciousness."[29]

In a different approach, Rudolf Bultmann also employs those materials of the Sayings Gospel Q that he used as the most original source for his book on Jesus.[30] In the preface to his book, Bultmann rejects all attempts to reconstruct the life of Jesus or to

---

cussion and bibliography of form criticism, see Helmut Koester, "Formgeschichte/Formenkritik II," *TRE* 11 (1983) 286–99.

26. See n. 1.

27. Schweitzer was deeply impressed by Wrede's work (thus the first title of his work "From Reimarus to Wrede"). But he essentially agreed with the older position that Mark had faithfully preserved the outline of the ministry of the historical Jesus, and he followed the insights of Johannes Weiß (Johannes Weiß, *Die Predigt Jesu vom Reiche Gottes* [Göttingen: Vandenhoeck & Ruprecht, 1992; 2nd ed. 1900; 3rd ed. 1964]) that Jesus' ministry and preaching was entirely dominated by ancient apocalyptic concepts but, although possibly historical, could not serve as a guide to today's appreciation of Jesus of Nazareth.

28. Heinrich Julius Holtzmann (*Die synoptischen Evangelien: Ihr Ursprung und geschichtlicher Character* [Leipzig: Engelmann, 1863]) is the father of the two-source hypothesis, affirming that Matthew and Luke had used, in addition to Mark, a second common source that consisted entirely of sayings of Jesus. However, in his own search for the historical Jesus, he so singularly focused on Mark, or a possibly even older Proto-Mark (*Urmarkus*), that he never seriously considered using Q as a primary source for the reconstruction of the original teachings of Jesus. See on this question Kloppenborg, "The Sayings Gospel Q and the Historical Jesus," 311–12.

29. Kloppenborg, ibid., 313; cf. Adolf von Harnack, *Sprüche und Reden Jesu: Die zweite Quelle des Matthäus und Lukas* (Beiträge zur Einleitung in das Neue Testament 2; Leipzig: Hinrichs, 1907); English translation: *The Sayings of Jesus: The Second Source of St. Matthew and St. Luke* (New Testament Studies 2; London: Williams & Norgate, and New York: Putnam's, 1908).

30. In 1925, within three years of Barth's commentary on the Epistle to the Romans and four years after his own *History of the Synoptic Tradition*, Rudolf Bultmann published a book with the title *Jesus* (Berlin: Deutsche Bibliothek, 1926; English translation: *Jesus and the Word* [New York: Scribner's, 1934]). Critics have remarked with some justified cynicism that this book, in its first edition, appeared in a series that had the title "The Immortal Persons [of Humankind])." How could Bultmann write such a book? It seems to me that this book must be understood as a work of dialectical theology—not far removed from Karl Barth's christology. Bultmann does, however, what Barth has not done: he presupposes a critical analysis of the gospel tradition that enables him to write his book on the whole on the basis of those sayings of Jesus that have survived relatively untouched and unaltered by their transmission in the Christian community. If—to speak with Barth—Jesus Christ is the revelation of the Word of God in this world, then it would be worthwhile to ask the question what it was that he said.

inquire into Jesus' self-consciousness or to fix in any objectifying way external data of Jesus' ministry. If one tried to do that, one would end up with only the additional question of the time-transcending truths of Jesus' words, that is, describing a significance of Jesus that is not anchored in a specific historical context. Essential for a historical inquiry is the specific contingency of something that happens at a particular time. Bultmann says, "Therefore, my presentation does not say anything about Jesus as a great human being or a genius or a hero; Jesus will not appear as fascinating or demonic, his words will not be characterized as deep, his faith will not be called magnificent, his character will not be described as pure like that of a child. Moreover, nothing will be said about the eternal character of his words or about the depth of his human soul, or anything else like that. My interest is exclusively to attend to that what Jesus demanded and what can therefore become present for us as the demand of his historical existence."[31]

Bultmann is not interested in the personality of Jesus but in his work. His work, however, is exclusively what he has taught: his proclamation. We cannot unearth eternal truths from this proclamation and apply these truths to ourselves, because Jesus spoke only to the people of his own time in their language and concepts. His proclamation must be understood within the context of the concrete human situation of Jesus' own time, in which it called human beings into a decision about their own existence. Only then can we understand his teaching as the opening of the possibility of genuine human existence. In this encounter with the Jesus of history, we may also encounter the question of how we ourselves want to understand our existence—insofar as we ourselves are indeed moved by the question of the meaning of our own existence. It is evident that this is an existentialist terminology describing the call for the renewal of our own life. In more traditional terminology, this would be understood as a call for repentance and conversion in the encounter with the proclamation of the historical Jesus.

In his book about Jesus, Bultmann assumes that the materials contained in the synoptic tradition, even if they do not go altogether back to Jesus himself, still contain much of a congenial understanding of Jesus' message. With respect to the eschatological expectations of the Synoptic Gospels, Bultmann says that they can hardly be understood unless one assumes that they have their origin ultimately in the historical Jesus. This enables him to understand Jesus fully within the context of the eschatological expectation of his time. Without such an expectation of the future fulfillment of the will of God, Jesus' message of radical obedience to God's will would simply become another ethical demand that we could easily pry loose from its historical context and present as an eternally valid moral truth. To allow Jesus' proclamation to stand as a truly historical phenomenon, it should not be stripped of all those elements, which appear to our modern mind as outdated mythology. Thus Bultmann avoids a modernization of Jesus' message. As a person of his time, Jesus shared the worldview of his time with all its mythological eggshells.

As Bultmann and von Harnack relied almost exclusively on the sayings of the Synoptic Sayings Gospel Q, this source played a central role in British scholarship of the

---

31. Bultmann, *Jesus and the Word*, 8.

first half of the twentieth century in the search for the voice of the historical Jesus.[32] But here, as also in the work of the German scholar Joachim Jeremias, the primary concern was the search for the original voice of Jesus (the *ipsissima vox*), which Jeremias pursued especially in his work on Jesus' parables[33] and his investigation of the extracanonical sayings.[34] All these works, however, did not face the basic problems and fallacies involved in the Old Quest; they are therefore not more than a continuation of the Old Quest with a shift from the narrative materials to the sayings.

III. The New Quest for the Historical Jesus

The most important problem of the nineteenth-century quest for the historical Jesus was its positivistic understanding of "history" and "historical." "History" was generally conceived of as the bare facts of things that happened in the past. What did actually and in fact happen when Jesus taught and acted in Palestine in the beginning of the first century? Since the images of the Christ of faith and of the Christian confessions were seen as secondary, a product of the later Christian community of believers, it seemed indispensable to isolate the historical Jesus from this later interpretation. Therefore, "historical" becomes something that is neither related to what preceded the ministry of Jesus nor to the subsequent course of events and the understanding of reality in the memory of the past.

The second problem of the Old Quest lies in its individualism. Already Pietism had a stake in the individual. Illumination of each and every individual by the Holy Spirit or by a personal encounter of each individual human being with the Savior Jesus was its central message. As the pietists believed that every single individual must be saved in order to create the ideal community, so the disciples of enlightenment from Reimarus to Ralph Waldo Emerson[35] proclaimed the illumination of the individual by the insights of rational truth. This also involved the view that personal, individualistic insight into the existence of, and communication with, a supreme divine being and individual moral perfection must have been the primary goal of Jesus' message. Nothing is said here about community and social structures that determine the individual's existence and the understanding of being a part of a nation, of a social group or race or gender, or of a religious movement.

A third problem of the Old Quest was its fascination with the question of the self-consciousness of Jesus. It was especially raised in connection with the christological titles (Messiah/Christ, Son of Man, Son of God, Lord) that the gospels assign to him.

---

32. See Kloppenborg, "Q and the Historical Jesus," 317.

33. *The Parables of Jesus* (2nd rev. ed.; New York: Scribner's, 1972).

34. *Unknown Sayings of Jesus* (2nd ed.; London: S.P.C.K., 1964). For an evaluation of this work of Jeremias, see chapter 6, "The Extracanonical Sayings of the Lord as Products of the Christian Community" pp. 84–99.

35. See my essay "Thomas Jefferson, Ralph Waldo Emerson, the *Gospel of Thomas,* and the Apostle Paul," in Helmut Koester, *Paul and His World: Interpreting the New Testament in Its Context* (Minneapolis: Fortress Press, 2007) 195–206.

Whenever it was accepted as historical that Jesus thought of himself as the Messiah, additional questions arose: when did he discover that he was the Messiah? Was Jesus thinking of himself as the Messiah who would be victorious, or did he think of himself as the suffering Messiah and thus anticipated his eventual death? At other times, the Old Quest denied that Jesus used any of these titles for himself, and sometimes it tried to understand them as categories that could be applied to human beings in general. This is, for example, the case with respect to the title Son of God. It was argued that Jesus spoke of himself as the Son of God only in that sense in which it could be applied to all human beings, provided that they were able to achieve the same understanding of themselves as children of God.[36]

What has been called "The New Quest of the Historical Jesus," which began in the fifties of the twentieth century, tried to avoid these pitfalls, and it also did not immediately resume the search for Jesus' voice in the Sayings Gospel Q. In fact, it was very critical of the renewed attempts to find the authoritative message of Jesus of Nazareth in the original words of Jesus (the *ipsissima vox*). It began in the year 1953 with Ernst Käsemann's lecture on "The Historical Jesus and the Christ of the Kerygma" that was presented at the annual meeting of the "Old Marburg Students" (the circle of Rudolf Bultmann's friends and former students).[37] When three years later the Heidelberg New Testament scholar Günther Bornkamm published his *Jesus von Nazareth* in 1956,[38] it became the landmark of a new period of interest in the historical Jesus. The book was immediately successful, was republished in as many as eleven new German editions and translated into English,[39] Dutch, Japanese, Danish, Italian, French, Portuguese, and Spanish. Soon after its first publication, this new interest in Jesus was hailed and discussed programmatically in America by James M. Robinson under the title "A New Quest for the Historical Jesus."[40] Bornkamm's book about Jesus of Nazareth eschews any attempt to write a "life" of Jesus. The work begins with the sentence, "No one is any longer in the position to write a life of Jesus." What is central for the writing of a biography, and what had dominated the Old Quest for the historical Jesus, namely the inquiry into the social conditions and psychological motivations of the work, life, and fate of the historical person Jesus, did not play any role in the beginning of this New Quest. Rather,

---

36. There are two problems with this approach to the personality of Jesus. (1) All our sources show no interest in any of the questions that concern Jesus' inner life and development or personal motivation. (2) It is questionable to make any historical figure subject to such inquiry because persons of past history, be it Moses or Jesus or Socrates or Caesar, should be understood in terms of their deeds and accomplishments and thus with respect to the effect of their actions upon their own world and upon future historical developments, not with respect to their psychological disposition and inner development. However intriguing such psychological interests might be, the course of history is affected by what people do and how they act. Their motivations matter only insofar as they steer the course of their actions.

37. Published in *ZThK* 51 (1954) 125–53; reprinted in Käsemann, *Exegetische Versuche und Besinnungen* (2 vols.; Göttingen: Vandenhoeck & Ruprecht, 1960–1964) 1. 184–214; ET: "The Problem of the Historical Jesus," in Käsemann, *Essays on New Testament Themes* (SBT 41; London: SCM, 1964) 15–47.

38. Günther Bornkamm, *Jesus von Nazareth* (Urban Taschenbücher; Stuttgart: Kohlhammer, 1956).

39. *Jesus of Nazareth* (London: Hodder & Stoughton, 1960), with a brief translator's preface by James M. Robinson; republished, Minneapolis: Fortress Press, 1995, with a preface by Helmut Koester.

40. James M. Robinson, *A New Quest for the Historical Jesus* (SBT 25; London: SCM, 1960); cf. Robinson, *Kerygma und historischer Jesus* (Zurich: Zwingli, 1967).

the New Quest was motivated by a theological problem, namely, the search for the historical foundation of the Christian proclamation, the kerygma of the early church. In
this proclamation, Jesus' coming and fate were announced as the events of salvation that
made God and his kingdom a present reality among the believers. Was this proclamation related simply to the naked historical fact of Jesus' death and resurrection? Or was
there an essential connection between the intention of Jesus' works and words on the
one hand, and the preaching of the church, on the other hand? Only if this question
could be answered positively did the historical foundation of the kerygma seem secure.
What Jesus of Nazareth had done and said and suffered should have some continuity
with the Jesus Christ, who became the object of Christian faith and the content of the
Christian proclamation—despite all the misunderstandings and reinterpretations of the
tradition about him. Bornkamm endeavored to demonstrate that Jesus of Nazareth and
the kerygma of the early church were constituent parts of one and the same historical
process.

The same distancing of the New Quest from the Old Quest was voiced in Rudolf
Bultmann's reaction to the beginnings of the New Quest. In 1960, in a lecture delivered before the Academy of Arts and Sciences at Heidelberg,[41] Bultmann characterized
the beginnings of the New Quest as follows:

> In the time of the life-of-Jesus research (that is, in the so-called liberal theology
> [of the 19th century]) the question was inspired by the attempt to liberate the his-
> torical Jesus from the secondary layer of theological interpretation, through which
> he had been obscured by means of the proclamation of the early church.... Today
> the direction of the inquiry has been reversed: the new quest is interested in the
> demonstration of the unity of the historical Jesus with the Christ of the
> kerygma.[42]

The intention of this New Quest, as it began with Käsemann's essay and Bornkamm's
book, is best understood in the subsequent debate of Käsemann with Joachim Jeremias.
It appears in a lecture that was first published in English translation in the year 1969
under the title "Blind Alleys in the 'Jesus of History' Controversy."[43] What is said here
against Jeremias's confidence in the rediscovery of the *ipsissima vox* of Jesus himself and
about his implications with respect to Christian faith is an appropriate note of caution
concerning the new flood of works on the historical Jesus that has inundated especially
the American landscape.

For Jeremias, an increasing knowledge of the historical Jesus is identical with a better understanding of the object of Christian faith. Käsemann correctly characterizes
Jeremias's position as follows:

> We are (Jeremias says) better equipped today than previous generations were. Lit-
> erary criticism of sources and tradition, form criticism, the history of the age and

---

41. "Das Verhältnis der urchristlichen Botschaft zum historischen Jesus," *SHAW.Philosphisch-historische
Klasse 1960.3*, 5–27 = Rudolf Bultmann, *Exegetica* (Tübingen: Mohr/Siebeck, 1967) 445–69 [translation
mine].

42. Bultmann, *Exegetica*, 445–46.

43. In Bultmann, *New Testament Questions of Today* (Philadelphia: Fortress Press, 1969) 23–65.

its environment, new knowledge about Jesus' native tongue and, above all, about his eschatology have refined our methods and kept us from making mistakes which were once unavoidable. We can no longer modernize Jesus and create him in our own image as easily as our fathers did.[44]

Käsemann rejects the hubris of the claim that we are so much better [equipped?] than our fathers and no longer subject to the same mistakes. Moreover, he makes mockery of the courage of the statement that more refined historical research will easily lead us to the discovery of the voice of Jesus and thus confront us with the unique presence of God himself in the history of the one and unique Jesus, for whom there are no parallels in the history of religions. If it is only the voice of Jesus that can give authority to our beliefs, and if we then continue to claim the superiority of our historical research and its result as the foundation of a new existence, we are worshiping a golden image with feet of clay. Are we the first generation of human beings whose historical research is no longer fallible, and for whom a religious commitment is no longer an adventure that is subject to trial and error and eventual failure? Is the "real" and "truly historical" Jesus of our scholarly endeavors no longer a human product but an everlasting truth that is confirmed by archaeology and will last beyond the day on which we have to leave the face of the earth? Käsemann asks, "Can we ply our trade otherwise than in the knowledge that the feet of those who will carry us out have already long been at the door and indeed are there all the time?"

Then, why inquire into the historical Jesus? Certainly not to attain an objective truth that is beyond the critical quest of another generation as well as more reliable than the proclamation of the church, past and present, nor to argue that the historical Jesus was so different from any of the claims of the Christian proclamation that the latter can only be characterized as a secondary invention, if not a complete fraud. All that is known about Jesus of Nazareth is known through documents written by people for whom this Jesus was at the same time the very object of a faith—faith to be understood as the venture of a new life, the creation of a new people, the move from injustice to justice, from an authoritarian society to a new society in which there was neither Jew nor Greek, neither slave nor free, neither male and female. Has this early Christian proclamation (not necessarily the Christian church and its proclamation in general) a right to insist that the object of its faith is Jesus of Nazareth in his message, ministry, life, and death? And to what degree is this Jesus, a Jesus who not only had a special message but also died as a political criminal, a critical yardstick of an early church and of its attempts of accommodation to the social and political structures of its time—or also to the accommodations of the churches to cultural structures of our time?

IV. The Sayings Gospel Q, the *Gospel of Thomas,* and Jesus of Nazareth

It was exactly during the years of this New Quest, that is, in the middle of the twentieth century, that the interest in the original sayings was newly awakened. Two factors

---

44. Ibid.

contributed to this new departure: (1) a fresh assessment of the development of the Sayings Gospel Q and the theological factors that dominated its composition and development;[45] (2) the discovery and publication of the *Gospel of Thomas*.[46] This resulted in a renewed quest for the historical Jesus, now once more based on the sayings of Jesus— a quest, however, that seems to be strangely unaware of Albert Schweitzer's devastating critique of the Old Quest and that scarcely heeds the warnings raised by the first scholars who had initiated the New Quest.

Regardless of the possibility of reconstructing earlier layers of the Sayings Gospel Q and of the *Gospel of Thomas,* it must be remembered that the earliest evidence for the circulation of sayings of Jesus comes primarily from the apostle Paul[47] and also from other early Christian literature, especially 1 Peter,[48] the Epistle of James, and the *First Epistle of Clement*.[49] It is also striking that these references often are not identified as sayings of Jesus. In Romans 12, Paul quotes sayings that have close parallels to those of the Sermon on the Mount without ever indicating that these admonitions go back to words of Jesus. As Paul can also occasionally quote a word of Jesus and clearly distinguish it from his own opinion, we must assume that he knew them as Jesus' sayings but did not feel that he had to appeal to Jesus' authority.

A very interesting use of sayings appears in 1 Corinthians 1–4. Paul's general terminology here is striking; a number of key terms used by Paul in these chapters are never or rarely used by Paul elsewhere: "to keep secret," "to hide," "to uncover," "to reveal," "the wise," "childish." Not only such key words but also the formulation of several sentences point to sayings that are found especially in the *Gospel of Thomas* (with some parallels in Q).[50] The conclusion is that the Corinthians indeed knew sayings like those

---

45. The most important works at that time were Heinz E. Tödt, *Der Menschensohn in der synoptischen Überlieferung* (Gütersloh: Mohn, 1959), and Dieter Lührmann, *Die Redaktion der Logienquelle* (WMANT 33; Neukirchen-Vluyn: Neukirchener Verlag, 1969); see also Kloppenborg, "Q and the Historical Jesus," 315–18.

46. For the story of the discovery, see James M. Robinson, "The Discovery of the Nag Hammadi Codices," *BA* 42 (1979) 206–24. The first publication of the Coptic text with English translation appeared in 1959 (A. Guillaumont, H.-Ch. Puech, W. Till, and Yassa 'Abd al Masih, eds., *The Gospel according to Thomas: Coptic Text Established and Translated* (Leiden: Brill, 1959; reduced reprint of the editio princeps of 1959 with only English translation: San Francisco: Harper & Row, 1984). The final critical edition was presented by Harry W. Attridge, Helmut Koester, and Thomas O. Lambdin, "The Gospel of Thomas (Introduction, Text, Translation, Greek Fragments, and Testimonia)," in Bentley Layton, ed., *Nag Hammadi Codex II, 2–7 Together with XIII, 2*, Brit. Lib. Or. 4926(1) and P. Oxy. 1, 654, 655* (NHS 20–21; Leiden: Brill, 1987) 37–128.

47. Koester, *Ancient Christian Gospels: Their History and Development* (Philadelphia: Trinity Press International; London: SCM, 1990; 2nd printing Philadelphia: Trinity Press International, 1991; paperback/3rd printing 1992) 52–62.

48. Ibid., 64–66.

49. Ibid., 66–71.

50. One of the pieces quoted here by Paul (as "scripture") appears in the *Gospel of Thomas* as a saying of Jesus:

I shall give you what eye has not seen
and what no ear has heard,
and what no hand has touched,
and what has never occurred to the human mind (*Gos. Thom.* 17).

Cf. 1 Cor 2:9:

. . . what eye has not seen
and what ear has not heard

in the *Gospel of Thomas* and claimed that these sayings were the source of religious inspiration and esoteric knowledge and wisdom. This observation also helps to date the existence of this special wisdom tradition of the sayings of Jesus to the time of Paul's ministry, no later than ca. 50 CE.

Puzzling is the relationship of the Epistle of James to the tradition of the sayings of Jesus.[51] The closest parallels are found in the Sermon on the Mount. Of the eight passages in question from the Epistle of James, five appear in Matthew 5 and one in Matthew 7. In no instance is there a reference in James that would indicate that these sayings were spoken by Jesus. It is possible that in some of these instances, rules of the community were adopted as sayings of Jesus only at a later stage of the tradition. That also may be true in the case of regulations for wandering apostles in the *Didache (Teaching of the Twelve Apostles)* that have several parallels in the mission speeches of Q, Luke, and Matthew.[52]

It is evident in all this early usage of sayings of Jesus that the emphasis is upon community regulations and parenesis. The only exception is the employment of Jesus' sayings as words of saving wisdom and immortality among the Corinthians. To what degree such sayings already were collected into smaller units—most likely transmitted orally, for example, in the form of catechisms—is difficult to determine. Evidently the composition of the Sayings Gospel Q and of the *Gospel of Thomas* presuppose such smaller collections.

How did a piece of literature eventually emerge from the sayings traditions that had been circulating in Paul's and other early communities? John Kloppenborg has argued persuasively that the Sayings Gospel Q that was used by both Matthew and Luke is a revised edition of an older writing that he identifies as a wisdom book.[53] This wisdom book, he argues, began with an "Inaugural Sermon of Jesus." This sermon is essentially preserved in Q 6:20–49—what later was used by Luke for the composition of the Sermon on the Plain. Second are instructions for discipleship and a mission speech, Q 9:57–10:16—further developed by Luke into the speech for the Sending of the Seventy. The third part consists of instructions on prayer, including the Lord's Prayer, Q 11:2–4 and 9–13, followed by exhortation to fearless preaching, Q 12:2–7 and 11–12. The fifth part is called "On Anxiety" and was composed of some sayings that are now found in Luke 12:13–34. Finally, there is a "Didache," an admonition to discipleship, to which several sayings belong that are now scattered in Luke 13 and 14. Therefore, it was

---

nor has it risen in the human heart
what God has prepared for those who love him.

There also is a direct allusion to *Gos. Thom.* 2 (in the version preserved in the Greek text of *Pap. Oxy.* 654.2), when Paul tells the Corinthians that "they have already become kings." See Helmut Koester, "Gnostic Writings as Witnesses for the Development of the Sayings Tradition," in Bentley Layton, ed., *The Rediscovery of Gnosticism,* vol. 1: *The School of Valentinus* (NumenSup 41; Leiden: Brill, 1980) 239–61.

51. Koester, *Ancient Christian Gospels,* 71–75.

52. Ibid., 16–17; Koester, *Synoptische Überlieferung bei den apostolischen Vätern* (TU 65; Berlin: Akademie-Verlag, 1957) 209–17.

53. John Kloppenborg, *The Formation of Q: Trajectories in Ancient Wisdom Tradition* (SAC; Philadelphia: Fortress Press, 1987).

essentially a book of instructions and regulations, prefaced with a programmatic statement, namely, the inaugural sermon of Q/Luke 6. This wisdom book was later expanded, primarily by adding sayings about the judgment and about the coming of the Son of Man. The original composition may tentatively be dated in the middle of the first century (ca. 50 CE), while the later redaction, producing the common source "Q" of both Matthew and Luke, was probably made shortly after 70 CE.

There was, however, a second early Christian writing that must have been composed at about the same time, namely, the earliest version of the *Gospel of Thomas*—note well that I am not talking about the *Gospel of Thomas* as it appears now in its third-century Coptic translation! What is most remarkable about the *Gospel of Thomas* is the fact that it presents numerous sayings of Jesus with parallels in the Synoptic Gospels and in the Gospel of John, but that in almost all instances, the *Gospel of Thomas* preserves these sayings in forms that are more original than the forms of the Synoptic and Johannine parallels.[54] Redactional features, introduced by the writers of the canonical gospels, are missing throughout. In fact, sayings of the *Gospel of Thomas* that have parallels in Matthew and Luke usually resemble the respective sayings as they must have appeared in the Sayings Gospel Q. Moreover, all materials that Kloppenborg has assigned to the later redaction of the Sayings Gospel, especially the sayings about the coming of the Son of Man, are absent in the *Gospel of Thomas*. My conclusion is therefore that the *Gospel of Thomas* rests on an older sayings gospel or wisdom book that was composed essentially on the basis of the same traditional sayings that were used by the author of the first version of Q, but including also sayings of Jesus that have found their way, independently of Q, into the Gospels of Matthew, Mark, and John.[55]

It is understandable that a number of scholars have used the hypothetical reconstruction of one, possibly two, wisdom books with sayings of Jesus around the year 50 CE—that is, twenty years before the most commonly accepted dates for the composition of the canonical gospels—as an opportune step for a reconstruction of the original preaching of Jesus. Some have argued that the predominance of wisdom sayings in these early sayings collections allows the conclusion that Jesus was a wisdom teacher, perhaps even in the style of a Cynic preacher.[56] Others, however, have used the Sayings Gospel Q and its materials to reconstruct the preaching of Jesus as that of a revolutionary prophet.[57] There are numerous other recent reconstructions of the historical Jesus, though not all of them are exclusively dependent upon a reconstruction of the Sayings Gospel Q.[58]

---

54. I have tried to demonstrate that in detail in my *Ancient Christian Gospels,* 75–128.

55. It is my opinion that sayings of Luke that have parallels in the *Gospel of Thomas* but not in Matthew also should be assigned to Q; see Helmut Koester, "Q and Its Relatives," in James E. Goehring, Charles W. Hedrick, Jack T. Sanders, eds., *Gospel Origins & Christian Beginnings: In Honor of James M. Robinson* (Forum Fascicles 1; Sonoma, Calif.: Polebridge Press, 1989) 49–63.

56. For literature regarding this hypothesis, see pp. 253–54, notes 16–22.

57. Richard Horsley, *Bandits, Prophets and Messiahs: Popular Movements at the Time of Jesus* (with John S. Hanson; Minneapolis: Winston-Salem, 1985); Horsley, *Jesus and the Spiral of Violence* (San Francisco: Harper & Row, 1987); Horsley, *Sociology and the Jesus Movement* (New York: Crossroad, 1989).

58. For essays considering the recent status of these works, see Bruce Chilton and Craig A. Evans, eds., *Studying the Historical Jesus: Evaluation of the State of Current Research* (NTTS 19; Leiden: Brill, 1994).

It must be said, however, that very serious obstacles exist to such reconstructions of the historical Jesus. Under the heading of "Invention and Arrangement," John Kloppenborg has warned in an essay that even in the earliest accessible written sources the sayings of Jesus have been shaped and molded according to the social situation and rhetorical strategies of the authors.[59] If the formative genre of the original composition of the Sayings Gospel Q was the wisdom book, it follows that all the traditional materials that were incorporated into its composition were "inscribed" according to that genre. It does not, however, follow that these materials were originally wisdom sayings. On the contrary, it is possible to show that, in their earlier form, some of these materials were rather prophetic and eschatological.

Even in the earliest stage of the Sayings Gospel, although it did not contain the expectation of the coming of the Son of Man on the clouds of heaven, some of its materials are evidently adaptations of prophetic sayings. The beatitudes, which were originally the opening lines of the inaugural speech of Jesus in the Sayings Gospel, cannot be classified simply as wisdom beatitudes. They are prophetic. It is the prophet who gives his blessings to those who are poor, hungry, and weeping (Luke 6:20–22). Other sayings from the earliest form of the Sayings Gospel must also be understood as prophetic announcements of the turning of the ages: to love one's enemies, to bless one's persecutors, and to lend to those who will not repay. These are not commendations of wise and moral behavior; they announce an eschatological moment (Luke 6:27–28, 34). John the Baptist is praised as the greatest among those who were born by women because he called for the final repentance before the coming of God's kingdom (Luke 7:28). And Jesus calls himself the one who has come to light a fire on earth (Luke 12:49). Those who can interpret the signs of the time will recognize that the kingdom of God has already come upon them.[60] The speech of the sending of the disciples speaks of the harvest at the turning point of the ages: "The harvest is plentiful but the laborers are few" (Luke 10:2). To announce that those who come from east and west and north and south will eat at the table of the kingdom of God (Luke 13:29) presupposes a prophetic authority that even transcends the boundaries of Israel as heir of God's promise.

A second caution concerns those materials that were incorporated into the Sayings Gospel Q only at the time of its later redaction, like the sayings about the future coming of the Son of Man. That a saying entered into a written document only in the secondary stage of its development does not necessarily mean that it did not exist earlier.[61] While most of the Son of Man sayings with their strongly apocalyptic orientation from the later stage of the Sayings Gospel may indeed have been created as late as the time of the Jewish War (66–70 CE),[62] at least one of these sayings belongs to an earlier stage

---

59. "Q and the Historical Jesus," 326–27.

60. Luke 17:20–21. One could argue that this saying, because it lacks a parallel in the Gospel of Matthew, does not belong to the Synoptic Sayings Source. However, the parallel in *Gos. Thom.* 113 demonstrates that it was part of the earliest stages of the sayings tradition.

61. Kloppenborg, "Q and the Historical Jesus," 329–34 (under the heading "The Silence of Q").

62. For further documentation, see the chapter, "The Sayings of Q and Their Image of Jesus," especially p. 256.

of the tradition, namely Q/Luke 12:8–9: "Whoever confesses me before people, the Son of Man will confess before the angels of God." At first glance it seems to be a secondary addition to a group of wisdom sayings (Q 12:2–7) and a most likely candidate for assignment to the redactor of Q because of the use of the title Son of Man and because of what may be called an "apocalyptic" notion of reward and punishment.[63] The saying in its Q-form, however, does not identify the Son of Man with Jesus; Matthew achieves this identification by replacing "the Son of Man" with the first person singular.[64] In Q 12:8–9, the Son of Man is not Jesus but an angelic figure in the divine court who functions as the advocate for the faithful—a concept that is quite different from the coming of the Son of Man on the clouds of heaven.

The *Gospel of Thomas*, although its sayings in general represent what may be called wisdom mysticism—or a Gnostic version of wisdom theology—is also a witness to an earlier eschatological orientation of the materials that were used in its composition. This is especially evident in the several sayings about the "kingdom (of the Father)," and particularly in sayings of *Thomas* for which parallels exist in Q or Luke. A few examples must suffice. *Gos. Thom.* 113 = Q?[65]/Luke 17:20–21 (When will the kingdom come?) is without doubt originally an eschatological saying, even if Thomas attaches a Gnostic explanation ("The kingdom of the father is spread out upon the earth and human beings do not see it"). *Gos. Thom.* 10 = Q?[66]/Luke 12:49 ("I have come to kindle a fire on earth"), *Gos. Thom.* 16 = Q/Luke 12:51–53 ("I did not come to bring peace, but the sword"), and *Gos. Thom.* 91 = Q/Luke 12:54–56 (The signs of the time) are clearly eschatological in their original orientation. Thus both the Sayings Gospel Q and the *Gospel of Thomas* are witnesses to a strong eschatological component in the sayings tradition that they used in the composition of their works and "inscribed" according to their own rhetorical strategy.

What does this imply about our knowledge of the historical Jesus of Nazareth? It is methodologically wrong to conclude that therefore the original preaching of Jesus must be seen as that of an eschatological prophet. We are still not dealing with the original words of Jesus of Nazareth, but with characteristic symbols of an early oral tradition that some of the earlier communities had fashioned (inscribed) to express their own, and possible quite distinctive, understanding of Jesus. Other very early traditions are clearly wisdom sayings that were understood by some followers of Jesus as challenges to discover in those sayings the deep religious wisdom hidden in them and thus to understand oneself as divine; such interpretation is clearly present in the initial statement of the *Gospel of Thomas* that "those who find the understanding of these sayings will not taste death." Again, other communities preserved, as we have seen, a memory of Jesus

---

63. Kloppenborg, *Formation of Q*, 207–8.

64. Matt 10:32–33; also the variant in Mark 8:38 presents that (secondary) identification of the Son of Man with Jesus and includes a secondary reference to "this generation," which is absent in Q 12:8–9.

65. On the question of the inclusion of this saying in Q, see Koester, *Ancient Christian Gospels*, 155–56.

66. On the question of the inclusion of this saying in Q, see Kloppenborg, *Q Parallels*, 142; Kloppenborg, *Formation of Q*, 151, n. 213. The following saying, Luke 12:50 ("I must be baptized with a baptism . . ."), however, is certainly a Lukan addition.

as one who anticipated in the common meal with his disciples the celebration of the messianic banquet.

To declare any one of these different strands of the earliest traditions to be the only genuine and direct continuation of Jesus' own ministry disregards the evident diversity of Christian beginnings. All these different and distinct early traditions are specific formations that were dependent upon the particular cultural, linguistic, and religious milieu in which the diverse groups of followers of Jesus found themselves after his death. None of these particular situations is necessarily identical with that of Jesus himself; in fact, all of them are several steps removed from the situation of Jesus' life and ministry. Even considering the very earliest life situation of the communities of the followers of Jesus, there is no reason to assume that they were identical with the life situation of Jesus himself—something we shall never fully know. Even if it were possible to prove that the community of the Sayings Gospel Q was located in Galilee, its tradition was fixed well before even the first composition of Q in Greek rather than in Aramaic, the language of Jesus.

There is never a one-to-one correspondence between the original activity and pronouncements of a teacher or prophet with the tradition of his utterances, because the rhetorical situations are fundamentally different. The preaching of prophets or the teaching of philosophers are designed directly to influence their audiences. That is their life situation (*Sitz im Leben*), which can never be fully reconstructed. On the other hand, traditions are inscribed for very different purposes and different rhetorical situations; they want to utilize a memory for the purpose of community organization, catechetical instruction, propaganda, and theological or philosophical reflection in life situations that may be fundamentally different.

This, however, does not imply that we cannot know anything about Jesus. There is quite a lot that is known about the eschatological and revolutionary temperament of the Jewish people at the time of Jesus and about their eschatological disposition, about prophets like John the Baptist, about expectations of the coming of messianic figures and the celebration of meals in anticipation of the messianic meal. We also know quite a bit about the beginnings of the proclamation and celebrations of the early followers of Jesus in Jerusalem, Galilee (where the Sayings Gospel Q may have been composed), and Antioch.

Jesus' preaching and ministry must be placed within the trajectory that leads from this Jewish milieu of his time to his memory in the communities of his followers. Earlier we discussed the role of the story of Jesus in its relation to the celebration of the Eucharist. It is striking how often "bread" is mentioned in Q, beginning in Q1: the poor, who shall be fed; the close connection between the petition of God's will being done on earth and the petition for the daily bread in the Lord's prayer; the parable of the Great Banquet, to which all are invited from the highways and byways; perhaps also the setting of some of the discourses of Jesus at scenes of banquets; and certainly the criticisms of those who only invite those who are like themselves. If there was realized eschatology in the Q community, it is not unlikely that its tangible celebration was the common meal of the members and its insistence that these meals should be inclusive. Is this meal understood as the banquet in the coming kingdom of God? The saying about those who will come from the east and the west and the north and the south to eat with Abraham in the kingdom of God[67] provides a positive answer. Looking for theological and doctrinal continuities may be the wrong question. If the continuity from Jesus of Nazareth to the formation of early Christianity is sought in the continuity of ritual rather than in the continuity of doctrine, the story of the Q community may not be too far removed from that of the Hellenistic community of Barnabas and Paul. It should also be remembered that the major conflict between Paul on the one side and Peter and James on the other side was about the question of whether Jewish and Gentile Christians could eat together.

A reconstruction of Jesus' life, ministry, and proclamation is not possible. All that the multitude of new books on the historical Jesus are doing is, at best, to select a single component of the various traditions about Jesus and combine it with a specific modern agenda[68] or, at worst, to weave together several components into some imaginary grand portrait, however based on critical investigations of the materials.[69]

The traditions about Jesus of Nazareth must be positioned within the trajectory that leads from the Hebrew Bible through Second Temple Judaism to John the Baptist and to the early reception of Jesus' message and mission and finally to the early Christian gospels, especially those of the New Testament canon. Who Jesus was and what his ministry wanted to accomplish cannot be understood apart from the image of Jesus in these later sources. It is therefore the most important part of the search for the historical Jesus to consider the reception of Jesus in their presentation of Jesus. It should never be isolated from that later perception.

---

67. Q 13:28–30—why is it not included in Q1 in Kloppenborg, *Formation of Q?*

68. Marcus Borg ("Portraits of Jesus in Contemporary North American Scholarship," *HTR* 84 [1991] 1–22) has demonstrated that very well, and not much has changed in more recent publications. For the general dependence of these portraits upon the cultural and social situation of the modern West, see Georgi, "The Interest in Life of Jesus Theology as a Paradigm for the Social History of Biblical Criticism," *HTR* 85 (1992) 51–83; reprinted in Georgi, *The City in the Valley* (SBL 7; Atlanta: Society of Biblical Literature, 2005) 221–54.

69. E.g., John P. Meier, *A Marginal Jew: Rethinking the Historical Jesus* (2 vols.; The AB Reference Library; New York: Doubleday, 1991–1994).

20

ESCHATOLOGICAL THANKSGIVING MEALS

From the Didache *to* Q *and Jesus*

I. The *Didache* as a Compilation of Older Church Order Materials

The *Didache* or *Teaching of the Twelve Apostles* must have been composed sometime during the second century. A specific date within this time period cannot be established with certainty. It is, however, advisable to assume a date early in that century because the author still considers the older archaic materials that he incorporates in his compilation as relevant. The interest in this chapter is not with the author of the *Didache* himself, but with some of the archaic, probably written, materials that he uses. They can quickly be characterized as follows:[1]

1. The Two Ways in chapters 1–6. This section will not be considered in this chapter. It mostly rests on an originally Jewish manual. The origin of the *sectio evangelica* in 1.3–4 need not concern us here.

2. A collection of liturgical materials relating to baptism, fasting, prayer, and the celebration of the Eucharist in chapters 7–10. Most of the material here is part of an older liturgical manual. The author of the *Didache* has added very little. From his hand certainly comes the reference to the gospel in 8.2a and the ruling that only baptized persons may share the Eucharist in 9.5. Everything else can be ascribed to the older liturgical manual. The only problem that remains is the question of the ending of the thanksgiving prayer after the meal. It can be assumed that *Did.* 10.6a is still part of the archaic Eucharistic tradition. *Did.* 10.6b with its invitation that those who are holy should come, is problematic, while *Did.* 10.7 certainly stems from the hand of the redactor.

3. Rules about the treatment of wandering missionaries (apostles and prophets) in chapter 11. Probably 11.1–2 and certainly 11.3 are redactional. What follows in chapters 12–15 also may contain some older rules, but they have been incorpo-

---

1. I am on the whole following the excellent and persuasive analysis of Kurt Niederwimmer, *The Didache: A Commentary* (Hermeneia; Minneapolis: Fortress Press, 1998) 42–52.

rated into a section that is mostly written by the author of the *Didache*. Most characteristic for the hand of the author are the references to the gospel in 11.3 and 15.3 and 4.

4. A small apocalypse at the end of the composition (chap. 16). This last section will not be discussed here, except to say that 16.3–8 may be independent of New Testament passages.[2]

A note is necessary here about the references to the gospel, which all come from the hand of the author of the *Didache*.[3] The author certainly does not mean by gospel the proclamation of Jesus' suffering, death, and resurrection. The alternative would be that he refers to something called gospel from which he draws some materials for the instructions for the ordering of the life of the community and the treatment of its leaders. If that is a written gospel, like Matthew, there are two problems: (1) why are references to any narrative materials completely missing, not to speak of the Passion Narrative? (2) there is no evidence that any of these written documents have been called gospels in the early second century. The first known designations of these writings as gospels are found in some casual references in Justin Martyr—but even Justin normally uses the term "Remembrances of the Apostles." The best solution of this problem seems to me that the gospel is the proclamation of Jesus, in whatever oral or written form that proclamation was available. This is most clearly the meaning in the first of these four gospel references in *Did.* 8.2, introducing the quotation of the Lord's Prayer: "Pray as the Lord has commanded in his gospel (=proclamation)." The following wording of the Lord's Prayer is almost identical with the one found in Matthew 6. There are, however, some suggestive differences that may indicate that this "Matthean" form of the Lord's Prayer is more original than the one found in our manuscripts of Matthew.[4] The concluding doxology in the *Didache* has only two members ("power" and "glory") as opposed to the threefold doxology that has been added in most manuscripts of the Gospel of Matthew.

II. The Instructions for Wandering Apostles and Prophets

This collection of instructions does not depend on any known written gospels. But in its genre it can be called a variant of the instructions found in the mission speech in Q 10:2–16.[5] There is also some resemblance in detail. *Did.* 11.4: "Every apostle who comes

---

2. See Helmut Koester, *Synoptische Überlieferung bei den Apostolischen Vätern* (TU 65; Berlin: Akademie-Verlag, 1957) 173–90.

3. I have treated that question in *Synoptische Überlieferung* (10–11) and have seen little reason to change my judgment.

4. See Koester, *Synoptische Überlieferung*, 203–9.

5. In the reconstruction of the Synoptic Sayings Gospel Q, I am following James M. Robinson, Paul Hoffmann, and John S. Kloppenborg, *The Critical Edition of Q* (Hermeneia. Supplements; Minneapolis: Fortress Press, 2000). The numbering of the passages quoted as "Q" corresponds to the chapter and verse numbers of the Gospel of Luke.

to you should be received like the Lord"; cf. Q 10:16: "Whoever takes you in takes me in." The instruction that any apostle who comes to you should only receive food but not any money (*Did.* 11.6) can be compared to Q 10:4: "Do not take any purse," and Q 10:7: "Eat and drink what is set before you."

Most striking is the command in *Did.* 11.7 that a prophet speaking in the Spirit should not be tested, followed by the statement that "every sin will be forgiven, but this sin will not be forgiven." This is certainly the most original form of a community rule attested in Mark 3:28–29 as well as in Q 12:10, where the rule says that blasphemies against a human being (Q: υἱὸν τοῦ ἀνθρώπου) or any sins and blasphemies (Mark) can be forgiven. It was later understood, probably by Luke and certainly by Matthew, that sins against the Son of Man, that is, Jesus, can be forgiven (see also *Gospel of Thomas* 44). The *Didache* has preserved the most archaic form of this community rule. Compare also the discussion of prophets speaking in the Spirit in 1 Corinthians 14.

The rules concerning apostles and prophets, which the *Didache* presents in this chapter, are part of a very archaic collection of community rules. They reflect a situation of the very early mission of apostles in which the authorization by prophetic inspiration was very much alive. This also includes the entirely enigmatic instructions regarding the "prophet, who performs the 'cosmic' mystery of the church" in *Did.* 11.11. The instructions are introduced by the author of the *Didache* as "according to the command of the 'gospel.'" The author of the *Didache* sees these rules as part of the commandments handed down by Jesus in his preaching.

III. The Thanksgiving Prayers

The phrase "About the Eucharist, you should give thanks in the following way" introduces three prayers. The first prayer concerns the "cup" (9.2), and the second prayer is about the "bread" (9.3–4). After an interpolation by the redactor (9.5), the third prayer follows and is explicitly introduced as prayer after the meal (10.1). All three prayers are based on regular Jewish meal prayers, as they must have been used in the Greek-speaking Jewish diaspora but can also be presupposed for Palestinian Judaism at the time of Jesus.[6] It is especially evident in the first two prayers; but also the third prayer follows the typical Jewish thanksgiving after the meal, although the sequence of the various phrases is somewhat different. The evidence for all this and quotes of respective Jewish meal prayers have been presented in numerous scholarly publications; there is no reason to repeat any of the arguments here.[7]

The prayers over cup and bread have been adapted for use in communities of the followers of Jesus in several ways. Instead of the traditional "blessing" (εὐλογία) of the cup and the bread, the term "thanksgiving" or "we give thanks" (εὐχαριστία,

---

6. I am aware of the fact that parallels to these prayers in rabbinic traditions are often dated to a time after the middle of the second century CE. That, however, does not exclude the probability of a use of such prayers at a much earlier time.

7. Cf. Niederwimmer, *Didache*, 141 (with literature).

εὐχαριστοῦμεν) is used. The prayers are not addressed to "Lord our God, Creator of the Universe," but to "Our Father" (9.2, 3) as in the Lord's Prayer (8.2). The blessing over the cup does not thank the creator for the "fruit of the vine" but for "the holy vine of David, your servant, that has been made known through Jesus, your servant" (9.2). The thanksgiving for the bread (originally probably ἄρτος and not κλάσμα) does not give thanks for the bread itself but for "wisdom and knowledge (ὑπὲρ τῆς ζωῆς καὶ γνώσεως) that has been made known through Jesus, your servant" (9.3). This is partic-ularly striking because of the disharmonious interpretation of the bread. Only in the next sentence (9.4) does the genuine symbolism of the "bread" appear: "As this [bread] was scattered on the mountains and been brought together into one, so may your church be brought together from the ends of the earth into your kingdom." The doxologies fol-lowing each prayer, "to you belongs the glory" and "to you belongs the glory and power for ever," are traditional; "through Jesus Christ" seems to be an addition of the redactor.

Analogous interpretations of the original Jewish meal prayers also appear in the prayer after the meal. Here the prayer is first addressed to God as "Holy Father" (10.2); the traditional Jewish address to God as "Lord, Ruler of the All" (δέσποτα παν-τοκράτωρ) appears in the next petition (10.3). Again, the thanksgiving does not specifi-cally concern the food that has been shared, but is rather for "the indwelling of God's holy name in our hearts" and for "knowledge, faith, and immortality" (ὑπὲρ τῆς γνώσεως καὶ πίστεως καὶ ἀθανασίας), which have been made known to us through Jesus, your servant" (10.2). Thanksgiving for the food itself only appears in the follow-ing petition (10.3), supplemented by an additional thanksgiving for the "spiritual food and eternal life through (Jesus?) your servant." Parallel to the interpretation of the bread in 9.4, a general petition follows on behalf of the holy church that it may be brought together from the four winds into God's kingdom (10.5).

IV. The Relationship of the Thanksgiving Prayers to Jesus

The conclusion of these thanksgiving prayers (10.6) is problematic. This conclusion consists of several liturgical sentences: "May grace come and may this world pass away." "Hosanna to the God of David." "If anyone is holy, let him come, if anyone is not, let him repent." "Lord come" (μαρὰν ἀθά). This conclusion has been interpreted as an invitation to the "Lord's Supper" that would have followed the fellowship meal, at which the above thanksgiving petitions would have been spoken. But this can be questioned on good grounds. The fellowship meal has been explicitly identified as the Eucharist. And while the author is clearly interested in the exact wording of the prayers to be spoken in this context, why does he not add instructions for the Lord's Supper, or at least quote the words of institution?

What has led scholars to this hypothesis is the assumption that the followers of Jesus, whenever they celebrated the Eucharist, must have made reference to the words of institution. To be sure, the words of institution quoted by Paul as a tradition (1 Cor 11:23–25) must have been formulated very early, apparently before Paul's call as an apostle. But we should not assume that, whenever and wherever followers of Jesus cel-ebrated the Eucharist in memory of Jesus, they would have used the words of institution. First, these words were formulated only after the death of Jesus. Second, they are clearly an interpretation of the suffering and death of Jesus. That an understanding of the Eucharist, however, is intrinsically tied to the proclamation of Jesus' death and resurrection as the central saving event is an unwarranted assumption. Nowhere in the archaic form of the Eucharistic prayers in the *Didache* is there any indication for an understanding of the saving significance of Jesus' death and resurrection. Even for the *Didache* as a whole, such understanding of the salvation through Jesus' death and resurrection is problematic, unless one wants to interpret the term "sacrifice" (θυσία) in *Didache* 14 as a reference to Jesus' death on the cross.[8]

My suggestion is that the interpretation of the Eucharist as a memory of Jesus' suffering and death is a secondary understanding of a fellowship meal that was originally celebrated as a continuation of meals celebrated by Jesus himself and his followers during the life and ministry of Jesus. If Jesus ever shared food, that is, bread and wine with his disciples and friends, he would have spoken the usual thanksgiving prayers, with the blessing of the cup at the beginning of the meal and a concluding prayer after the meal—according to the regular Jewish custom of the time. It is evident that the thanksgiving prayers are based upon such customary Jewish meal blessings.

As such meal celebrations were continued after Jesus' death, the prayers were not necessarily reinterpreted with reference to Jesus' suffering and death. Rather, as such prayers appear in the *Didache,* Jesus is remembered as the Servant of God, who has revealed life and knowledge, faith and immortality, which are now not present in the memory of what Jesus has suffered but in the memory of what Jesus has said. In other words, the sayings of Jesus communicate knowledge and life. Moreover, the eschatological perspective that is present in these prayers also may have been part of the prayers during Jesus' lifetime. On the other hand, the reference to the gathering of the church (ἐκκλησία) instead of the gathering of Israel reflects a later understanding. If the call "Lord come!" (μαρὰν ἀθά) belongs to the traditional prayers and is not an addition of the redactor, the "Lord" would refer to God and not Jesus; this call also reveals an Aramaic substratum. The enigmatic "holy vine of David, your servant" may result from the attempt to establish a relationship to the tradition of Israel; but it does not imply a reference to Jesus as the royal heir of David's kingship. Jesus is not the royal messiah but the servant of God, like Moses, David, and the prophets.

V. The Prayers of the *Didache* and the Words of Institution

These archaic Eucharistic prayers are, however, parallel to the Pauline understanding of the Lord's Supper in some respect, in spite of the absence of the words of institution. In both instances, the bread is the symbol of the community. In Paul, the "body" of the Lord is understood as the body of Christ, that is, the church.[9] The reference to the

---

8. Niederwimmer (196–97) argues against such an understanding and suggests that θυσία refers to the speaking of the Eucharistic prayers, which requires that the speaker be morally pure.

9. Cf. 1 Corinthians 12; cf. 1 Cor 10:15–16; 11:27, 29.

"holy vine of David" can be paralleled to Paul's understanding of the cup as a symbol for the covenant. Both texts also share the eschatological perspective; cf. Paul's "As often as you eat this bread and drink this cup, you shall proclaim the death of the Lord until he comes" (1 Cor 11:26). Paul also shares the call "Lord, come!" with the *Didache* in a formula closely resembling *Did.* 10.6: "If someone does not love the Lord, he stands condemned; Lord, come!" (1 Cor 16:22). Also note that both the *Didache* and 1 Cor 11:25 speak about the "cup," not about the "blood." Finally, although the designation of Jesus as the "Servant of God" does not appear in Paul, the words of institution are introduced in 1 Cor 11:23 with "In the night in which he was handed over"—a sentence that recalls the servant song of Isaiah 53. It is safe to conclude that both otherwise very different interpretations of the Eucharist are based on the same tradition, consisting of a symbolic interpretation of the cup and the bread and an eschatological perspective that is ultimately based on the meal practice of Jesus.

VI. The *Didache* and Q

While Paul's understanding of the Eucharist belongs to the kerygma of Jesus' death and resurrection as the primary saving event, the turning point of the ages, the Eucharistic prayers of the *Didache* belong in an understanding of Jesus' words as the saving event as it is present in the tradition of the Synoptic Sayings Gospel Q. As has been observed before, the community of Q also must have celebrated a Eucharistic meal. The term Eucharist is missing, but the Lord's Prayer closely connects the petition for the will of God to be done on earth with the petition for the bread. Q envisions an eschatological meal fellowship in the kingdom of God for those coming from the east and the west (Q 13:28–29). Christological titles are largely missing in both Q and the *Didache* prayers, except for the title "Servant" in *Didache* 9–10 and the title "Son of Man" in the later redaction of Q. "Son of God" rarely appears in Q,[10] and never in the *Didache* prayers. In Q and the *Didache* prayers, Jesus is never called "Christ" or "Lord"; in Q the title *Lord* is always reserved for God;[11] wherever κύριος is used for Jesus in Q, it always means "master".[12] The *kingdom* is always the Kingdom of God. In both instances, God is called "Father."[13] For the revelation of knowledge through Jesus, compare Q 10:21–22. To be sure, there are also differences. While the term πίστις appears in Q (7:9; 17:6), ἀθανασία and ζωή are missing. The term *church* never appears in Q, nor does its epithet *holy*.

Nevertheless, the archaic Eucharistic prayers of the *Didache* must have originated in a community for which the sayings of Jesus were considered as having the power to save, and in which there was no recourse to Jesus' suffering, death, and resurrection. Q is the most eminent witness for this understanding of the saving significance of Jesus' ministry.

---

10. It appears only twice in the story of the temptation of Jesus: 4:3, 9; it is implied in Q 10:21
11. See Q 4:12; 10:21; 13:35.
12. See Q 6:46; 7:6; 9:59; 10:2.
13. For Q see 6:39; 10:21, 22; 11:2; 12:30.

Resemblance in the instructions for the treatment of wandering prophets and apostles with the speech of the sending of the disciples in Q further underlines the close relationship of the archaic traditions of the *Didache* with the tradition of Q. That the Son of Man sayings are missing in the prayers of the *Didache* would point to a relationship at the earlier stage of the development of Q.[14] With their emphasis upon the "knowledge" (γνῶσις) revealed through Jesus, these prayers have developed this understanding of Jesus' ministry in the direction of the *Gospel of Thomas,* although the eschatological expectation of Q as well as of Jesus' sayings about the coming kingdom is still strongly emphasized.

---

14. Cf. here the work of John S. Kloppenborg, *The Formation of Q: Trajectories in Ancient Wisdom Collections* (Studies in Antiquity and Christianity; Philadelphia: Fortress Press, 1987).

PUBLICATIONS OF HELMUT KOESTER, 1991–2007

For the bibliography until 1990, see Birger A. Pearson, ed., *The Future of Early Christianity: Essays in Honor of Helmut Koester* (Minneapolis: Fortress, 1991) 477–87.

1991

1. (with François Bovon) *Genèse de l'écriture chrétienne* (Mémoires premières; Brepols, 1991) 138 pp.
2. "Epilogue: Current Issues in New Testament Scholarship," in Birger A. Pearson, ed., *The Future of Early Christianity: Essays in Honor of Helmut Koester* (Minneapolis: Fortress, 1991) 467–76.
3. "Macedonia," in *Holman Bible Dictionary* (Nashville: Holman, 1991) 907–8.

1992

4. "Secret Gospel of Mark: Translation, Introduction, Notes," in Robert J. Miller, ed., *The Complete Gospels* (Sonoma, CA: Polebridge Press, 1992) 402–5.
5. "Jesus the Victim," Presidential address at the annual meeting of the Society of Biblical Literature, November 23, 1991, *JBL* 111 (1992) 3–15.
6. "Writings and the Spirit: Authority and Politics in Ancient Christianity," *HTR* 84 (1991) 353–72.
7. "The Story of the Johannine Tradition," *Sewanee Theological Review* 36 (1992) 17–32.
8. "Luke's Holy Land and Jesus' Company," *Bible Review* 8,3 (June 1992) 22, 52.
9. "Finding Morality in Luke's Disturbing Parables," *Bible Review* 8,5 (October 1992) 5, 10.
10. "Let us all Become Benefactors," *Religious Studies News* 7,1 (January 1992) 1 and 3.
11. "SBL Members Pledge over $100,000," *Religious Studies News* 7,2 (May 1992) 7.

1993

12. "Jesu Leiden und Tod als Erzählung," in Rüdiger Bartelmus, Thomas Krüger and Helmut Utzschneider, eds, *Konsequente Traditionsgeschichte: Festschrift für Klaus Baltzer zum 65. Geburtstag* (Göttingen: Vandenhoeck & Ruprecht, 1993) 199–204.
13. "The Passion Narratives and the Roots of Anti-Judaism," *Bible Review* 9,1 (1993) 5, 46.

14. "Recovering the Original Meaning of Matthew's Parables," *Bible Review* 9,3 (1993) 11, 52.

15. "The Future Is Now," *Bible Review* 9,5 (1993) 8, 17.

16. "Redirecting the Quest for the Historical Jesus," *Harvard Divinity Bulletin* 23 (1993) 9–11.

1994

17. *Athens A* (with Christopher Matthews and Erika Schluntz) in Helmut Koester and Ann Graham Brock, eds., *Archaeological Resources for New Testament Studies,* vol. 1 (2nd ed.; Philadelphia: Trinity Press International, 1994

18. *Isthmia* (with Eric Sorenson) in: Helmut Koester and Ann Graham Brock, eds., *Archaeological Resources for New Testament Studies,* vol. 2 (Philadelphia: Trinity Press International, 1994).

19. "The Historical Jesus and the Historical Situation of the Quest: An Epilogue," in Bruce Chilton and Craig A. Evans, eds., *Studying the Historical Jesus: Evaluation of the State of Current Research* (New Testament Tools and Studies 19; Leiden: Brill, 1994) 535-45.

20. "Archäologie und Paulus in Thessalonike," in Lukas Bormann, Kelly del Tredici, Angela Standhartinger, eds., *Religious Propaganda and Missionary Competition in the New Testament World: Essays Honoring Dieter Georgi* (Leiden: Brill, 1994) 393-404.

21. "Written Gospels and Oral Tradition," *JBL* 113 (1994) 293–97.

22. "Secret Gospel of Mark: Translation, Introduction, Notes," in Robert J. Miller, ed., *The Complete Gospels* (2d. ed.; Sonoma, CA: Polebridge Press, 1994) 408–10.

23. (with Stephen J. Patterson) "The Gospel of Thomas: Does it Contain Authentic Sayings of Jesus?" in Harvey Minkoff, ed., *Approaches to the Bible: The Best of Bible Review,* vol. 1: *Composition, Translation and Language* (Washington, DC: Biblical Archaeology Society, 1994) 89–107; reprint from *Bible Review* 6,2 (1990) 28-39.

24. "Jesus before Pilate," *Bible Review* 10,1 (1994)

25. "Mark and the Life—and Death—of Jesus," *Bible Review* 10,3 (1994) 17, 55.

26. "A Political Christmas Story," *Bible Review* 10/5 (1994) 23, 58.

27. Editor (with Ann Graham Brock): *Archaeological Resources for New Testament Studies,* vol. 1: *Athens, Corinth, Olympia, Thessalonike* (2nd ed.; Philadelphia: Trinity Press International, 1994) 350 pp. and 282 slides, indices, glossary.

28. Editor (with Ann Graham Brock): *Archaeological Resources for New Testament Studies,* vol. 2: *Athens, Corinth, Isthmia, Philippi, Ephesos* (Philadelphia: Trinity Press International, 1994) 360 pp. and 302 slides, indices, glossary.

1995

29. *History, Culture, and Religion of the Hellenistic Age* (Introduction to the New Testament, vol. 1; 2nd edition; New York: De Gruyter, 1995) 409 and xxxiv pp.; second edition of #116.

30. "Jesus' Presence in the Early Church," *Cristianesimo nella Storia* 15 (1994) 541–57.
31. "The Red Hall in Pergamon," in L. Michael White and O. Larry Yarbrough, *The Social World of the Early Christians: Essays in Honor of Wayne A. Meeks* (Minneapolis: Fortress, 1995) 265–74.
32. "Foreword" to Günther Bornkamm, *Jesus of Nazareth* (Minneapolis: Fortress, 1995) 3–6.
33. "Historic Mistakes Haunt the Relationship of Christianity and Judaism," *Biblical Archaeology Review* 21,2 (1995) 26–27. Responses to readers' comments in *Biblical Archaeology Review* 21,4 (1995) 14–18.
34. Statement on New Testament and Archaeology in "Scholars Speak Out," *Biblical Archaeology Review* 21,3 (1995) 28–29.
35. "The Historical Jesus and the Cult of the Kyrios Christos (The Annual Faculty Research Lecture at Harvard Divinity School)," *Harvard Divinity School Bulletin* 24,3 (1995) 13–18.
36. "Where God Can Be Found: The Radical Message of Jesus' Death," *Bible Review* 11,1 (1995) 18, 47.
37. "Explaining Jesus' Crucifixion," *Bible Review* 11,3 (1995) 16, 48.
38. "What Is——and Is Not—Inspired," *Bible Review* 11,5 (1995) 18, 48.
39. Editor: *Ephesos: Metropolis of Asia: An Interdisciplinary Approach to its Archaeology, Religion, and Culture* (Harvard Theological Studies 41; Valley Forge, PA; Trinity Press International, 1995) xix and 357 pp.
40. "Preface" to *Ephesos: Metropolis of Asia* (Harvard Theological Studies 41; Valley Forge, PA; Trinity Press International, 1995) xvii–xix.
41. "Ephesos in Early Christian Literature," in *Ephesos: Metropolis of Asia* (Harvard Theological Studies 41; Valley Forge, PA; Trinity Press International, 1995) 119–40.

1996

42. "The Son of David and the King of the Jews," *Bible Review* 12,1 (1996)18, 44.
43. "Paul, the Christian Community and the Jews," *Bible Review* 12,3 (1996) 20, 44.
44. "The Second Coming Demythologized," *Bible Review* 12,5 (1996) 20, 51.
45. "The Sayings Gospel Q and the Quest for the Historical Jesus: A Response to John S. Kloppenborg," *Harvard Theological Review* 89 (1996) 345–49.

1997

46. "Rediscovering the Message of Lent," *Bible Review* 13,1 (1997) 16, 46.
47. "A történeti Jézus és a 'Küriosz Khristosz' kultusza," *Keresztyén Igazság* 34 (1997) 10–18; 35 (1997) 6–13. Hungarian translation of unpublished essay "The Historical Jesus and the Cult of the Kyrios Christos" (see above #35; republication without notes).
48. "The Sayings of Q and Their Image of Jesus," in: William L. Petersen, Johan S. Vos,

and Henk J. de Jonge, eds., *Sayings of Jesus: Canonical and Non-Canonical: Essays in Honor of Tjitze Baarda* (NovT Sup. 89; Leiden: Brill, 1997) 137–54.

1998

49. "The Memory of Jesus' Death and the Worship of the Risen Lord," *HTR* 91 (1998) 335–50.

50. "Paul and Philippi: The Evidence from Early Christian Literature," in Charalambos Bakirtzis and Helmut Koester, eds., *Philippi at the Time of Paul and After His Death* (Harrisburg, PA: Trinity Press International, 1998) 49–66.

51. "The Cult of the Egyptian Deities in Asia Minor," in Helmut Koester, ed., *Pergamon, Citadel of the Gods: Archaeological Record, Literary Description, and Religious Development* (HTS 46; Harrisburg, PA: Trinity Press International, 1998) 111–35.

52. (with Charalambos Bakirtzis) "Introduction," in Charalambos Bakirtzis and Helmut Koester, eds., *Philippi at the Time of Paul and After His Death* (Harrisburg, PA: Trinity Press International, 1998) 1–4.

53. Editor (with Charalambos Bakirtzis): *Philippi at the Time of Paul and After His Death* (Harrisburg, PA: Trinity Press International, 1998) xv and 87 pp, 7 figures and XVI plates.

54. "Preface," in Helmut Koester, ed., *Pergamon, Citadel of the Gods: Archaeological Record, Literary Description, and Religious Development* (HTS 46; Harrisburg, PA: Trinity Press International, 1998).

55. Editor: *Pergamon, Citadel of the Gods: Archaeological Record, Literary Description, and Religious Development* (HTS 46; Harrisburg, PA: Trinity Press International, 1998).

1999

56. "Associations of the Egyptian Cult in Asia Minor," in Peter Scherrer, Hans Taeuber, and Hilke Thür, eds., *Steine und Wege: Festschrift für Dieter Knibbe zum 65. Geburtstag* (Österreichisches Archäologisches Institut, Sonderschiften Band 32; Wien, 1999) 315–18.

57. "Ephesus und Paulus in der frühchristlichen Literatur," in H. Friesinger and F. Krinzinger, *Hundert Jahre Österreichische Forschungen in Ephesos: Akten des Symposions Wien 1995* (Österreichische Akademie der Wissenschaften: Wien, 1999) 1. 297–305.

58. Editor: Carolyn Osiek, *Shepherd of Hermas; A Commentary* (Hermeneia: Minneapolis: Fortress, 1999).

2000

59. *History and Literature of Early Christianity* (Introduction to the New Testament, vol. 2; 2nd edition; New York: De Gruyter, 2000) xxxvii + 375 pages.

60. "Evangelium I: Begriff," *Die Religion in Geschichte und Gegenwart* (4th ed.; Tübingen: Mohr/Siebeck, 2000) 2. 1735–36.

61. "Evangelium II: Gattung," *Die Religion in Geschichte und Gegenwart* (4th ed.; Tübingen:Mohr/Siebeck, 2000) 2. 1736–41.

62. "An Intellectual Biography of James M. Robinson: Speech at the Occasion of His Retirement," in Jon Ma. Asgeirson, Kristin de Troyer and Marvin Meyer, ed., *From Quest to Q: Festschrift James M. Robinson* (BETL 146; Leuven: Peeters, 2000) xii–xxi.

2001

63. "Paul's Letters as Theology for the Community," in Adela Yarbro Collins and Margaret M. Mitchell, eds., *Antiquity and Community: Essays on Ancient Religion and Philosophy Presented to Hans Dieter Betz on His 75th Birthday* (Tübingen: Mohr/Siebeck, 2001) 215–25.

64. "On Heroes, Tombs, and Early Christianity: An Epilogue," in Jennifer K. Berenson Maclean and Ellen Bradshaw Aitken, trans. and notes, *Flavius Philostratus: Heroikos* (SBL Writings from the Greco-Roman World 1; Society of Biblical Literature, 2001) 257–64.

65. Editor: Ulrich Luz, *Matthew 8–20: A Commentary* (Hermeneia: Minneapolis: Fortress, 2001).

2002

66. "Markusevangelium, geheimes," *Die Religion in Geschichte und Gegenwart* (4th ed.; Tübingen:Mohr/Siebeck, 2002) 5. 846.

67. "Milet," *Die Religion in Geschichte und Gegenwart* (4th ed.; Tübingen:Mohr/Siebeck, 2002) 5. 1224–25.

68. Editor: François Bovon, *Luke 1: A Commentary on the Gospel of Luke 1:1–9:56* (Hermeneia; Minneapolis: Fortress, 2002).

2003

69. "The Synoptic Sayings Gospel Q in the Early Communities of Jesus' Followers," in David H. Warren, Ann Graham Brock, and David Pao, eds., *Early Christian Voices in Texts, Traditions, and Symbols: Essays in Honor of François Bovon* (Biblical Interpretation Series 66; Leiden, Brill, 2003) 45–58.

70. "Nock, Arthur Darby," *Die Religion in Geschichte und Gegenwart* (4th ed.; Tübingen: Mohr/Siebeck, 2003) 6. 351–52.

71. "Pergamon," *Die Religion in Geschichte und Gegenwart* (4th ed.; Tübingen: Mohr/Siebeck, 2003) 6. 1107–09.

2004

72. "Suffering Servant and Royal Messiah: from Second Isaiah to Paul, Mark, and Matthew," *Theology Digest* 51 (2004) 102–24.

73. Editor: *The Cities of Paul: Images and Interpretations from the Harvard Archaeology Project* (Minneapolis: Fortress Press, 2004) [CD-Rom].

2005

74. "The Silence of the Apostle," in Daniel N. Schowalter and Steven Friesen, eds., *Urban Religion in Roman Corinth* (HTS 53; Harvard University Press, 2005) 339–49.
75. "Paul's Proclamation of God's Justice for the Nations," *Theology Digest* 51 (2005) 303–14.
76. "Gospels and Gospel Traditions in the Second Century," in Andrew Gregory and Christopher Tucket, eds., *Trajectories through the New Testament and the Apostolic Fathers* (Oxford: Oxford University Press, 2005) 27–44.
77. "Foreword" to Dieter Georgi, *The City in the Valley: Biblical Interpretation and Urban Theology* (Studies in Biblical Literature; Atlanta: Society of Biblical Literature, 2005) vii–x.
78. "Harvard Divinity School and the Future of Theological Education," in Warren Lewis and Hans Rollmann, *Restoring the First-century Church in the Twenty-first Century: Essays on the Stone-Campbell Restoration Movement: In Honor of Don Haymes* (Eugene, OR: Wipf and Stock, 2005) 435–42.
79 "Wilder, Amos," *Die Religion in Geschichte und Gegenwart* (4th ed.; Tübingen: Mohr: Siebeck, 2005) 8 1547–49.
80. Editor: Ulrich Luz, *Matthew 21–28: A Commentary* (Hermeneia; Minneapolis: Fortress, 2005).
81. *introdução ao novo testamento,* volume 1. *história, cultura e religião do período helenístico* (coleção biblia e sociologia; Sao Paulo [Brasil]: Paulus, 2005). [Portugese translation of *History, Culture, and Religion of the Hellenistic Period.* #29 above]
82. *introdução ao novo testamento,* volume 2. *história e literatura do cristianismo primitivo* (coleção biblia e sociologia; Sao Paulo [Brasil]: Paulus, 2005). [Portugese translation of *History and Literature of Early Christianity.* # 59 above]

2006

83. "The Apostolic Fathers and the Struggle for Christian Identity," *Expository Times* 117/4 (2006) 133–39 = Paul Foster, ed., *The Writings of the Apostolic Fathers* (London and New York: T&T Clark /Continuum, 2007)
84. "Eschatological Thanksgiving Meals: from the Didache to Q and Jesus," in Ἁγία Γραφὴ καὶ σύνχρονο' ἄνθρωπο': Τιμητικὸ' Τόμο' στὸν Καθηγητὴ Ἰωάννη Δ. Καραβιδόπουλο *[Festschrift for Professor IoannesD. Karavidopoulos]* (Thessaloniki: P. Pournara, 2006) 539–46.
85. "Messias oder leidender Gottesknecht," in *Emlékkönyv Tökés Istvan kilencvenedik születésnapjara [Festschrift für Istvan Tökés zum 90. Geburtstag]* (Protestantisch-theologisches Institut in Klausenburg; Kolozsvar/Rumania, 2006) 166–79.

2007

86. *Paul and His World: Interpreting the New Testament in its Context* (Minneapolis: Fortress, 2007) 301 pp.

87. *From Jesus to the Gospels: Interpreting the New Testament in its Context* (Minneapolis: Fortress, 2007) 295 pp.

88. "The Apostolic Fathers and the Struggle for Christian Identity," in Paul Foster, ed., *The Writings of the Apostolic Fathers* (London and New York: T&T Clark /Continuum, 2007) 1–12; reprint of # 84 above.

89. "Revelation 12:1–12: A Meditation," in William H. Brackney and Craig Evans, *From Biblical Criticism to Biblical Faith: Essay in Honor of Lee Martin McDonald* (Maco, Georgia: Mercer University Press, 2007) 138–44.

90. Editor of Ulrich Luz, *Matthew 1–7: A Commentary* (Hermeneia; Minneapolius: Fortress, 2007).

INDEX OF ANCIENT LITERATURE

INDEX OF NAMES AND SUBJECTS

INDEX OF GREEK TERMS

INDEX OF MODERN AUTHORS

Paul and His World

Interpreting the New Testament in Its Context

Helmut Koester

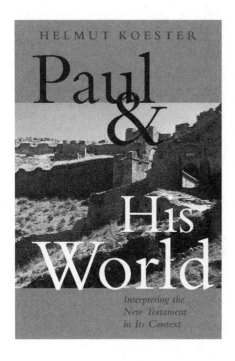

Cloth
320 pages
$39.00
ISBN 978-0-8006-3890-0

Critical essays on Paul's theology and eschatology, his religious and cultural context, and the interaction between Christianity and its Greco-Roman environment—from one of the most renowned scholars in the field. The companion volume to *From Jesus to the Gospels*.